ANGLO-SAXON WILLS

Edited
with Translation and Notes
by

DOROTHY WHITELOCK, M.A.

Allen Scholar of the University of Cambridge; sometime
Marion Kennedy Student of Newnham College

Wm. W. Gaunt & Sons, Inc.
Holmes Beach, Florida
1986

WM. W. GAUNT & SONS, INC.

First published 1930
Reprinted by permission of
Cambridge University Press

International Standard Book Number: 912004-54-1

Library of Congress Catalog Card Number: 85-82256

Reprint 1986

WM. W. GAUNT & SONS, INC.
Gaunt Building
3011 Gulf Drive
Holmes Beach, Florida 33510-2199
U.S.A.

CAMBRIDGE STUDIES
IN ENGLISH LEGAL HISTORY
Edited by
HAROLD DEXTER HAZELTINE, LITT.D., F.B.A.
Of the Inner Temple, Barrister-at-Law;
Downing Professor of the Laws of England in
the University of Cambridge

First published 1930

Reprinted by permission of

Cambridge University Press

International Standard Book Number: 912004-54-1

Library of Congress Catalog Card Number: 85-82256

Reprint 1986

WM. W. GAUNT & SONS, INC.
Gaunt Building
3011 Gulf Drive
Holmes Beach, Florida 33510-2199
U.S.A.

CAMBRIDGE STUDIES
IN ENGLISH LEGAL HISTORY

Edited by HAROLD DEXTER HAZELTINE, LITT.D., F.B.A., of the
Inner Temple, Barrister-at-Law, Downing Professor of the Laws of England
in the University of Cambridge.

THE HISTORY OF CONSPIRACY AND ABUSE OF LEGAL
PROCEDURE. By PERCY HENRY WINFIELD, LL.D., of the Inner
Temple, Barrister-at-Law; Fellow of St John's College, and Rouse
Ball Professor of English Law, Cambridge. 1921.

STATUTES & THEIR INTERPRETATION IN THE FIRST
HALF OF THE FOURTEENTH CENTURY. By THEODORE
F. T. PLUCKNETT, M.A., LL.B., Assistant Professor of Legal
History in Harvard University; late Choate Fellow in Harvard
University and Research Student of Emmanuel College, Cambridge.
1922.

INTERPRETATIONS OF LEGAL HISTORY. By ROSCOE
POUND, PH.D., LL.D., Carter Professor of Jurisprudence in Harvard
University. 1923.

IOANNIS SELDENI *AD FLETAM DISSERTATIO.* Reprinted
from the edition of 1647 with parallel translation, introduction and
notes by DAVID OGG, Fellow and Tutor of New College, Oxford.
1925.

A MANUAL OF YEAR BOOK STUDIES. By WILLIAM
CRADDOCK BOLLAND, M.A., LL.D., of Lincoln's Inn, Barrister-at-
Law; late Sandars Reader in the University of Cambridge, and
Scholar of Magdalene College, Cambridge. 1925.

ANGLO-SAXON WILLS. Edited with translation and notes by
DOROTHY WHITELOCK, M.A., Allen Scholar of the University of
Cambridge; sometime Marion Kennedy Student of Newnham
College. 1930.

ANGLO-SAXON WILLS

Edited

with Translation and Notes

by

DOROTHY WHITELOCK, M.A.

Allen Scholar of the University of Cambridge, sometime
Marion Kennedy Student of Newnham College

CAMBRIDGE

AT THE UNIVERSITY PRESS

1930

Cambridge University Press
Fetter Lane, London

New York
Bombay, Calcutta, Madras
Toronto

Macmillan

Tokyo
Maruzen Company, Ltd

CONTENTS

COMMENTS ON THE WRITINGS KNOWN AS ANGLO-SAXON WILLS

Through Miss Whitelock's skilful editorship some of the most important private documents of the later Anglo-Saxon age have been made easily accessible to scholars. Not only are these scattered documents, written in Anglo-Saxon, now ready to hand; they are illumined both by the editor's faithful translation and by her learned notes. Especially by means of the notes, which are based on much painstaking research, the 'wills' have been placed in their environment of time and place; and, in addition, they have been minutely explained as evidences of the growth of Anglo-Saxon as a living language. Miss Whitelock has taken pains to give us information as to the sources from which the wills in their present form have been derived; and she has also dealt with some of the diplomatic problems raised by the documents. She has made, in fact, a most welcome and valuable addition to our knowledge of a part of that priceless heritage of documents in which so much of Anglo-Saxon social, legal, and institutional history is enshrined.

While these present writings, by the accepted terminology of scholars, bear the name of 'wills', they are not wills in the later juridical meaning of that term. The true will is not only a uni-lateral written disposition of property to take effect on the death of the testator; it possesses also the qualities of revocability and ambulatoriness; and, in addition, it names an executor. While the germs of one or more of these features of the later will are to be found in some of these Anglo-Saxon documents, no one of them possesses all the requisite qualities. They are in fact the predecessors of the will; and as such they are of great interest to the student of legal history. They picture to us, among other things, some of the earlier stages of the growth of testamentary power. For a long time the claims of kindred and lords had to be reckoned with: and in the documents now before us we can watch certain features of that long process whereby men ultimately acquired the right freely to alienate their property by 'last will and testament'.

These documents are not wills; and, moreover, they are not even the actual gifts, the dispositions, made by the donors. The gifts as found in the documents are of varied character; but the one that is most distinctive and general is the gift *post obitum*. The donor says: 'I *give...after* my death'; or he says: 'I *give... after* my death and the death of X and Y'; or he uses a formula similar to these. One of the main problems in regard to Anglo-Saxon wills is to find the correct interpretation of gifts which are thus phrased, strangely enough it may well appear to us, both in the present and in the future tense. However this problem may be resolved—and to that we shall return—the writings are only the evidence, the documentation, of these gifts; they are not the gifts themselves. Nor is there any line of distinction to be drawn between writings which evidence death-bed gifts *mortis causa* and the writings which evidence gifts *mortis causa* made by persons in full health and with no thought of death. In both cases the dispositive act of giving *mortis causa* is an oral and formal act; and this act, done before witnesses, is one which needs no documentation to make it valid and binding in the law. The transaction itself, the juristic act, is complete without the writing. The writing, in other words, is not a document combining in itself both dispositive and evidentiary qualities; it is merely an evidence-document[1]. The making of the oral or nuncupative will is evidenced by living witnesses; it is also evidenced by a parchment upon which the scribe has reproduced the oral will. Living witnesses forget and die; a documentary witness, a written *testimonium*, never forgets and never dies[2].

This view as to the character of the Anglo-Saxon 'will' may seem strange to the man of to-day who rightly regards the modern will as a dispositive instrument; but, if he be surprised, let him but project his mind into the early periods of Roman and Germanic legal development. In those far-off times men concluded

---

[1] On the distinction between these two types of documents, see Bresslau, *Urkundenlehre*, pp. 44, 45.

[2] It may, however, be lost or destroyed.

their legal transactions in oral speech and by the use of forms
and symbols[1]; and only by gradual processes of change did they
come to employ dispositive and evidentiary documents[2]. The
Anglo-Saxons inherited the legal traditions of Germanic peoples
on the Continent; and, like those peoples, they adopted Graeco-
Roman writings, under ecclesiastical influence, and at the same
time transformed them to suit their own purposes within a
native Germanic environment of oralism, formalism, and symbolism. The Anglo-Saxon documents, and not least of all our
so-called wills, must be studied, therefore, in their relation to
these characteristics of Germanic legal transactions before early
custom had been touched by Romanic practices. The introduction of documents based on Graeco-Roman models did
not displace the oral, formalistic, and symbolical features of
Germanic legal transactions in the England of pre-Conquest
times. While they received written instruments as a new feature
of their legal life the Anglo-Saxons did not use them in all
respects as the later Romans had used them; on the contrary,
in the process of adopting them, they adapted writings to the
requirements of their own native customary transactions in the
law of contract and property. Early Germanic custom demanded
that these transactions be not only capable of being heard and
seen, but that they be actually heard and seen[3]; and, hence,
spoken words and manual acts that were formal and symbolical
dominated the law in regard to the formation of contracts and
the conveyance of property. Nor were these features of primitive
Germanic custom absent in the case of Anglo-Saxon transactions
of legal import. They ruled, not least of all, the gift of property
mortis causa.

The Anglo-Saxon 'will', as contained in a writing, generally

---

[1] See von Ihering, *Geist des römischen Rechts*, II, 2, 5th ed. §§ 43–47 *d*, for
a brilliant illumination of transactions in early Roman law. On early Germanic law, see Heusler, *Institutionen des deutschen Privatrechts*, I, §§ 11–19;
Schröder, *Lehrbuch der deutschen Rechtsgeschichte*, 4th ed. §§ 11, 35, 61;
von Amira, *Grundriss des germanischen Rechts*, 3rd ed. §§ 69–71.

[2] On the use of writings by Germanic peoples, see Heusler, *op. cit.* § 19;
Schröder, *op. cit.* § 33; von Amira, *op. cit.* § 71; Brunner, *Zur Rechtsgeschichte der römischen und germanischen Urkunde* (bibliography, pp. xiii–
xvi). Bresslau's *Urkundenlehre* gives valuable information on the diplomatic
aspects of the development.

[3] Von Amira, *op. cit.* § 70.

embraced a number of these gifts, both of land and chattels, to a variety of lay and ecclesiastical persons; it was in fact, if one may use the term, a bundle of gifts *mortis causa*. The document which tells us of this bundle of gifts possessed, however, a unity of its own; not only did it assume one or another of the several diplomatic forms known to the age, but it had relations to other documents, more particularly the land-book[1]. If for a moment, therefore, we look not at the separate gifts mentioned in the written will, but if we keep our eyes on the instrument itself and view it in its entirety as a documentary unit, we shall gain clearer notions as to the diplomatic and juridical nature of the writing which contains the gifts and is known as the will. But, while looking on the writing as a unit, we should not consider it in isolation. Not only ought we to study its relation to other instruments of the time, such as the land-book; we should also envisage the writing in its environment of custom in respect of oral, formal, and symbolic transactions in general[2]. It is only by applying these methods in our study of the written will that we can see this documentary entity in its true light. It is not the will itself; it is only evidence of the will.

There are indeed clear indications in these writings described by historians as wills, and there are further and valuable proofs in other legal sources of the age, that the will itself, the act in the law, is oral; and that, while in some instances this jural act appears to be unilateral, in most cases at least it is bilateral and is in fact a contract between the donor, or *quasi*-testator, and one or more of the principal donees. Even when the will appears to be unilateral it may be doubted whether, in the majority of instances, this is truly the case. Wills in Anglo-

---

[1] The relation of the written will to the land-book will be considered briefly in later paragraphs.

[2] For aspects of this environment in Anglo-Saxon times, see Pollock and Maitland, *History of English Law*, 2nd ed. I, pp. 25–63; Holdsworth, *History of English Law*, 3rd ed. II, pp. 56–118. Similarly, the English writ-system, a written formalism, can be understood only by studying it in its relation to the traditional oral formalism in procedure which it supplanted; and the nature and purpose of written pleadings can be grasped only by considering them in their historical relation to the oral pleadings which they displaced.

Saxon times, as in contemporary Germanic law on the Continent[1], are *donationes irrevocabiles post obitum*; and the reason why they are irrevocable is because the donor has contractually promised by the making of his will, by the conclusion of a transaction *inter vivos*, that on his death the donees are to have conveyed to them the properties which form the subject-matter of his gift[2]. When, therefore, the will as embodied in the writing appears to be unilateral it is nevertheless, in most instances, based on a contract, express or implied, with one or more of the donees. Even when it can be shown that the will is truly unilateral the gift *mortis causa* is but a promise; it is a promise which can only be fulfilled *post obitum*. The Anglo-Saxon oral will, viewed as an entity, is only one of the several species of the great genus Gift[3]; and many of the gifts of that genus are not present gifts, but promises to give. In the Germanic Gift contract and conveyance are in truth closely interwoven; but in that species known as the *donatio post obitum* contract predominates. The complete *donatio* is composed of two jural acts: the gift-

---

[1] See Heusler, *op. cit.* II, §§ 195–199; Brunner, *Grundzüge der deutschen Rechtsgeschichte*, 5th ed. § 57; Brissaud, *History of French Private Law* (Continental Legal History Series), §§ 486–513.

[2] The burning of his former wills by King Alfred is clearly an exceptional case, owing to the fact that the *quasi*-testator is the King himself; and this instance cannot be cited as proof that wills were in general revocable in Anglo-Saxon times. For King Alfred's will, see Harmer, *English Historical Documents of the Ninth and Tenth Centuries*, No. XI, pp. 15–19. It is to be observed, moreover, that King Alfred refers in his will to the fact that when he made his earlier wills he had "more money and more kinsmen." It would seem that the death of certain kinsmen, who were donees under his former wills, was one of the chief reasons why he revoked these and made a new will. Whether *quasi*-testators in general could revoke their wills, and, if so, only in the event of the death of donees, must be left an open question. Attention may be drawn to five instances in the present collection where the donor seems to consider the possibility of his wishing to "alter (*wendan*)" his will: in four of these cases this possibility is expressed in the anathema. See No. II, p. 8, lines 25 *et seq.*; No. IV, p. 16, line 20; No. XXIX, p. 78, line 8; No. XXXI, p. 82, line 25; No. XXXV, p. 92, lines 6 *et seq.*, *infra*. This does not necessarily mean that alteration could take place without the consent of the donee. In all cases where the will took the form of a contract between the donor and the donee, the consent of the donee to an alteration made by the donor would mean that the parties modified the original contract by a later agreement.

[3] The broad scope of Gift (*Gabe*) in Germanic law may be studied in von Amira's *Nordgermanisches Obligationenrecht*, I, §§ 72–74, II, §§ 64–66. 'Gift' in English medieval law also illustrates the Germanic conception. See Pollock and Maitland, *op. cit.* Index, *s.v.* Gift.

contract and the gift-transfer. Even though in the contract the donor may use the present tense and say that he 'gives', his gift is but a promise to give until the property has been transferred to the donee[1]. The oral will of Anglo-Saxon times is a bundle of these Germanic contractual *donationes irrevocabiles post obitum*.

The validity of the oral *verba novissima*, the Anglo-Saxon death-bed will, at least from the eighth century onwards, has always been admitted[2]; and the evidence furnished by our sources points irresistibly to the fact that oral wills made by persons who were in good health and had no fear of imminent death were also recognised by Anglo-Saxon law as binding. The written will, not less than the land-book, was an exotic in England. Ecclesiastical in origin, it was not only developed under clerical influence for the material benefit of Anglo-Saxon churches and convents, but it was ultimately brought in a later age within the scope of the jurisdiction of ecclesiastical courts. At least from the beginning of the eighth century onwards ecclesiastical policy furthered the idea that spoken words were sufficient for gifts and contracts. Lest, however, spoken words fade from the memory, declare ecclesiastical draftsmen in the preambles to eighth-century Anglo-Saxon charters, it is best to have evidence of these words in a writing[3]. To the proof of oral acts furnished by transactions-witnesses, which was already a feature of Anglo-Saxon law, there was now the added evidence. of writings; and, so far as one can see, it is this new species of proof introduced by the ecclesiastics which helps us more than perhaps anything else to understand the legal nature and purpose of the documents that are now known as Anglo-Saxon 'wills'. These documents were not the wills themselves, the dispositive acts in the law. The wills were the oral declarations before witnesses; the writings were merely evidentiary. From one point of view too much stress has been laid upon the term *cwide* by writers on the history of Anglo-Saxon 'wills'; and from another point of

---

[1] Von Amira, *op. cit.* I, § 72 (at pp. 510–512), II, § 64 (at pp. 620–622).

[2] Pollock and Maitland, *op. cit.* II, p. 318. For a good example of the death-bed will, see Domesday Book, I, f. 177 *a*.

[3] See Brandileone, 'Anglo-Saxon Documents of the Eighth and Ninth Centuries' (*Wigmore Celebration Essays*, pp. 384–393, at pp. 386–387).

view too little importance has been attached to it. Although in later Anglo-Saxon times the term *cwide* was frequently used to indicate the document which we know as a 'will', other terms, especially 'writing' (*gewrit*), were also employed in the same sense; and, in fact, *gewrit* was not only used earlier, but also more generally, than *cwide*. The original meaning of *cwide*, and a meaning which it always retained, points clearly to orality; for in this basic sense *cwide* is simply speech, discourse, *dictum*. By a natural process in the development of thought the writing in which the oral *cwide* was embodied for purposes of evidence was itself called the *cwide*[1].

In the literature dealing with Anglo-Saxon wills too much stress, it may be thought, has also been laid upon the ecclesiastical origin of the writings; it has been too often assumed that the importation of written instruments implied the wholesale reception of Romano-ecclesiastical legal ideas in regard to the dispositive, as well as the evidential nature of documents. This assumption colours much of the literature on the land-book[2]; it also gives its tone to some of the historical accounts of the written will. On examination it is found, however, that this assumption carries us too far. One of the most important contributions of the Church to the legal polity of the Anglo-Saxons was the introduction of writings for the purposes of evidence; and, so far as one can see, in pre-Conquest days churches and

---

[1] The naming of a document after the oral transaction which it evidences is a well-known phenomenon in legal history. Thus, for example, when the *maldage*, or oral contract, of western Scandinavian law was embodied in a document, the document itself acquired the name *maldage*. See von Amira, *op. cit.* II, pp. 274–275, 334–338. In Anglo-Saxon times the writing which evidenced the oral will might consist of an entry in a church-book. For an illustration, see Kemble, *C.D.* 755, where an oral will, which was not a death-bed disposition, was upheld by the gemot and then entered in a church-book for purposes of permanent evidence. The entry was merely a *notitia*, an evidence-document. No legal significance attaches to the fact that an evidence-document is called a *cwide*. Any kind of writing, by whatever name it may call itself, is sufficient if it has legal efficacy as an evidence-document, such as an entry in a church-book. Certain kinds of writings, such as *chirographa*, have unusual strength as evidence-documents owing to the mode of their execution. Of this hereafter.

[2] Maitland, more cautious, seems never to have taken a definite position on the question as to whether the land-book was dispositive and evidential or merely evidential.

convents were themselves content if they had merely evidence-documents to prove title to the gifts that were made to them orally and never pressed for the acquisition of dispositive instruments. While, however, ecclesiastics recognised the adequacy of spoken words for gifts and contracts, since it was a part of Church policy to further formlessness in legal transactions, and while they were satisfied, apparently, by documents which merely evidenced those verbal transactions, the Germanic custom of the Anglo-Saxons required that oral contracts and gifts be confirmed by the use of certain formalities and symbols. Both native custom and ecclesiastical legal doctrine were at one in their recognition of the validity of oral transactions; and the point on which they differed chiefly concerned formalism and symbolism. In this matter custom proved to be stronger than ecclesiastical policy. We shall miss many features of Anglo-Saxon legal history if we do not grasp the point that to the very end of the epoch traditional employment of formalities and symbols retained its full control of the rules governing oral dispositive acts. To this aspect of our problem in regard to oral wills we shall return presently. For the moment it is important to establish the fact that, with the firm support of the Church, the Anglo-Saxons continued on their own traditional Germanic course and made their wills, just as they concluded all their other jural acts, by word of mouth.

The oral character of the Anglo-Saxon will is proved by many statements found not only in the written wills, but also in documents which recount the history of transactions in regard to certain properties. The donor, using the vernacular, 'bequeathes in spoken words[1]'; and no doubt some of these words are spoken formally in order that the oral disposition may be strengthened or confirmed[2]. The donor 'speaks his saying', he

---

[1] Thorpe, *Diplomatarium Anglicum*, p. 495 (at p. 497): Ic cweþe on wordum. Cf. Thorpe, *D.A.* p. 139 (at p. 141): ꝥ word gecwæð (he said that word). Bosworth-Toller, *s.v. becweðan*: Swa ðu worde becwist (as thou sayest by word). In Anglo-Saxon sources *word-riht* has the sense of a spoken law, a law expressed in spoken words.

[2] Cf. *word and wedd* in Æthelred's laws. Here, as Gierke has remarked, *word* means the formal word which confirms or strengthens the promise. See *Schuld und Haftung*, p. 184, n. 48. Thorpe, *D.A.* p. 176: ic...mid wordum afæstnige.

'speaks his *cwide*[1]': and his *cwide*, spoken in Anglo-Saxon, is reproduced in the written will. The very fact that the written wills are in the vernacular is some proof, although of course not conclusive proof, that the scribe has merely taken down what he heard[2]. This point, however, need not be pressed; for there are many confirmatory proofs of orality. In some of the documents it is stated that the *quasi*-testator 'declares and commands to be written what are his wishes as to the disposal of his property after his time[3]'; and in many of the other instruments there are statements of similar import. The donor *mortis causa* 'makes known' or 'declares' by the 'writing' how he grants, or has granted, his property; and there is no doubt, as we shall see later, that in these and similar instances an oral declaration of the will has either preceded or accompanied the writing of the document[4]. The will may take, and indeed generally does take, the form of a contract; and here too, as we shall see presently, the will-agreement is spoken[5]. In one way or another the written wills disclose to us the fact that the will itself, in contrast with the writing which enshrines it, is a will declared orally in the presence of witnesses: the writing is merely the documentation of the oral will[6].

[1] Thorpe, *D.A.* p.271 (at p. 272): he cwæð his cwide beforan him. P. 26, lines 11–12, *infra*: Ðis is Byrhtrices 7 Ælfswyðe his wifes nihsta cwide ðe hi cwædon on Meapaham on heora maga gewitnæsse. P. 22, lines 8–9, *infra*: Ælfheah...his cwidæ gecwæðen hæfð. Harmer, *English Historical Documents of the Ninth and Tenth Centuries*, No. xx, p. 33, lines 22–24: 7 eall þæt yrfe þæ ic hæbbe on lænelandum, þonne wylle ic þæt þæt sie gedeled for mine sawle swa swa ic nu þam freondum sæde þæ ic to spræc. See also Harmer, *E.H.D.* No. xi, p. 16, lines 28–30 (cydde...gecwædon).

[2] The documentary wills in Latin all appear to be later versions of the originals. Some wills are contained in Latin documents which are not primarily versions of the wills, but include the wills together with other matter.

[3] See, e.g., Thorpe, *D.A.* pp. 469, 476, 480; Harmer, *E.H.D.* No. ii, p. 3, lines 3–4.

[4] Illustrations will be found in the present as well as in other collections of Anglo-Saxon written wills.

[5] The terms *word-gecwide* and *cwid-ræden* mean oral contracts in Anglo-Saxon sources; while *cwide* sometimes indicates an oral decree or ordinance.

[6] See, e.g., No. ii, p. 8, lines 19–22; No. v, p. 18, lines 5–9; No. ix, p. 22, lines 8–9; No. xi, p. 26, lines 11–16; No. xx, p. 56, lines 10–13; No. xxii, p. 66, lines 1–2; No. xxiii, p. 66, lines 16–24; No. xxxii, p. 84, lines 8–16, *infra*. For illustrations, see also Thorpe, *D.A.* pp. 462, 469, 476, 480; Harmer, *E.H.D.* No. xx, p. 33, lines 22–25. In this last case the witnesses

Support for the view that the will was spoken is to be found in some of the Latin documents. Thus, Æthelric, the son of Æthelmund, states[1], in 804, that at the synod of Clofeshoh the archbishop, *cum testimonio* of the king and his *optimates*, gave a decision that Æthelric was free to give his land at Wæstmynster [Westbury, Glos.] and the title-deeds (*libellos*) to whomsoever he wished. Æthelric then pledged the land before he went to Rome; but, on returning, he redeemed it. A few years later at the synod of Acle, in the presence of the king, bishops, and *principes*, he reminded them of the decision of the former council; and, with their permission, he testified to whom he wished to give his inheritance. In the document this statement is followed by the will, which is introduced by the words: *et sic dixi*. The will, which is mainly composed of gifts to Worcester, includes a clause to the effect that there are three copies of the document and ends with an anathema and a list of witnesses[2].

In another Latin document[3] the donor declares that she makes gifts of certain lands to certain churches. She concludes her *dispositio* with the words: *sicut prædictus vir meus Alfwoldus eas adhuc vivens viva voce eidem ecclesie concessit.* While it is not altogether easy to interpret this document as a whole, a possible

---

of the oral declaration are at the same time the 'protectors' of the will; that is, they are charged with the duty of distributing at the death of the donor, in accordance with the oral directions of the donor, the property that is granted.

[1] Birch, *Cartularium Saxonicum*, 313 (preserved in Worcester cartularies: Tiberius A, xiii: Nero E, 1) = Thorpe, *D.A.* p. 54. The present writer is much indebted to Miss Whitelock for drawing his attention to this document and for her observations upon it.

[2] Possibly this document was touched up a little by the Worcester scribe, but that he should have invented the whole seems improbable. Worcester was engaged a little later in a dispute over the estate (Birch, *C.S.* 379, dated 824, from the same sources as the document containing the will) and the compiler of the cartulary may have wished to make their title as strong as possible. But, since passages like that about pledging the land have a genuine ring, one seems entitled to use the document as at least supporting evidence in favour of the view that the Anglo-Saxon will was oral. It may be added that the reference to three copies means that the document is a chirograph. Chirographic written wills come under observation in later paragraphs.

[3] Birch, *C.S.* 1061 = Thorpe, *D.A.* p. 516. This document is a copy of a chirograph of about the middle of the tenth century.

view is that the donor's husband had given the lands to the churches by his oral will, but with the reservation of usufruct for the life of his wife, the present donor; and that title to the lands had been conveyed to the grantees with this reservation. On this view the present gift appears to be in the nature of a release (*resignatio*)[1].

The first of these two Latin documents, the one containing the will of Æthelric, the son of Æthelmund, is evidence for the view that wills were sometimes made orally before the witan[2]. It is also possible that in some cases the will in its written form was read out to those who had witnessed the making of the oral will; but under these circumstances the oral reading of the writing would appear to have constituted what one may describe as a secondary orality which, although not part of the jural act of making the will, had as its purpose the strengthening of the earlier oral declaration, or announcement, of the will[3]. Towards the end of the written will of the Ætheling Æthelstan[4] is the statement: 'Now I pray all the councillors, both ecclesiastical and lay, who may hear my will (*cwide*) read, that they will help to secure that my will may stand, as my father's permission is stated in my will'. It is clear that this is a special case[5], for Æthelstan was a great man in the realm, the son of King Ethelred; and, moreover, the will itself may have belonged to the category of *verba novissima*. Whether or not the oral will was made before the witan, that is, 'the councillors, both ecclesiastical and lay', it seems impossible to tell; but if it was a will made during illness, and hence a case of *verba novissima*, this hardly seems likely. The more natural explanation is that the will was read before the witan because of Æthelstan's high rank; and, as Miss Whitelock remarks, 'it is hardly likely that the wills of

[1] The release (*resignatio*) as a form of gift *mortis causa* will be mentioned in a later paragraph.

[2] There are instances which imply that the king was sometimes present at the making of wills. See, e.g., Nos. VIII, XIII, XV, *infra*. In some cases he is named as a witness. See Nos. XXX, XXXII, *infra*.

[3] Cf. Brunner's suggestion as to the reading out of the text of the land-book in the process of booking land. See his *Urkunde*, p. 161; and cf. von Amira, *Grundriss des germanischen Rechts*, p. 228.

[4] No. XX, *infra*.

[5] See pp. 167–174, *infra*.

lesser people were read there[1]'. In old Scandinavian law the publicity of transactions could be effected by one or the other of two modes. Either the transaction was itself concluded before an assembly; or the transaction, already complete and binding, was announced to an assembly. After the introduction of writings into Northern legal life this announcement (*lýsing*) was closely associated with the document in which the transaction was embodied; and it often consisted of reading the document to the assembly[2]. It is possible, therefore, that in the instance of Æthelstan's will we have to do with an announcement to the Anglo-Saxon *witan* comparable with the announcement to the assembled *thing* in Scandinavia[3].

While it has seemed important to mention at the outset certain proofs of the oral character of the Anglo-Saxon will, attention should be drawn to the point that they are supported by other proofs which will come under our observation in later paragraphs. For the moment, however, let us take account of the fact that Anglo-Saxon wills were not only oral dispositions of property *mortis causa*, but that many of them, perhaps most of them, were contractual dispositions. The contractual character of early Germanic gifts *mortis causa*, as predecessors of the unilateral and revocable will or testament in the later and true sense of that term, has long been recognised by scholars[4]; and it need occasion no surprise, therefore, that contractual gifts *mortis causa* were also known to Anglo-Saxon law. They are in truth but a further illustration of the large part played by contract in the Anglo-Saxon age. Status and contract were two of the main foundations of social life; but, although many relationships were based on status, contract became ever more important as time

---

[1] See p. 173, *infra*.

[2] See von Amira, *Nordgermanisches Obligationenrecht*, II, §§ 33, 34; and also *op. cit.* I and II, register, *s.v. lýsing*.

[3] Cf. the case of King Ethelred's *confirmation* of Æthelric's will, where an oral declaration was 'straightway written and read before the king and his witan'. See No. XVI (2), p. 44, lines 22–24, *infra*. By concluding and also by announcing transactions before the witan the widest publicity and the highest authority were obtained. See Liebermann, *National Assembly in the Anglo-Saxon Period*, p. 71.

[4] See, e.g., Brissaud, *History of French Private Law* (Continental Legal History Series), §§ 486, 489; Hübner, *History of Germanic Private Law* (Continental Legal History Series), §§ 110–113.

went on and tended in fact to displace status. The Grant (or Gift) of property was one of the chief forces making for this progress to contractual conditions. Grant, however, was one of the broadest general conceptions known to Anglo-Saxon law and custom; and these broad general conceptions, such as Grant and Wrong, were characteristic of early stages of legal growth in all parts of Europe. In Anglo-Saxon times Grant, or Gift, included within itself both the idea of conveyance and the idea of contract. Conveyance and contract were aspects of Grant; and in some grants one or the other of these two characteristics predominated. Only gradually, in the course of long centuries, were these two juridical ideas, conveyance and contract, finally differentiated by legal reasoning and given their separate and distinct places in the general scheme of jurisprudence. One of the reasons why Contract in Anglo-Saxon times has been partly concealed from our gaze is because it so often played its rôle behind the mask of Grant. Although the purchase of land was a transaction in which the contractual element was prominent, the transaction itself did not take the form of a contract of sale; it took the form of a grant[1]. If, moreover, we look only at the higher ranks of society we can now see that grants, or gifts, of land were the main foundation of relationships. The gradual feudalisation of land in Anglo-Saxon times was accomplished by gifts of land which had their contractual as well as their conveyancing features. The feudal *nexum* was created by gift; and it seems in fact never to have lost the duality of conveyance and contract involved in gift. The gift of land, even the gift of bookland by the king, and even more so, perhaps, the gift of loan-land by the owner of book-land, had marked contractual aspects. The Anglo-Saxons think in terms of grantor and grantee; and by grant they mean both conveyance and contract. The king and leading laymen form a large part of the class of grantors; while the ecclesiastics and ecclesiastical institutions are one of the

---

[1] Professor Chadwick has kindly supplied the following examples. Birch, *C.S.* 146: Ego Aeðilbold pro redemptione animae meae largitus sum terram.... contra eius pecuniam.... Birch, *ibid.*, 348: ...ego Coenuulfus...Vulfredo archiepiscopo...pro intimo caritatis affectu...seu etiam pro commodo pecunio illius, hoc est vii libras auri et argenti...terram. For other examples see Birch, *ibid.*, 373, 455, 509.

largest, perhaps the largest, class of grantees. These grantors
and grantees are traffickers. The subject-matters of their bar-
gaining are not, however, spears and chasubles: these two groups
of men are concerned with things of far greater durability and
value. The men of this world want things in the next; while the
men of the next world want things in this. By their gifts the
lay folk buy things in the spiritual world; and by their counter-
gifts and counter-performances the clerical folk buy things in
the corporeal world. Rights in terrestrial possessions are exchanged for rights in the heavenly mansions; and these rights
are exchanged by grants which at the same time are contracts.
In Anglo-Saxon law, as in other Germanic customary systems,
gift is not gratuitous; gift requires counter-gift or counter-performance. When, therefore, lay folk and clerical folk bargain,
they exchange gifts. The gift of the laymen is land; the gift of
the clergy is the care of the soul by spiritual services. In these
gifts and counter-gifts there is the intermingling of conveyance
and contract; and sometimes these two inherent qualities, or
aspects, of gift seem almost inextricably interwoven. Nor is
there any difference, in this respect, between gifts *inter vivos*
and gifts *mortis causa*; and, moreover, be it noted, donors by
their gifts *mortis causa*, not less than by their grants *inter vivos*,
are thinking of their souls and buying a secure and lasting place
for them in the world to come. Many gifts *mortis causa* are
primarily contracts; they are promises that on the death of the
donors the donees shall have conveyances. Some of them are
present conveyances which still leave the donor a promisor; as
when the donor himself conveys book-land to the donee, with
a reservation of usufruct for one or more lives. The transaction
here is *inter vivos* and at the same time it is *mortis causa*; the
conveyance is a present conveyance which can be perfected only
at a later time. It is in fact perfected only when, on the death
of the donor and of others who have the usufruct, the donor's
promise is fully performed by the final surrender of the land to
the donee.

The approach to gifts *mortis causa* must be by this gateway
of the Germanic Grant of Anglo-Saxon law and custom; for
gifts *mortis causa* are grants and they are, moreover, grants in

which both conveyance and contract are mingled. For the moment let us pay particular attention to the contractual aspect of these grants; and, first of all, let us consider a notable feature of many wills. The writings in which wills are embodied prove to us that in fact many a donor, or *quasi*-testator, confirms by his will agreements which he has already concluded with his wife, members of his kindred, or other persons, in regard to the devolution on their death of properties which belong to them[1]. These contracts (*forword, gecwide, wordgecwide, maldage, pactum*) were concluded orally in the presence of witnesses; and they were confirmed by the parties by formal acts, such as solemn promises to God and the saints or the mutual delivery of symbolic pledges (*wedd*)[2]. The written wills leave us in no doubt as to the nature of these contracts: they were 'spoken' agreements made binding by the use of formalities and symbols. Since they were concluded in such a way as to be not only capable of being heard and seen, but actually heard and seen by witnesses, these agreements complied with the general requirements of Germanic custom in regard to legal transactions[3]; and there is at least some evidence that in certain instances they

[1] A provision as to survivorship is a usual feature of these agreements: that is, the parties stipulate that the one who outlives the other is to have property belonging to the deceased. See p. 166, *infra*.

[2] Examples of these oral agreements *mortis causa* confirmed by will are to be found in Nos. IV, X, XIII, XV, XIX, XXIV, XXXI, XXXIII, XXXIV, XXXIX, *infra*; Thorpe, *D.A.* pp. 576, 586 (two); Harmer, *E.H.D.* Nos. X, XI. The terms *forword* and *maldage* are of Scandinavian origin. While *maldage* is rarely found in Anglo-Saxon sources, *forword* is used frequently in the sense of contractual agreement. See Thorpe, *D.A.* pp. 1–455, *passim*, for examples of *forword* in documents that are not written wills. Cf., on the use of '*vorwort*' in other Germanic sources, Puntschart, *Schuldvertrag und Treugelöbnis*, § 19 (at pp. 379–80). In Nos. XXXIII and XXXIV, *infra*, both of which must be read together, there is an instructive instance of a partnership agreement (*felageschipe*), confirmed by will, in regard to the devolution of property. As Miss Whitelock points out, *felageschipe* corresponds to the old Icelandic *felagskapr*, which means any kind of partnership. See pp. 194, 203, *infra*. Indeed the term *felag* has reference to the several kinds of partnership known to the old law of Sweden, Norway, Iceland, and Greenland. In some instances the devolution of partnership property was the subject-matter of the agreements. See von Amira, *op. cit.* I, pp. 670–680, II, pp. 1, 807–822.

[3] See the writings of von Amira and other historians of Germanic law and custom. The witnessing of a legal transaction was a formality; and it was also a means of proof.

were reduced to writing[1]. The chief points to observe, however, are that by their formal contracts, concluded orally, parties made gifts *mortis causa*; and that these contracts, confirmed by will, were themselves, in all essential particulars, 'wills' in the Anglo-Saxon sense[2]. Be it noted especially that these contractual gifts are *donationes post obitum*[3]; and, moreover, since they are based on binding contracts they are *donationes irrevocabiles post obitum*. The contractual *grant* or *dispositio* is sometimes phrased in the same way as are grants in the case of gifts *post obitum* in the 'wills': the famous formula in the wills—'after my day'—also appears in the contracts. Other *formulae*, such as 'if I outlive X' and 'if X survive me', are also used; and these are especially appropriate to contractual gifts *post obitum*. The contracting party expresses, furthermore, his concern about the 'standing', the performance, of the agreement[4]; and here, again, there is a parallel with the anxiety voiced by *quasi*-testators in regard to the 'standing' of their wills. In truth these contracts confirmed by will are themselves 'wills': later wills confirm earlier wills. When, therefore, we think and talk about Anglo-Saxon 'wills' we should think and talk about these contracts *mortis causa* as being true 'wills' in the Anglo-Saxon sense of that term.

There is, moreover, a still more important point to consider. Not only are many oral contracts *mortis causa* confirmed by oral will; some, and indeed most, of our Anglo-Saxon 'wills', including those of the present collection, are themselves oral contracts *mortis causa*. There is, indeed, no essential difference between these two categories of oral contract *mortis causa*: both of them are contractual *donationes irrevocabiles post obitum*. Restricting our attention for the moment to those writings which are known as wills, let us observe two things: first, some of the writings are not only framed in terms of contract, but are called contracts (*forword, geþinge, gerednes, conventio*[5]); secondly, the contractual character of many of the other writings is disclosed,

---

[1] See Harmer, *E.H.D.* No. XI (King Alfred's will).

[2] The contracts were confirmed by the oral will; but no doubt the will in its written form, since it bore the Christian crosses, further confirmed them.

[3] See the passages mentioned in note 2, p. xxi, *supra*.

[4] See, e.g., No. XIII, p. 32, lines 14–16, *infra*.

[5] For examples, see Nos. V, XXIII, XXXIX, *infra*; Thorpe, *D.A.* pp. 459, 465, 468, 492, 509, 585, 593.

not by the fact that they are called contracts, but by other documentary features. In all these cases, however, the writings
which embody the contracts are not the contracts themselves.
The contracts, like many other contracts of Anglo-Saxon times,
are oral contracts concluded formally; the writings, even though
they may call themselves contracts, are only evidence of the
agreements that are already valid and binding without the use
of documentation.

In this connection it is to be noticed that some of the writings
which contain wills, or, in other words, some of the wills in their
written form, are executed in duplicate or triplicate as *chirographa*[1]; and no doubt were we in possession of their originals,
instead of later versions, many more of the writings known as
wills could be shown to have been *chirographa*[2]. The fact that
an Anglo-Saxon written will was executed in duplicate or triplicate points to the contractual character of the oral will itself[3].
Whenever a written will was executed in triplicate one copy was
always held by the donor, while the two remaining copies were
held by two of the principal donees; or, as in some cases, one
of these two remaining copies was held by one of the principal
donees, while the other was held by a disinterested monastery
or by the king in his *haligdom*[4]. If the history of the *chiro-*

---

[1] For chirographic wills, see Nos. XIII, XIX, XX, XXIV, XXV, XXIX, XXX,
XXXI, XXXIII, and the notes thereon, *infra*; Thorpe, *D.A.* pp. 476, 586,
593. No. XVI (2), *infra*, which is not a written will but the royal *confirmation* of a will, was executed in triplicate. In making Anglo-Saxon chirographs the subject-matter of the transaction was written three times
on one skin of parchment with the word '*chirographum*' blazoned large
between the copies; the knife was then passed through the middle of the
words *chirographum*, thus cutting the parchment into three pieces. By
bringing two of these pieces, or all three of them, together the oneness of
the copies could be established. See, further, Bresslau, *op. cit.* pp. 502–
511; Earle, *Land Charters and other Saxonic Documents*, p. xliii. On the
writing of fines in triplicate in days after the Conquest, see Turner, *Feet
of Fines*, pp. cxxiv–cxxvii.

[2] Bresslau, *op. cit.* p. 505, has observed that Anglo-Saxon chirographic
writings rarely contain an express statement that they are in fact chirographs. Since the chirograph began with the sign of the cross, a con-
siderable number of the 'wills' in Thorpe's collection appear to have been
chirographs. See Galbraith, 'An Episcopal Land-Grant of 1085', *E.H.R.*
XLIV, p. 355; Thorpe, *D.A.* pp. 459–601.

[3] See Brunner, *op. cit.* pp. 200, 202.

[4] In the case of one of our chirographic wills the writing was executed
in duplicate: one was held by the principal donee, the other by the donor's

graphum in Greek and Roman law[1], from which the Anglo-Saxons derived it, be any guide to the nature of the Anglo-Saxon documentary will in duplicate or triplicate, we should be entitled to conclude that these *chirographa* were not both dispositive and evidentiary instruments, but that they were merely evidence-documents; or, to phrase it in other terms, that they were not dispositive *cartae*, but merely memoranda, documents *memoriae causa*, *notitiae*[2].

It is possible that the *chirographum*, in the sense of a document executed in duplicate or triplicate for purposes of evidence, may have an ancient origin in the primitive Germanic *festuca notata*, the small notched stick, the tally stick, which was broken in two pieces in order that each party might have one as

heirs. Thorpe, *D.A.* p. 476. The reason for placing a third copy in a place of safety was that one single copy was not proof of the transaction. In case one of the two parties lost his copy, or refused to produce it, the third copy could then be brought forward and compared with the copy of the party who did produce his. Bresslau, *op. cit.* pp. 508–9. Cf. also Keller, 'Cyrographum und Hautgemal' (*Festschrift für Brunner*, 1910, pp. 187–211, at p. 192).

[1] See Vinogradoff, *Historical Jurisprudence*, II, pp. 238–245; Girard, *Manuel Élémentaire du Droit Romain*, 3rd ed. pp. 496, 497; Buckland, *Manual of Roman Private Law*, pp. 270, 271, *Roman Law from Augustus to Justinian*, p. 458, n. 5; Heumann, *Handlexikon zu den Quellen des römischen Rechts*, 8th ed. *s.v. chirographarius*, *chirographum*; Bresslau, *op. cit.* pp. 45–46; Brunner, *op. cit.* pp. 44–57, 145–148.

[2] The introduction of *chirographa* and other evidence-documents into eighth-century England appears to have been due, in part at least, to the Graeco-Byzantine culture among the Roman clergy. See Kemble, *Codex Diplomaticus*, 169 (A.D. 781); Brandileone, *loc. cit.* p. 387. The term *chirographum* does not necessarily point, however, to a purely evidentiary document as distinct from a document which is both dispositive and evidential. In Greece and at Rome the term was used for both types of documents: in matter of historical development, as the literature indicated in the preceding note will show, the evidential *chirographa* were earlier than the dispositive documents which bore the same name. The term *chirographum* was used in Anglo-Saxon times for all kinds of documents; while in Norman times it was a *terminus technicus* for the Anglo-Saxon as distinct from the Norman document. See Bresslau, *op. cit.* p. 503. In the form of *cartae excisae* (*indentatae*) the Anglo-Saxon *chirographa* may well have been the origin of the later English *indenture*. See Bresslau, *op. cit.* p. 508. The use of the *chirographum*, as a document made in duplicate or triplicate, seems to have spread from Anglo-Saxon England to the Continent. See Bresslau, *op. cit.* pp. 502–511. It may be added that in his account of the *chirographum* as used by Germanic peoples in the medieval epoch Bresslau appears to look upon the document, when executed in duplicate or triplicate, as an evidential *notitia*. See *op. cit.* pp. 502–511.

evidence[1]; but, so far as the Anglo-Saxon evidential *chirographum* is concerned, an origin in the Graeco-Romanic document of the same name is more easily traced. The evidentiary function of the chirograph is in the mind of the scribe. In one document he tells us that the *testimonium chirographorum* is designed to keep acts in perpetual memory[2]; while in another writing, itself a chirograph, he remarks, putting the words into King Eadgar's mouth, that the three chirographs, for purposes of evidence (*to swyte-lungum*)[3], have been placed in the three monasteries[4]. At least in respect of the Anglo-Saxon written will one seems justified in concluding that the presence of chirographic copies indicates three things: first, that the dispositive act in the law, the will itself, was oral; secondly, that it was evidenced not only by the living witnesses, but also by the chirographic writings; and, thirdly, that the oral will, evidenced by the *chirographa*, was in essence a contractual agreement between the donor and the principal donee or donees[5]. The fact that the principal donee is in possession of one of the *chirographa* is of prime significance; for it shows us not only that he has written evidence of the oral will, but that he has possession of the document as a contractual promisee.

There is, moreover, an additional fact which indicates the contractual character of many Anglo-Saxon wills: the fact, namely, that the principal donee is a promisor as well as a promisee. It was a deep-seated Germanic idea that a gift required a counter-gift or counter-performance, however slight that might be, as in the case of the Lombardic *launegild*[6]. Many

---

[1] See Heusler, *op. cit.* 1, pp. 76–79, 91–92; Brissaud, *op. cit.* § 366; Bresslau, *op. cit.* p. 511. Cf. Henry, *Contracts in the Local Courts of Medieval England*, Index, *s.v.* Tally. [2] Thorpe, *D.A.* p. 16 (at p. 17).

[3] Liebermann, *Gesetze der Angelsachsen*, II, *s.v.* swutulung [=Beweis].

[4] Thorpe, *D.A.*, p. 231 (at p. 233). Thorpe's translation is slightly different from the one presented, which was suggested to the present writer by Miss Whitelock. The Old English as it stands in Thorpe can hardly be correct: a verb is apparently missing after *cyrografum*.

[5] Earle, *Land Charters and other Saxonic Documents*, p. xliii, has indicated that in Anglo-Saxon times chirographs were chiefly used for contracts.

[6] The best exposition of the history and juridical nature of the counter-gift (*Gegengabe*) in Germanic law will be found in von Amira's *Nordgermanisches Obligationenrecht*, I, §§ 72–74, II, §§ 64–66. For a criticism of some of von Amira's views, in so far as they apply to old Swedish law, see Beauchet, *Propriété Foncière en Suède*, pp. 321–335.

of the gifts made by Anglo-Saxon *quasi*-testators to all sorts of persons are based on this early Germanic notion of counter-gift: and the written wills deserve special study from this point of view[1]. For the moment attention may be drawn to the principal donee who, in Anglo-Saxon wills, is nearly always an ecclesiastical donee, usually a church or a convent. In return for the promise of the gift by the *quasi*-testator, the donee promises to give him burial[2], or, as in many cases, he promises to care for his soul, and sometimes also the souls of his ancestors and kindred, by masses, psalters, prayers, and other religious services[3]. Since the donor and the principal donee have exchanged mutual promises, and since accordingly each of them is a promisor as well as a promisee, it is natural that each should possess one of the *chirographa*, for in that writing the terms of the contract are embodied.

Many Anglo-Saxon wills were, therefore, bilateral contracts concluded orally in the presence of witnesses by the exchange of promises and the use of certain formalities; and, in respect of their formation and validity alike, they were contracts of the same nature as the agreements which, as we have found, were frequently confirmed by will. They were contracts, moreover, similar in character to the contracts of other systems of Germanic law; and they should be studied not only in their historical relation to Frankish, Burgundian, Lombardic, Scandinavian, and other forms of Germanic contractual obligation, but also, since the Anglo-Saxon law of contract was merely a branch of the Germanic law of obligations in its widest sense, as one of the special manifestations of the Anglo-Saxon contract. As in

---

[1] The idea of the counter-gift seems in fact to permeate much of English medieval law and custom.

[2] See, e.g., Nos. v (and pp. 116, 144), XXIII (and pp. 176–178), *infra*. For similar gifts in post-Conquest times, see Pollock and Maitland, *op. cit.* II, pp. 322–323. While the line which separates these gifts from the payment of *soul-scot* is not clear, it would seem that if a man desired to be buried in a church other than the one which had the right to *soul-scot*, he was then obliged to contract with that other church by promising a gift in return for burial.

[3] From the donor's view-point this is the 'soul-gift' (*Seelgabe*). See pp. 1–97 (*passim*), *infra*. Cf. von Amira, *op. cit.* I, pp. 504–517, especially pp. 506, 508–509. Similar to the soul-gift of Christian times were the earlier gifts to heathen gods for long life.

the case of other Germanic contracts the will-contract of Anglo-
Saxon times rested for its validity on oral agreement confirmed
by formal acts, such as the exchange of symbolic pledges (*wedd*),
in the presence of witnesses; and, as in other Germanic contractual systems, the embodiment of the oral and formal contract in writing was not essential to the completion of the contract
as a binding obligation. The writings which evidence oral wills
form, in fact, only one of several groups of Anglo-Saxon
evidence-documents. Apart from the land-books, which may
or may not have been dispositive documents[1], most, if not all,
of the private documents of the age seem to have been merely
of evidential value. Acts in the law, including the formation
of contracts in general[2], acts unconnected in any way with the
making of wills, were oral and formal in their character. Only
after the acts had become legally complete and binding were
they reduced to writing[3]; and in the case of contracts some at
least of these evidence-documents, like many written wills, were
in the form of *chirographa*. Thus to formulate the matter in terms
of documentary evidence is, however, merely to give expression
in a different phraseology to the historical truth that legal transactions in Anglo-Saxon times were concluded orally and formally. Although this truth is important in itself, it has an especial
value as showing us the historical environment within which the
oral will, either as a unilateral declaratory act or as a bilateral
contractual act, originated and developed. The oral will was not
an exotic in England; it was native to the Germanic custom of
the Anglo-Saxon period of our legal history. The writing, exotic
in every sense, was simply a new and a better form of testimony;
from its very nature it was a permanent record of what the
parties had said and done. For the introduction of that novel
testimonium into their legal life the Anglo-Saxons were indebted
to the ecclesiastics.

Inasmuch as the Anglo-Saxon donor *mortis causa* was a con-

---

[1] This problem will be mentioned later.
[2] On the Anglo-Saxon law of contracts, see Pollock and Maitland, *op. cit.* I,
pp. 56–58, II, pp. 184–233 (*passim*); Holdsworth, *op. cit.* II, pp. 82–87; Hazeltine, *Geschichte des englischen Pfandrechts*, pp. 69–113.
[3] See, e.g., Thorpe, *D.A.* pp. 147, 166, 169, 191, 312, 320, 328, 331, 346,
349; Harmer, *E.H.D.* No. VIII, p. 12, lines 5–7.

tractual promisor, we are driven to ask the question as to the effect of his promise. Did it bind him personally in liability? Did it bind in liability the property that was the subject-matter of his gift? In early medieval Germanic law *solus consensus* created only a legal duty without liability—*Schuld* without *Haftung*. To create a liability, either of the person or of property, formalities in addition to bare promises were essential; and perhaps the chief function of the Germanic formal contract was to establish legal liability in addition to legal duty. Only during the last few decades has this fundamental distinction between *Schuld* and *Haftung* emerged into clear light as one of the distinctive characteristics of early Germanic law; and its discovery has meant the re-writing of the history of the formal contract from the new view-point. It is now seen indeed that the reason why contracts were concluded, or confirmed, by formal words and by formal acts, such as the oath and the delivery of symbolic pledges, was to bind in liability either the person of the promisor or his property; and it has been partially proven that this was not less true of Anglo-Saxon formal contracts than of similar contracts in other parts of the Germanic world[1]. When we bear in mind that the contractual will of Anglo-Saxon times was a contract concluded formally, and that it differed in no essential particular from other formal contracts of the time, we may not unreasonably surmise that it had the effect of binding either the donor personally or his property, or both, in legal liability. There is much in the written wills, and even more in other legal sources of the age, to lead us to infer that by the delivery of a symbolic *wedd*, or by some other formality, the donor-promisor had bound his property; and that in fact the donee-promisee, by the acceptance of the symbolic *wedd*, had acquired a right in the nature of a *ius ad rem* in the subject-matter of the gift[2]. If we may go as far as this, we must continue to the end and conclude that when, on the death of the donor-promisor, the subject-matter of the gift (Blackacre, shall we say) was conveyed to the donee in ful-

---

[1] See Hazeltine, *op. cit.* pp. 109–113; Gierke, *Schuld und Haftung*, pp. 182–186, 314–317, 365.

[2] Cf. Pollock and Maitland, *op. cit.* II, pp. 86, 88. On the so-called *ius ad rem* see, Heusler, *op. cit.* I, § 77; Heymann, 'Zur Geschichte des *jus ad rem*' (*Festschrift für Gierke*, 1911, pp. 1167–1185).

filment of the donor's promise, the symbolic pledge (*wedd*) was thereby redeemed. This, however, is only one of many thoughts that arise in the mind through a perusal of the interesting documents known as wills[1]. To establish this suggested property-liability as in fact one of the legal effects of the making of a will, or, on the other hand, to prove that such a liability has no basis in the law of Anglo-Saxon times, is one of the matters which can find no place in these brief comments. Here one may only hint that the problem of liability is a valuable clue which, if followed up by research, might ultimately help us better to grasp the inner meaning of the Anglo-Saxon contractual will.

A study of the land-books has shown that the act of creating and transferring book-land was done in such a way that the witnesses both heard and saw it. The grant was spoken; the sanction was also oral; the *caraxare signa* was effected by 'tongue' and 'finger'. The scribe has played a merely passive rôle; he has transferred to the document the things that were said and done by those engaged in the transaction. An examination of the orality, formality, and symbolism in the act of booking land[2] is in fact a valuable introduction to the study of that group of documents known as Anglo-Saxon wills. By holding the scribe's parchment will up to the light, and thus making it luminous and transparent, behind it we can see the living parties themselves as they act their parts in the

---

[1] The significance of the terms of a contract *mortis causa*, to be found in the Medhamstead memoranda, should not be overlooked:—...and on his *wedde* gesealde þet land æt Wermingtune æfter his dæg into Sancte Petre for his saule on hyra gewytnesse. See Vinogradoff, *Collected Papers*, I, p. 159, n. 1. Cf. also the delivery of a document as a symbol in *substitution* for the delivery of a symbolic *wedd*: the formal delivery of such a document bound the transferor's property. See p. xxxi, n. 2, *infra*. It is clear from Cnut's proclamation that the one who broke oaths (*aðas*) or pledge (*wedd*) incurred God's displeasure and hence ecclesiastical punishment. See Earle, *Land Charters*, p. 229 (at p. 231); Stubbs, *Select Charters*, 9th ed. (Davis), p. 90 (at p. 91). This personal liability, enforced by ecclesiastical authorities, may well have been combined with property-liability enforced by lay authorities. A study of litigation over wills would help us to understand better the conflicting claims of the family and the donee; and from such a study an answer to the question as to property-liability might emerge.

[2] See Brunner, *op. cit.* pp. 153–166, 185–190.

transaction; for it is clear that, apart from certain sentences which he has written largely for explanation, the scribe has merely reproduced what the witnesses have themselves heard and seen. From the diplomatic point of view the written wills are miscellaneous in character. Some of them begin with the solemn invocation which we associate with the charter; some begin in the form of writs; many others begin with a bald statement that 'this is the will of X' or that 'this is the contract of X and Y[1]'. Practically all these writings are in fact combinations and variations of two or more of the recognised diplomatic forms; but, however miscellaneous our group of Anglo-Saxon written wills may be, nearly all of them contain at least three of the several parts usually found in early medieval diplomas: the *notificatio*, the *dispositio*, the *sanctio*. The several parts of the written will correspond in fact to the several stages in the oral and formal act of making the will. The declaration or announcement, characteristic of the opening part of the instrument, corresponds to the oral declaration or announcement; the written grant is a copy of the verbal grant; the written sanction is a report of the spoken sanction[2]. The fluctuation in the personal pronoun and in the tense, which is a marked feature of the

---

[1] These statements are clearly the scribe's own explanations.
[2] An instructive illustration of the oral announcement and oral grant is found in the nuncupative will of Eanwen reported in Kemble, *C.D.* 755. In the presence of Leofled and three witnesses Eanwen said, apparently in a loud voice, for she was angry: 'Here sits Leofled, my kinswoman, whom I grant both my land and my gold, both raiment and garment, and all that I own, after my day'. Then to the three thanes, who were witnesses, she said: 'Declare my errand to the gemot before all the good men, and make known to them whom I have granted my land to, and all my property'. The announcement was duly made verbally to the gemot, which upheld the oral will; and the will was then recorded as a *notitia*, for purposes of evidence, in a church-book. With this oral announcement and grant an oral death-bed will, which will be found in Domesday Book, may be compared. A dying man called to his bed his wife, his son, and several friends, and then addressed them as follows: 'Hark, my friends. I will that my wife shall hold this land which I bought from the Church as long as she lives, and after her death let the Church from which I had it take it. And should anyone encroach on this land let him be excommunicated'. Here we have not only the oral announcement and grant, but also the oral sanction. See D.B. I, f. 177 a. These two nuncupative wills help us to form a mental picture of the oral making of all wills in Anglo-Saxon times. The diplomatic parts of the writing correspond to the stages in the oral transaction.

writings, is to be explained only if we remember that the scribe, acting a passive rôle, has sometimes taken down the words as from dictation; while, at other times, giving perhaps his own version of the transaction, he has indicated the grantor by using the third personal pronoun and has employed the past tense instead of the present in referring to the transaction as a whole[1].

Studies of the written will from the diplomatic view-point reveal, therefore, the purely evidentiary character of the document itself. Nor is a different result produced by an examination of the question as to the significance of the delivery of the chirographic copy of the written will to the principal donee. In this matter, again, a comparison with the land-book is helpful. The delivery of the land-book was a formal act because the donor was conveying land to the grantee; but the delivery of the chirographic will to the donee appears to have been informal because the donor had already concluded his contract with the donee and hence formality in the delivery of the evidence-document was not essential[2]. Even as to the delivery of the

---

[1] The relation between the making of the oral will and the scribe's documentation of it may be studied in the writings of the present volume as well as in other collections of written wills. On the scribe's use of tense, especially the future tense, in land-books, see Brunner, *op. cit.* pp. 165–166. For the view that Brunner's explanation of the use of the future tense is unsatisfactory, see Napier and Stevenson, *Crawford Charters*, pp. 37–38; and cf. Bresslau, *op. cit.* p. 5, n. 3. On the use of first and third personal pronouns and of tense in early medieval documents, see Bresslau, *op. cit.* pp. 3–5.

[2] In Germanic law on the Continent, even as early as Frankish times, documents were used as a *substitute* for the more ancient symbolic pledges (*wadia*, A.-S. *wedd*). The delivery of the document, not less than the delivery of a symbolic chattel, as pledge, was treated as a formal act; the document in which the contract was embodied was itself pledged by its formal delivery to the creditor. By this formal act of delivering the document as a symbol the property of the transferor, the debtor, was bound in liability; while the payment of the debt was at the same time the redemption of the document as a symbolic pledge. See Gierke, *Schuld und Haftung*, pp. 130, 330–333. Cf. also Tangl, 'Urkunde und Symbol' (*Festschrift für Brunner*, 1910, pp. 761–773). While it is possible that a like idea underlies the delivery of the chirographic will by the donor to the donee in Anglo-Saxon times, no proof of this has been found. The one who wishes to research on this point, if indeed there be such a person, should not forget that the chirographic will embodied the terms of a contract and that it was especially contract-documents which were used as symbolic pledges in Germanic law on the Continent.

land-book questions may be asked which have not as yet been satisfactorily answered. Brunner maintained half a century ago that the *traditio cartae,* the formal delivery of the land-book, meant that the *carta* itself was dispositive[1]. This view needs thorough examination in the light of later research[2]. There is much support in the sources for the position that the conveyance of book-land was not by the Romanic *traditio cartae,* but by the Germanic *traditio per cartam*; that the land-book was used, like the sod taken from the land, merely as a symbol which represented the land; that the conveyance was in fact a symbolic transfer *per cartam* similar to the symbolic transfer *per cespitem* or *per ramum*; and that, therefore, the land-book itself was not dispositive, but merely an evidence-document. Recent research has shown us that in the fusion of Roman law and Germanic custom on the Continent during the early middle age customary rules as to spoken words, formalities, and symbols were firmly retained; and that the Germanic peoples, adding the document to their long list of more ancient symbols, transformed the Roman *traditio* of a dispositive *carta* into the symbolic *traditio per cartam*. This form of symbolic transfer differed in no essential particular from symbolic transfer *per cespitem* or *per ramum*; and, since the transfer was symbolic, the *carta* itself had merely evidential value[3]. The verbal, formal, and symbolic features in the transfer of book-land, already mentioned in an earlier paragraph, have been largely overlooked, or treated too lightly, by scholars[4]. Something at least may be said for the view that the

---

[1] Brunner, *op. cit.* pp. 147–208.

[2] In still other respects Brunner's account of the land-book needs examination and possibly correction. Thus, on the assumption that there was no Anglo-Saxon chancery, he classed royal charters among private documents. *Op. cit.* pp. 158–159. See, however, Larson, *King's Household in England before the Norman Conquest,* Index, *s.v.* chancellor, chancery, charters.

[3] On Continental *traditio per cartam,* see Brissaud, *op. cit.* §§ 294–298 (cf. §§ 362–370); Wigmore, *op. cit.* § 2426.

[4] These features may be studied in Brunner, *op. cit.* pp. 153–166, 185– 190. On the symbols, including hand-grasp, see also Pollock, *Land Laws,* 3rd ed. pp. 199–200. For the use of the term *traditio per cartam,* see Kemble, *C.D.* 1089. For a procedure similar to the Frankish *levatio cartae,* see Kemble, *C.D.* 45. The statement in some of the land-books that the donor placed ' *terras et libros* ' on the altar means that he placed sods or other symbolic things taken from the land and also the land-books on the altar. See

Anglo-Saxons conveyed book-land by symbolic *traditio per cartam*; but this is not the place to argue the point. Was there not, possibly, a direct continuity in the history of English conveyancing throughout Anglo-Saxon and Anglo-Norman times? If the dispositive act in Anglo-Saxon times was dual in character, a conveyance composed of oral *dispositio* and symbolic *traditio per cartam*, then the Anglo-Norman conveyance of freehold can be explained in the light of at least one of its non-Norman origins. In post-Conquest days the charter of feoffment was not a dispositive instrument; it was a pure evidence-document. It evidenced both the oral *donatio*, the feoffment, and the *traditio*, the real, as opposed to a symbolic, livery of seisin. True to the Germanic custom of Anglo-Saxon times this dual transaction was one which could be and was both heard and seen; and the newness in the Anglo-Norman conveyance did not consist either in orality or in the use of formalities and symbols, for these were present in rich abundance. The new and Norman feature was the rigorous requirement that, however many were the formalities and symbols, there must be an actual change of possession, a real and not a merely symbolic livery of seisin; and this, it may be suggested, was the main contribution of the Normans to the English conveyance of land. Although the

Brunner, *op. cit.* p. 189; Liebermann, *G.d.A.* II, Bocland (1 *d*). Cf. Harmer, *E.H.D.* No. XXIII, p. 38, lines 17–23. Brandileone's contention, in opposition to Brunner, that the delivery of the *carta primitiva* was not essential would seem to make the delivery of '*libros*' merely the transfer of symbols similar to the '*terras*'; and, indeed, Brandileone's stress upon the importance of the oral *dispositio* and the evidentiary character of documents leads to the view that the land-book was merely symbolical and evidential. See Brandileone, *loc. cit.* pp. 384–393. Cf. Gierke, *op. cit.* p. 330. Oral restrictions on the alienation of book-land, declared by the donor before witnesses, had validity even though they were not included by the scribe in the book. See Pollock, *op. cit.* p. 200. Land-books were executed, at least in some cases, in duplicate or triplicate as *chirographa*; and *chirographa* of this character were at least generally of only evidential value. See Schmid, *G.d.A.* Glossar, *s.v.* bôc; Lodge, 'Anglo-Saxon Land-Law' (*Essays in Anglo-Saxon Law*, p. 110); Brunner, *op. cit.* p. 174. Brunner's comparison of the Anglo-Saxon land-book with the Anglo-Norman deed of feoffment (*op. cit.* p. 152, n. 5) was not a happy one; for that deed was purely evidential. The vast extension of the use of evidence-documents in Europe after the dissolution of the Carlovingian empire was at the expense of the dispositive *carta*. The ever-increasing use of the writ-form in the making of Anglo-Saxon land-books may have been due to the influence of this Continental tendency. Documents in the writ-form were usually of only evidential value.

historical relation between the Anglo-Saxon land-book and the Anglo-Norman charter of feoffment falls outside the scope of these present paragraphs, we are entitled to ask questions about the land-book itself. Both the land-book and the written will were of ecclesiastical origin; and they were both drafted by ecclesiastical scribes. If the land-book was dispositive, what force, we may inquire, gave it that character? Clearly not the force of Anglo-Saxon Germanic custom. The force may have been pressure on the part of the Church; but, so far as one can see, the Church in Anglo-Saxon times not only never insisted on having dispositive as distinct from evidentiary documents, but actually stressed the need for instruments that were purely evidential. The force may have been the insistence of the parties; but one may gravely doubt whether donors and donees cared two straws whether the land-book was dispositive and evidential or merely evidential. Our studies of the land-book and the written will should run on parallel lines. In solving problems as to the nature of the land-book, just as in answering questions as to the character of written wills, we should go behind the documents themselves and look at their environment; we must, in fact, interpret the land-books, just as we read the written wills, in the light of the custom that was shaping them to its own ends. Since the pressure of Germanic custom in Anglo-Saxon days made for orality, formality, and symbolism in all legal transactions, such as the making of a will, one may at least hazard the suggestion that, although the land-book may masquerade before us in the Roman garb of dispositiveness, it was in truth, not less than the written will, a document which merely evidenced a Germanic oral transaction that was complete without a writing.

However that may have been, we must return to the written will by taking account of the fact that its delivery to the donee played no rôle in the making of the will. The scribe contents himself with the bare statement: 'There are three of these documents'. He tells us that one is in the hands of the principal donee; that another is in the custody of a disinterested monastery or of the king; that the third is retained by the donor. Had delivery of the instrument been a formal act essential in the making of the will the scribe would have been at pains to tell us this and perhaps to describe the act. His failure to do so is further proof that the making of the will was an oral and formal act complete without the documentation.

When we turn to a study of the gifts made by the donor[1] it is equally apparent that the written will is not a dispositive document; it conveys no titles to the donees, but merely evidences the donor's contractual promises. The donor himself expresses his anxiety concerning the fulfilment of his promises 'after his day'. He charges all and sundry to see to it that his will be executed; and he actually expresses in the will his knowledge that execution can only be by conveyance of titles to the donees. He looks forward to conveyances of title because he knows that as yet he has only promised to give and that his gifts can be completed, and thus his will be made to 'stand', only by transfers.

There are instances where, at the time of the making of the will, land that is the subject-matter of a gift is already in the legal and actual possession of the donee. Examples of this are where the donee already holds under a contract of sale (*landceap*) or under a mortgage[2]; and in such cases the gift of the *quasi*-testator is in the nature of an *Auflassung* (*resignatio, abdicatio*)[3]. A somewhat different case is where the donee is already in legal possession of the land under a prior gift *post obitum* which is to be perfected on the death of the present donor; and where, at the same time, the present donor is in actual possession under

---

[1] The reader may be reminded, in passing, that the power to dispose of land by will rests on royal authority. The power to dispose of book-land is conferred in the *carta primitiva*; whereas in the case of folk-land the power must be given by special grant. In many of the written wills there is the statement that the donor has obtained the king's permission to make his will; while in others there is the prayer that the king will regard the donor as worthy to make his will or that the king will allow his will to stand. The significance of these statements is that only by the king's special permission can the donor dispose of his folk-land by will. See Vinogradoff, *Collected Papers*, I, pp. 168–191.

[2] See No. xxxix, *infra*. On *landceap*, see Vinogradoff, *op. cit.* I, pp. 154–157.

[3] This form of gift in the Anglo-Saxon oral will is in essence the release (*relaxatio*), or quit-claim, of English law after the Conquest. See Pollock and Maitland, *op. cit.* II, pp. 90, 91, 187.

a lease (*on gafollande*)[1]. In such a case the donor naturally makes no gift of the land itself; but he can and sometimes does make a gift to the one in legal possession of the land, under the former gift *post obitum*, of the chattels on the land and the peasants dwelling on the land[2].

Apart from special cases, such as those mentioned, the *quasi*-testator himself sometimes transfers book-land to the donee with the reservation of usufruct for one or more lives; and in such cases he conveys the book-land by delivery of the book or books to the donee[3]. When the donor retains the book or books, together with the title and possession, but promises that on his death the donee shall have the land[4], title to the book-land must be conveyed to the donee after the donor's death. In such cases it would seem that the conveyance can take one or the other of two forms: either the heir or the 'protector' of the will uses the recognised mode of transferring title to book-land or the king himself transfers by writ. The same principle is true of gifts of folk-land and of chattels: only by employing the customary modes of transfer can title be vested in the donee[5]. It may well have been one of the chief duties of the 'protector', the predecessor of the true executor, either to transfer title to the donees or to see to it that other parties conveyed title in accordance with the donor's promises.

Still another way to test the character of the written will is to observe how it was regarded by the courts. Anglo-Saxon litigation in regard to wills deserves a more careful study than it has hitherto received[6]: our knowledge of it is still fragmentary. It may be pointed out, however, that in at least one case the

---

[1] See Liebermann, *G.d.A.* II, *s.v. gafolland*.

[2] See No. III, *infra*.

[3] For illustrations, see Nos. V, VII, *infra*. Some of the gifts in the written wills may be interpreted to mean that the *quasi*-testator himself transfers folk-land to the donee with reservation of usufruct for one or more lives; and, if this be in fact the case, there is here an interesting parallel to similar transfers of book-land by the *quasi*-testator.

[4] See Brunner, *op. cit.* pp. 201–202.

[5] On transfer of folk-land by customary modes, see Vinogradoff, *op. cit.* I, pp. 149–167. It would seem that title to folk-land could also be conveyed to the donee by the king's writ. See Holdsworth, *op. cit.* II, p. 77. Title to chattels passed by *traditio* before witnesses.

[6] See, e.g., Holdsworth, *op. cit.* II, pp. 114–116.

court upheld a purely oral will which was not a death-bed disposition[1] and that in another case the tribunal treated the writing in which an oral will was embodied as merely evidential[2]. Further research would no doubt reveal other instances where the court reached similar results.

With only one or two further remarks one must, and should, leave the reader in peace and quietude to peruse the documents which Miss Whitelock has placed before him. The theory advanced in these paragraphs that the Anglo-Saxon oral will was a contract may not, and probably does not, explain all the gifts in the will. It gives us a thread, however, upon which to string many of the gifts; and, above all, it enables us to differentiate between contract and conveyance as the two main factors in the transfer of titles to the donees. That the grant *post obitum* is sometimes regarded by theorists of our own day as a 'present gift[3]' is primarily due to the fact that the donor has bound himself by his contract; by a transaction *inter vivos* he has promised to give property to the donee. Even more clearly is it a 'present gift' when in partial fulfilment of his promise the donor himself conveys title to the donee with reservation of usufruct. The chief meaning of the will-contract, however, is that it makes all the gifts *donationes irrevocabiles post obitum*; and these contractual gifts *mortis causa* are perfected, as we have seen, only when, on the death of the donor, conveyances are made to the donees in fulfilment of the promises that have been made to them. In cases where the donor has himself conveyed land to the donee with reservation of usufruct for the donor's life, or for his life and the lives of other persons, there is naturally no need for a conveyance to the donee on the cessation of the life or lives in question; here, since death terminates the temporary right of usufruct, a delivery of possession to the donee seems to be all that is required to make his title complete and absolute. While one should not be too dogmatic, there appear

---

[1] Kemble, *C.D.* 755 (before A.D. 1038); *Essays in Anglo-Saxon Law*, appendix of select cases, p. 365.

[2] Kemble, *C.D.* 256 (a case of the early ninth century); *Essays in Anglo-Saxon Law*, appendix of select cases, p. 331. In this document the words 'altera kartula' refer to the written will.

[3] Cf. Pollock and Maitland, *op. cit.* II, pp. 314–356, *passim.*

to be no cases where the donor himself transfers possession, as distinct from title, to the donee. The contracts by which donors make *donationes irrevocabiles post obitum* all appear to be 'formal contracts' as distinct from so-called 'real contracts'. Donors may indeed give legal possession to donees as part of their title; but the donors always appear to retain actual or physical possession. The formal contracts of donors *mortis causa* are obligations; and, apart from special cases, such as the conveyance of title by the donor with reservation of usufruct, the donees' rights *in personam* become rights *in rem* only through the efficacy of conveyances after the death of the donors. Even if it be true, as suggested in a former paragraph, that the formal contract binds the donor's *res* in legal liability, the right of the donee, apart from the case where the donor himself conveys title, seems to be at most a *ius ad rem* and not a full proprietary *ius in rem*. It is not the oral will, nor is it the written *testimonium* of that will, which gives the donee his *iura in rem*. It is only conveyance in fulfilment of the donor's obligation which transmits the donor's *iura in rem* to the donee.

The Anglo-Saxons themselves do not seem to have had any theory in regard to their 'will' and its gifts. In practice, however, they were thoroughly familiar with that duality of contract and conveyance which was characteristic of gifts *post obitum* and of all other forms of Germanic grant; and with practice they were content. It is only men of later ages, trying to penetrate into the mind and custom of the Anglo-Saxons, who have been concerned to frame theories. Any theory, so long as it explains the historical sources, is a good theory; but the one which not only explains the sources, but also illumines them, as by the flare of a torch, is the best theory. The contractual theory of the 'will' of the Anglo-Saxons may not be the best theory; it probably is not. But at least it may throw light upon some of the features incident to those puzzling documents which Miss Whitelock has given us to read.

While it would be out of place to consider, in the present paragraphs, the history of the Anglo-Saxon oral will and the Anglo-Saxon written will in the periods of our legal history after the Norman Conquest, it may be asserted with some confidence that the principles established before the Conquest persisted for a long time[1]. The rise of common law and ecclesiastical jurisdictions meant, however, that the history of dispositions of property *mortis causa* was to run in new channels. Under ecclesiastical jurisdiction a true unilateral and revocable will of personal property was developed and enforced; but the common law courts, while condemning gifts *post obitum*, evolved no will of land. Only by later legislation was the will of land established as a part of English law; and only through legislation of a still later time was the will of realty and personalty as we know it to-day finally recognised and enforced by the courts. Here, in concluding these desultory comments, let it be remarked only that the student of writings, including written wills, must ever bear in mind the relation between orality and documentation; and, moreover, he must always ask himself the question as to whether documents which appear to be dispositive are not after all merely the evidence of transactions already constituted and legally binding without any writing. The unwritten common law, the common law apart from statute, made no requirement that legal transactions of any kind 'be done in writing as a condition of jural validity[2]'. The common law remained in fact true to its Germanic origins; and only by legislative action were requirements of written form introduced into our system. Even when documents are required by statute there is the further question, however, as to whether those writings are both dispositive and evidential or merely evidential. No doubt in present-day English law both the will and the deed are dispositive documents[3]; and no doubt also those instruments represent the

[1] On the law of wills from the Norman Conquest to the end of the middle ages, see Pollock and Maitland, *op. cit.* II, pp. 323–356; Holdsworth, *op. cit.* III, pp. 534–595. On the relation between the orality and documentation of wills in later English law, see Williams, *Law of Real Property*, 24th ed. (Eastwood), pp. 289–316; Williams, *Law of Personal Property*, 18th ed. pp. 545–586.

[2] Wigmore, *op. cit.* § 2454. On the principles of the early common law as to proof by writings, see Salmond, *Essays in Jurisprudence and Legal History*, pp. 3–69 (*passim*), 173–224 (*passim*); Thayer, *Evidence at the Common Law*, Index, *s.v.* Writings.

[3] See, e.g., Holdsworth, *Historical Introduction to the Land Law*, p. 116. Even at the present day, however, documents like leases and wills are both contracts and conveyances. The mingling of contract and conveyance,

culmination of a long development from conditions in which orality and formality and symbolism were the rule to conditions under which documentation is viewed as the abstract embodiment of rights that pass with the passing of the writing. In the middle ages, even in the later part of that epoch of our history, legal transactions were fundamentally of the same nature as in the primitive days of Germanic custom; they were required to be both heard and seen before they were accorded a legal efficacy. What view did the ecclesiastical courts of the later middle ages take as to the nature of the will which they were enforcing? Did they look upon the written will of personalty as dispositive; or, on the contrary, did they still cling, at least for a time, to the Germanic and ecclesiastical idea of earlier days that the writing had merely evidential value? The answer to these and similar questions would help us to trace the historical relation between the oral contractual will of the Anglo-Saxons and the written unilateral will of a later age.

H. D. H.

characteristic of the Germanic Grant in Anglo-Saxon times, has been preserved. Vestiges of the Anglo-Saxon contractual will are to be found in the well established principle of present-day English law that 'a man may validly bind himself or his estate by contract to make any particular disposition (if in itself lawful) by his own will'. See Pollock, *Principles of Contract*, 9th ed., p. 423.

PREFACE

Over fifty English wills of the Anglo-Saxon period have come down to us, and in addition to these there are about a dozen Latin documents in medieval cartularies which are probably translations or abstracts of Old English wills. Only a small proportion of the wills, however, fifteen in all, are preserved in a contemporary form. Of the majority we possess only later copies by monastic scribes.

The thirty-nine wills in the present edition all belong to the period between about the middle of the tenth century and the end of the Anglo-Saxon period. Four wills of this period, those of the Ealdorman Æthelwold, King Edred, Bishop Ælfwold of Crediton and Leofwine, have not been included, as these have already been edited with translation and commentary, the two first by Miss Harmer in *Select English Historical Documents of the Ninth and Tenth Centuries*, the others by Napier and Stevenson in *Crawford Charters*. Before the period covered by this edition, wills are rare. Less than a dozen have been preserved, the earliest dating from the first half of the ninth century. All the more interesting of these have been edited by Miss Harmer. The rest, contained in Thorpe's *Diplomatarium*, are short documents and lack the characteristic features of the Anglo-Saxon will, such as reference to heriot and *sawolsceatt* or mention of royal permission.

That great numbers of wills from Anglo-Saxon times have perished is shown not only by fairly frequent references in Anglo-Saxon documents from the ninth century onwards to wills no longer extant, but also by the distribution of those wills which have survived. For the period after the reign of Ethelred all the wills belong to the eastern counties, the rest of England being entirely unrepresented. Earlier, the localities are more varied, but there are only a few wills which do not owe their preservation to the fact that they contain bequests to the abbeys of Abingdon, Bury, Christchurch in Canterbury, or Winchester.

The majority of the wills here printed were first published

by Kemble in his *Codex Diplomaticus Ævi Saxonici*, completed in 1848. Thorpe collected together all the wills in Kemble and published them with a translation in his *Diplomatarium Anglicum Ævi Saxonici* in 1865. He included several documents which technically are not wills. Sometimes he uses different manuscripts from Kemble, but in the main he prints direct from the latter. Four wills, Nos. IV, VI, X, XII, first appeared in print in 1866, when Edwards edited the *Liber Monasterii de Hyda* for the Rolls Series. Finally, from 1885 to 1893, Birch published his *Cartularium Saxonicum*, a collection of charters to the end of Edgar's reign, and several wills are included in this. A few wills have been printed separately, mainly in local journals. Reference to these is made in the notes.

Facsimiles of Nos. III, XIV, XV, XIX and XXVI are contained in Bond's *Facsimiles of Ancient Charters in the British Museum*, 1873 to 1878; of Nos. XIII, XVI, XVII, XX and XXX in the *Ordnance Survey Facsimiles of Anglo-Saxon MSS.*, edited by Sanders, 1878 to 1884.

The text of all the wills in this edition has been collated with the original manuscripts, with the exception of those contained in the *Liber Monasterii de Hyda* and No. XXIII, from the *Red Book of Thorney*, as these manuscripts were unfortunately inaccessible to me, and also of No. XXII, as the cartulary in which it is contained cannot now be found. The spelling and punctuation of the manuscripts have been preserved, except that I have supplied capital letters for proper names, and that, while retaining the ordinary Old English abbreviations, *e.g.* for *and*, *þæt*, *bisceop*, I have expanded in italics the abbreviations in texts from medieval cartularies and have throughout supplied *m* or *n* in place of the horizontal stroke denoting a nasal consonant. Insertions in the manuscripts have been enclosed in ' ', supplied readings between square brackets. The more important variants in other manuscripts and in the texts of earlier editions have been given in the textual notes.

As these documents are preserved in versions covering a period of nearly four centuries, it is clear that the transcription of personal names presents a certain amount of difficulty. To retain in the translation the spelling of the manuscript in names which appear in a multitude of forms would only be confusing to readers not versed in English philology. The system I have in general adopted has been to give the name in the form which seems to me the most usual during the last century of the Anglo-Saxon period. For example, *Æðelmær*, *Eðelmer*, *Ailmer*, *Aylmer*, *Ailmar*, are all levelled under the first form, but I have not thought it necessary to reinsert the original *w* in such names as *Osulf*, when it is consistently omitted in texts of the period. As, however, it seemed to me pedantic to follow this system in the case of names still current, or of familiar names like those of the English kings, I have given such names in their modern form.

In conclusion, I should like to take this opportunity of expressing my sincere thanks to all who have assisted me in this work; and first and foremost to Professor and Mrs Chadwick for their unfailing interest and encouragement throughout my studies. Professor Chadwick first turned my attention to this subject and has generously placed his time and great store of learning at my disposal. I am also indebted to him for undertaking the laborious work of proof-reading. My thanks are also due to Professor A. Mawer of Liverpool for assistance with the identification of some place-names; to Professor F. M. Stenton of Reading for advice and help with proofs; to Miss H. M. Taylor for collating the text of No. XXXII with the manuscript, and to the librarians and staffs of the Cambridge University Library, the British Museum, Corpus Christi College, Cambridge, Canterbury, Rochester and St Paul's Cathedrals, and the Society of Antiquaries of London, for facilities afforded me when collating the manuscripts. Finally, I desire to acknowledge my obligations to Professor H. D. Hazeltine for including this edition in his series and supplying an introductory preface and for the sympathetic interest he has taken in my work; to the Syndics of the Cambridge University Press for undertaking the publication and the staff for the care taken in the printing; and to the Council of Newnham College for the award of the Marion Kennedy Studentship which enabled me to work on this subject.

D. W.

October 1929

LIST OF ABBREVIATIONS

(a) IN THE TEXT

aƀb	abbud.
7	and.
ƀ	bisc(e)op.
p̃	preost.
sc̄e	sancte.
ꝥ	þæt.
Xp̄es	Cristes.

(b) IN THE NOTES

B.	Birch, *Cartularium Saxonicum*, quoted by number of document.
Björkman	Björkman, *Nordische Personennamen in England in alt- und frühmittelenglischer Zeit.*
B.T.	Bosworth and Toller, *Anglo-Saxon Dictionary.*
B.T. *Suppl.*	Supplement to the same.
Chadwick	Chadwick, *Studies on Anglo-Saxon Institutions.*
Chronicle	Anglo-Saxon Chronicle. The letters A, C, D, E, F, refer to the different MSS. according to the nomenclature adopted in Earle and Plummer, *Two of the Saxon Chronicles Parallel.*
Crawford Charters	*Crawford Collection of Early Charters, etc.,* edited by Napier and Stevenson.
D.B.	Domesday Book.
Dugdale	Dugdale, *Monasticon Anglicanum*, 1846 edition.
E.	Earle, *A Handbook to the Land Charters and other Saxonic Documents.*
E.H.R.	*English Historical Review.*
F. and L.	Foster and Longley, *The Lincolnshire Domesday and the Lindsey Survey.*
Fl. Wig.	Florence of Worcester.
G.P., G.R.	See W.M.
Grein	Grein, *Sprachschatz der angelsächsischen Dichter.*
Harmer	Harmer, *Select English Historical Documents of the Ninth and Tenth Centuries.*
K.	Kemble, *Codex Diplomaticus Ævi Saxonici*, quoted by number of document.
Liebermann	Liebermann, *Gesetze der Angelsachsen.*

LIST OF ABBREVIATIONS

L.V.H. *Liber Vitae of Hyde Abbey*, edited by Birch, in *Register of New Minster and Hyde Abbey*.

M.E. Middle English.

N.E.D. New English Dictionary.

O.E. Old English.

O.Icel. Old Icelandic.

R.S. Rolls Series.

Searle Searle, *Onomasticon Anglo-Saxonicum*.

T. Thorpe, *Diplomatarium Anglicum Ævi Saxonici*.

V.C.H. *Victoria County History*.

W.M., *G.P.*; *G.R.* William of Malmesbury, *De Gestis Pontificum Anglorum*; *De Gestis Regum Anglorum*.

Wright-Wülker Wright, *Anglo-Saxon and Old English Vocabularies*, edited and collated by Wülker, 1884; quoted by page and line.

NOTE. In the citation of the laws the numbering of the divisions and sections corresponds with that of Liebermann, which in general is also adopted in Attenborough's *Laws of the Earliest English Kings* and in Robertson's *Laws of the Kings of England from Edmund to Henry I*.

ADDENDA

p. 24, ll. 17 f. *XIII hida landes.* These are shown by a charter of Ethelred's in the *Liber Monasterii de Hyda,* pp. 217 ff., to consist of estates at *Heantune, Beadingaburnan, Meolocdune, Staðe, Frodincgtune* and *Suggincgwyrþe,* with a meadow by the River Meon. These places are not easy to identify. The first four are said to be in the Isle of Wight, but this cannot be true of *Staðe,* as Tichfield occurs in the boundaries. I cannot identify this place or *Meolocdune. Beadingaburnan* is Bathingbourne near Shanklin, but *Heantune,* which must be near to it, has disappeared. *Frodincgtune* is Fratton in the Isle of Portsea. *Suggincgwyrþe* can hardly be Segenworth near Tichfield as this place is too far from Fratton to occur in the boundaries.

As this charter is dated 982 we must take this as the date of Æthelmær's death (see p. 126) and assume the date of K. 638 to be a copyist's error.

p. 40, l. 8 and p. 144, *morgangyfu.* On p. 144 I have erroneously assumed that the author of the *Liber Eliensis* used *dos* in the Roman sense (see Du Cange, *Glossarium Mediae et Infimae Latinitatis,* s.v. *dos,* 1; Buckland, *Text-Book of Roman Law,* pp. 107–111), whereas in his day it was a provision for the wife's widowhood made by the husband at the time of the marriage (see Du Cange, *loc. cit.* 2; Pollock and Maitland, *History of English Law,* II, pp. 420–428). For the view that the later dower (*dos*) was derived from the Germanic bride-price and 'morning gift', see Young, in *Essays in Anglo-Saxon Law,* p. 174; Buckstaff, *Essay on Married Women's Property,* in *Annals of the American Academy of Political and Social Science,* IV, pp. 35, 51; Brissand, *History of French Private Law* (Continental Legal History Series), §§ 521, 529. The relation of the Anglo-Norman *dos* to the *morgengifu* of Anglo-Saxon times, is however, not clear. Buckstaff, *op. cit.* pp. 57 f., suggests that many features of the former are of Norman origin.

ANGLO-SAXON WILLS

I. THE WILL OF BISHOP THEODRED.

[I]n nomine domini nostri Ihesu Christi.

Ic Þeodred Lundeneware Biscop wille biquethen mine quiden
mines erfes. Þe ic begeten habbe 7 get bigete godes Þankes and
his halegen for mine soule 7 for min louerde Þat ic vnder bigeat
and for min Eldrene. and for alle Þe mannes soule Þe ic fore-
5 Þingiae. And ic almesne vnderfongen habbe and me sie rithlike
for to bidden Þat is Þan erst Þat he an his louerd his heregete.
Þat is Þanne tua hund marcas arede goldes and tua cuppes
siluerene. and four hors so ic best habbe. and to suerde so ic
best habbe. 7 foure schelda. and foure spere. and Þat lond Þat
10 ic habbe at Dukeswrthe[1]. and Þat lond Þat ic habbe at Illyntone.
And Þat lond Þat ic habbe at Earnningtone[2]. 7 ic an Eadgiue
fifti marcas redes goldes. And into scē Paules kirke mine to
beste messehaclen. Þe hic habbe mid alle Þe Þinge Þe Þereto
biriỗ mid calice and on cuppe. and mine beste masseboc. and
15 alle mine reliq*uias* Þe ic best habbe into Paules kirke. And ic
an Þat lond aet Tit[3] into seynte Paules kirke Þen hewen to
bedlonde mid al Þat Þe Þeron stant buten Þe men Þe Þer aren
fre men alle for mine soule. and ic an Þat lond at Suthereye mid
alle Þe fiscoỗe Þe Þerto bireỗ Þen hewen into scē Paules kirke.
20 and frie men Þo men for Þe Bisscopes soule. and Þeodred bisscop
an Þat lond at Tillingham into scē Paules kirke Þo hewen to
hare[4]. and fre men Þo men for mine soule. And ic an Þat lond
at Dunemowe ouer mine day into scē Paules kirke Þen hewen.
And ic an Þat lond at Mendham Osgote mine sustres sune ouer
25 mine day. buten ic wille Þat se minstre. And[5] hide londes at
Myndham to Þere kirke. And ic an Þat lond at Scotforỗ. and
Mydicaham into Myndham kirke Þo godes hewen. And ic an
Osgot Þat lond at Silham. 7 at Isestede. 7 at Chikeringe. 7 at
Aysfeld[6] and at Wrtinham. and alle Þe smale londe Þat Þereto
30 bereỗ. And ic an Þat lond at Horham and at Elyngtone into
Hoxne into scē Aethelbrichtes kirke Þer[7] godes hewen. And ic
an Þat lond at Luthinglond Offe mine sustres sune and his

---

[1] K. *Ankeswrỗ.*
[2] K., T. *Earmingtone.*
[3] Sic MS. for *Cic.* K. *Tit.* T. *Cic.*
[4] Sic MS. for *are.* K. *here.*
[5] Sic MS.
[6] K. *Æysfeld.*
[7] K., T. *Þen.*

I. THE WILL OF BISHOP THEODRED.

In nomine domini nostri Iesu Christi.

I, Theodred, Bishop of the people of London, wish to announce my will concerning my property, what I have acquired and may yet acquire, by the grace of God and his saints, for my soul and for that of my lord under whom I acquired it and for my ancestors' souls, and for the souls of all the men for whom I intercede, and from whom I have received alms, and for whom it is fitting that I should pray.

First, he grants his lord his heriot, namely, two hundred marks of red gold, and two silver cups and four horses, the best that I have, and two swords the best that I have, and four shields and four spears: and the estate which I have at Duxford, and the estate which I have at Illington, and the estate which I have at Arrington. And I grant to Eadgifu fifty marks of red gold.

And to St Paul's church I grant the two best chasubles that I have, with all the things which belong to them, together with a chalice and one cup. And my best mass-book, and the best relics that I have [are to go] to St Paul's church. And I grant to St Paul's church the estate at St Osyth, as an estate to provide sustenance for the community, with all that is on it, except the men who are there; they are all to be freed for my soul's sake. And I grant the estate at Southery, with all the fishing which belongs to it, to the community at St Paul's church, and the men are to be freed for the bishop's soul. And Bishop Theodred grants the estate at Tillingham to St Paul's church to be the property of the community, and the men are to be freed for my soul. And I grant the estate at Dunmow after my death to St Paul's church for the community.

And I grant the estate at Mendham to my sister's son Osgot after my death, except that I desire that the minster and a hide of land at Mendham [shall belong?] to the church. And I grant the estate at Shotford and Mettingham to God's community at Mendham church. And I grant to Osgot the estates at Syleham, and at Instead, and at Chickering and at Ashfield, and at *Wortinham*, and all the small estates which are attached to these.

And I grant the estates at Horham and at Athelington to God's

broþer. and fre men þo men halue. and at Mindham also for þe
Bisscopes soule. And ic an Osgote mine mey Eadulfes sune þat
lond at Bertune and at Rucham[1]. and at Pakenham. And ic an
þat lond at Newetune. and at Horninggeshæthe. and at Ikewrthe.
5 and at Wepstede into sc̄e Eadmundes kirke þen godes hewen to
are for Þeodred bisscopes soule. And ic an þat lond at Waldringfeld Osgote mine Sustres sune. and min hage þat ic binnin
Gypeswich bouhte. And ic[2] Wlstan þat lond at Wrtham so it
stant. And ic an into eueri bisscopes stole fif pund to delen for
10 mine soule. And ic an þen Archebiscope fif Markes goldes.
And ic an þat men dele at mine biscopriche binnen Lundene
and buten Lundene . x . pund for mine soule. And ic an at
Hoxne at mine biscopriche þat men dele . x . pund for mine
soule. 7 Ic wille þat men nieme þat erfe þat at Hoxne stand.
15 þat ic þerto bigeten habbe. and dele it man on to. half into þe
minstre 7 dele for min soule. And lete men stonden so mikel
so ic þeron fond. and fre man[3] þo men alle for mine soule. And
ic wille þat men lete stonden at Lundenebyri so mikel so ic
þeron fond. 7 nime[4] þat ic þerto bigat and dele on to. half into
20 þe minstre 7 half for mine soule. and fre men alle þo men. 7 do
men þat Ilke at Wunemannedune 7 on Sceon 7 lete[5] men stonden
at Fullenham so it nu stant buten hwe[6] mine manne fre wille
7 on Denesige let stonden so mikel so ic þeron fond. And dele
it man on to half[7] into þe minstre 7 half for mine soule. And
25 ic an into Glastingbiri . v . pund for mine soule. and ic an
Þeodred min wite massehakele þe ic on Pauie bouhte and 'al'
þat þerto bireð. 7 simbelcalice 7 þere messeboc þe Gosebricht
me biquaþ. And ic an Odgar[8] þere gewele massehakele þe ic on
Pauie bouhte. 7 þat þerto bireð. And ic an Gundwine þer oþer
30 gewele massehakele þat is ungerenad. 7 þat þe þerto bireð.
and ic spracacke[9] þe rede messehakele. 7 al þat þe þerto bired.
And wo so mine cuyde ofte✓ god him ofte heuene Riches buten
he it er his ende it bete.

---

[1] K. *Bucham.*
[2] Sic MS.
[3] T. *men.*
[4] K. *mine.*
[5] T. *let.*
[6] K. *hwye.*
[7] An *e* has been half-erased.
[8] K., T. *Ordgar.*
[9] K., T. *Spratacke.*

community at St Ethelbert's church at Hoxne. And I grant the estate at Lothingland to Offa my sister's son and his brother, and half the men are to be freed there, and also at Mendham, for the Bishop's soul. And I grant to my kinsman Osgot, Eadulf's son, the estates at Barton, and at Rougham, and at Pakenham.

And I grant the estates at Nowton and at Horningsheath and at Ickworth and at Whepstead to St Edmund's church, as the property of God's community, for Bishop Theodred's soul. And I grant to Osgot my sister's son the estate at Waldringfield and my messuage in Ipswich, which I bought. And I grant to Wulfstan the estate at Wortham just as it stands.

And I grant to every bishop's see five pounds to be distributed for my soul. And I grant to the Archbishop five marks of gold. And I grant that ten pounds be distributed for my soul at my episcopal demesne, in London and outside London. And I grant that ten pounds be distributed for my soul at my episcopal demesne at Hoxne. And it is my will that the stock which is at Hoxne, which I have acquired there, be taken and divided into two parts, half for the minster, and [half] to be distributed for my soul. And as much as I found on that estate is to be left on it, but all the men are to be freed for my soul. And it is my wish that at London there be left as much as I found on the estate, and that what I added to it be taken and divided into two, half for the minster and half for my soul, and all the men are to be freed. And the same is to be done at *Wunemannedune* and at Sheen. And at Fulham everything is to be left as it now stands, unless one wishes to free any of my men. And at Dengie let there be left as much as I found on the estate and let the rest be divided into two, half for the minster and half for my soul.

And I grant to Glastonbury five pounds for my soul. And I grant to Theodred my white chasuble which I bought in Pavia, and all that belongs to it, and a chalice for festivals and the massbook which Gosebriht bequeathed to me. And I grant to Odgar the yellow chasuble which I bought in Pavia, and what belongs to it. And I grant to Gundwine the other yellow chasuble which is unornamented, and what belongs to it. And I...... the red chasuble and all that belongs to it. And whosoever detracts from my testament, may God deprive him of the kingdom of heaven, unless he make amends for it before his death.

II. THE WILL OF ÆLFGAR.

[I]N nomine domini.

Þis is Alfgares[1] quide þat is erst þat ic an mine louerd tueye
suerde fetelsade and[2] tueye bege ayther of fifti mancusas goldes.
and þre stedes. and þre scheldes[3]. and þre speren. And me
kidde Þeodred bisscop and Edric Alderman þa ic selde mine
5 louerd þat suerd þat Eadmund king me selde on hundtuelftian
mancusas goldes. and four pund silueres on þam fetelse þat ic
moste ben mine quides wirde. And ic nefre forwrouht ne habbe
on godes witnesse wið mine louerd buten ic[4] so mote. And ic
an Athelflede mine douhter þe lond at Cokefelð. and at Dittone.
10 and þat at Lauenham. ouer min day. on þe red þat heo be þe bet
for mine soule. and hire moder soule 7 for hire brother soule.
7 for hire seluen[5]. And þanne ouer vre aldre[6]day ic an þat lond
at Cokefeld into Beodricheswrthe to seynt Eadmundes stowe.
And ic wille þat Athelfled vnne ouer 'hire' day þo londes at
15 Dittone into suilke halegen stowe: suilk hire redlikest þinge for
vre aldre soule. And ouer vre[7] aldreday: ic an þat lond at
Lauenham mine douhter childe gif þat god wille þat heo ani
haueð. buten Atelfled her wille him his vnnen[8]. and gif heo non
ne habbe: gange it into Stoke for vre aldre soule. and ic an
20 þat lond at Babingþirne Atelflede mine douhter. And after hire
day: min other douhter hire day. And ouer here bothre day:
mine douhter berne gif he[9] bern habbe. And gif he[9] bern[10] ne
habbe: þanne go it into sc̄e Marie Stowe at Berkynge for vre
aldre[11] soule. And ic an þat lond at Illeye[12] mine ginger douhter
25 hire day. and ouer hire day: Berthnoðe his day gif he leng libbe
þanne heo. gif he[9] bern habben þanne an ic[13] hem. gif he[9] non
ne habbeþ[14]: þanne an ic it Athelfleð mine douhter. ouer here
day. and after hire day: into Cristes kirke at Caunterbiri þen
hirde de brite[15]. And þe lond at Colne and at Tigan[16] ic an min

[1] T. *Ælfgares*.	[2] Addit. MS. *an*.
[3] Ibid. *cheldes*.	[4] Ibid. *it*.
[5] Ibid. omits from *on þe red þat* to *seluen*.	[6] Ibid. *alderne*.
[7] Ibid. *hure*.	[8] Ibid. *hunnes*.
[9] T. *heo*.	[10] Addit. MS. inserts *non*.
[11] Ibid. *alderne*.	[12] Ibid. *Illeyge*.
[13] Ibid. inserts *it*.	[14] Ibid. *habben*.
[15] For *to brice*.	[16] Addit. MS. *Tygan*

II. THE WILL OF ÆLFGAR.

In nomine domini.

This is Ælfgar's will. First I grant to my lord two swords with sheaths, and two armlets, each of fifty mancuses of gold, and three stallions and three shields and three spears. And Bishop Theodred and the Ealdorman Eadric told me, when I gave to my lord the sword which King Edmund gave to me, which was worth a hundred and twenty mancuses of gold and had four pounds of silver on the sheath, that I might have the right to make my will; and God is my witness that I have never done wrong against my lord that I may not have this right.

And I grant to my daughter Æthelflæd the estates at Cockfield and Ditton and that at Lavenham after my death on condition that she be the more zealous for the welfare of my soul and of her mother's soul and of her brother's soul and of her own; and then after our lifetime I grant the estate at Cockfield to St Edmund's foundation at Bedericesworth. And it is my wish that Æthelflæd shall grant the estate at Ditton after her death to whatever holy foundation seems to her most advisable, for the sake of our ancestors' souls. And I grant the estate at Lavenham after our lifetime to my daughter's child if it be God's will that she have any, unless Æthelflæd wishes to grant it to him before; and if she has no child, the estate is to go to Stoke for our ancestors' souls. And I grant the estate at Baythorn to my daughter Æthelflæd, and after her death to my other daughter for her time; and after the death of both of them, to my daughter's child, if she has a child; and if she has no child, then it is to go to St Mary's foundation at Barking for the souls of our ancestors.

And I grant the estate at Eleigh to my younger daughter for her life, and after her death to Brihtnoth for his life if he live longer than she. If they should have children, then I grant it to them. If they have none, then I grant it to my daughter Æthelflæd after their death, and after her death to Christchurch at Canterbury for the use of the community. And I grant the estates at Colne and Tey to my younger daughter, and after her death, if she has a child, to her child; and if she has no child, I bequeathe

gingere douht*er*. and ouer[1] day gif heo bern habbe. hire bern.
and gif heo bern[2] ne habbe: bequeðe it[3] Bernothe his day. and
ouer his day: into Stoke for vre aldre soule And ic an þat lond
at Piltendon*e* and at Mereseye into Stoke. And ic an þat Athelfled
5 bruke þe lond þer wile þe hire lef beth one raða[4] heo it[5] on riht
helde. and on þe red þat heo do þan hirde so wel so heo best may
into Stoke for mine soule and for ure aldre. And ic an þat lond
at Grenstede into Stoke for mine soule 7 for Athelwardes 7 for
Wiswiðe[6]. And ic Athelfled þere brice wille hire lif beth on þe
10 red þat heo do for þa[7] saule so wel so heo[8] best may. nu his me
god uþe 7 min lauerd. And ic an þat lond at Tidwoldingtone[9]
Alfwold[10] ouer mine day þe he formige ilke ihere þen hird at
Paulesbiri for vre aldre soule. And ic an[11] þat lond at Totham[12]
Berchnoðe and mine gingere douht*er* here day. and aft*er* here
15 day: wudelond[13] into Mereseye Athelfled mine douht*er*. And
ic an þat wudelond at Aisfeld[14] into Stoke also Eakild[15] self it
her bouhte. And ic mine moder þat lond at Ryssebroc gif heo
leng liuið þan hic. þanne aft*er* vnker bother day ic an it Winelme
gif heo Athelfled on richte hird. And ic wille Bidden suilc
20 louerd so þanne beth for godes luuen[16] and for alle hise halegen.
werken min bern þat he[17] werken þat he nefre ne mugen for-
werken mine quide þe ic for mine soule cueden habbe. and gif
it wo awende: habbe him wið god gemaene and wið þe holi
scas[18] þe ic it to becueþen habbe. þat he it nefre ne bete buten
25 on helle wite se þis quide awende boten it me seluen wende[19]
er min ende[20]. And ic Athelgar an an hide lond þes þe Aeulf
hauede be hundtuelti acren ateo so he wille.

---

[1] Addit. MS. adds *hire*.
[2] Ibid. omits *bern*.
[3] Ibid. *ic*.
[4] Ibid. *rathan*.
[5] Ibid. *ic*.
[6] T. *Wifwiðe*.
[7] Addit. MS. *þat*.
[8] Ibid. *he*.
[9] Ibid. *Tidweldington*.
[10] T. *Ælfwold*.
[11] Addit. MS. *and*.
[12] T. *Cotham*.
[13] The Addit. MS. reading, *wende lond*, is obviously the correct one.
[14] Ibid. *Asfeld*.
[15] Ibid. *Aylkil*.
[16] Ibid. *louen*.
[17] Ibid. omits *he*.
[18] Ibid. *stans*.
[19] Ibid. adds *it*.
[20] Ibid. *endinge*.

it to Brihtnoth for his time, and after his death to Stoke for our ancestors' souls.

And I grant the estate at Peldon and that at Mersea to Stoke. And I grant that Æthelflæd is to have the use of the estates as long as is agreeable to her, on condition that she holds it lawfully, and on condition that she does the best she can for the community at Stoke for the sake of my soul and of our ancestors' souls. And I grant the estate at Greenstead to Stoke for my soul and for Æthelweard's and for Wiswith's. And I grant to Æthelflæd the use of it for as long as her life lasts, on condition that she does the best she can for those souls. Now may God grant me this, and my lord.

And I grant the estate at Heybridge to Ælfwold after my death [on condition] that he pay a food-rent every year to the community at St Paul's for our ancestors' souls. And I grant the estate at Totham to Brihtnoth and my younger daughter for their time; and after their death the estate is to go to Mersea for my daughter Æthelflæd. And to Stoke I grant the woodland at Ashfield as Eakild himself bought it. And I [grant] the estate at Rushbrooke to my mother if she live longer than I; then after the death of both of us I grant it to Winehelm if he (?) serve Æthelflæd loyally.

And I beseech whoever may then be king, for the love of God and all his saints, that let my children do what they may, they may never set aside the will which I have declared for my soul's sake. And if anyone alter it, may he have to account for it with God and the holy saints to whom I have bequeathed my property, so that he who shall alter this will may never repent it except in the torment of hell, unless I myself alter it before my death.

And I grant to Æthelgar a hide of a hundred and twenty acres of land which Aeulf held. He is to dispose of it as he wishes.

III. THE WILL OF WYNFLÆD.

Wynflæd cyð hu hio wile ymbe þæt hio hæfð ofer hyre dæg
hio becwiþ into cyrcan hyre ofring...u[1] 7 hyre beteran ofr'i'ng-
sceat 7 hyre rode 7 into beodern[2] hiwun twa selefrene cuppan 7
hyre to saulsceatte ælcon godes þeowe mancos go[ld]es 7 butan
5 þam Ceoldryþe I mancus 7 Oðelbryhte 7 Else 7 Æþel...þe[3] 7 an
pund to Wiltune þam hiwum 7 Fugele anne mancus 7 hio
becwið Æðelflæde hyre dehter hyre agrafenan beah 7 'hyre
mentelpreon' 7 þ̄ land æt Ebbelesburnan 7 þa boc on ece yrfe
to ateonne swa hyre leofosð sy 7 hio [an h]yre þara manna 7 þæs
10 yrfes 7 ealles þæs þe þær þenne on bið butan þæt man scel for
hyre saulle þærof don ægþer ge an mannon ge an yrfe 7 æt
Ceorlatune hio hyre an ealswa þere manna 7 þæs yrfes b[ut]an
þam freotmannon 7 þæt man finde of þam yrfe æt Ceorlatun[e
healfes][4] pundes wyrþne saulsceat to Mylenburnan 7 healfes
15 pundes wyrþne saulscet fram Cinnuc[5] to Gyfle 7 Eadmære þæt
land æt C[ol]les[h]ylle 7 æt Inggeneshamme 7 hio an him eac
þæs landes æt Faccancu[mbe þe][6] hyre morgengyfu wes his dæg
7 ofer his dæg gyf Æþelflæd leng lybbe þonne he þonne fo hio to
þam lande æt Faccancumbe and ofer hyre dæ[g g]a hit eft an
20 Eadwoldes hand 7 gif god wille þæt Eadwold weorþe to þam
ge[w]exen a'n' his fæder dæge[7] þæt he land healdan mæge
þene bid ic Eadmær þæt he him læte þara twega landa oþer to[8]
oþþe æt Colleshyll[e] oð æt Ead[b]urggebyrig 7 ofer his dæg buta
7 hio wile þæt man finde æt Inggenesham[me h]ealfes. pundes
25 wyrþ'n'e saulsceat to Waneting for hy 7 æt Colleshylle 7 finde
man of þam yrfe . LX . pene'g'ga wyrð to S'c'rifenanhamme
. LX . to Colleshylle . LX . to Cillariðe 7 freoge man Wulfware
folgyge þam þe hyre leofo[st sy...][9]ttryðe ealswa 7 freoge man
Wulfflæde on þæt gerad þæt hio folgige Æþelflæde 7 Eadgyfe
30 7 hio becwið Eadgyfe ane crencestran 7 ane sem[estra]n[10] oþer

---

[1] K., T. read the first missing letter as *f*.   [2] K. *Bedern.*
[3] Three letters missing. The first may be *w, f, s, r* or *þ*.
[4] Hole in MS. Kemble's emendation.   [5] K. *Cynnuc.*
[6] Space for about six letters.   [7] K. omits *dæge*.
[8] K., T. assume omission after *to*.
[9] Hole in MS. Space for about eight letters.
[10] Tear in MS. Kemble's emendation.

III. THE WILL OF WYNFLÆD.

Wynflæd declares how she wishes to dispose of what she possesses, after her death. She bequeathes to the church her offering—......and the better of her offering-cloths, and her cross; and to the refectory two silver cups for the community; and as a gift for the good of her soul a mancus of gold to every servant of God, and besides that one mancus to Ceolthryth and Othelbriht and Elsa and Æthel...th; and one pound to the community at Wilton and one mancus to Fugel.

And she bequeathes to her daughter Æthelflæd her engraved bracelet and her brooch, and the estate at Ebbesborne and the title-deed as a perpetual inheritance to dispose of as she pleases; and she grants to her the men and the stock and all that is on the estate except what shall be given from it both in men and stock for the sake of her soul. And at Charlton, also, she grants her the men and the stock except the freedmen, and except that a gift for her soul to the value of half a pound be supplied for Milborne from the stock at Charlton, and from Chinnock a gift for her soul to the value of half a pound for Yeovil.

And to Eadmær [she grants] the estates at Coleshill and Inglesham (?), and she grants to him also the estate at Faccombe, which was her marriage-gift, for his lifetime, and then after his death, if Æthelflæd survive him, she is to succeed to the estate at Faccombe, and after her death it is to revert to Eadwold's possession. And if it is God's will that Eadwold be old enough in his father's lifetime to hold land, then I ask Eadmær to relinquish to him one of two estates, either Coleshill or Adderbury, and after his lifetime, both. And at Inglesham (?) she wishes that there be furnished on her behalf for Wantage a gift for her soul worth half a pound, and [the same] at Coleshill; and that from the stock the equivalent of sixty pence be supplied for Shrivenham, sixty for Coleshill and sixty for Childrey.

And Wulfwaru is to be freed, and she is to serve whom she pleases, and ...ttryth also. And Wulfflæd is to be freed on condition that she serve Æthelflæd and Eadgifu. And she bequeathes to Eadgifu a woman-weaver and a seamstress the one called Eadgifu, the other called Æthelgifu. And Gerburg is to

hatte Edgyfu[1] oþer hatte Æþelyfu 7 freoge man 'Gerburge'
7 Miscin 7 hi...l[2] 7 Burhulfes dohtur æt C[in]nuc 7 Ælfsige
7 his wif 7 his yldran dohtor 7 Ceolstanes wif 7 æt Ceorlatune
freoge man Pifus 7 Edwyn[3]...7...n[4] wif 7 æt Faccancumbe
5 frioge man Edelm[5] 7 Man 7 Iohannan 7 'Sprow 7 his wif'
7 En. f...[6]7 Gersande 7 'Snel'[7] 7 æt Colleshylle freoge man
Æþelgyþe 7 Bican[8] wif 7 Æffan 7 B[e]dan 7 Gurhannes wif
7 freoge man Wulfware[9] swystor Byrhsigis wi[f] 7......[10]
þysne wyrhtan 7 'Wulfgyþe Ælfswyþe dohtor' 7 gif þær hwylc
10 witeþeow 'man' sy butan þyson þe hio geþeowede hio gelyf'ð'
to hyre bearnon þæt hi 'h'ine willon lyhtan for hyre saulle
7 Ælfwolde hyre twegen wesendhornas 7 an hors 7 hyre re'a'de
ge[t]eld [7] hio becwyð[11] Eadmære ane hlidfæsþe cuppan oþre
Æðelflæde 7 bit þæt hi findon betweox him twa smicere scencing-
15 cuppan [i]nto beodern for hi oþþe hyre ahgene ieredan cuppan
geiccon hy sy......[12] an anon punde þonne wolde hio þæt man
dyde 'inn'on ægþere cuppan healf pund penega 7 agyfe man
Eadwolde his ag[e]ne . II . sylerenan cuppan; 7 hio becwið him
hyre goldfagan treowena[n] cuppan þæt he ice his beah mid þam
20 golde oþþe hi mon æt him gehweorfe mid . XVI . mancussum
reades reades[13] goldes swa micel þær is to gedong 7 hio becwiþ
him twa mydrecan 7 þæraninnan an bedreaf eal þæt to anum
bedde gebyreð 7 a'g'yfe Eadmær Eadwolde swa micel yrfe 7 swa
fela manna swa...[14] him ær æt Hafene becwæð 7 [h][15]e his
25 fæder syððan swa he wille 7 be þan lande æt Cinnuc hit agon
þa hiwan æt Sceaftesbyrig ofer hyre dæg 7 hio ah þæt yrfe 7 þa
men þenne an hio þan hywum þara gebura þe on þam gafollande
sittað 7 þera þeowra manna hio an hyre syna dehter Eadgyfe 7
þæs yrfes butan þam saulsceatte þe man to Gifle syllan sceal
30 7 hio wile þ man læte on þan lande standan . VI . ox's'an 7
. IIII . cy mid feower cealfon. 7 of [þa]m þeowan mannan æt

---

[1] K. *Eadgyfu.*   [2] Hole in MS. Space for seven or eight letters.
[3] K. *Eadwyne.*   [4] Gap and tear in MS.   [5] K. *Æðelm.* T. *Ædelm.*
[6] Hole in MS. K., T. *En[e]fætte.*   [7] K. *Suel.*
[8] K. *Biccan.*   [9] Last letter uncertain. T. *-a.* K. *-es.*
[10] Long gap and tear in MS.   [11] *y* written over *e.*
[12] Gap for twelve or more letters, and tear. K. [*n....ec...an*], not now
visible.   [13] Sic MS.   ·
[14] Small hole in MS. Space for two or possibly three letters.
[15] Small hole. Space for one letter.

be freed, and Miscin and Hi...... and the daughter of Burhulf at Chinnock, and Ælfsige and his wife and elder daughter, and Ceolstan's wife. And at Charlton Pifus and Eadwyn and ...'s wife are to be freed. And at Faccombe Eadhelm and Man and Johanna and Sprow and his wife and En...... and Gersand and Snel are to be freed. And at Coleshill Æthelgyth and Bica's wife and Æffa and Beda and Gurhann's wife are to be freed; and Wulfwaru's sister, Brihtsige's wife, and......the wright, and Wulfgyth, Ælfswith's daughter are to be freed. And if there be any penally enslaved man besides these whom she has enslaved, she trusts to her children that they will release him for her soul's sake.

And [she grants] to Ælfwold her two buffalo-horns and a horse and her red tent. And she bequeathes to Eadmær a cup with a lid, and another to Æthelflæd, and prays that between them they will furnish two fair goblets to the refectory for her sake, or augment her own ornamented cups......worth one pound. Then she would like half a pound of pence to be put into each cup, and that Eadwold should be given back his own two silver cups. And she bequeathes to him her gold-adorned wooden cup in order that he may enlarge his armlet with the gold, or that he may receive sixteen mancuses of red gold in exchange; that amount has been put on it. And she bequeathes to him two chests and in them a set of bed-clothing, all that belongs to one bed.

And Eadmær is to pay to Eadwold as much stock and as many men as he (?) has bequeathed to him at Avon, and he afterwards [is to pay] to his father what he wishes. And with regard to the estate at Chinnock, the community at Shaftesbury possess it after her death, and she owns the stock and the men; this being so, she grants to the community the peasants who dwell on the rented land, and the bondmen she grants to her son's daughter Eadgifu, and also the stock, except the gift for her soul which must be rendered to Yeovil; and she wishes that six oxen and four cows with four calves be allowed to remain on the estate. And of the bondmen at Chinnock she bequeathes to Eadwold, Ceolstan, Eadstan's son, and Æffa's son, and Burhwyn [and] Martin and Hisfig; and in their place she bequeathes to Eadgifu,

Cinnuc hio becwið Eadwolde Ceolstan Etstanes[1] sunu 7 Æffan
sunu 7 Burhwynne Mærtin 7 Hisfig[2] 7 hio becwiþ Ead[gy]fe
þærangean Ælfsige þene coc 7 Ælfware Burgan[3] dohtor 7
Herestan 7 his wif 7 Ecelm 7 his wif 7 hiora cild 7 Cynestan
5 7 Wynsige 7 Byrhtrices sunu 7 Edwynne[4] 7 Buneles sunu 7
Ælfferer[5] dohtor 7 hio becwið Æðelf[læde][6] Elhhelmmes dehter
Ælfferes dohtor 'þa geonran' 7 hyre twilibrocenan cyrtel 7 oþerne
linnenne oþþe linnenweb 7 Eadgyfe twa mydrecan 7 þæranin[n]an
hyre be't'sþe bedwahrift 7 linnenne ruwan 7 eal þæt bedref þe
10 þærto gebyreð 7[7] hyre betstan dunnan tunecan 7 hyre 'beteran'
mentel 7 hyre twa tr'e'owenan gesplottude cuppan 7 hyre ealdan
gewiredan preon is an . VI . mancussum 7 sylle man hyre . IIII .
mancussas of hyre sa . . . . . .[8] bege 7 an lang healwahrift 7 oþer
sceort 7 þrio sethrægl 7 hio an Ceoldryþe hyre blacena tunecena
15 swa þer hyre leofre beo 7 hyre be't's'ð haliryft 7 hyre betsþan
bindan [7 Æþelf][9]læde þisse hwitan hyre cincdaðenan[10] cyrtel
7 cuffian 7 bindan 7 finde Æðelflæd syþþan an hyre nun's'crude
loce hwæt hio betsð mæge Wulfflæde 7 Æþelgife 7 ice mid golde
þæt hyra ægþer hyru hæbbe . LX . peneng[a wyr]þ 7 Ceolwynne
20 7 Edburge[11] þæt sy . XXX . penega wyrþ 7 þær synt twa micle
myd'e'rcan 7 an hræglcysð 7 an lytlun towmyderce 7 eac twa
ealde mydercan þenne an hio Æþelflæde on ælcum þingum þe
þær unbecweden bið on bocum 7 an swilcum lytlum 7 hio
gelyfð [þ]æt hio wille hyre saulle geþencan 7 þær synt eac
25 wahriftu sum þe hyre wyrðe bið 7 þa læstan hio mæg syllan
hyre wimmannon 7 hio becwið Cynelufe hyre dæl þera wildera
horsa þe mid Eadmære's' synt 7 hio an Æþelflede hyre hy . . .
ppe[12] 7 þara andlumena 7 ealra þera getæsa þet þærbinnan beoð
7 eac ðæs worþiges gif his hyre se cing an swa swa Eadweard
30 cing ær his Byrhtwynne hyre meder geuþe 7 hæbbe Eadwold
7 his sweostor hyre taman hors g[e]'mæn' . . .[13] his agene toforan.

---

1. K. *Eastanes.*   2. K., T. *his wif.*   3. K. *Tefl Wareburgan.*
4. K. *Eadwynne.*   5. K. *Ælfweres.*
6. Hole in MS. This is a little wider than the space usually occupied by -*læde.*
7. There is a long gap in the MS. here, perhaps an erasure.
8. A long horizontal tear in MS. K., T. *sa[ulesceatte. . .].*
9. Hole in MS. Kemble's emendation.   10. K., T. *cinewaðenan.*
11. K. *Eadburge.*
12. Corner of MS. missing. K. [*sa . . . . cu*] but there is now no trace of this.
13. Corner of MS. missing.

Ælfsige the cook and Ælfwaru, Burga's daughter, and Herestan and his wife, and Ecghelm and his wife and their child, and Cynestan and Wynsige and Brihtric's son and Eadwyn and Bunele's son and Ælfhere's daughter.

And she bequeathes to Æthelflæd, daughter of Ealhhelm, Ælfhere's younger daughter, and her double badger-skin (?) gown, and another of linen or else some linen cloth. And to Eadgifu two chests and in them her best bed-curtain and a linen covering and all the bed-clothing which goes with it, and ......and her best dun tunic, and the better of her cloaks, and her two wooden cups ornamented with dots, and her old filagree brooch which is worth six mancuses. And let there be given to her four mancuses from her......and a long hall-tapestry and a short one and three seat coverings. And she grants to Ceolthryth whichever she prefers of her black tunics and her best holy veil and her best headband; and to Æthelflæd the White her......gown and cap and headband, and afterwards Æthelflæd is to supply from her nun's vestments the best she can for Wulfflæd and Æthelgifu and supplement it with gold so that each of them shall have at least sixty pennyworth: and for Ceolwyn and Eadburg it shall be thirty pennyworth. And there are two large chests and a clothes' chest, and a little spinning box and two old chests.

Then she makes a gift to Æthelflæd of everything which is unbequeathed, books and such small things, and she trusts that she will be mindful of her soul. And there are also tapestries, one which is suitable for her, and the smallest she can give to her women. And she bequeathes to Cynelufu her share of the untamed horses which are with Eadmær's. And to Æthelflæd she grants her......and the utensils and all the useful things that are inside, and also the homestead if the king grant it to her as King Edward granted it to Brihtwyn her mother. And Eadwold and his sister are to have her tame horses in common....

IV. THE WILL OF BISHOP ÆLFSIGE.

Þis is Ælfsiges biscopes cwide. Þæt is þonne ærest þæt ic wille
þæt man gefreoge ælcne witeþeowne mannan þe on þam
biscoprice sie for hine and for his cynehlaford. And minum
cynehlaford mine heregeatya and þæs landes æt Tantune þe he
5 me ær to let. And ic gean þæs landes æt Crundelan ofer mine dæg
Ælfheage and ofer his dæg gange hit into ealden mynstere. And
Io[1] gean minum mægcnafan þæs landes æt Anne his dæg, and
ofer his dæg into niwan mynstere; and þæs landes æt þan twan
Worþigum minre magan þa hwile þe hyre lif biþ, and siþþan
10 minre swistlr[2] and minum magcnafan—ægþer ge þara landa ge
þæs æt Cleran and þa oþerra lalra[3] þe mine fæder ahte; and þæs
landes æt Tioceburnan Wlfrice Cufing his dæg and ofer his dæg
into ealdun mynstere. And þæs landes æt Runcwuda swa hit ær
gecweden wæs to ealdun mynstere; and Ælfwige þæs landes æt
15 Ciltrigtune ofer þære wuduwan dæg; and Wlfrice æt Wicham
þæs æt Lætanlia. Þonne bidde ic minnan leofan freond Ælfheah
þæt bewite ægþer ge þa land ge þa þe mine mgas[4] sien, and þæt
þu ne geþafige þæt man þis on ænig oþer wænde. Gif hit þonne
hwa do God hine fordo ge mid sawle ge mid lichoman ge her
20 ge on þan to feondan[5] buton Io[6] hit self on oþer wænde.

V. THE BEQUEST OF ORDNOTH AND HIS WIFE
TO WINCHESTER CATHEDRAL.

Her is geswutelod on þisum gewrite hú Ordnoð. 7 his Wif
geuðan þara . x . hida æt Cendefer into þæra ealdan cyrican to
Wintanceastre ofer heora begra deg. 7 þa boc þyderinnan sealdan
to swutelunge on þa gerad. þ seo boc heam sy geara gyf hy
25 hyre hwer beþurfan tó ænire rihtinge. 7 gange seo bóc æft into
þære stowe 7 dæle man swylcne del héora æhta swylce hy

---

[1] For *ic*.
[2] For *swister*.
[3] For *ealra*.
[4] For *magas*.
[5] For *toweardan*.
[6] For *ic*.

IV. THE WILL OF BISHOP ÆLFSIGE.

This is Bishop Ælfsige's will. First, I wish that each man penally enslaved who is on the episcopal demesne be freed for my sake and my royal lord's. And I grant to my royal lord my heriot and the estate at Taunton which he has let to me. And I grant the estate at Crondall after my death to Ælfheah, and after his death it is to go to the Old Minster. And I grant to my young kinsman the estate at Ann for his lifetime, and after his death to the New Minster; and the estate at the two Worthys to my kinswoman as long as her life lasts, and then to my sister and my young kinsman—both those estates and that at Clere and the others, all which my father possessed; and the estate at Tichborne to Wulfric Cufing for his time and after his death to the Old Minster. And [I grant] the estate at Ringwood to the Old Minster, as was settled before; and to Ælfwig the estate at Cholderton (?) after the widow's death; and to Wulfric of Wickham that at Netley.

Then I pray you, my dear friend Ælfheah, that [you] will watch both over the estates and those who are my kinsmen, and that you will never permit anyone to alter this in any way. If anyone do so, may God destroy him both soul and body, both here and in the future, unless I myself change it.

V. THE BEQUEST OF ORDNOTH AND HIS WIFE
TO WINCHESTER CATHEDRAL.

Here in this document it is declared how Ordnoth and his wife granted the ten hides at Candover to the old church at Winchester after the death of both of them, and gave to it the title-deed as evidence, on condition that the title-deed shall be ready for them if they need it at any time for any correction; but the title-deed is to be returned to the minster. And such portion of their goods as they have specified is to be distributed after their death, and the surplus is to go to the minster with the estate.

On these terms is the estate given to the minster: that on

gecwedan æfter heora dege 7 gange seo ofereáca into þære stowe
mid þam lande. on ða gereðnesse is þæt land geseld to þam
mynstre þ man unc gefecce. æt uncrum ændedege mid þes
mynstres crafte 7 unc swylce legerstowe forescewian swylc unc
5 for gode þeárflice sý. 7 for weorulde gerysenlic. Þis is seo
gewitnes ðe Ordnod. Wile habban godæs 7 his hiredes on ealdan
mynstre. þ is þ he 7 is wif cwædan on heora gewitnesse þ is
æhta gangan on his freonda hand ofer his deg se ðel þe he cweþe
7 se oþer dæl into þære stowe þær hi restað.

VI. ÆTHELGEARD'S BEQUEST TO THE
NEW MINSTER, WINCHESTER.

10   Ic Æðelgeard an þæs landes æt Stottanwelle ofer mine dæge
minra wifan hera dæge and þonne on niwan mynstera on
Wintanceaster uncer begea sawle þarfa þæm to brocon and
næfre utan seallan.

VII. BRIHTRIC GRIM'S BEQUEST TO
WINCHESTER CATHEDRAL.

Her is geswutulad þet Brichtric Grim gean þes landes æt
15 Rimtune into ealdan mynstre æfter his dege. mid þere hide þe
he syþþan begeat into þan lande. 7 agyfþ þa bóc ðe Eadred
cyning him gébocode into þam ealdan mynstre to þere ealdan
bǽc. þe Æþestan cyning ær gebocode on þet gerad þet he hæbbe
þone bryce þes landes swa lange swa his tyma sy. 7 gange
20 syððan into þære stowe swa gewered swa hit stande mid mete
7 mid mannum. 7 mid ælcum þingan his sawle to frófre. 7 þyses
is to ywitnesse. Dunstan arcebisceop. 7 Aþelwold bisceop 7
Ælfstan bisceop. 7 Æþelgar abbod. 7 se hired on Glestingabyrig.
7 þa twegen hiredas. on ealdan mynstre. 7 on niwan mynstre on
25 Wintanceastre.

the day of our death they will fetch us with the minster's resources and provide for us such resting-place as is necessary for us in God's sight and fitting in the eyes of the world.

It is for this that Ordnoth wishes to have the testimony of God and his community at the Old Minster: namely, that he and his wife announced in their presence that the part of his possessions which he stated was to go into his friends' possession after his death, and the other part to the place where they shall be buried.

VI. ÆTHELGEARD'S BEQUEST TO THE NEW MINSTER, WINCHESTER.

I, Æthelgeard, grant the estate at Sotwell after my death to my wife for her lifetime, and then for the need of the souls of both of us to the New Minster in Winchester, for them to use and never to alienate.

VII. BRIHTRIC GRIM'S BEQUEST TO WINCHESTER CATHEDRAL.

It is here declared that Brihtric Grim grants the estate at Rimpton to the Old Minster after his death, together with the hide which he afterwards acquired in addition to that estate; and he presents to the Old Minster, the title-deed which King Edred granted, as a supplement to the old title-deed which King Athelstan granted; on condition that he is to have the use of the estate as long as his life lasts, and afterwards it is to go to that foundation, stocked as it is with cattle and men and all things, for the comfort of his soul.

Of this the following are witnesses: Archbishop Dunstan, and Bishop Æthelwold, and Bishop Ælfstan, and Abbot Æthelgar, and the community at Glastonbury, and the two communities of the Old and New Minsters in Winchester.

VIII. THE WILL OF ÆLFGIFU.

ÞIS ys Ælfgyfæ gegurning to hiræ cinehlafordæ. þæt is þæt
heo hyne bítt for godæs lufun and for cynescypæ þæt heo mote
beón hyre cwydes wyrðæ. Þonnæ cyð heo þæ leóf bæ þinre
geþafiunga hwæt heo for þæ and for þyræ sawlæ to godæs
5 ciricean dón wýlæ. Þæt is æræst þæt héo ánn into ealdan mynstær.
þær heo hiræ licaman ræstan þæncþ þæs landæs æt Hrisanbeorgan
eallswa hit stænt buton þæt heo wylæ bæ þinre geþafunga þæt
man freóge on ælcum tunæ ælne witæþæownæ mann þæ undær
hiræ geþeowuð wæs. and twa hund mandcussa goldæs to þam
10 mynstær. and hire scrín mid hiræ haligdomæ. And heo an innto
nigean mynstær þæs landæs æt Bleddanhlæwe. and hund mancussa goldæs. And annæ offringdisc into nunna mynstær. and
þæs landæs æt Hwætædunæ into Rummæsigæ xriste & sanctan
Marian. and æt Cæstæleshammæ Into Abbandunæ. And æt
15 Wicham into Baþum. And ic ánn minæn cinæhlafordæ þæs
landæs æt Weowungum and æt Hlincgeladæ. and æt Hæfæresham. and æt Hæðfælda. and æt Mæssanwyrðæ and æt Gyssic
and twegea bæagas æigþær ýs ón hundtwælftigu*m*. mancussum
and anræ sópcuppan and syx horsa and swa fala[1] scylda and
20 spæra. and þam æþelingæ þæs landæs æt Niwanhám. and anæs
beages on þritægum mancussum. And þæra hlæfdigan anæs
swyrbeages on hundtweltifgum[2] mancussum and anæs beages
on þritegum mancussum. and anre sopcuppan. And ic ann
Aþelwoldæ[3] bisceopæ þæs landæs æt Tæafersceat. And bidde
25 hinæ þæt hæ symlie þingiæ for minæ modor an for me. And ic
ánn bæ minæs hlafordæs geþafiungæ þæs landæs æt Mundingwillæ. and æt Beorhþanstædæ. Ælfwerdæ and Æþelwærdæ and
Ælfwaræ him to gemanan hira dǽg. and ofær hira dæg into
ealdan mynstær for minnæ cynehlaforð and for mæ. And
30 syllan hi ælcæ geáre twa dǽgfæorman into þam twam mynstrum.
þa wilæ þæ hi his brucæn. And ig[4] án Ælfwæræ[5] miræ swystær
eallæs þæs þæ ic hiræ álenæð hæfdæ. And Æþælfledæ minæs
broþur wifæ þæs bændes þæ ic hire alæneð hæfdæ. And ælchum
abbodæ fif pund pæniga to hira mynstres bote. And leof be

---

[1] T. *fela.*   [2] Sic MS.   [3] K. *Æþelwoldæ.*
[4] T. *ic.*   [5] K. *Ælfwaræ.*

VIII. THE WILL OF ÆLFGIFU.

This is Ælfgifu's request of her royal lord; she prays him for the love of God and for the sake of his royal dignity, that she may be entitled to make her will.

Then she makes known to you, Sire, by your consent what she wishes to give to God's church for you and for your soul. First, she grants to the Old Minster, where she intends her body to be buried, the estate at Risborough just as it stands, except that, with your consent, she wishes that at each village every penally enslaved man who was subject to her shall be freed; and [she grants] two hundred mancuses of gold to that minster and her shrine with her relics. And she grants to the New Minster the estate at Bledlow, and a hundred mancuses of gold; and a paten to the Nunnery and the estate at Whaddon to Christ and St Mary at Romsey; and Chesham to Abingdon, and Wickham to Bath.

And I grant to my royal lord the estates at Wing, Linslade, Haversham, Hatfield, Masworth and Gussage; and two armlets, each of a hundred and twenty mancuses, and a drinking-cup and six horses and as many shields and spears. And to the Ætheling the estate at Newnham and an armlet of thirty mancuses. And to the queen a necklace of a hundred and twenty mancuses and an armlet of thirty mancuses, and a drinking-cup.

And I grant to Bishop Æthelwold the estate at *Tæafersceat* and pray him that he will always intercede for my mother and for me. And with my lord's permission I grant the estates at Mongewell and Berkhampstead to Ælfwēard and Æthelweard and Ælfwaru in common for their lifetime, and after their death to the Old Minster for my royal lord and for me. And they are to pay a two-days' food-rent every year to the two minsters, as long as they possess the estates.

And to my sister Ælfwaru I grant all that I have lent her; and to my brother's wife Æthelflæd the headband which I have lent her.

And to each abbot five pounds of pence for the repair of their minster. And, Sire, with your consent, [I wish] that I may

þinre geþafiunga þæt ic motæ bætæcen þam bisceope. and þam
abbodæ. þonæ ofæreacan to þære stowe botæ. and earmum
mannum for me to dælænne swa swa him þincæ þæt mæ for godæ
þearflucustþ[1] si. And ic biddæ minnæ cinelaford for godæs
5 lufum. þæt[2] næ forlæte minæ mænn þe hinæ gesæcen. and him
wyrðæ syn. and ic ann Ælfwerdæ anræ sópcuppan. and Æþelwerdæ anæs gerænodæs drincæhornæs.

IX. THE WILL OF THE EALDORMAN ÆLFHEAH.

HER is geswutelod an ðis gewrite hu Ælfheah ealdorman his
cwidæ gecwæðen hæfð. be his cynehlafordæs geþafuncge þæt is
10 þonnæ æræst þæt he geán his drihtne for his sawlæ þæarfæ þæs
landæs æt Ællændune and þæs æt Crundelom to ealdan mynstære
to Winticeastræ. And þæra twæntiga hida æt Ceorlatunæ into
Mealdælmæsbyrig and þæra fiftyna hida æt Suðtune into Baðan
and he geán his cynehlafordæ þæra hundtwæntiga[3] hida æt
15 Wyrðæ and þæs landæs æt Coccham and æt Þæcham. and æt
Ceolæswyrðæ. And æt Incgenæsham. and æt Ægelesbyrig and
æt Wændofron. And þreo hund mancusa goldæs. and annæ
dícs an þrym pundom. And anæ sóppcuppan an þrym pundan
7 an handsex. and þæræ lecge is hundeahtati mancussa goldæs.
20 7 seax swurð and seax hors. mid geredan. and swa fæla spæra
and scylda. And he geán Ælfriðæ ðæs cyninges wifæ his
gefæðeran. þæs landæs æt Scyræburnan ealswa hit stænt. And
þam yldran æþælingæ þæs cyngæs suna. and hiræ þritiga mancussa goldæs and anæs swurdæs. And þam gincgran ðæs landes
25 æt Wolcnæsstedæ. And he gean Ælfhære his breðær þæs
landæs æt Færndunæ. and æt Ealdincburnan. And Godwinæ
his suna þæs æt Tudincgatunæ. and Ælfwerdæ æt Wyritunæ.
And Æþelwerdæ his mege æt Wicumun[4]. And Ælfwine his
swustur suna þæs æt Froxafelda. Þonnæ an ic Ælfsiþæ minon
30 wifæ gyf heo leng beoð þonne ic and it swa gehylt swa ic hiræ
truwan to hæbbe ealra þara oðæra landa þæ ic læfæ. And heo

---

[1] T. -liicustþ. K. -liicust.   [2] T. inserts he.
[3] K. -twyntiga.   [4] K. Wicurnun. T. Wicuman.

entrust the surplus to the Bishop and the Abbot for the repair
of the foundation, and for them to distribute for me among poor
men according as seems to them most profitable for me in God's
sight.

And I beseech my royal lord for the love of God, that he will
not desert my men who seek his protection and are worthy of
him. And I grant to Ælfweard a drinking-cup and to Æthelweard an ornamented drinking-horn.

IX. THE WILL OF THE EALDORMAN ÆLFHEAH.

Here in this document it is declared how the ealdorman
Ælfheah has declared his will with his royal lord's consent.
Firstly, that for his soul's need he gives to his Lord the estate
at *Ellandun*, and that at Crondall to the Old Minster at
Winchester; and the twenty hides at Charlton to Malmesbury;
and the fifteen hides at Sutton to Bath.

And he grants to his royal lord the hundred and twenty hides
at Worth and the estates at Cookham, Thatcham, Chelworth,
Inglesham (?), Aylesbury and Wendover; and three hundred
mancuses of gold and a dish of three pounds and a drinking-
cup of three pounds and a short sword; and [on] the scabbard (?) there are eighty mancuses of gold; and six swords and
six horses with trappings and as many spears and shields.

And to Ælfthryth the King's wife, his *gefædere*, he grants the
estate at Shirburn (?) just as it stands; and to the elder Ætheling,
the King's son and her's, thirty mancuses of gold and a sword;
and to the younger the estate at Walkhampstead. And he grants
to his brother Ælfhere the estates at Faringdon and Aldbourne.
And to his son Godwine the estate at *Tudingatun* and Purton (?)
to Ælfweard and Wycombe to his kinsman Æthelweard; and
Froxfield to his sister's son Ælfwine.

Then to my wife Ælfswith, if she live longer than I and
maintains the property in accordance with the confidence I have
in her, I grant all the other estates which I leave; and she is to
remember God zealously [with almsgiving] from the property,
and be zealous for the welfare of our souls. And she is to possess

þanne gæornlicæ of þam god geþæncæ and for uncre sawle
geornlicæ beo and brucæ heo þæs landæs æt Batancumbæ hyræ
dæg and æfter hire dæge ga hit an Ælfwærdes hand uncres suna
gif hæ lifæs beo gyf hæ næ beo gyf hæ næ beo[1] for[2] mine broðorn
5 to þa hwilæ þæ hi beón and æfter hyra dege ga into Glæstinga-
byrig for urnæ fædær and for uræ modor and for us eallæ. And
ic wullan þæt man gefreogen ælcne witeþeowne man on ælcum
þæra landæ þæ ic minon freondon bæcwedden hæbbæ. And
þisseræ geþafiuncga þæ sæ cyning geuþæ is to gewitnæssæ
10 Ælfþryþ þæs cynincges wif and Aþelwold[3] bisceop. and Ælfhære
ealdorman and Æþelwine ealdorman and Ælfwinæ and Æscwig
abbod.

X. THE WILL OF THE EALDORMAN ÆTHELMÆR.

Æðelmær ealdorman cyð on dysum gewrite his cynehlaforde
and eallum his freondum his cwyde wæs to his nyhstan dæge.
15 Þæt is þonne þæt ic gean Gode ærest for mine sawle to Wintanceastre into Niwan Mynstre, þære ic me restan wille, an hund
mancesa goldes and tyn pund peneta and min scrin and XIII hida
landes ðær þe Lufa ahte, mid mete and mid mannum salswa[4] hit
stent, and ic æt minum hlaforde gebohte ða hit to his handa
20 forwyrht[5] mid hundtwelftigum mancesum goldes æt Cyrthugtune
on Aþelwoldes bysceopes gewitnesse and ealra minra geferena.
And ic gean þæs landes æt Tudanwyrðe minum wife hire dæg
and æfter dæge gange mid hire lice þær ic reste for uncere begra
sawle. And ic gean into Ealdan Mynstre into sce Trinitate an
25 hund mancesa goldes and tyn pund penaga; and II pund into
Nunnena Mynstra; and II pund into mæssepreosta gylde and
I pund into diacona gylde. And into Cristes cyricun on Cantu-
warabyrig III pund; and II pund into sce Agustyne; and II pund
into Hrofeceastere: and II pund into Abbandune; and II pund into
30 Rumesige; and II pund into Wiltune; and II pund into Sceaftesbyrig; and VI pund into Glæstyngabyrig; and II pund into
Mealdelmesbyrig; and I pund into Baðan; and I pund into Cracgelade; and I pund into Burnan. And minum hiredcnihtum V pund

---

[1] Sic MS.   [2] For *fon*. Sic K., T.
[3] K. *Æþelwold*.   [4] For *ealswa*.
[5] *wæs* has been omitted here.

the estate at Batcombe for her time and after her death it is to
pass into the possession of our son Ælfweard if he is still alive.
If he is not, my brothers are to succeed to it for as long as they
live, and after their death it is to go to Glastonbury for the sake
of our father and of our mother and of us all.

And I wish that every penally enslaved man be freed on each
of the estates which I have bequeathed to my friends.

And the witnesses of this permission which the King has
granted to me are: Ælfthryth the King's wife, and Bishop
Æthelwold and the Ealdorman Ælfhere and the Ealdorman
Æthelwine and Ælfwine and the Abbot Æscwig.

X. THE WILL OF THE EALDORMAN ÆTHELMÆR.

The ealdorman Æthelmær in this document informs his
royal lord and all his friends [what] his will was on his last day.
In the first place, for my soul I grant to God, to the New
Minster at Winchester, where I wish to be buried, a hundred
mancuses of gold and ten pounds of pence, and my shrine; and
thirteen hides of land which Lufa possessed, with the produce
and the men just as it stands, and as I bought it from my lord
at Chirton (?), in the presence of Bishop Æthelwold and all my
companions, for a hundred and twenty mancuses of gold, when
it came into my lord's possession by confiscation.

And I grant the estate at Tidworth to my wife for her time,
and after her death it is to go at her funeral to the place where
I shall be buried, for the souls of both of us.

And I grant to the Holy Trinity at the Old Minster a
hundred mancuses of gold and ten pounds of pence; and two
pounds to the Nunnery; and two pounds to the priests' gild
and one pound to the deacons' gild. And to Christchurch at
Canterbury [I grant] three pounds; and two pounds to St
Augustine's; and two pounds to Rochester; and two pounds to
Abingdon; and two pounds to Romsey; and two pounds to
Wilton; and two pounds to Shaftesbury; and six pounds to
Glastonbury; and two pounds to Malmesbury; and one pound
to Bath; and one pound to Cricklade; and one pound to Bourne.

to gedule[1]. And ic becweðe minum cynehlaforde to heregeatuwum
IIII beagus on ðrym hund mancesum goldes and IIII sweord and
VIII hors feower gerædode and IIII ungerædode and IIII helmas
and IIII byrnan and VIII speru and VIII scyldas. And ic and[2]
5 minan yldran suna ðæs landes æt Igeneshamme and þam
gingran þæs æt Cottesmore and þæs ðe ðær[3]. And ic an minum
bearnum to gedale þreo hund mancesa goldes. And ic gean
syððan minum wife ealles ðæs ðe ic gean ge on lande ge on
æhtum to þam forewordun þe wit mid wedde unc betweonan
10 gefæstnodon.

XI. THE WILL OF BRIHTRIC AND ÆLFSWITH.

✠ Þis is Byrhtrices 7 Ælfswyðe his wifes nihsta cwide. ðe hi
cwædon on Meapaham on heora maga gewitnæsse. þ wæs
Wulfstan Úcca. 7 Wulfsie his broðor. 7 Sired Ælfredes suna:̷
7 Wulfsie se blaca. 7 Wine preost:̷ 7 Ælfgar on Meapaham:̷
15 7 Wulfeh Ordeges suna:̷ 7 Ælfeh his broðor. 7 Byrhtwara[4]
Ælfrices laf. 7 Bryhtric hyræ mæg. 7 Ælfstan bisceop; Ærest his
kynehlaforde[5] ænne beah. on hundeahtotigan mancysan goldes:̷
7 an handsecs. on ealswa miclan. 7 feower hors:̷ twa gerædede.
7 twa sweord gefetelsode[6]. 7 twegen hafocas:̷ 7 ealle his
20 heador[7]hundas; 7 ðære hlæfdian. ænne beah on ðrittigan
mancysan goldes:̷ 7 ænne stedan. to forespræce. þ se cwyde
standan moste[8]; 7 for his sawle 7 his yldrena. into[9] sce Andreæ.
twa sulung æt Denetune:̷ 7 hio for hire sawle 7 hire yldrena:̷
twa æt Langanfelda. 7 þiderin for hy. ðrittig mancys goldes.
25 7 ænne sweorbeah:̷ on . XL . mancysan. 7 ane cuppan seolfrene.
7 healfne bænd gyldenne. 7 ælce geare to heora gemynde.
twegra daga feorme. of Hæslholte. 7 . II . of Woðringaberan. 7
. II . of Bærlingan. 7 . II . of Hærigeardeshamme. 7 to Cristes

---

[1] For *gedale*.   [2] For *an*.
[3] Some expression such as *to hyrð* has been omitted here.
[4] K. -*waru*.   [5] Written over an erasure. K. *cyne-*.
[6] T. *gefelsode*.   [7] K. *heahdeor*.
[8] K. *mihte*.   [9] T. *in*.

And to my household servants [I grant] five pounds to be divided among them. And I bequeathe to my royal lord as my heriot four armlets of three hundred mancuses of gold, and four swords and eight horses, four with trappings and four without, and four helmets and four coats of mail and eight spears and eight shields.

And I grant to my elder son the estate at Inglesham (?) and to the younger that at Cottesmore, and whatever [is included] in it. And I grant three hundred mancuses of gold for my children to divide. And finally, all that I grant to my wife, whether estates or goods, I grant according to the terms which we settled by a compact between us.

XI. THE WILL OF BRIHTRIC AND ÆLFSWITH.

This is the last will of Brihtric and his wife, Ælfswith, which they declared at Meopham, in the presence of their relations, namely, Wulfstan Ucca, and his brother Wulfsige, and Sired, Alfred's son, and Wulfsige the Black and Wine the priest, and Ælfgar of Meopham, and Wulfheah, Ordheah's son and his brother Ælfheah, and Brihtwaru, Ælfric's widow, and her kinsman Brihtric, and Bishop Ælfstan.

First, to his royal lord an armlet of eighty mancuses of gold and a short sword of the same value, and four horses, two with harness, and two swords with sheaths, and two hawks and all his staghounds. And to the queen an armlet of thirty mancuses of gold, and a stallion, for her advocacy that the will might stand.

And to St Andrew's two ploughlands at Denton for Brihtric's soul and for his ancestors' souls; and Ælfswith grants for her soul and her ancestors' souls two ploughlands at Longfield; and to the same church on their behalf thirty mancuses of gold and a necklace of forty mancuses, and a silver cup and half a gold headband; and each year in commemoration of them, two days' food-rent from *Hæslholt*, two from Wateringbury, two from Birling and two from Harrietsham. And to Christchurch sixty mancuses of gold, thirty for the bishop and thirty for the

circan . LX . mancys goldes . XXX . ðam biscope . XXX . ðam
hirode:⁄ 7 ænne sweorbeah. on . LXXX . mancys:⁄ 7 twa cuppan
seolfrene. 7 ðæt land æt Meapaham; 7 to sc̄e Augustine. ðrittig
mancys goldes. 7 twa cuppan seolfrene. 7 healfne[1] bænd
5 gyldenne. 7 ꝥ land æt Dæræntan. Byrhwara[2] hire dæg:⁄ 7 æfter
hire dæge. into sc̄e Andree. for unc. 7 uncre yldran; 7 Bærlingas
Wulfehe:⁄ 7 he selle . x . hund pænega. into sc̄e Andree:⁄ for
unc 7 uncre yldran; 7 Wulfsie Woðringabyras. innon ꝥ gecynde;
7 Sirede. Hæslholt. innon ꝥ gecynde; 7 Wulfege. 7 Ælfege his
10 breðer Herigeardeshamme. innon ꝥ gecynde. Wulfege ꝥ inland.
7 Ælfege ꝥ utland. 7 Wulfstane Uccan. Wolcnesstede. innon
ꝥ gecynde; 7 án handsecs on ðrim pundan:⁄ 7 ða tyn hyda on
Strættune. into þæm mynstre. to Wolcnesstede; 7 ꝥ land æt
Fealcnaham. æfter Byrhwara[3] dæge. into sc̄e Andree. for Ælfric
15 hire hlaford. 7 his yldran. swa heora cwide wæs. 7 Bromleah.
æfter Brihtwara dæge. into sc̄e Andrea:⁄ swa Ælfric hire hlaford
hit becwæð. for hine[4] 7 his yldran. 7 Snodingcland[5] eac:⁄ into
sc̄e Andrea. æfter hire dæge. swa Ælfere hit becwæð Ælfrices
fæder. 7 he[6] seoððan. on gewitnesse. Eadgife ðære hlæfdian.
20 7 Odan arcebisceopes[7]. 7 Ælfeges Ælfstanes suna. 7 Ælfrices his
broðor. 7 Ælfnoþes Pilian. 7 Godwines æt Fecham. 7 Eadrices
æt Hó. 7 Ælfsies preostes on Crogdæne; 7 Wulfstane . LX .
mancos goldes to dælanne for unc 7 uncre yldran. 7 oðer swilc
Wulfsige to dælanne. 7 hæbban heom wið god gemæne gif hy[8]
25 hit ne don; 7 Wulfsige. Tydiceseg. 7 ða boc:⁄ innon ꝥ gecynde.
7 . II . spuran. on . III . pundan; 7 ic bidde for godes lufan minne
leofan hlaford. ꝥ he ne ðafige ꝥ ænig man uncerne cwide awænde.
7 ic bidde ealle godes freond ꝥ hi ðarto filstan. hæbbe wið god
gemæne þe hit brece. 7 god him sy symle milde þe hit healdan
30 wille;

---

[1] K. *twa* instead of *healfne*.
[2] K. *Byrhtwara.*
[3] K., T., B. *Byrhtwara.*
[4] K. *hire.*
[5] Hearne, *Snodingeland.*
[6] B. *be.*
[7] K. *arceopisceopes.*
[8] B. *hig.*

community, and a necklace of eighty mancuses and two silver cups, and the estate at Meopham. And to St Augustine's thirty mancuses of gold and two silver cups and half a gold headband.

And the estate at Darenth to Brihtwaru for her life, and after her death to St Andrew's for us both and for our ancestors. And Birling to Wulfheah, and he is to pay a thousand pence to St Andrew's on behalf of us and our ancestors. And Wateringbury to Wulfsige, to remain in his family. And *Hæslholt* to Sired, to remain in his family. And Harrietsham to Wulfheah and Ælfheah his brother, to remain in their family, to Wulfheah the *inland* and to Ælfheah the *utland*. And Walkhampstead, to Wulfstan Ucca, to remain in his family, and a short sword worth three pounds. And the ten hides at Stratton to the minster at Walkhampstead.

And after Brihtwaru's day, the estate at Fawkham [is to go] to St Andrew's for her husband Ælfric and his ancestors, in accordance with their will; and Bromley after Brihtwaru's day to St Andrew's as her husband Ælfric bequeathed it, for him and his ancestors; and Snodland also to St Andrew's after her day, as Ælfhere, Ælfric's father, bequeathed it, and Ælfric afterwards in the presence of the Lady Eadgifu, and Archbishop Oda, and Ælfheah, Ælfstan's son, and his brother Ælfric, and Ælfnoth Pilia, and Godwine of Fetcham, and Eadric of Hoo, and Ælfsige the priest in Croydon.

And forty mancuses of gold [is to be given] for Wulfstan to distribute for us and for our ancestors; and the same for Wulfsige to distribute; and may they have to account with God if they do not do it. And Titsey with the title-deed to Wulfsige, to remain in his family, and two spurs worth three pounds.

And I pray my dear lord, for the love of God, that he will not allow any man to alter our will. And I pray all God's friends that they will give their support to it. May he who violates it have to account with God, and may God be ever gracious to him who wishes to uphold it.

XII. THE WILL OF ÆTHELWOLD.

Þis is Aþelwoldis cwyde. Þæt is ærest þæt he bitt his cynehlaford for godes lufon and for his cynescipe þæt his cwyde
standen mote on þæm þingon þe he æt þe gegearnod hæfþ and
æt þinum foregengan. Þæt is ærest þæt he gean for his sule[1]
5 xx mancusas goldes into Niwan Menstre and ane cuppan him
to sawelsceatte and xx mancusas goldes his gebroþrun into
Abbandune. And he becwæþ his cynehlaford him to heregeattewan ænne beah on xxx mancusas and twu lecga and II hors and
II sweord and II scyldas and twa speru. And he becweæþ his wife
10 þa x hida æt Maningforda þa hwile þe hire dæg wære and aftær
hire dæge into Niwan Mynftre for heora begra sawle. And he hire
becwæþ xxx mancusas goldes and ane cuppan. And ic gean
minum suna anre hide landes æt Uptune and anre lecge and ic
gean þæm ealdermen anre crusnan and ic gean Leofwine oþere
15 crusnan.

XIII. THE WILL OF ÆLFHELM.

Hér is on[2] sio[3] swutelung hu Ælfhelm his are. 7 his æhta
geuadod hæfð. for gode. 7 for wurulde[4]. þæt is þonne ærest his
hlaforde. an hund mancosa goldes. 7 twa swurd. 7 feorwer[5]
scyldas. 7 feower speru. 7 feower hors. twa gerædode. twa
20 ungerædode. 7 he gean for his sawle þæs landes. æt Wrættincge.
into sce Æþeldryðe[6]. buton þam twam hydon þe Æþelric hæfð.
7 ic gean þæs landes. æt Brycandune. into sce Petre. to Westmenstre. buton ic wylle þ man mæste minum wiue. twa hund
swyna[7]. þænne þær mæsten sy. þider hire leouest sy. 7 ic gean
25 Ælfgare minum suna. þæs landes æt Hwipstede. 7 'þæs' æt
Wealtune. his dæg. 7 æfter his dæge. ga hyt[8] for uncra begra
sawle þider him leouest sy. 7 ic cyþe[9] hwæt ic minum wiue to

---

[1] For *saule*. [2] K., T. omit *on*. [3] K., T. *seo*.
[4] K., T. *worulde*. [5] Sic MS. K., T. *feower*. B. *feowur*.
[6] K., T. *-ðryðe*. [7] K., T. *swina*.
[8] K., T. *hit*. [9] B. *cype*.

XII. THE WILL OF ÆTHELWOLD.

This is Æthelwold's will. First he prays his royal lord for the love of God and the sake of his kingly dignity that his will relating to those things which he has acquired from you and from your predecessors may stand.

First he grants for his soul twenty mancuses of gold to the New Minster, and a cup as his burial fee; and twenty mancuses of gold to Abingdon for his brothers. And he has bequeathed to his royal lord as his heriot an armlet of thirty mancuses, and two scabbards (?) and two horses and two swords and two shields and two spears.

And he has bequeathed the ten hides at Manningford to his wife for as long as her life shall last, and after her death to the New Minster for the souls of both of us. And he has bequeathed her thirty mancuses of gold and a cup. And I grant to my son one hide of land at Upton and one scabbard (?). And I grant to the ealdorman a fur robe and I grant the other fur robe to Leofwine.

XIII. THE WILL OF ÆLFHELM.

Herein is the declaration of how Ælfhelm has disposed of his property and his goods in fulfilment of his duties both to God and men. First to his lord a hundred mancuses of gold and two swords and four shields and four spears and four horses, two of them harnessed and two unharnessed.

And for his soul he grants to St Etheldreda's the estate at Wratting except the two hides which Æthelric has. And I grant the estate at Brickendon to St Peter's at Westminster, but it is my wish that when there is mast, two hundred pigs be fed for my wife's sake, to benefit whatever foundation she pleases.

And I grant to my son Ælfgar the estate at Whepstead and that at Walton for his lifetime; and after his death they are to go wherever he pleases, for the souls of both of us. And I declare what I gave to my wife as a marriage-gift, namely, Baddow and Burstead and Stratford and the three hides at Enhale. And

morgengyue[1] sealde. Þ is Beadewan. 7 Burgestede. 7 Strætford.
7 þa þreo hyda æt Heanhealan. 7 ic gef hire þa wyt[2] ærest
togædere comon. þa twa hyda æt Wilburgeham. 7 æt Hrægenan.
7 Þ þærto lið. 7 ic gean hire Carletunes. 7 ic gean hire þæs
5 heauodbotles æt Gyrstlingaþorpe. 7 ealra þara[3] æhta þe þæron
standað. mid mete. 7 mid mannum. buton ic gean Godrice.
7 minre dehter healues þæs landes. be wuda. 7 be felda. buton
þam þe ic minum preoste gean. 7 ic gean minum wiue. 7 minre
dehter healues þæs landes. æt Cunningtune. to gedale. buton
10 þam feower hydon þe ic Æþelrice 7 Alfwolde[4] gean. 7 þa
healuan hyde þe ic gean Osmære minum cnihte. 7 ic gean
Ælfmære. 7 his breðer Ælfstane. þara twegra landa. to gedale.
æt Hættanlea. 7 æt Pottune. buton þam þe ic Osgare gean. 7 ic
gean Godere þæs þe ic æt Wimunde gebohte. 7 ic gean Leofsige
15 Lytlanbyrig æfter minum dæge. on Þ gerad þe þæt stande. þe
wyt beforan þan[5] ealdormen lucan[6]. 7 ic gean him 7 his wiue
þæs landes æt Stoctune. wið án hund mancosa goldes. 7 ic wylle
Þ man selle minum hlaforde Þ gold. to minum heregeatum. 7 ic
gean minum þrym broþron.[7] to gedale þæs landes æt Trosting-
20 tune. buton þam þe ic gean Alfwolde[8]. þæs þe Æþelric hæfde.
7 ic gean Ælfhelme. þære hyde æt Icelingtune. 7 þæs æt
Mawyrþe[9]. 7 ic gean Wulfmære þæs þe ic æt Byornham[10] hæfde.
7 ic gean minre scæðe. for mire[11] sawle into Hramesege. healfe
þan[12] abbode. 7 healue þam hirede. 7 ic gean minum wiue heal-
25 ues þæs stodes æt Trostingtune. 7 minan[13] geferan healues þe
me mid[14] ridað. 7 fó min wíf[15] to healuan[16] þe on wealde is. 7 min
dohter to hea'l'uan. 7 ic wylle[17] Þ min wíf fó æfre to healfan[18]
æhtan[19] on ælcon[18] tune fó to lande se þe fó. swa. hio to forgyuen[20]
wæs; Nu bydde[21] Ic þe leof hlaford. Þ mín cwyde[22] standan mote.
30 7 Þ þu ne geþauige. Þ hine man mid wuo wende. god is mín

[1] K., T. -gife.
[2] K., T. wit.
[3] K. ðæra. T. þæra.
[4] K., T. Ælfwolde.
[5] T. þam.
[6] K. Lucan.
[7] K., T. -um.
[8] K., T. Ælf-.
[9] K., T. Mawurðe.
[10] K., T. Biornham.
[11] K., T. minre.
[12] K., T. þam.
[13] K., T. minum.
[14] T. mid me.
[15] T. inserts æfre.
[16] K., T. healfum.
[17] K., T. wille.
[18] K., T. -um.
[19] T. omits æhtan.
[20] K., T. -gifen.
[21] K., T. bidde.
[22] K., T. cwide.

when we first came together, I gave her the two hides at Wilbraham, and Rayne and whatever pertains to it. And I grant her Carlton and I grant her the chief messuage at Gestingthorpe, and all the possessions that are on it, including produce and men; but I grant to Godric and my daughter half the woodland and open land, except that which I grant to my priest. And I grant to my wife and my daughter half the estate at Conington, to divide between them, except the four hides which I grant to Æthelric and Ælfwold, and the half hide which I grant to my servant Osmær.

And I grant to Ælfmær and his brother Ælfstan, to divide between them the two estates, Hatley and Potton, except what I grant to Osgar. And I grant to Godhere what I bought from Wimund. And I grant Littlebury to Leofsige after my death, on condition that the agreement which we concluded before the ealdorman shall hold good. And I grant to him and his wife the estate at Stockton for a hundred mancuses of gold, and I wish that the gold be given to my lord in payment of my heriot.

And I grant to be divided among my three brothers the estate at Troston, except that I grant to Ælfwold that which Æthelric had. And I grant Ælfhelm the hide at Ickleton and the property at *Maworth*. And I grant Wulfmær what I had at Barnham.

And for my soul's sake I grant my long-ship to Ramsey, half for the abbot, and half for the community. And I grant to my wife half the stud at Troston, and half to my companions who ride with me. And my wife is to succeed to half of what is on the woodland, and my daughter to half. And I wish that my wife shall in all cases receive half the stock at each village, whoever may succeed to the land, as it was granted to her.

Now I pray you, dear lord, that my will may stand, and that you will not permit it to be wrongfully altered. God is my witness that I was as obedient to your father as ever I could be, and thoroughly loyal in thought and in deed, and was ever faithful to you with perfect loyalty and devotion; of this God is my witness.

That man who shall alter my will (unless it be you, Sire, and I am confident that you will not), may God drive him from his kingdom, unless he will quickly alter it back again; and may God

gewyta[1] ic wæs þinum fæder swa gehyrsum swa ic fyrmest
myhte[2]. 7 fullice hold on mode. 7 on mægene. 7 þe æfre on
fullon[3] hyldon[3] hold. 7 on fulre luue. þæs me is god gewyta[1].
se man se þe minne cwyde[4] wende. buton þu hyt[5] sy leof.
5 7 ic hæbbe geleauan ꝥ þu nelle. god afyrre hine of his rice. buton
he þe hraþor ongén wende. 7 god 7 ealle his halgan gehealde
æcne[6] þara þe þærto gefyrþryge[7] ꝥ he standan mote[8];

Endorsed.

Gif hwa æfre ænig þinc[9] of þysum[10] cwyde[4] awende oþþe
ætbrede. sy him godes ár 7 his ece edlean æfre ætbroden. 7 he
10 næfre ne wurþe on his myltse gemet. ac he sy amansumod of
þam gemanan ealra gecorenra Cristes heapa. ge nu ge on ecnysse
buton he þe hrædlicor þæt forlæte. 7 on riht eac eft gewende.

XIV. THE WILL OF ÆTHELFLÆD.

Þis is Æþelflæde cwyde ꝥ is ærest ꝥ ic gean minum hlaforde
þes landes æt Lamburnan 7 þæs æt Ceolsige 7 æt Readingan.
15 7 feower beagas on twam hund mancys[11] goldes. 7 . IIII . pellas.
7 . IIII . cuppan. 7 . IIII . bleda. 7 . IIII . hors. 7 ic bidde minne
leouan hlaford for godes lufun. ꝥ min cwyde Standan mote.
7 ic nan oðer nebbe geworht on godes gewitnesse. 7 ic gean þæs
landes æt Domarhame into Glestingabyrig. for Ædmundes
20 cinges sawle. 7 for Æadgares cinges. 7 for mire sawle[12]. 7 ic gean
þes landes æt Hamme into Cristes cyrcan. æt Cantwarebyrig for
Eadmundæs cinges sawle. 7 for mire sawle. 7 ic gean þes landes.
æt Wuda[13]ham Bæorhtnoðe. æaldormen. 7 mire swustær hyre
dæg. 7 ofer[14] hire deg into sca Marian cyrcan. æt Byorcingan.
25 7 ic gean þes landes. æt Hedham[15] Bæorhtnoðæ ealdormen.
7 mire swuster hæora dæg. 7 æfter hæora dæge into Paulusbyrig.
æt Lundænæ. to bisceophamæ. 7 ic gean þæs landæs. æt Dictunæ

---

[1] K., T. *gewita*.   [2] K., T. *mihte*.   [3] K., T. *-um*.   [4] K., T. *cwide*.
[5] K. *hit*.   [6] K., T. *ælcne*.   [7] K., T. *gefyrðrige*.
[8] In the bottom right-hand corner of the parchment is written *Gif hwa*.
[9] K., T. *þing*.   [10] K., T., B. *þisum*.
[11] Cambridge MS. *markes*.   [12] Ibid. omits two preceding clauses.
[13] *a* written over *e*.   [14] *e* written over *o*.   [15] Cambridge MS. *Haddam*.

and all his saints maintain each of those who give their support that the will may stand.

Endorsed.

If anyone ever alters or removes anything in this will, may God's grace and his eternal reward be taken from him for ever; and may he never be found in his favour, but be excommunicated from the society of all Christ's chosen companies, both now and in eternity, unless he will quickly desist from that and also make full restitution.

XIV. THE WILL OF ÆTHELFLÆD.

This is Æthelflæd's will. First, I grant to my lord the estate at Lambourn and those at Cholsey and at Reading, and four armlets of two hundred mancuses of gold, and four robes and four cups and four bowls and four horses. And I pray my dear lord for the love of God that my will may stand, and I have made no other, by God's witness.

And I grant the estate at Damerham to Glastonbury for King Edmund's soul and for King Edgar's and for mine. And I grant the estate at Ham to Christchurch at Canterbury for King Edmund's soul and for my soul. And I grant the estate at Woodham to the Ealdorman Brihtnoth and my sister for her life; and after her death to St Mary's church at Barking. And I grant the estate at Hadham to the Ealdorman Brihtnoth and my sister for their lifetime, and after their death to St Paul's in London as episcopal property. And I grant the estate at Ditton to Ely, to St Etheldreda and her sisters. And I grant the two estates, Cockfield and Chelsworth, to the Ealdorman Brihtnoth and my sister for her life; and after her death to St Edmund's foundation at Bedericesworth. And I grant the estate at Fingringhoe to the Ealdorman Brihtnoth and my sister for her life; and after her death to St Peter's church at Mersea. And I grant the estate at Polstead to Ealdorman Brihtnoth and my sister for her life; and after her death to

into Ylig¹ to scæ Æþælðryð. 7 to hire geswustran. 7 ic gean þara
twegra landa æt Cohhanfeldæa² 7 æt Cæorlesweorþe³ Bæorhtnoðæ æaldormen. 7 miræ swuster hire dæg. 7 ofer hire dæg
into scæ Eadmundes stowe to Bydericeswyrðe⁴. 7 ic 'ge'an þæs
5 landes æt Fingringahó Bæorhtnoðe æaldermen. 7 mire swuster
hiræ deg 7 ofer hire dæg into scæ Pætres cyrcan æt Myresigæ.
7 ic gæan þæs landes æt Polstede Bæorhtnoðe æaldormæn.
7 mire swuster hire deg. 7 ofor hira dæg into Stocy. 7 ic gæan
þæs landæs æt Hwifersce into Stocy ofer minnæ deg 7 ic gæan
10 Bæorhtnoðæ æaldermen. 7 mire swuster þæs landes æt Strætforda hire dæg. 7 ofer hire dæg. Ic his gæan into Stocy. 7 ic
willæ þ Lauanham ga into Stoce ofær þes æaldermannes dæg.
7 mire swuster. 7 ic gean þæs landes æt Byligesdynæ into Stocy
ofer þæs æaldermanes dæg. 7 mire swuster 7 ic gean þara landa
15 æt Pelta⁵ndune. 7 et Myresige. 7 æt Grenstede⁶ into Stocy ofer
minnæ dæg. 7 ofer Bæorhtnoðes æaldormannæs. 7 ofær mire
swuster. 7 ic gean þes landes æt Ylmesæton⁷ Beorhtnoðe
æaldormen. 7 mire swuster hira dæg. 7 ofær hira dæg. ic his
gæan Æadmundæ. 7 ic an þæræ. aræ hide æt Þorpæ into Hed-
20 læge⁸. for mire sawle. 7 for mira eldrena ofer [minne dæg]⁹ 7 ic
gean ðæra . x . hida æt Wicforda Sibrihte minum mægæ ofer
minne dæg. 7 ic gean Ægwinæ minum geræfan. þara . IIII¹⁰ . hida
æt Hedham. ofer miminne¹¹ deg. swa hit on æalddagum gestod.
7 ic gæan Brihtwolde minum cnihtæ þara twegra hida. on
25 Dunninclande ofer minnæ dæg. ¹²7 ic an Alfwolde minum preoste
twægra hida on Dunninglande ofer minne dæg. 7 ic gean
Æþælmære minum præoste twægra hida on Dunninglandæ
ofæ[r]¹³ minne dæg. 7 ic gæan Ælfgæate minum megæ. twegra
hida on Dunninglande ofar minnæ dæg. 7 ic gæan ðæs landæs æt
30 Wæaldingafælda Crawa mira magan ouær minnæ dæg. 7 ic wille þ
man frigæ hæalue mine men on elcum tune for mine sawlæ. 7 þ man
dele æal healf þ yrue þ ic hæbbæ on ælcum tune for mire sawle.

---

¹ Cambridge MS. *Ely.*   ² Ibid. *Cokefeld.*   ³ Ibid. *Cherleswerth.*
⁶ There is a dot under the final *e* of this word, as if the scribe meant to
delete it.   ⁵ *a* written over *e.*   ⁶ Omitted from Cambridge MS.
⁷ Cambridge MS. *Elmesete.*   ⁸ Ibid. *Hadlege.*   ⁹ Gap in MS.
¹⁰ Cambridge MS. *four.* B. and British Museum Facsimiles have VII. There
seems to be a very faint stroke joining the first two strokes of the number.
¹¹ Sic MS. for *minne.*
¹² Cambridge MS. omits the following bequests of Donyland.
¹³ The MS. omits the *r.*

Stoke. And I grant the estate at Withermarsh to Stoke after my death, and I grant to the Ealdorman Brihtnoth and my sister for their lifetime the estate at Stratford; and after their death I grant it to Stoke. And it is my wish that Lavenham should go to Stoke after the ealdorman's death and my sister's. And I grant the estate at Balsdon to Stoke after the ealdorman's death and my sister's. And I grant the estates at Peldon and at Mersea and at Greenstead to Stoke after my death, and after the death of the Ealdorman Brihtnoth and my sister. And I grant the estate at Elmsett to the Ealdorman Brihtnoth and my sister for their lifetime, and after their death I grant it to Edmund. And I grant the one hide at Thorpe to Hadleigh after my death, for my soul and the souls of my ancestors.

And I grant the ten hides at Wickford to my kinsman Sibriht after my death. And to my reeve Ecgwine I grant the four hides at Hadham after my death, as it was settled in former times. And I grant to my servant Brihtwold two hides in Donyland after my death. And I grant to Ælfwold my priest two hides in Donyland after my death. And I grant to Æthelmær my priest two hides in Donyland after my death. And I grant to Ælfgeat my kinsman two hides in Donyland after my death. And I grant the estate at Waldingfield to my kinswoman Crawe after my death.

And I wish that half my men in every village be freed for my soul; and that half the stock which I have be distributed in each village for my soul.

XV. THE WILL OF ÆLFFLÆD.

Ælflæd[1] gæswytelaþ on þis gewrite hu hæo wile habban ge-
fadad hiræ æhta for gode. 7 for worldæ. Ærest þ ic an minum
hlaforde þara . VIII . landa æfter minum dege þ is erest æt
Douorcortæ. 7 æt Fulanpettæ. 7 æt Ælesforda. 7 æt Stanwægun.
5 7 æt Byrætune[2]. 7 æt Læxadyne. 7 æt Ylmesætun. 7 æt Bucyshealæ. 7 twægra bæha on twera punda gewihte. 7 twa sopcuppan. 7 an sæolfran fæt; 7 þæ leof æadmodlice bidde for godes
luuan. 7 for mines hlafordæs sawle lufan. 7 for minræ swystor
sawlæ lufan þ þu amundie þa halgan stowæ et Stocæ þæ mine
10 yldran on restaþ. 7 þa are þæ hi þiderin sæadon[3] a to freogon[4]
godæs rihte; þ is þonno[5] þ ic gean æalswa mine yldran his 'er'
gæuþan þ is þonne þ land æt Stoce into þeræ halagan stowæ.
7 æal þ þ þær to tunæ gæhyrð. 7 þonæ wuda æt Hæpfælda þæ
min swystar gæuþæ. 7 mine yldran. þonne synd þis þa land þæ
15 minæ yldran þærto bæcwædon ofær minre swystor dæg. 7 ofær
minne. þ is ðonne Stredfordæ. 7 Fresantun. 7 Wiswyþetun.
7 Lauanham. 7 Byliesdyne. 7 Polstyde. 7 Wifærmyrsc. 7 Grænstydæ. 7 Peltandune. 7 Myræsegæ. 7 þ wudæland æt Totham þæ
min fæder geuþæ into Myresiæ. 7 Colne. 7 Tigan; þonne synd
20 þis þa land þe minæ yldran becwædon into oþrum. halgum
stowum. þ is þonne into Cantwarabyrig to Cristæs circan þan
hired to brece þes landes æt Illanlege 7 into Paules mynstre into
Lundene. þes lan'des' æt Hedham to biscophame. 7 þes landes
æt Tidwoldingtune þan hirede to brece into Paules mynstre.
25 7 into Beorcingan þam hirede to brece þes landes æt Babbingþyrnan[6]. 7 ic gean Ælfþ'r'æðe[7] minæs hlauordæs medder
Wuduhamæs æftær minum dæge. 7 æfter hiræ dege gange hit
into sc̄a Marian stowæ into Beorcingan æalswa hit stænt mid
mæte. 7 mid mannum; 7 ic gæan into [s]c̄e Æadmunde. þara
30 twegra landa Cæorlesweorþæ. 7 Cochanfelde þam hirede to
bre[ce] æalswa mine yldran his er geuþan. 7 þæs landes æt
'H'nyddinge[8] æftær Crawan degæ miræ magan. 7 ic gæan into

---

[1] Cambridge MS. *Aethelfled*.   [2] Ibid. *Byreton*.
[3] o written over *e*.
[4] Cambridge MS. *and þer þe hi þiderin saidon 7 ofregan*.
[5] Sic MS.   [6] T. *Bobbingþyrnan*.
[7] Cambridge MS. *Alfwrað*.   [8] Ibid. *Wenlynge*.

XV. THE WILL OF ÆLFFLÆD.

Ælfflæd declares in this document how she wishes to have her property disposed of, in fulfilment of her duties to God and to men.

First I grant to my lord after my death the eight estates, namely Dovercourt, Beaumont, Alresford, Stanway, Barton, Lexden, Elmset and Buxhall; and two armlets of two pounds in weight, and two drinking-cups and a silver vessel. And I humbly pray you, Sire, for God's sake and for the sake of my lord's soul and for the sake of my sister's soul, that you will protect the holy foundation at Stoke in which my ancestors lie buried, and the property which they gave to it as an immune right of God for ever: which property I grant exactly as my ancestors had granted it, that is the estate at Stoke to the holy foundation with everything that belongs to the village there, and the wood at Hatfield which my sister and my ancestors gave. Then these are the estates which my ancestors bequeathed to it after my sister's lifetime and after mine: Stratford, Freston, Wiston, Lavenham, Balsdon, Polstead, Withermarsh, Greenstead, Peldon, Mersea and the woodland at Totham which my father granted to Mersea, and Colne and Tey.

Then these are the estates which my ancestors bequeathed to other holy places: namely the estate at Eleigh to Christchurch at Canterbury for the use of the community; and the estate at Hadham·to St Paul's minster at London as episcopal property, and the estate at Heybridge for the use of the community at St Paul's minster; and the estate at Baythorn for the use of the community at Barking.

And I grant Woodham after my death to Ælfthryth, my lord's mother, and after her death it is to go to St Mary's foundation at Barking just as it stands, with the produce and with the men. And I grant for the use of the community at St Edmund's the two estates Chelsworth and Cockfield, just as my ancestors have granted them, and the estate at Nedging after the death of Crawe my kinswoman. And I grant to Mersea after my death everything that my lord and my sister granted, that is Fingringhoe and the six hides on which the minster stands. And I grant

Myresie. æfter minum degæ ealswa min hlaford 7 min swester
geuþan. þ is Fingringaho. 7 þara six hida þæ þ mynstær on
stent; 7 ic gæan ef[te]r Crawan dege þes landes æt Wealdingafelda into Suðbyrig to scæ Gregoriæ ealswa min swestar hit er
5 foræwyrde; 7 ic gean into Ælig¹ scæ Petre. 7 scæ Æþældryþe.
7 scē Wihtburhe. 7 scæ Sexburhe. 7 scē Æormenhilde þer mines
hlafordes lichoma rest þara þreo landa þe wit buta geheotan gode.
7 his halga[n]². þ is æt Rettendune þe wes min morgangyfu.
7 æt Sægham. 7 æt Dictune ealswa min hlaford. 7 min swæstar
10 his er geuþan. 7 þaræ anre hide æt Cæafle³ þe min swystar
begeat. 7 þes bæahges gemacan þe man sæalde minum hlaforde
to sawlescæatte. 7 ic gean Æðelm[æ]re æaldorman þes landes æt
Lellinge ofer mine deg mid mete. 7 mid mannum. æalswa hit
stent on þet gerad þ he beo on minum life min fulla freod. 7
15 forespreca. 7 mira manna. 7 efter minum dege beo þara halgan
stowe. 7 þeræ are ful freod. 7 forespeca æt Stocæ þe mine yldran
on restaþ. 7 ic gean þes landes æt Lissingtune Eðelmere mines
......e⁴ mid mete. 7 mid mannum ealswa hit stent. 7 hine
eadmodlice bi'd'de þ he min fulla freod. 7 mundiend beo on
20 minum dege. 7 efter minum dege gefelste þ min cwide 7 mira
yldran standan mote: þis sind þa landmearca to Byligesdyne of
ða burnan. æt Humelcyrre. fra[m]⁵ Humélcyr[re......]⁶ Heregeresheafode. fram Heregeresheafode æfter ðam ealdan hege to
ðare grene &c. þonne forð þ hit cymð to þare stanstræte. of
25 þare stanstræte 7lang scrybbe⁷ þ hit cymð to Acantune fram
Acyntune þ hit cymð to Rigendune⁸. fram Rigindune æft to þara
burnan. 7 þær. Is. landes fif hida. þis sind þa landgemæra to
Hwifermirsce 7 to Polestede. of Loppandune to Scelfleage. fram
Leage to Mercyl 7lang Mercyle into Sture. 7lang Sture to
30 Leofmannes gemære. 7lang Leofmannes gæmære to Amalburnan. fram Amalburnan to Norðfelda. ðonne forð to Bindhæcce.
fram Bindhæcce to T⁹udanhæcce. fram Tudanhæcce to Gid-

---

¹ T. *Elig.*
² The MS. omits *n*, or the stroke over the *a* representing a nasal consonant.
³ Cambridge MS. *Chenele.* T. *Cæfle.*
⁴ Gap in MS. B. and British Museum Facsimiles supply *hlafordes mege.*
Cambridge MS. has *mey* only.
⁵ MS. omits *m.*   ⁶ K. supplies *þ hit cymð to.*
⁷ Cambridge MS. *ribbe.* K., B. *sorybbe.*
⁸ Cambridge MS. *Reydone.*   ⁹ *d* first written, but deleted.

after Crawe's death the estate at Waldingfield to St Gregory's at Sudbury according to the agreement my sister made about it.

And I grant to St Peter and St Etheldreda and St Wihtburg and St Sexburg and St Eormenhild, at Ely, where my lord's body lies buried, the three estates which we both promised to God and his saints; namely, Rettendon, which was my marriage gift, Soham and Ditton, just as my lord and my sister have granted it; and the one hide at Cheveley, which my sister obtained, and the pair to the ring which was given as burial fee for my lord.

And I grant to the ealdorman Æthelmær the estate at Lawling after my death, with its produce and its men, just as it stands, on condition that during my life he shall be a true friend and advocate to me and to my men, and after my death, be a true friend and advocate of the holy foundation at Stoke, where my ancestors lie buried, and its property. And I grant the estate at Liston to Æthelmær my [lord's kinsman?] with the produce and with the men just as it stands, and humbly pray him that he will be my true friend and protector during my life, and after my death will help to secure that my will and my ancestors' wills may stand.

These are the boundaries of Balsdon: from the stream at *Humelcyrre*; from *Humelcyrre* to *Heregeresheafod* from *Heregeresheafod* along the old hedge to the green oak; then on until one comes to the paved road; from the paved road along the shrubbery until one comes to Acton; from Acton until one comes to Roydon; from Roydon back to the stream. And there are five hides of land.

These are the boundaries of Withermarsh and Polstead: from *Loppandun* to Shelley; from Shelley to the Brett; along the Brett to the Stour; along the Stour to Leofman's boundary; along Leofman's boundary to the *Amalburn*; from the *Amalburn* to *Northfield*; then on to *Bindhæcc*; from *Bindhæcc* to *Tudanhæcc*; from *Tudanhæcc* to Giffords Hall; from Giffords Hall to

dincgforda fram Giddingforda to Hnutstede fram Huntstede to
Hwitincghó fram Hwitingho to Wudemannestune. fram Wudemannestune to [Cær]esige gæmære. fram. Cæresige gemære to
Hædleage gemære. fram Hædleage gæmære to Hligham gemære.
5 Fram Hligham gemære eft to Loppandun¹.

XVI (1). THE WILL OF ÆTHELRIC.

Her cyð 'Æþeric' on þissum gewrite hwam he géann ofor his
dæig þæra æhta þe him god alæned hæfð. þ is ærest sona minum
hlaforde. syxti mancusa² goldes. 7 mines swyrdes mid fetele.
7 þarto twa hors. 7 twa targan. 7 twegen francan. 7 ic geann
10 Leofwynne minan wife ealles þæs þe ic læfe hire dæig. 7 ofor
hire dæg. gange þ land on Boccinge into Cristes circean þam
hirede for uncera saule 7 for mines fæder þe hit ær begeat eall
buton anre hide ic gean into þære cyrcean þam preoste þe þar
gode þeowaþ. 7 ic geann þæs landes³ æt Rægene⁴ be westan⁵.
15 into sce Paule þam bisceope to to⁶ geleohtenne. 7 þar on godes
folce cristendom to dælenne. 7 ic geann þarto twegra hida þe
Eadric gafelaþ ælce geare mid healfum punde 7 mid anre garan.
7 ic geann be eastan stræte ægþer ge wudas ge feldas Ælfstane
bisceope into Coppanforde. 7 þæs heges on Glæsne⁷. 7 ic geann
20 þæs landes æt Norðho. healf into sce Gregorie. on Suþbyrig.
7 healf into sce Eadmunde on Bedericeswyrþe. Nu bidde ic þone
bisceop Ælfstan. þ he ámundige mine lafe 7 þa þincg þe ic hyre
læfe. 7 gif him god lifes geunne lencg þonne unc þ he gefultumige
þ ælc þara þinga stande þe ic gecweden hæbbe:

---

¹ The rest of the last line is illegible. The Cambridge MS. stops at this
point.
² Cambridge MS. *markes*.   ³ K. omits *landes*.
⁴ T. *Regene*.   ⁵ Cambridge MS. inserts *strete*.
⁶ K. omits the second *to*.   ⁷ Cambridge MS. *Glesene*.

Nurstead; from Nurstead to *Hwitingho*; from *Hwitingho* to *Wudemannestun*; from *Wudemannestun* to Kersey boundary; from Kersey boundary to Hadleigh boundary; from Hadleigh boundary to Layham boundary; from Layham boundary back to *Loppandun*.

XVI (1). THE WILL OF ÆTHELRIC.

Here in this document Æthelric makes known to whom after his day he grants the possessions which God has lent to him. First of all, to my lord sixty mancuses of gold, and my sword with the belt, and in addition two horses, two round shields and two javelins.

And I grant all that I leave to my wife for her lifetime; and after her death the estate at Bocking is to go to the community at Christchurch, for our souls and for that of my father who obtained it; all except one hide which I give to the church for the priest who serves God there. And I grant the estate to the west of Rayne to St Paul's for the Bishop, for the provision of lights and for the communication of Christianity to God's people there; and I grant in addition two hides for which Eadric pays a yearly rent of half a pound and one ....
And I grant to Copford for Bishop Ælfstan both woods and open lands east of the high-road, and the enclosure at Glazenwood. And half the estate at *Northho* I grant to St Gregory's at Sudbury, and half to St Edmund's at Bedericesworth.

Now I pray Bishop Ælfstan that he will protect my widow and the things which I leave her, and, if God grant him longer life than us, that he will help to secure that each of the bequests which I have made may stand.

XVI (2). KING ETHELRED'S CONFIRMATION OF ÆTHELRIC'S WILL.

✠ Her swutelað on þison gewrite hu Æðelred kyning geuðe
þ Æþerices cwyde æt Boccinge standan moste. hit wæs manegon
earon ær Æðeric forðferde þ ðam kincge wæs gesæd þ he wære
on þam unræde þ man sceolde on Eastsexon Swegen underfón
5 ða he ærest þyder mid flotan com. 7 se cincg hit on mycele
gewitnysse Sigerice arcebisceope cyðde þe his forespeca þa wæs
for ðæs landes þingon æt Boccinge ðe he into Cristes cyrcean
becweden hæfde. þa wæs he þisse spæce ægþer ge on life. ge
æfter ungeladod ge ungebétt oð his laf his hergeatu þam cincge
10 to Cócham brohte þær he his witan widan gesomnod hæfde.
þa wolde se cing ða spæce beforan eallon his witan uphebban.
7 cwæð þ Leofsige ealdorman. 7 mænige men þære spæce
gecnæwe wæron. þa bæd seo wuduwe Ælfric arcebisceop ðe hire
forespeca wæs. 7 Æðelmær þ hig þone cincg bædon þ heo moste
15 gesyllan hire morgengyfe into x͞pes cyrcean for ðone cincg.
7 ealne his leodscype wið ðam ðe se cing ða egeslican onspæce
alete. 7 his cwyde standan moste þ is swa hit herbeforan cwyð.
þ land æt Boccinge into x͞pes cyrcean. 7 his oðre landare into
oðran halgan stówan swa his cwyde swutelað. þa god forgylde
20 þam cincge getiðode he ðæs for x͞pes lufan. 7 sc͞a Marian. 7 sc͞e
Dunstanes. 7 ealra þæra haligra ðe æt x͞pes cyrcean restað. þæs
costes ðe heo þis gelæste. 7 his cwyde fæste stode. þeos swutelung
wæs þærrihte gewriten[1]. 7 beforan þam cincge and þam witon
gerædd; þis syndon ðæra manna naman ðe ðises to gewittnesse
25 wæron. Ælfric arceb̄ . 7 Ælfheh b̄ on Wintaceastre. 7 Wulfsige b̄
on Dorsæton. 7 Godwine b̄ on Hrofeceastre. 7 Leofsige ealdorman[2]. 7 Leofwine ealdorman. 7 Ælfsige abb̄. 7 Wulfgar abb̄.
7 Byrhtelm abb̄. 7 Lyfincg abb̄. 7 Alfwold[3] abb̄. 7 Æðelmær.
7 Ordulf. 7 Wulfget. 7 Fræna. 7 Wulfric Wulfrune sunu: 7 ealle

---

[1] K. gewiten.   [2] T. omits this witness.
[3] K. Ælfwold.

XVI (2). KING ETHELRED'S CONFIRMATION OF ÆTHELRIC'S WILL.

It is shown here in this document how King Ethelred granted that the will of Æthelric of Bocking should stand.

It was many years before Æthelric died that the King was told that he was concerned in the treacherous plan that Swegn should be received in Essex when first he came there with a fleet: and the King before many witnesses, informed Archbishop Sigeric of it, who was then his advocate for the sake of the estate at Bocking which he had bequeathed to Christchurch. Then both during his life and afterwards, he was neither cleared of this charge, nor was the crime atoned for, until his widow brought his heriot to the King at Cookham, where he had gathered his council from far and wide. Then the King wished to bring up the charge before all his council, and said that the Ealdorman Leofsige and many others were cognisant of the charge. Then the widow begged Archbishop Ælfric, who was her advocate, and Æthelmær, that they would beseech the King that she might give her marriage-gift to Christchurch, for the sake of the King and all his people, to the end that the King would give up the terrible accusation, and Æthelric's will might stand; that is, as it says above, the estate at Bocking to Christchurch, and his other landed property to other holy places as his will specifies. Then may God repay the King! He consented to this for the sake of Christ and of St Mary and of St Dunstan and of all the saints who rest at Christchurch, the terms being that she should carry out this and his will should remain valid.

This declaration was straightway written and read before the King and the council. These are the names of the men who witnessed this:

Archbishop Ælfric, and Ælfheah, Bishop of Winchester, and Wulfsige, Bishop of Dorset, and Godwine, Bishop of Rochester, and the Ealdorman Leofsige, and the Ealdorman Leofwine, and Abbot Ælfsige, and Abbot Wulfgar, and Abbot Brihthelm, and Abbot Ælfwold, and Æthelmær and Ordulf and Wulfgeat and Fræna and Wulfric, Wulfrun's son; and all the thegns who were

ða ðegnas ðe þær widan gegæderode wǽron ægðer. ge of Westsexan. ge of Myrcean. ge of Denon. ge. of Englon. ¹þissa gewrita
syndon þreo. an is æt xp̄es cyrcean. oðer æt þæs cinges haligdome.
þridde hæfð seo wúduwe.

XVII. THE WILL OF WULFRIC.

IN NOMINE DOMINI.

5   Her swutelað Wulfric his hleofan hlaforde his cwyde 7 eallon
his freon[do]n. þ is þ ic geann minon hlaforde twa hund mancessa goldes. 7 twa seolforhilted sweord. 7 feower hors. twa
gesadelode. 7 twa ungesadelode. 7 þa wæpna þe þærto gebyriað.
7 ic geann ælcum bisc[eope] . v . mancessa goldes. 7 þam twam
10 arcebisceopan. heora ægþran tyn mancses goldes. 7 ic geann into
ælc[um] munucregole. i . pund. 7 ælcon abbode. 7 ælcon
abbatissan . v . manxes goldes. 7 ic geann Ælfrice arcebis[ceope
þ]æs landes æt Dumeltan forð mid þon oðran for minon sawle.
wið þan þe he freond. 7 fultum. ðe betere sy [into] þære stowe
15 þe ic gew[o]rht hæbbe. 7 ic gean Ælfhelme. 7 Wulfage þæra
landa betwux Ribbel. 7 Mærse. 7 [on Wir]halum. þ heo hig
dælan him betweonan. swa hig efnost magon. butan heora
ægðer his agen habban w[ille on þ] gerad þonne 'sceadd'genge
sy. þ heora ægðer sylle . iii . þusend sceadda. into þæra stowa
20 æt Byrtune. 7 ic gean[n] Ælfhelme Rólfestun. 7 Héorlfestun².
7 ic geann Wulfage þæs landes æt Beorelfestune. 7 æt Mærcham-
tune. 7 ic geann Ælfhelme þæs landes æt Cunugesburh. wið þon
þe he do þ þa munecas habban ælce geare þridd[an] dæl þæs
fisces. 7 he ða twa dæl. 7 ic geann Wulfage þæs landes æt
25 Alewaldestune. 7 ic geann Ufegeate þ[æs] landes æt Norðtune.
on þ gerád þ he freond. 7 fultum þe betere sy into þære stowe.
7 ic geann minre ear[m]an dehter þæs landes æt Elleforda.
7 þæs æt Ácclea³. mid eallon þam þe þær nu to herð⁴. þa hwíle
hire [dæg] bið. 7 ofer hire dæg gá þ land into þære stowe æt
30 Byrtune. 7 heo hit náge mid nanon þinge to forwyrcenne ac

---

¹ The rest is written smaller, but in the same hand.
² Burton Reg. *Heorelfestun.*
³ Burton Reg. *Aclea.*   ⁴ Ibid. *hyrð.*

gathered there from far and wide, both West Saxons and Mercians, Danes and English.

There are three of these documents: one is at Christchurch, the second at the King's sanctuary; the widow has the third.

XVII. THE WILL OF WULFRIC.

In nomine domini.

Wulfric here declares his will to his dear lord and to all his friends. First I grant to my lord two hundred mancuses of gold, and two silver-hilted swords and four horses, two saddled and two unsaddled, and the weapons which are due with them. And I grant to every bishop five mancuses of gold and to each of the two archbishops ten mancuses of gold. And I grant to every monastic order one pound and to every abbot and every abbess five mancuses of gold. And I grant to Archbishop Ælfric the land at Dumbleton along with the other, for my soul, in the hope that he may be a better friend and supporter of the monastery which I have founded.

And I grant to Ælfhelm and Wulfheah the lands between the Ribble and the Mersey, and in Wirral, that they may share them between them as evenly as they can—unless either of them wishes to have his own—on condition that when it is the shad season, each of them shall pay three thousand shad to the monastery at Burton. And I grant to Ælfhelm Rolleston and Harlaston. And I grant to Wulfheah the estates at Barlaston and Marchington. And I grant to Ælfhelm the estate at Conisbrough, on condition that he arrange that the monks shall have each year a third of the fish, and he two thirds. And I grant Wulfheah the estate at Alvaston, and I grant Ufegeat the estate at Norton in the hope that he may be a better friend and supporter of the monastery.

And I grant to my poor daughter the estate at Elford and that at Oakley, with all that now belongs there, as long as her life lasts, and after her death, the land is to go to the monastery at Burton. And she shall not possess it on such terms that she can forfeit it for any reason, but she is to have the use of it as long

hæbbe heo ðone bryce þa hwile þe heo hit geearnigean[1] cann.
7 gá hit syððan into þæra stowe æt By[rtune] fórðon þe hit wæs
mines godfæder gyfu. 7 ic wille 'þ̄ Ælfhelm' si hire múnd.
7 þæs landes. 7 þ̄ æt Tamwurþin hire to [nan]on þeowdome. ne
5 nánon geborenan men. butan þ̄ hie[2] þone ealdordom hæbbe.
7 ic geann Wulfgar[e] minan cnihte þæs landes æt Baltryðeleage.
ealswa his fæder hit him begeat. 7 ic becweðe Morcare þ̄ [lan]d
æt Waleshó. 7 þ̄ æt Þeogendeþorpe. 7 þ̄ æt Hwitewylle. 7 þ̄ æt
Clune. 7 þ̄ æt Barleburh. 7 þ̄ æt Ducemannestune. 7 þ̄ æt
10 Moresburh. 7 þ̄ æt Eccingtune. 7 þ̄ æt Bectune. 7 þ̄ æt Doneceastre[3]. 7 æt Morlingtun. 7 ic geann his wife Aldulfestreo.
ealswa hit nu stont mid mete. 7 mid mannon. 7 ic geann
Ælfhelm[e] minan mæge[4]. þæs landes æt[5] Paltertune. 7 þæs ðe
Scegð[6] me becwæð. 7 ic geann Æþelrice þ̄ land æt Wibbe[to]fte.
15 7 þ̄ æt Twongan. his dæg. 7 ofer his dæg. ga þ̄ land for mine
sawle. 7 for minre meder[7]. 7 for his into [Byrtune]. And þys
synd þa land[8] þe ic geann into Byrtune. þ̄ is ærest Byrtun þe þ̄
mynster on stent. 7 Stræt[tu]n. 7 Bromleage. 7 Bedintun.
7 Gageleage. 7 Witestan. 7 Langanford. 7 Styrcleage. 7 Niwantun
20 æt þære wi[c] 7 Wædedun 7 þ̄ lyttle land þe ic ah on oðer
Niwantune. 7 Wineshylle. 7 Suttun. 7 Ticenheale. 7 þ̄ æt[9]
Scen[ct]une. 7 þ̄ æt[9] Wicgestane. 7 þ̄ æt[9] Halen 7 Hremesleage[10].
7 þ̄ æt Sciplea. 7 þ̄ æt Suðtune. 7 þ̄ æt Actune tw[egra] manna
dæg ealswa þa foreword sprecað. 7 Deorlafestun. 7 þ̄ þærto
25 hereð. þ̄ is Rudegeard. 7 min ly[t]tle land on Cotewaltune.
7 Lege mid eall[on] þam þe[11] þærto hereð. Ácofr[e mid] þam þe[11]
þærto hereð[12] Hílum. 7 Celfdun. 7 Cætesþyrne[13]. 7 þ̄ heregeatland
æt Suðtune[14]. 7 Morlege. 7 Bregdeshale[15]. 7 Mort[u]n. 7 eall seo
socna þe ðærto hereð. 7 þ̄ land þyderin æt Pilleslege[16]. 7 Oggodes-
30 tun. 7 Wynnef[eld] 7 Snodeswic into Mortune. 7 þ̄ æt Taðawyllan. 7 þ̄ land æt Æppebbyg[17] þe ic gebohte mid minum féó.
7 þ̄ æt[9] Westune. 7 Burhtun. 7 seo hid æt Scearnforda into
[W]iggestane. 7 þ̄ æt Hereburgebyrig. 7 Ealdeswy[rðe] 7

[1] Burton Reg. *geearnian.* [2] Ibid. *heo.* [3] Ibid. *Donecestre.*
[4] Ibid. *meage.* [5] Ibid. *on.* [6] Ibid. *Sægð.*
[7] Ibid. *for his moder.* [8] Ibid. omits *land.* [9] Ibid. omits þ̄ æt.
[10] Ibid. *Remesleage.* [11] Ibid. *þ̄.* [12] Ibid. inserts þ̄ *is.*
[13] Ibid. *Cætesþyrne.* [14] Ibid. *Suttune.* [15] Ibid. *Brægesheale.*
[16] T. *Wyllesleage.* [17] Burton Reg. *Æppelby.*

as she can deserve it, and afterwards it is to go to the monastery at Burton because it was my godfather's gift. And I desire that Ælfhelm may be protector of her and of the land. And the land at Tamworth is not to be subject to any service nor to any man born, but she is to have the lordship.

And I grant to my servant Wulfgar the estate at Balterley just as his father acquired it for him. And I bequeathe to Morcar the estates at *Walesho*, *Theogendethorp*, Whitwell, Clowne, Barlborough, Duckmanton, Mosbrough, Eckington, Beighton, Doncaster and *Morlingtun*. And to his wife I grant Austrey, just as it now stands with the produce and the men. And I grant to my kinsman Ælfhelm the estate at Palterton, and that which Scegth bequeathed to me. And I grant to Æthelric the estate at Wibtoft, and that at Tong, for his day, and after his day it is to go to Burton for my soul and for my mother's and for his.

And these are the estates which I grant to Burton: first Burton on which the monastery stands, and Stretton and Bromley and *Bedintun* and Gailey and Whiston and Longford and Stirchley and Newton by the *wic*, and *Wædedun*; and the little estate which I have in the other Newton; and Winshill and Sutton and Ticknall, and Shangton, and Wigston, and Hales and Romsley, and Shipley and Sutton; and Acton for two lives as the terms state; and Darlaston and what belongs to it, namely, Rudyard and my little estate in Cotwalton; and Leigh with all that belongs to it; Okeover with what belongs to it, Ilam, and Caldon and Castern; and the heriot-land at Sutton, and Morley and Breadsall, and Morton and all the jurisdiction which belongs to it, and the land included in it at Pilsley, and Ogston and Wingfield and *Snodeswic* along with Morton; and the estate at Tathwell; and the estate at Appleby which I bought with my money, and that at Weston and Burton; and the hide at Sharnford along with Wigston; and Harbury and Aldsworth and Alvington and Eccleshall and *Waddune* and one hide at Sheen.

And I grant to the community at Tamworth the estate at Longdon just as they have let it to me, and they are to have half the usufruct, and the monks of Burton half, both of the produce, and the men and the stock, and of all things.

Ælfredingtune. 7 Eccleshale. 7 æt Waddune. 7 an hida æt
Sceon. And ic geann þam hirede in Tom[wy]rðin. þ land æt
Langandune. ealswa hi hit ær me[1] to [l]eton. 7 habban hi þone
bryce healfne. 7 healf[ne] þa munucas into Byrtune. ge on mete.
5 ge on mannon. 'ge on yrfe'. ge on eallon[2] þingon. 7 se bisceop
fó to his lande æt Buba'n'dune. 7 fon ða munucas into Byrtune.
to þam þe on þam land is. ge on méte[3] ge on mannon. ge on
eallon þin[gon] 7 þ land þam bisceope æt þære sýle. 7 ic wylle
þ se cyning[4] beo hlaford. þæs mynstres ðe ic getimbr[ede].
10 7 þæra landára þe ic ðyderinn becweden hæbbe gode to lofe.
7 to wurðmynta[5] minan hlafor[de] 7 for minra sawla. 7 Ælfric
arceb. 7 Ælfhelm min broðor. þ hig beon mund. 7 freond.
7 forespreocan. into ðære stowe wið ælcne geborenne mann.
heom to nanre agenre æhta. butan into sa[nctus] Benedictus
15 regole. 7 ic geann minre goddeht[e]r Morkares[6] 7 Aldgyðe[7].
þ land æt Strættune. 7 ðo[ne] búle þe wæs hire ealdermoder.
7 into þam mynstre æt Byrtune. an hund[8] wildra horsa. 7 sexte[ne]
tame hencgestas. 7 þærto eall þ ic hæbbe on libbendan. 7 on
licgendan. butan 'þan' ðe ic becweden hæbbe 7 god ælmihtig
20 hine awende of eallum godes dreame. 7 of ealra cristenra
gemanan. se ðe ÞIS awende. butan hit min án[9] cynehlaford sy.
7 ic hópyge to him swa gódan. 7 swa míldheortan [þ] he hit
nylle sylf dón. ne eac nanum oþrum menn[10] geþafian. VALETE .
IN . X . Þ . O . AME[N].

Endorsed.

25 Þis is seo freolsboc to þam mynstre æt Byrtune þe Æþelred
cyning[11] [æf]re écelice gefreode. gode to lofe. 7 eallon his halgan
to weorþunge. Swa swa Wulfric hit geédstaðelode[12]. for hine
sylfne[13]. [7 fo]r his yldrena sawla. 7 hit mid munecon gesette.
þ þær æfre inne þæs hades menn under heora abbude. gode
30 þeowian. æfter [san]ctus Benedictus tæcincge[14]. Sic Fiat.

[1] Burton Reg. *me ær.*	[2] Ibid. *ælcon.*	[3] Ibid. omits *ge on mete.*
[4] Ibid. *cyng.*	[5] Ibid. inserts *for.*	[6] Ibid. *goddohtor Morcares.*
[7] Ibid. *Ealdgyðe.*	[8] Ibid. *hundred.*	[9] Ibid. *ane.*
[10] Ibid. omits *menn.*	[11] Ibid. *cyng.*	[12] Ibid. *gestaðelode.*
[13] Ibid. omits *sylfne.*	[14] Ibid. *tæcinge.*	

And the bishop is to take possession of his estate at Bupton, and the monks at Burton are to take what is on the land, both produce and men, and all things; and the land at the mire [is to go] to the bishop.

And I desire that the king be lord of the monastery which I built and the estates which I have bequeathed to it to the glory of God and the honour of my lord and for my soul; and that Archbishop Ælfric and my brother Ælfhelm be protectors and friends and advocates of that foundation against any man born, not as their own possession, but [as belonging] to St Benedict's order.

And I grant to my goddaughter [the daughter] of Morcar and Ealdgyth, the estate at Stretton and the brooch(?) which was her grandmother's. And to the monastery at Burton a hundred wild horses, and sixteen tame geldings, and besides this all that I possess in livestock and other goods except those which I have bequeathed.

And whoever perverts this, may God Almighty remove him from all God's joy and from the communion of all Christians, unless it be my royal lord alone, and I believe him to be so good and so gracious that he will not himself do it, nor permit any other man to do so.

Valete in Christo. Amen.

Endorsed.

This is the charter of freedom to the monastery at Burton which King Ethelred freed eternally, to the glory of God and the honour of all his saints, just as Wulfric re-established it for his own sake and for the souls of his ancestors, and filled it with monks in order that men of that order under their abbot might ever serve God in that place, according to St Benedict's teaching. *Sic fiat.*

XVIII. THE WILL OF ARCHBISHOP ÆLFRIC.

Her sutelað hu Alfric[1] arcebisceop his cwyde gedihte þ is
ærest him to saulsceate he becwæð into χp̄es cyrcan þ land æt
Wyllan 7 æt Burnan. 7 Risenbeorgas. and he becwað his laford
his beste scip 7 þa segelgeræda ðarto. 7 LX. healma. 7 LX. beor-
5 nena. 7 he wilnode gif hit his lafordes willa wære þ he gefaestnode
into sc̄e Albane þ land æt Cyngesbyrig 7 fenge sylf wið þam. eft
to Eadulfingtune. An[2] he becwæð þ land æt Dumeltun into
Abbandune 7 Ælfnoðe ðarof. III. hida his dæg and suððan[3] to
þan oþaran to Abbandune. 7 X. oxan 7 II. men he him becwæð
10 7 filgan hi þam lafordscype þe þ land to hyre. And he cwæð þæt
land æt. Wealingaforda þe he gebohte Celewærde 7 hofer his
dæg into Ceolesige. 7 he becwæð into sc̄e Albane þ land æt
Tiwan[4] 7 standan þa forword betweonan þan abbode 7 Ceolrice
ðe ær wið ðæne arcebiscop geforwyrd wæron þ is þ Ceolric
15 habbe ðæne dæl þæs landes þe he hæfð his dæg 7 eac ðæne dæl
þe se arceb for his sceatte him to let. þ wæs ehtoðe healf hid
wið v pundun 7 L mancusum goldes. 7 ga hit ofer his dæg eall
togædere into sc̄e Albæne. 7 heora forewyrd wæron þ Osanig
æfter Ceolrices dæge gange eac þyderin. 7 þ land on Lundene
20 þe he mid his feo gebohte. he becwæð into sc̄e Albæne. 7 his bec
ealle he cwæð eac þyderin. 7 his geteld. And he becwæð þ man
fenge on þe feoh ðe man hæfde 7 ærest ælcne borh agulde 7
suððan tilode to his hergeatwæn þæs ðe man habban sceolde.
And anes scipes he geuðe þam folce to Cent. 7 oþres to Wiltune-
25 scire. 7 elles on oðrum þingum gif þæs hwæt wære⸴ he bæd þ
Uulfstan bisceop 7 Leofric abbud dihton swa heom best þuhte.
And þe land be westan æt Fittingtune 7 æt Niwantune he
becwæð his sweostrun 7 heora beornun 7 Ælfheages land Esnes
suna ga à on his cyn. And he becwæð Uulfstane ærcebiscope

---

[1] K. *Ælfric*.　　　　　　[2] K., T. *and*.
[3] K., T. *siiððan*.　　　　[4] K. *Ripan*.

XVIII. THE WILL OF ARCHBISHOP ÆLFRIC.

Here it is made known how Archbishop Ælfric drew up his will. First as his burial fee, he bequeathed to Christchurch the estates at Westwell and Bourne, and Risborough. And he bequeathed to his lord his best ship and the sailing tackle with it, and sixty helmets and sixty coats of mail. And if it were his lord's will, he wished that he would confirm to St Alban's the estate at Kingsbury, and himself retake possession of *Eadulfington* in return.

And he bequeathed to Abingdon the estate at Dumbleton, and three hides of it to Ælfnoth for his life, which afterwards [are to belong] to Abingdon with the rest. And he bequeathed him ten oxen and two men, and they are to be subject to the lordship to which the land belongs. And he bequeathed the estate which he bought at Wallingford to Ceolweard, and after his death to Cholsey.

And he bequeathed to St Alban's the estate at Tew, and the terms were to remain unchanged between the abbot and Ceolric which had been agreed upon with the Archbishop; namely that Ceolric was to hold the portion of the estate which he has for his life, and also that portion which the Archbishop let to him in return for his money; that was seven and a half hides for five pounds and fifty mancuses of gold; and after his day all of it together is to go to St Alban's. And their terms were that Osney also should go to that monastery after Ceolric's day. And he bequeathed to St Alban's the estate in London which he bought with his money, and all his books he also bequeathed there and his tent.

And he arranged that what money there was should be taken and first every debt paid, and afterwards what was due was to be provided for his heriot. And he granted a ship to the people of Kent and another to Wiltshire. And as regards other things besides these, if there should be any, he bade that Bishop Wulfstan and Abbot Leofric should act as seemed best to them. And the estates in the west, at Fiddington and Newton, he bequeathed to his sisters and their children. And the land of Ælfheah, Esne's son, is always to remain in his family.

ane sweorrode. 7 anne ring 7 anne psaltere. 7 Alfheage[1] biscope
anne rode. And he forgeaf on godes est Centingan þæne borh
þe hy hym sceoldan 7 Middelsexon. 7 Suðrion þ feoh þ heom
foresceat. And he wyle þ man freoge æfter his dæge ælene
5 witefæstne man þe on his timan forgylt wære. Gif hwa þis[2]
awende hæbbe him wið god gemaene. amen.

XIX. THE WILL OF WULFGEAT.

✠ Þis is Wulfgates gecwide æt Dunnintune þ is þonne þ he
geann ærest gode his sawelscættas þ is . I . hid æt Tærdebicgan.
7 . I . pund penega. 7 VI 7 twentig freotmonna for his sawle.
10 7 into Wigeracæstre an bryþen mealtes hea'l'f of Dunnintune
healf of Cylleshale. 7 into sc̄e Æþelbrihte healfes pundes weorð.
7 into sc̄e Guðlace healfes pundes weorð. 7 into Leomynstre
. IIII . aldhryðra. 7 into Bromgearde . I . hryðer oðer into Cliftune
7 into Heantune . IIII . hryðra 7 to Pencric . II . hryðra 7 into
15 Tweongan . II . hryðra 7 he geann forgifnesse ælcan þara þe wið
hine agylt hæbbe for his sawle þearfe. 7 he geann anes geares
gafol his monnum to gyfe. swa heo þa are brucon swa heo þa
ælmessan gelæstan þa ðer to londe foð. 7 he geann his hlaforde
. II . hors. 7 . II . sweord 7 . IIII . scyldas 7 . IIII . spera. 7 . X .
20 mæran. mid . X . coltan. 7 he bit his hlaford for godes lufan þ he
beo his wifes freond 7 his dohter 7 he ann his wife þæs landes
æt Cylleshale. 7 æt Eowniglade. 7 æt Hrodene þa hwile hire
dæg beo. 7 ofer hire dæg ga þ land eft in min cynn þa ðær
nehste[3] syn. 7 Wulfgyfe minre dohter þ land æt Dunnintune
25 swa hit stont. 7 æt Þornbyrig þæt land þe wæs mid hire moder
golde geboht æt Leofnoðe. 7 Wulfgyfe suna mire dohter þ land

---

¹ K. *Ælfheage.*   ² Sic. MS.   B. *ne liste.*

And he bequeathed to Archbishop Wulfstan a pectoral cross, and a ring and a psalter; and to Bishop Ælfheah a crucifix. And in accordance with God's will, he forgave the people of Kent the debt which they owed him, and the people of Middlesex and Surrey the money which he paid on their behalf. And it is his will that after his day every penally enslaved man who was condemned in his time be set free.

If anyone change this, may he have it to account for with God. Amen.

XIX. THE WILL OF WULFGEAT.

This is the will of Wulfgeat of Donington; namely, that he grants to God his burial fee, namely, one hide at Tardebigge and one pound of pence, and twenty-six freedmen, for his soul; and to Worcester a brewing of malt, half from Donington and half from Kilsall; and to St Ethelbert's the equivalent of half a pound; and to St Guthlac's the equivalent of half a pound; and to Leominster four full-grown bullocks; and to Bromyard one bullock; and another to Clifton; and four bullocks to Wolverhampton; and two bullocks to Penkridge; and two bullocks to Tong.

And for his soul's need, he grants forgiveness to each of those who have sinned against him. And he grants a year's rent to his men as a gift. May they who succeed to land there enjoy the income according as they carry out the charitable bequests.

And he grants to his lord two horses and two swords and four shields and four spears and ten mares with ten colts. And he prays his lord for the love of God that he will be a friend to his wife and daughter. And he grants to his wife the estates at Kilsall and Evenlode and Roden for as long as her life lasts, and after her death the land is to revert to my kindred, those who are nearest. And to my daughter Wulfgifu [I grant] the estate at Donington as it stands, and the estate at Thornbury which was bought from Leofnoth with her mother's gold; and to the son of my daughter Wulfgifu the estate at Ingwardine; and to my daughter Wilflæd the other hide at Tardebigge; and

æt Ingewyrðe. 7 Wilflede minre dohter þa oðre hide æt Tærde-
b'i'cgan 7 Ælfilde mire magan þa hide beneoþan wuda eall swa
wit on wedd gesealdon. 7 gif ic lengc beo þonne heo þonne
hæbbe ic þ land æt Wrotteslea. 7 ealle þa ðe to mire ahte fon
5 gylde Brune . xx . mancses goldes. 7 ic geann him . vi . mæran.
mid . vi . coltan to þance. 7 þa hors þa þe þær to hlafe beon mine
wife 7 minre dohtran eallum gelice fela. 7 þeo wellinc æt þære
wíc into Dunnintune. 7 Æþelsige. leof cyð þis mine hlaforde
7 ealle mine freondum.

XX. THE WILL OF THE ÆTHELING ÆTHELSTAN.

10 ✠ On godes ælmihtiges naman. Ic Æþestan[1] æþeling.
geswutelige on þysum gewrite. hu ic mine áre. 7 míne æhta.
geunnen hæbbe. gode to lofe. 7 minre saule to[2] alysednysse.
7 mines fæder Æþelredes cynges. þe ic hit æt geearnode. þ is
ærest þ ic geann. þ man gefreoge. ælcne witefæstne mann. þe ic
15 on spræce[3] ahte. 7 ic geann in mid me. þær ic me reste. Criste.
7 sce Petre. þæs landes æt Eadburgebyrig. þe ic gebohte æt
minan fæder. mid twam hund mancosan goldes be gewihte.
7 mid . v . pundan[4] seolfres. 7 þ land æt Mereláfan. þe ic
gebohte æt minum[5] fæder mid þridde healf hund mancosan
20 goldes. be gewihte[6]. 7 þ lánd æt Mórdune. þ min fæder me to
lét. Ic gean into þære stowe. for uncer[7] begra saule. 7 ic hine
þæs bidde for godes lufan. 7 for sca Marían. 7 for sce Petres.
þ hit stándan mote. 7 þæs swúrdes[8] mid þam sylfrenan[9] hiltan.
þe Wulfric worhte. 7 þone gyldenan fetels. 7 þæne beh þe
25 Wulfric worhte. 7 þone dréncehórn[10]. þe ic ær æt þam hirede
gebohte[11]. on ealdan mynstre. 7 ic wille þ man nime þ feoh. þe
Aþelwoldes[12] láf me ah to gyldene[13]. þe ic for hyre are gesceoten[14]

---

[1] Addit. MS. (d) Æþelstan.
[3] Ibid. spæce.
[5] MS. (b) minan.
[7] Ibid. uncra.
[9] Ibid. seolfrenan.
[11] MS. (b) bohte.
[13] MS. (b) gyldanne.

[2] Canterbury MS. (b) to minre saule.
[4] T. inserts be gewihte.
[6] Ibid. omits be gewihte.
[8] Ibid. swyrdes.
[10] Ibid. and MS. (d) drenchorn.
[12] T. Æðel-.
[14] Ibid. gescoten.

to my kinswoman Ælfhild the hide below the wood, just as we both pledged ourselves to do; and if I live longer than she, then I am to have the estate at Wrottesley.

And all those who succeed to my property are to pay to Brun twenty mancuses of gold; and I grant to him in gratitude six mares with six colts. And the horses which are left are to be for my wife and my daughters, to each the same number. And the spring at Droitwich (?) is to belong to Donington.

And, dear Æthelsige, make this known to my lord and to all my friends.

XX. THE WILL OF THE ÆTHELING ÆTHELSTAN.

In the name of Almighty God. I, Æthelstan the Ætheling, declare in this document how I have granted my estates and my possessions, to the glory of God and for the redemption of my soul and of my father's, King Ethelred's, from whom I acquired the property.

First, I grant that every penally enslaved man whom I acquired in the course of jurisdiction be freed. And to Christ and St Peter, at the place where I shall be buried, I grant along with my body the estate at Adderbury which I bought from my father for two hundred mancuses of gold, by weight, and for five pounds of silver. And the estate at Marlow which I bought from my father for two hundred and fifty mancuses of gold, by weight; and the estate at Morden which my father let to me, I grant to that foundation for the souls of us both; (and I beseech him, that for God's sake and for St Mary's and for St Peter's, my bequest may stand); and the sword with the silver hilt which Wulfric made, and the gold belt and the armlet which Wulfric made, and the drinking-horn which I have bought from the community at the Old Minster.

And I desire that the money which Æthelwold's widow ought to pay me, which I have contributed towards her income, that is twelve pounds by tale, be taken and entrusted to Bishop Ælfsige at the Old Minster for my soul. And I grant to Christchurch in Canterbury the estate at Hollingbourne and

hæbbe. 7 betæce Ælfsige bisceope. into ealdan mynstre. for
mine saule. þ synd . XII . pund be getale. 7 ic geann into Cristes
cyrican on Cantwarabyrig. þæs landes. æt Holungaburnan.
7 þǽs þe þærto hyrð. buton þære. anre sulunge þe ic Siferðe[1]
5 geunnen hæbbe. 7 þæs landes æt Garwaldintune[2]. 7 ic ann þæs
landes æt Hryðerafelda Into nunnan[3] mynstre. Sca Marian
þances. 7 ænne sylfrene[4] mele[5]. on fif pundon. 7 Into niwan
mynstre ænne sylfrene[4] hwer on fif pundon. on þære halgan
þrymnesse[6] naman þe seo stow is forehalig. 7 Ic geann to
10 Sceaftenesbyrig[7] to þære halgan rode. 7 to sce Eadwearde.
þara . VI . punda þe Ic Eadmunde minon breðer gewissod hæbbe.
7 Ic geann minon fæder Æþelræde cynge. þæs landes æt
Cealhtune[8] buton þam ehta hidan þe Ic Ælmære minon cnihte
geunnennen[9] hæbbe. 7 þæs landes æt Norðtune. 7 þæs landes
15 æt Mollintune. 7 þæs seolferhiltan swurdes[10] þe Ulfcytel ahte.
7 þære byrnan. þe mid Morkære[11] is. 7 þæs horses þe Þurbrand
me geaf. 7 þæs hwitan horses þe Leofwine[12] me geaf. 7 Ic geann
Eadmunde minon breðer þæs swurdes[13] þe Offa cyng ahte.
7 þæs swurdes[13] mid þam pyttedan hiltan. 7 anes brandes. 7 ænne
20 seolforhammenne blædhorn[14]. 7 þara landa þe ic ahte on East
Englan. 7 þæs landes æt Peácesdele. 7 Ic wylle. þ mon gelæste
ælce geare ane dægfeorme þam hirede into Elig[15] of þysse áre
on Sce Æþeldryðe mæssedæg. 7 gesylle þær to[16] mynstre an
hund penega. 7 gefede þǽr on þone dæg. c.[17] þearfena. 7 sý æfre
25 seo ælmesse gelæst gearhwamlice. age land se þe age. þa hwile.
þe Cristendom stande. 7 gif þá nellað þa[18] ælmessan geforðian þe
þa land habbað. gange seo ár. into sce Æþeldryðe. 7 Ic geann
Eadwige minon breðer anes seolforhiltes[19] swurdes[20]. 7 Ic geann
Ælfsige. bisceope. þære gyldenan rode. þe is mid Eadrice
30 Wynflæde suna; 7 anne blacne[21] stedan. 7 Ic geann. Ælmære
þæs landes æt Hamelandene þe he ær ahte. 7 ic bidde minne

---

[1] MS. (b) Sifyrðe.
[2] Ibid. nunnena.
[3] T. male.
[4] Ibid. Scæft-.
[5] Sic MS.
[6] MSS. (b) and (d) Morcere.
[7] MS. (b) swyrdes.
[8] T. Ælig.
[9] MS. (b) an hund.
[10] Ibid. sylfer-.
[11] Ibid. -ingtune.
[12] Ibid. seolfrenne.
[13] MS. (b) þrynnesse.
[14] Ibid. Cealctune.
[15] MS. (b) swyrdes.
[16] MS. (b) Leowine.
[17] Ibid. anes seolforhammenes blædhornes.
[18] T. supplies þam.
[19] Ibid. þas.
[20] Ibid. swyrdes.
[21] Ibid. anes blacan.

what belongs to it, except the one ploughland which I have given to Siferth; and the estate at *Garwaldingtun*. And I grant the estate at Rotherfield to the Nunnery, for St Mary's sake, and a silver cross of five pounds; and to the New Minster a silver cauldron, of five pounds, in the name of the Holy Trinity, to whom the foundation is dedicated. And I give to the Holy Cross and St Edward at Shaftsbury, the six pounds about which I have given directions to my brother Edmund.

And to my father, King Ethelred, I grant the estate at Chalton except the eight hides which I have granted to my servant Ælfmær; and the estate at Norton; and the estate at Mollington; and the silver-hilted sword which belonged to Ulfketel; and the coat of mail which Morcar has; and the horse which Thurbrand gave to me; and the white horse which Leofwine gave to me.

And to my brother Edmund I grant the sword which belonged to King Offa; and the sword with the 'pitted' hilt; and a blade and a silver-coated trumpet; and the estates which I obtained in East Anglia; and the estate in the Peak valley (?). And I wish that each year there shall be paid one day's food-rent from this property to the community at Ely on the festival of St Etheldreda; and that a hundred pence shall be given to that monastery, and a hundred poor people fed there on that day; and may this charitable bequest be for ever performed yearly, whoever shall hold the estates, as long as Christianity shall last. And if they who have the estates will not discharge these charities, the property shall go to St Etheldreda's.

And I grant to my brother Eadwig a silver-hilted sword. And I grant to Bishop Ælfsige a gold crucifix which Eadric, Wynflæd's son, has, and a black stallion. And I grant to Ælfmær the estate at Hambledon which he had before: and I beseech my father, for God Almighty's sake and for mine, that he will permit this grant which I have made to him. And I grant to God-

fæder fur[1] godes. ælmihtiges lufan. 7 fur[1] minon. þ he þæs
geunne. þe Ic him. geunnen hæbbe. 7 Ic geann Godwine
Wulfnoðes suna. þæs landes. æt Cumtune. þe his fæder ǽr ahte.
7 Ic geann Ælfswyðe. minre fostermeder. for hire myclon.
5 geearnungon[2]. þæs landes æt Westune[3]. þe Ic gebohte æt minon
fæder. mid þridde healf[4] hund mancusan[5] goldes. be gewihte.
7 Ic gean Ælfwine minon mæssepreoste. þæs landes æt Heorulfestune. 7 þæs malswurdes[6]. þe Wiðer[7] ahte. 7 mines horses mid
minon gerædon. 7 Ic geann Ælmære minon discþene. þara ehta
10 hida. æt Cateringatune. 7 anes fagan stedan. 7 þæs sceardan
swurdes[6]. 7 mines targan. 7 Ic geann. Siferðe[8] þæs landes æt
Hocganclife[9]. 7 anes swurdes[6]. 7 anes horses. 7 mines bohscyldes[10]. 7 Ic geann. Æþelwerde Stameran 7 Lyfingce þæs
landes. æt Tywingan[11]. 7 Ic ann Leofstane Leofwines[12] breðer.
15 Cwattes. þære lan'd'are. þe Ic[13] of his breðer nam. 7 Ic geann
Leommære. æt Biggrafan þæs landes þe ic him ær of nam. 7 Ic
geann Godwine Dreflan[14]. þara þreora hida. æt Lutegaresheale.
7 Ic geann Eadrice Wynflæde Sunu þæs swurdes[15] þe seo hand
is on gemearcod. 7 Ic gean'n' Æþelwine[16] minon. Cnihte þæs
20 swurdes[15] þe he me ær sealde. 7 Ic geann. Ælfnoðe minon
swurdhwitan[17] þæs sceardan malswurdes[18]. 7 minon headeor-
hunton þæs stodes. þe is on Colungahrycge. 7 gehealde mon of
mino'n' golde. Ælfric æt Bertune. 7 Godwine Drefelan æt swa
miclon swa Eadmund min broðor wát. þ ic heom mid rihte to
25 gyldanne ah; Nu þancige Ic minon fæder mid ealre eadmodnesse
on godes ælmihtiges naman þære andsware. þe he me sende on[19]
frigedæg. æfter middessumeres[20]. mæssedæge. be Ælfgare.
Ælffan[21] suna. þ wæs. þ he me Cydde[22]. mines fæder worde.
þ ic moste be godes leafe. 7 be his. geunnan minre are. 7 minra
30 æhta. swá me mæst ræd þuhte. ægðer ge for gode. ge for worulde.

---

[1] MS. (b) and MS. (d) for.
[2] MS. (b) earnungan.
[3] MS. (d) Prestune.
[4] MS. (b) helf.
[5] Ibid. mancusa.
[6] Ibid. (-)swyrdes.
[7] Ibid. Wiðar.
[8] Ibid. Sifyrðe.
[9] Ibid. Hocgganclife.
[10] MS. (d) bocscyldes.
[11] Ibid. Tywinham.
[12] MS. (b) Leowines.
[13] Ibid. inserts ær.
[14] Ibid. Drefelan.
[15] Ibid. swyrdes.
[16] Ibid. Ægelwine.
[17] Ibid. swyrd-.
[18] Ibid. malswyrdes.
[19] MS. (d) inserts þone.
[20] MS. (b) middan sumeres.
[21] Ibid. Alfgare Æffan.
[22] MS. (d) inserts a.

wine, Wulfnoth's son, the estate at Compton which his father possessed. And I grant to my foster-mother, Ælfswith, because of her great deserts, the estate at Weston, which I bought from my father for two hundred and fifty mancuses of gold, by weight. And to my chaplain Ælfwine I grant the estate at Harleston and the inlaid sword which belonged to Withar, and my horse with the harness. And I grant to my seneschal Ælfmær the eight hides at Catherington, and a pied stallion and my round shield, and the notched(?) sword. And to Siferth I grant the estate at Hockliffe, and a sword and a horse and my curved (?) shield. And I grant to Æthelweard the Stammerer and Lyfing the estate at Tewin. And I grant to Leofstan, the brother of Leofwine Cwatt, the landed property which I have taken from his brother. And to Leofmær of Bygrave I grant the estate which I have taken from him. And I grant to Godwine the Driveller the three hides at Lurgashall (?). And I grant to Eadric, the son of Wynflæd, the sword on which the hand is marked. And I grant to my servant Æthelwine the sword which he has given to me. And I grant to Ælfnoth my sword-polisher the notched (?) inlaid sword, and to my staghuntsman the stud which is on *Colungahrycg*. And let Ælfric at Barton and Godwine the Driveller be paid from my money as much as my brother Edmund knows that I ought rightly to pay them.

Now I thank my father in all humility, in the name of Almighty God, for the answer which he sent me on the Friday after the feast of Midsummer by Ælfgar, Æffa's son; which, as he told me in my father's words, was that I might, by God's leave and his, grant my estates and my possessions as seemed to me most advisable in fulfilment of my duties to God and men. And my brother Edmund and Bishop Ælfsige and Abbot Brihtmær and Ælfmær, Ælfric's son are witnesses of this answer.

7 þysse andsware is to gewitnesse. Eadmund min broðor.
7 Ælfsige bisceop. 7 Byrhtmær abb. 7 Ælmær Ælfrices sunu.
nu bidde ic. ealle þa witan. þe minne cwyde gehyron rædan.
ægðer ge[1] gehadode. ge læwede. þ hi beon on fultume. þ min
5 Cwyde standan mote. Swa mines fæder leaf[2]. On minon Cwyde
stænt. Nu cyðe Ic. þ ealle þa þingc. þe Ic to gode. into godes
Cyrican. 7 godes þeowan geunnen hæbbe[3]. Sý gedon for mines
leofan fæder Sawle Æþelredes Cyncges[4]. 7 for minre[5]. 7[6]
Ælfþryðe minre Ealdemodor þe me afedde. 7 for ealra þara þe
10 me to þyson godan gefylstan. 7 Se. þe þysne Cwyde. þurh ænig
þingc. awende. habbe him wið god ælmihtigne gemæne. 7 wið Sca
Marían. 7 wið Sce Peter. 7 wið ealle þa. þe godes naman heriað;

XXI. THE WILL OF WULFWARU.

Ic Wulfwaru bidde minne leofan hlaford Æþelred kyning him
to ælmyssan. þ ic mote beon mines cwydes wyrðe. Ic kyðe þe
15 leof her on ðisum gewrite hwæs ic geann into Baðum to Sce
Petres mynstre. for mine earman sawle. 7 for minra yldrena
þe me min ar of com. 7 mine æhta. þ is þonne þ ic geann ðæder
into ðære halgan stowe anes beages is on syxtigum mancussum
goldes. 7 anre blede is on þriddan healfon punde. 7 twegea
20 gyldenra roda. 7 anes mæssereafes mid eallum þam ðe ðærto
gebyreð. 7 anes hricghrægles þæs selestan þe ic hæbbe. 7 anes
beddreafes mid wahryfte[7] 7 mid hoppscytan. 7 mid eallum þam
þe þærto gebyreð. And ic geann Ælfere abbode þæs landes æt
Ferscesforda[8]. mid mete 7 mid mannum. 7 mid eallre tylðe.
25 swa ðærto getilod bið. And ic geann Wulfmære minum yldran
suna þæs landes æt Clatfordtune. mid mete. 7 mid mannum.
and mid eallre tilðe. 7 þes landes æt Cumtune. mid mete. 7 mid
mannum. 7 mid eallre tilðe. 7 þes landes æt Budancumbe ic
geann him healfes[9]. mid mete. 7 mid mannum. 7 mid eallre
30 tilðe. healfes ic his geann Alfware[10] minre gyngran dehter. mid

---

[1] MS. (d) end.
[2] Ibid. inserts þ.
[3] Ibid. mine.
[4] K. mid ðam hryfte.
[5] T. healf.

[6] MS. (b) inserts ys 7.
[7] Ibid. Ægelredes cynges.
[8] Ibid. inserts for.
[9] K. Fersceforda.
[10] K. Ælfware.

Now I pray all the councillors, both ecclesiastical and lay, who may hear my will read, that they will help to secure that my will may stand, as my father's permission is stated in my will.

I now declare that all those things which I have granted to God, to God's church and God's servants, are done for the soul of my dear father King Ethelred and for mine, and for the soul of Ælfthryth my grandmother, who brought me up, and for the souls of all those who shall give me their help with these benefactions. And may he who by any means perverts this will, have to account with Almighty God, and with St Peter, and with all those who praise God's name.

XXI. THE WILL OF WULFWARU.

I, Wulfwaru, pray my dear lord King Ethelred, of his charity, that I may be entitled to make my will. I make known to you, Sire, here in this document, what I grant to St Peter's monastery at Bath for my poor soul and for the souls of my ancestors from whom my property and my possessions came to me; namely then, that I grant to that holy place there an armlet which consists of sixty mancuses of gold, and a bowl of two and a half pounds, and two gold crucifixes, and a set of mass-vestments with everything that belongs to it, and the best dorsal that I have, and a set of bed-clothing with tapestry and curtain and with everything that belongs to it. And I grant to the Abbot Ælfhere the estate at Freshford with the produce and the men and all the profit which is obtained there.

And I grant to my elder son Wulfmær the estate at Claverton, with produce and with men and all profits; and the estate at Compton with produce and men and all profits; and I grant him half the estate at Butcombe with produce and men and all profits, and half of it I grant to my younger daughter Ælfwaru, with produce and men and all profits. And they are to share the principal residence between them as evenly as they can, so that each of them shall have a just portion of it.

And to my younger son Ælfwine I grant the estate at Leigh,

mete. 7 mid mannum. 7 mid eallre tilðe. 7 dælon hi þ heafodbotl
him betweonan swa rihte swa hi rihtlicost magon. þ heora
ægðer his gelice micel habbon. And Ælfwine minum gyngran
suna ic geann þes landes æt Leage. mid mete 7 mid mannum.
5 7 mid eallre tilðe. And þes landes æt Healhtune. mid mete
7 mid mannum 7 mid eallre tilðe. And þes landes æt Hocgestune.
mid mete 7 mid mannum. 7 mid eallre tilðe. 7 ðritigra mancussa
goldes. And ic geann Godan minre yldran dehter þes landes æt
Wunfrod. mid mete. 7 mid mannum. 7 mid eallre tilðe. 7 twegea
10 cuppena on feower pundum. 7 anes bendes on ðritigum mancussum goldes. 7 twegea preonas. 7 anes wifscrudes ealles. And
Alfware minre gyngran dehter ic geann ealles þæs wifscrudes
þe þer to lafe bið. And Wulfmære minum suna 7 Ælfwine
minum oðrum suna. 7 Alfware[1] minre dehter heora þreoðra[2]
15 ælcum ic geann twegea cuppena on godum feo. And ic geann
Wulfmære minum suna anes heallwahriftes. 7 anes beddreafes.
Ælfwine minum oðrum suna ic geann anes heallreafes. 7 anes
burreafes. mid beodreafe. 7 mid eallum hræglum swa ðerto
gebyreð. And ic geann minum feower cnihtum. Ælmære[3].
20 7 Ælfwerde. 7 Wulfrice. 7 Wulfstane. anes bendes on twentigum
mancussum goldes. And ic geann eallum minum hiredwifmannum to gemanum anes godes casteneres wel gerenodes. And ic
wylle þ þa þe to minre are fon. þ hi fi[n]don[4] twentig freotmanna[5]. Tyne be eastan. 7 tune[6] be westan. and æfre ælce
25 geare ealle gemænelice ane feorme into Baðum swa gode swa
hi bezte þurhteon magon. to swylcre tide. swylce heom eallum
þince þ hi bezt. 7 gerisenlicost hi forðbringan magon. Swylc
heora swylce þis gelæste. hæbbe he Godes milze and mine. And
swylc heora swylce þis gelæstan nelleᴠ́ hæbbe he hit him wið
30 ðone héhstan gemæne. þ is se soðæ god. þe ealle gesceafta
gesceop. 7 geworhte.

[1] K. Ælfware.	[2] Sic ms. K., T. þreora.
[3] K. Ælfmære.	[4] K., T. fedon.
[5] K. freolsmanna.	[6] K. tyna. T. tyne.

with produce and men and all the profits; and the estate at Holton, with produce and men and all profits; and the estate at Hogston, with produce and men and all profits; and thirty mancuses of gold.

And I grant to my elder daughter, Gode, the estate at Winford, with produce and men and all profits; and two cups of four pounds; and a band of thirty mancuses of gold and two brooches and a woman's attire complete. And to my younger daughter Ælfwaru I grant all the women's clothing which is left.

And to my son Wulfmær and my second son Ælfwine and my daughter Ælfwaru—to each of the three of them—I grant two cups of good value. And I grant to my son Wulfmær a hall-tapestry and a set of bed-clothes. To Ælfwine my second son I grant a tapestry for a hall and tapestry for a chamber, together with a table-cover and with all the cloths which go with it.

And I grant to my four servants Ælfmær, Ælfweard, Wulfric and Wulfstan, a band of twenty mancuses of gold. And I grant to all my household women, in common, a good chest well decorated.

And I desire that those who succeed to my property provide twenty freedmen, ten in the east and ten in the west; and all together furnish a food-rent for Bath every year for ever, as good as ever they can afford, at such season as it seems to all of them that they can accomplish it best and most fittingly. Whichever of them shall discharge this, may he have God's favour and mine; and whichever of them will not discharge it, may he have to account for it with the Most High, who is the true God, who created and made all creatures.

XXII. ÆTHELFLÆD'S BEQUEST TO ST PAUL'S.

Her swutelað on ðam cwide ðe Ægelfled[1] gecweden hæfð[2] God[3] to lofe and hire saule to þerfe and hire hlafordes. þæt is ðonne ða feower hida landes at Lagefare and twa hida æt Cochamstede ðe hy gean for hire saule and for hire hlafordes 5 into sanctes Paules mynstre on Lundene ðam gebroðran to bigleofan, ðam ðe ðæs[4] dæghwamlice Gode þeniað, be ðes cynges fulle geleuen Æðelredes, on ðera manna gewitnesse ðe heora naman her standað: þæt is ðonne Ægelnoð[5] arcebiscop, and Wulfstan arcebiscop, and Ælfun biscop on Lundene, 10 and Ælfric abbot, and Wigard abbot, and Ælsi abbot on Cowwaforde[6], and Ælfere ealdorman, and Briðnoð ealdorman, and Eadric ealdorman, and Ælfsige cynges þegn, and Ufegeat scireman, and Frena cynges þegn. And swa hwilc man swa þisne cwide awende, sy he Iudas gefere ðe urne drihten 15 belewde on helle wite.

XXIII. THE WILL OF MANTAT THE ANCHORITE.

Mantat ancer godes wræcca greteð Cnut cing 7 Emma hlæfdie swiðe bliþelike mid godes blisse. And ic ciðe þ ic habbe ure almesse Crist betaht 7 his allen halgan ure sawle to frofre 7 to blisse þære it lengest wunian sculen. þæt is ærest. þæt land æt 20 Twiwell into Þornige. þær ure ban resteð. 7 þæt land æt Cunintun, prestes 7 diaknes þa þe hit æt me earnodon on mine life. And hi habbað god behaten 7 me on hande gesealde þ hi sculen elke geare don for us twa hundred messen 7 twa hundred sauters. 7 þertoeaken fele holy beden. Nu bidde ic inc for godes 25 lufe 7 for ure wreccan bene þat þis none man ne awende; þat wat[7] god þ inc ne wæs nen bescoran man nytter þænne[8] 7 þat inc sceal ben cuðe on þan towarden liue Gehealde inc here on liue heofan engle kinge. 7 geleade inc on his lihte mid him þer yt wiðuten sorhge euer wunian. Amen;

[1] T. *Egelfled*.   [2] T. *hæfd*.   [3] T. *Gode*.
[4] T. *ðær*.   [5] T. *Egelnoð*.   [6] T. *Cowwaford*.
[7] Collectanea Topographica, K., T. *þat*.
[8] Something has evidently been omitted here, probably an *ic*.

XXII. ÆTHELFLÆD'S BEQUEST TO ST PAUL'S.

Here in this bequest it is made known what Æthelflæd has bequeathed for the praise of God and the need of her soul and her lord's; namely, the four hides at Laver and two hides at Cockhampstead which she grants for her soul and for her lord's to St Paul's minster in London for the maintenance of the brethren who daily serve God there; with the full permission of King Ethelred, in the presence of those men whose names are given here; namely, Archbishop Æthelnoth and Archbishop Wulfstan and Ælfhun, Bishop of London, and Abbot Ælfric, and Abbot Wigheard, and Abbot Ælfsige of *Cowwaford* and the Ealdorman Ælfhere, and the Ealdorman Brihtnoth, and the Ealdorman Eadric, and Ælfsige, the king's thegn, and Ufegeat the sheriff, and Fræna, the king's thegn.

And whatsoever man shall alter this bequest, may he be a companion in the torment of hell of Judas who betrayed our Lord.

XXIII. THE WILL OF MANTAT THE ANCHORITE.

Mantat the Anchorite, God's exile, greets King Cnut and Queen Emma very joyfully with God's joy. And I make known to you that I have entrusted our charitable gift to Christ and all his saints where it shall remain longest, for the comfort and happiness of our soul. First, the estate at Twywell to Thorney, where our bones shall rest, and the estate at Conington, to priests and deacons who have deserved it of me during my life. And they have promised God and given pledge to me that each year they will recite for us two hundred masses and two hundred psalters and in addition many holy prayers.

Now I pray you for the love of God and on account of an exile's entreaty, that no man may alter this. God knows that no tonsured man has been more useful to you both than [I], and that shall be known to you in the future life.

May the King of the angels of heaven uphold you both in this life and lead you into his light where you may ever dwell with him without sorrow. Amen.

XXIV. THE WILL OF THURKETEL
OF PALGRAVE.

[H]er Switeleþ ihu Þurketel an his ahte after his day þat is erst
for his soule Palegraue into seynt Eadmund and Witingham
half and half þe bisscop. and alle mine men fre. and ilk habbe
his toft and his metecu 7 his metecorn. And ic an at Reydone-[1]
5 berh þat midleste forlong fre into þe kirke. and Scortland[2] 7 þe
prestes toft al into þe kirke fre. And ic an Lefwen min wif
Simplingham al þat ceaplond. 7 þat oþer þat ic mid hire nam
and half Reydone[1] mid mete and mid Erue to þat forwarde þat
we spreken habben 7 mine men fre. And ic an Wingefeld mine
10 broþeres sunes Vlfketel 7 Þurfketel. And ic an Lefquene
fiftene acres at Palegraue 7 an toft. and Wlwine habbe þat lond
þe he mines hafde. 7 Alfwold[3] habbe mid ton[4] þe he her hauede[5]
. XVI . acres mid tofte[6] mid alle[7]. And Osebern habbe þat lond
besiden Thrandestone þat ic þer hauede. And ic an Lefric mine
15 neue and Godwine mine mey and Wlwine 7 his brother
. XX . acres at Reydone[8]. and þe mor[9] þe ic 7 þo munekes soken[10]
ymbe min del fremannen to note so he[11] er deden. er daye 7 after
daye. Se þe þis awende. Wende him god fro heuene riche into
helle Witerbrogen bute he it þe deppere bete. er his ending day.
20 Þise write sinden þre. on is at seynt Eadmundesbiri. oþer haueð
þe bisscop. þridde haueð Þurketel himself.

---

[1] K. *Keydone*.   [2] K. *Scoreland*. Addit. MS. *Scortelond*.
[3] K. *Ælfwold*.
[4] The Addit. MS. reading *ten* is probably the correct one.
[5] K. omits from here until *hauede* on l. 14.
[6] *and* has been written here and deleted by writing dots underneath.
Addit. MS. retains *and*.
[7] Addit. MS. *halle*.   [8] K. *Keydone*.
[9] Addit. MS. *moer*. K. *mon*.   [10] K. *seken*.
[11] T. *hi*.

XXIV. THE WILL OF THURKETEL
OF PALGRAVE.

It is here made known how Thurketel grants his possessions after his death. First, for his soul, Palgrave to St Edmund's, and half Whittingham, and half to the Bishop. And all my men are to be free, and each is to have his homestead and his cow and his corn for food. And I grant the middle furlong at Roydon hill free to the church; and *Shortland* and the priest's homestead, all free to the church.

And to my wife Leofwyn I grant Shimpling, all the purchased estate and the other which I received when I married her; and half Roydon with produce and with livestock on those terms upon which we have agreed; and my men are to be free. And I grant Wingfield to my brother's sons, Ulfketel and Thurketel. And I grant Leofcwen fifteen acres at Palgrave and a homestead. And Wulfwine is to have that land of mine which he held. And Ælfwold, as well as the ten which he had before, is to have sixteen acres with a homestead and everything. And Osbeorn is to have the land near Thrandeston which I have had there. And I grant to Leofric my nephew and my kinsman Godwine and Wulfwine and his brother, twenty acres at Roydon. And [I grant] the moor about my part of which the monks and I contended, for freemen to use, as they did before, both before my death and after.

He who alters this—may God expel him from the kingdom of heaven to the torments of hell, unless he repent it all the more deeply before his last day.

There are three of these documents: one is at Bury St Edmunds; the second the Bishop has; the third Thurketel himself has.

XXV. THE WILL OF THURKETEL HEYNG.

[H]er kythet on þis write ihu ic Thurketel an min ahte after
min day. þat is erst þat ic an þat lond at Castre 7 at Thorpe mid
medwe and mid merisce and ingong and vtgong mine soule to
alisednesse god and sc̄e Benedicte and seynt Eadmunde to Biry
5 and to Holm[1]. and mine wyues del euere unbesaken to gyfen
and to habben þer hire leuest be. and mine lafard rithte heregete.
And Alfwen[2] mine douter habbe þat lond at Ormisby to þan
forwarde þat he[3] it ne may forwirken. and after hire day. go
þat lond into Holme for mine soule and for hire buten þat lond
10 þat Omund[4] ahte þat habbe Ketel mine nefe[5]. and þat lond at
Scrouteby habben mine nefe kild Swegner[6] sunen 7 Alemundes[7].
And an[8] pund habbe se Abbot on Holm. an other se Abbot on
Byri. and mine men fre þo it ihernen[9] wellen. And wo so þis
quides bereuen wille. bereue hym god heueriche. buten he it
15 her bete. þise write sinden þre. and is on Holme and oþer on
Byri. þridde mid Thurkitel seluen.

XXVI. THE WILL OF BISHOP ÆLFRIC.

✠ Her swytelað on þissum gewrite hu Ælfric ƀ wille his are
beteon þe he under gode geernode 7 under Cnute kyncge his
leofue laforde 7 siþþan hæfð rihtlice gehealdan under Haralde
20 cyncge; þ is þonne ærest þ ic gean þ land et Wilrincgawerþa[10]
into sc̄e Eadmunde for mira saule 7 for minas lafordas. swa ful
7 swa forð swa he hit me to handa let. 7 ic gean þ land æt
Hunstanestune be æstan broke 7 mid þan lande et Holme into

---

[1] Addit. MS. omits following passage till after *Alfwen*.
[2] K. *Ælfwen*.
[3] T. *heo*.
[4] Addit. MS. *Edmund*.
[5] Ibid. *neste*.
[6] K., T. *Swegnes*.
[7] Addit. MS. *Symon. 7 Alcmundes*.
[8] *and* first written and the *d* deleted.
[9] Addit. MS. *heruen*.
[10] Cambridge MS. *Wirlinworth*.

XXV. THE WILL OF THURKETEL HEYNG.

Here in this document it is made known how I, Thurketel, grant my possessions after my day. First, that I grant the land at Caister and at Thorpe with meadow and with marsh, with ingress and with egress, to God and St Benedict and St Edmund at Bury and at Holme, for the redemption of my soul. And my wife's portion is to be for ever uncontested, for her to hold or to give where she pleases. And to my lord his due heriot.

And my daughter Ælfwyn is to have the estate at Ormesby with the proviso that she may not forfeit it; and after her time the estate is to go to Holme for my soul and for hers, except the land which Omund had; that my nephew Ketel is to have. And my nephews' children, the sons of Swegn and of Ealhmund, are to have the estate at Scratby.

And the Abbot of Holme is to have a pound and the Abbot of Bury another. And my men are to be free, those who will work for it (?).

And whosoever wishes to despoil this will, may God deprive him of the kingdom of heaven, unless he repent it here.

There are three of these documents: one is at Holme and the second at Bury; the third with Thurketel himself.

XXVI. THE WILL OF BISHOP ÆLFRIC.

It is made known here in this document how Bishop Ælfric wishes to assign his property which he acquired under God and under King Cnut his dear lord, and has since held lawfully under King Harold. First, then, I grant the estate at Worlingworth to St Edmund's, for my soul and for my lord's, with the same rights as when he gave it into my possession. And I grant the estate at Hunstanton, east of the brook, and including the estate at Holme, to St Edmund's. And it is my will that the monks of Bury pay sixty pounds for the estates at Tichwell and at Docking and what belongs there. And I grant to Leofstan the dean the estate at Grimston with all the rights with which I have held it.

sc̄e Eadmunde. 7 ic wille ꝥ þa munecas on Byrig sellan[1] syxtig punde for þan lande et Ticeswelle 7 et Doccyncge 7 ꝥ þerto geherað[2]: 7 ic gean Leofstane dæcane þæt land et Grimastune swa ful 7 swa forð swa ic hit ahte[3]. 7 ic gean mine cynelaforde Haralde . II . marc gol[4]. 7 ic gean mire hlefdigen an marc gol[4]. 7 gelæste man Ægelrice . IIII . pund mire fatfylre[5]. 7 sela man mine cnihtas þa mina stiwardas witan . xxxx . punda. 7 fif pund into Elig. 7 fif pund into Holm. 7 fif pund Wulfwarde muneke minne mæge. 7 fif pund Ælffæh min sæmestre[6]. 7 ic wille ꝥ man sella ꝥ land et Walsingaham swa man derast mage[7]. 7 gelesta 'man ꝥ feoh[8]' swa ic gewissod hæbbe. 7 ic wille ꝥ man selle ꝥ land et Fersafeld swa man derast mæge. 7 recna man iung'ere[9]' Brun án marc gol. 7 mid þan laue scytte man mina borgas. 7 ic gean Ælfwiṇe minan preoste et Walsingaham . xxx . akera et Eggemera. 7 Uui prouast[10] habba þone ofaræcan. 7 'ic gean' Ædwine muneke. ꝥa mylne et Gæssæte[11] þe Ringware ahte. 7 ic gean Ælfwig preoste. ꝥ land et Rygedune[12] þe ic bohte to Leofwenne. 7 ic gean ꝥ myln þe Wulnoð ahte into sc̄e Eadmunde. 7 ic gean Sibriht ꝥ land þe ic gebohte on Mulantune. 7 ic gean ꝥ fen þe Þurlac me sealde into Ælmham þa preostas to foddan; 7 ic gean into Hoxne. þa preostas. an þusend werð fen. 7 ic gean ꝥ fen þe Ælfric me sealde into Holme. 7 ic gean þon hage binnon Norðwic for mire saule 7 for ealra þe hit me geuðon into sc̄e Eadmunde. 7 ic gean þan hage into sc̄e P*et*re binnon Lunden. 7 ic gean iungre Brun ꝥ healfe þusend fen.

[1] Addit. MS. *tellen.*

[2] There is a marginal note 7 *ic gean ꝥ mylne* at this point.

[3] The MS. has crosses at this point.

[4] There is a long gap in MS. here, with no trace of writing.

[5] Other MSS. *fat siluere.*

[6] *sesæmestre* first written, then *se* erased. Other MSS. have *sescemaistre.*

[7] *a* written over *e.* Other MSS. omit passage between this point and the next *derast mæge.*

[8] *mid þan feo* first written and then half erased.

[9] *ere* written over *a.*

[10] Addit. MS. *Oui min prest.*

[11] Cambridge MS. *Geysete.*

[12] Other MSS. *Reydone.*

And to my royal lord Harold I grant two marks of gold....
And I grant to my lady one mark of gold....And Æthelric
my cup-bearer, is to be paid four pounds. And forty pounds
are to be paid to my servants whom my stewards know; and
five pounds to Ely and five pounds to Holme and five pounds
to my kinsman Wulfweard the monk and five pounds to
Ælfheah my tailor. And I wish that the estate at Walsingham
be sold as dearly as possible, and the money be paid out as
I have directed. And I wish that the estate at Fersfield shall
be sold as dearly as possible, and one mark of gold shall be paid
to the younger (?) Brun, and with what is left let my debts be paid.

And to Ælfwine, my priest at Walsingham, I grant thirty
acres at Egmere, and Ufi the prior is to have the rest. And
I grant to Edwin the monk the mill at Guist which Ringwaru
owned. And I grant to Ælfwig the priest the estate at Roydon
which I bought from Leofwyn. And I grant the mill which
Wulfnoth owned to St Edmund's. And I grant to Sibriht the
estate in Moulton which I bought.

And I grant the fen which Thurlac gave me to Elmham for
the sustenance of the priests: and I grant to the priests at Hoxne
fenland worth a thousand [pence]. And I grant the fen which
Ælfric gave me to Holme. And I grant the messuage in Norwich
to St Edmund's for my soul and the souls of all those who
granted it to me. And I grant the messuage in London to
St Peter's. And I grant to the younger (?) Brun the fen worth half
a thousand [pence].

XXVII. THE WILL OF WULFSIGE.

[H]er switeleþ on þise write wam Wlsi an his[1] aihte. þat is
erst for his soule þat lond at Wiken into seynt Eadmundes biri
þa tweye deles 7 Alfric[2] Biscop þe þridde del. buten ane girde
and . XII . swine mesten þat schal habben Wlwine hire day. and
5 after hire day into seynt Eadmundes biri 7 alle þo men fre for
vnker bother soule. And ic an mine kynelouerd . II . hors. and
Helm and brinie. 7 an Swerd and a goldwreken spere. and ic
an mine lauedy half marc goldes. an mine Nifte ann ore[3] wichte
goldes. And habbe Stanhand[4] alle þinge þe ic him bicueðen
10 habbe. and mine brother bern here owen lond. 7 . II . hors mid
sadelgarun. and . I . brinie and on hakele. And se þe mine cuiðe
awende god almithtin awende his asyne from him on domesday
buten he it her þe rathere bete.

XXVIII. THE WILL OF ÆLFRIC MODERCOPE.

Þis is se quide þe Alfric[5] biquath er he ofer se ferde. þat is erst
15 Lodne into seynt Eadmunde be wude and by felde and be fenne
so ful 7 so forth so ic it formist ahte. And ic an þat lond at
Birthe into seynt Aþeldrithe so ful 7 so forth so ic it bigeten
hauede eyþer on wude oþer on felde. And into Holm to sce
Benedicte Berton al so ful 7 so forth so ic it ahte. And ic an into
20 Rameseye six marc silures. and þat schal Godric mine brother
lesten. 7 ic an Þurwineholm[6] into Lodne. and Fuglholm[7] into
Berhe. And þa schep delen[8] men on to half into Lodne 7 half into
Beorthe. And 'ic' biquethe to min heregete ane marc goldes. and
þat schal Godric mine brother lesten. And Alfric[9] biscop I bi-
25 quethe mine teld 7 min bedreaf þat ic best hauede vt on mi fare
mid me. 7 be Alfric[9] biscop 7 Tofi Prude. 7 Þrunni þese quides
mundes hureþinge. þat it no man awende. 7 gif it wa wille
awenden: god almithen awende is ansene fram hym on domesday.

[1] T. hi.
[2] K., T. Ælfric.
[3] K. æn nore.
[4] T. Standhand.
[5] K. Ælfric.
[6] K. ðus Wineholm.
[7] K. Fuglhelm.
[8] K. deden.
[9] K. Ælfric.

XXVII. THE WILL OF WULFSIGE.

Here in this document it is made known to whom Wulfsige grants his possessions. First, for his soul, two-thirds of the estate at *Wick* to Bury St Edmunds and the third part to Bishop Ælfric, except one yardland and mast for twelve swine which Wulfwyn shall have for her life, and after her death [it shall go] to Bury St Edmunds; and all the men are to be free for the sake of the souls of us both.

And I grant to my royal lord two horses and a helmet and a coat of mail, and a sword and a spear inlaid with gold. And I grant to my lady half a mark of gold, and to my niece an ore's weight of gold. And Stanhand is to have everything which I have bequeathed to him, and my brother's children their own land, and two horses with harness, and one coat of mail and one cloak.

And he who alters my will, may Almighty God turn away his face from him on the Day of Judgment unless in this life he will quickly make amends for it.

XXVIII. THE WILL OF ÆLFRIC MODERCOPE.

This is the will which Ælfric made before he went across the sea. First, to St Edmund's, Loddon—woodland, open land and fen—with as full rights as ever I owned it; and I grant the estate at Bergh to St Etheldreda's with all the rights with which I acquired it, both woodland and open land; and Barton to St Benedict's at Holme, with as full rights as those with which I owned it. And I grant to Ramsey six marks of silver, and that my brother Godric is to pay. And I grant *Thurwineholm* with Loddon and *Fuglholm* with Bergh. And the sheep are to be divided into two parts, half for Loddon and half for Bergh.

And for my heriot I bequeathe one mark of gold, and Godric my brother is to pay it. And I bequeathe to Bishop Ælfric my tent, and my bed-clothing, the best that I had out on my journey with me. And Bishop Ælfric, Tofi the Proud and Thrym, are to be executors of this will, especially in order that no one may alter it. And if anyone wishes to alter it, may God Almighty turn his face from him on the Day of Judgment.

XXIX. THE WILL OF LEOFGIFU.

[1][L]eofgiue gret hyre leuedi godes gretinge. And ic kithe þe
mine quide wat[2] ic Crist an and his halegan mine louerdes soule
to alisednesse and mine into þe holy stowe þer ic self resten wille
þat is at seynt Eadmundes byri. þat is þat lond at Hintlesham and
5 þat lond at Gristlyngthorp. buten þat lond þat Ailsi hauede þat
he at his lauerd ernede and at me. and ilc þridde aker on þan
wude at Hintlesham habbe Ailri[3]. and ingong and vtgong be
feld and be fenne. And ic wille þat Ailric[4] prest and Ailfric[4]
prest and Ailri[5] diacon habben þat minstre at Colne. so here
10 lofard it hem vthe. And ic wille þat Aylfric[6] prest ben on þat
ilke loh[7] þe Aignoð was. And be se mund ofer þan minstre þe
is ofer alle oþere. and ic an þan kinge to marc goldes for[8] min
eruenumen to[9] 7 gealaeste þat gold. and mine lauedi[10] þat lond
at Belhcham[11] buten þat lond þat Godric mine stiward haueð þat
15 habbe he. and Alfward[6] bisscop þat lond at Benetleye buten half
hide þe Osemund hauede[12]. þat ic an Alfwy[6] min stiward. and
þat he on sit. 7 Alfnoð[6] min stiward þat lond þat Berric hauede
vnder hande. And Alfgar[6] mine mei þat lond at Borham. [13]And
Alfric[6] mine mey Withgares sone þat lond at Bromforde. And
20 Stigand þat lond at Willauesham. And Ailric[14] mine brotheres
sone þat lond at Stonham and at Waldingfeld and at Lithtletic[15].
And Alflet[16] mine douhter þat lond at Hag'e'le. And Godwine
min aðum 7 mire meygan þa þre hide at Werle. And Lef-
kyld[17] þa to hide onfast his owen. And Aylmer[18] habbe þat
25 lond at Stonham þe ic hym er to hande let. to reflande[19].
And ic an Godric mine reue[20] at Walddingfeld þa þritti

---

[1] Space for capital left in MS: small *l* in the margin.
[2] K., T. *þat.*   [3] K., T. *Ailsi.*
[4] K. *Ælfric.*   [5] K. *Ælfsi.*
[6] K. *Ælf-.*   [7] Addit. MS. *soh.*
[8] K., T. *fon.*   [9] Addit. MS. *for min herunemei.*
[10] K. *laue[r]de.*   [11] Addit. MS. *Bolcham.*
[12] Ibid. inserts *hunder hande.*
[13] Ibid. alters the order of the next few clauses.
[14] Addit. MS. *Alfric.* K. *Ælfric.* T. *Æilric.*
[15] Addit. MS. *Licheletik.*   [16] K. *Ælfled.* T. *Alfled.*
[17] Addit. MS. *Leythfled.*   [18] K., T. *Æylmer.*
[19] Addit. MS. omits *to reflande.*
[20] Ibid. replaces this by the names of the next two legatees.

XXIX. THE WILL OF LEOFGIFU.

Leofgifu greets her lady with God's greeting. And I declare to you my will, what I grant to Christ and his saints for the redemption of my lord's soul and mine, to the holy place where I myself wish to be buried, namely, Bury St Edmunds. That is, the estate at Hintlesham and the estate at Gestingthorp, except the land which Æthelsige had, which he acquired from his lord and from me. And Æthelsige is to have every third acre in the wood at Hintlesham, and ingress and egress by open land and fen. And I desire that Æthelric the priest and Ælfric the priest and Æthelsige the deacon shall have the minster at Colne as their lord granted it to them. And it is my wish that Ælfric the priest shall be in the same position in which Æthelnoth was. And may he be guardian over the minster who is over all others.

And I grant to the king two marks of gold—my heirs are to succeed to the inheritance and pay the gold—and to my lady the estate at Belchamp except the land which my steward, Godric, has. He is to keep it. And to Bishop Ælfweard the estate at Bentley except the half hide which Osmund had; I grant that to my steward Ælfwig with that which he occupies, and to Ælfnoth my steward the land which was in *Berric's* possession. And to my kinsman Ælfgar the estate at Boreham. And to my kinsman Ælfric, Wihtgar's son, the estate at Bramford. And to Stigand the estate at Willesham. And to Æthelric my brother's son the estate at Stonham and at Waldingfield and at *Lithtletic*. And to my daughter Ælfflæd the estate at Haughley. And to my brother-in-law Godwine, and my kinswoman, the three hides at Warley. And to Leofcild the two hides next to his own. And let Æthelmær have the estate at Stonham which I have let to him as 'reeve land.' And I grant to Godric, my reeve at Waldingfield, the thirty acres which I have let to him. And the estate at Lawford to Æthelric my household chaplain, and Ælfric [and] my servants who will serve me best. And Æthelric the priest is to have one hide at *Forendale*. And I desire that all my men shall be free, in the household, and on the estate, for my sake and for those who begot me.

acre þe ic him er to hande let. ¹And Ailric min hirdprest
7 Alric² mine chihtes³ þat lond at Lalleford þe me best
heren willen. 7 Ailric⁴ prest habbe an hide at Forendale⁵.
And ic wille þat alle mine men ben fre on hirde and on tune for
5 me and for þo þe me bigeten. And ic bidde mine leuedien for
godes louen þat þu⁶ þolie⁷ þat ani man mine quide awende. And
se þe it awende. god almichin 'a'wende his ansene from him on
domesday. buten ic it self do. God þe healde. Nu sinden þise
write þre. on is mid þise kinges halidome. and oþer at seynt
10 Eadmunde. 7 þridde mid Leofgiue seluen.

XXX. THURSTAN'S BEQUEST TO CHRISTCHURCH.

✠ Her cyð on þisan gewritu þ Þurstan geann þæs landes æt
Wimbisc into χp̄es cyrcean for his sawle 7 for Leofware 7 for
Æþelgyðe⁸. þam hirede to fostre æfter Þurstanes dæge 7 æfter
Æðelgyþe. 7 ælcon geare an pund to fulre sutelunge þa hwile
15 þe we libban⁹. 7 gelæste se hired æt χp̄es cyrcean¹⁰ swa hwæder
swa he wille þam hirede into sc̄e Augustine þe twelf pund be
getale oððe twa hida¹¹. Þis syndon þa gewitnysse þæs cwydes.
Eadwerd kyncg. 7 Ælfgifu seo hlæfdige. 7 Eadsige arceb¹².
7 Godwine eorl. 7 Leofric eorl¹³. 7 Ælfwærd b on Lundene.
20 7 Ælfwine b on Winceastre. 7 Stigand p̄. 7 Eadwold p̄. 7 Leofcild scirgerefa. 7 Osulf Fila. 7 Ufic. 7 Ælfwine Wulfredes sunu.
7 Ælfric Wihtgares sunu. 7 ealle þa þegenas on Eastsexan.
7 beon heora menn frige æfter heora beira dæge. 7 na stinge nan
mann æfter heora dæge on þ land buton se hired æt χp̄es circean.
25 7 yrfan hi swa hi wyrðe witan. 7 þissera gewritu syndan þreo.
an is æt χp̄es cyrcean. oþer æt sc̄e Augustine¹⁴. 7 þridde biþ mid
heom sylfan.

¹ Addit. MS. omits following sentence.   ² K. Ælric. T. Ailric.
² K., T. cnihtes.   ⁴ K. Ælfric.
⁵ Addit. MS. Frendenhale.   ⁶ ne or neuere has been omitted.
⁷ Addit. MS. þurfolie.
⁸ Cotton MS. adds buton twam hidan.
⁹ Ibid. omits 7 ælcon geare...libban.
¹⁰ Ibid. adds for Þurstanes saule 7 for æþelgyðe instead of swa hwæder swa
he wille.
¹¹ Ibid. omits oððe twa hida.   ¹² Ibid. adds 7 ælfric arceb.
¹³ Ibid. inserts above the line Ælgar þes eorlles sune.
¹⁴ Ibid. Augustine has been erased and albane substituted.

And I pray my lady, for God's sake, that you will [not] permit anyone to alter my will. And he who alters it—unless it be myself—may God Almighty turn his face from him on the Day of Judgment. May God keep you.

Now there are three of these documents. One is in the king's sanctuary; and the second is at St Edmunds; and the third with Leofgifu herself.

XXX. THURSTAN'S BEQUEST TO CHRISTCHURCH.

Here in this document it is made known that Thurstan grants the estate at Wimbish, for his soul and for Leofwaru's and for Æthelgyth's, to Christchurch, for the sustenance of the community after Thurstan's death and after Æthelgyth's; but each year, as long as we live, a pound [shall be paid] as a sufficient proof [of this reversionary right]. And the community at Christchurch is to pay to the community at St Augustine's whichever they prefer, twelve pounds by tale or two hides.

These are the witnesses of the bequest: King Edward and the Lady Ælfgifu, and Archbishop Eadsige, [and Archbishop Ælfric], and Earl Godwine, and Earl Leofric, [and the Earl's son Ælfgar], and Ælfweard, Bishop of London, and Ælfwine, Bishop of Winchester, and Stigand the priest, and Eadwold the priest, and Leofcild the sheriff, and Osulf Fila, and Ufic, and Ælfwine, Wulfred's son, and Ælfric, Wihtgar's son, and all the thegns in Essex.

And their men are to be free after the death of both of them. And after their death no one is to have authority on that estate except the community at Christchurch, and those are to inherit whom they know to be entitled.

There are three of these documents: one is at Christchurch; the second at St Augustine's; the third with the testators themselves.

XXXI. THE WILL OF THURSTAN.

[1][O]n vre drichtines name ic Þurstan Wine sune kithe alle
manne ihu ic an þe þing þe me god haueð lent so longe so his
wille beth. þat is þat ic an þat lond at Wimbisc into Cristes
kirke for mine soule 7 for Lefwares and for Egelsithes[2] after
5 mine day. 7 after Egelsithes[2]. þo men fre. and leste man of
Cristes kirke . XII . pund be tale. into seynt Augustine. And ic
an þat lond at Herlawe into sc̄e Eadmunde buten þe halue hide
þe Alfwine hauede at Gildenebrigge. and buten þat tuft þe
Alfgor on sit and þat hóó. þerto. and alle þe men fre. And ic an
10 þat lond at Sculham[3] at þe Northhalle into seynt Eadmunde
after vnker bothre day. and þo men fre. And ic an þat lond at
Wetheringsete into Ely[4] buten þat lond þat Aylri haueð habbe
he þat fre his day and his wiues. and after here bothere day into
þe tunkirke. 7 þo men fre. and Ic an þat lond at Cnapwelle into
15 Ely buten þat lond þat Ordeh haueð 7 Aylric munek haueð and
þo men fre. And ic an þat lond at Westone Agilswiðe buten þat
lond þat Sewine haueð to earninge[5] þat schal into tunkirke and
after hire day into Ely. 7 þo men fre. And ic an þat lond at
Sculham at þe Middelhalle half into sc̄e Benedicte to Rameseye.
20 7 half into sc̄e Benedicte into Holm. so it þerto lith after vnker
bother day and þo men fre. And ic an mine kinelouerd for mine
Hergete to marc goldes and to hors. and sadelfate and Helm and
brinie and Suerd and to scheldes and to speren. And ic wille
þat men selle þat lond at Bidicheseye. and nime of þat lond to
25 marc goldes to þe kinges heregete. and half marc goldes þe erl
Harold. and half marc goldes Stigand bisscop. 7 an marc goldes
mine felage. And an marc goldes his berne[6]. Þorþes brother
7 an marc goldes Sendi Arfast[7] and þat þe þer ouer goð. delen
le eruene men[8] for his soule on his felawes witnesse, buten þat
30 vttreste Milne into sc̄e Aethelburg at Berkynge. And wille þat

---

[1] Space in MS. but small *o* written in the margin.
[2] T. *Egelgithes*.   [3] Addit. MS. *Stucham*.
[4] Except for the anathema, the version in the Addit. MS. ends here.
[5] T. *Earninge*.   [6] T. *Hisberne*.
[7] MS. has *Bisscop* here, but with dots underneath to show that it should be
deleted.
[8] For þe eruenumen. *pouere* has been written over *eruene* in a different hand.
T. has *ermene*.

XXXI. THE WILL OF THURSTAN.

In our Lord's name. I, Thurstan, Wine's son, make known to all men how I grant the things which God has lent to me for as long as it shall be his will.

That is, that I grant the estate at Wimbish to Christchurch, for my soul and Leofwaru's and Æthelgyth's, after my day and after Æthelgyth's; the men are to be free, and twelve pounds by tale is to be paid by Christchurch to St Augustine's.

And I grant to St Edmund's the estate at Harlow, except the half hide which Ælfwine had at Ealing Bridge, and except the homestead which Ælfgar occupies and the spur of land which belongs to it; and all the men are to be free. And I grant the estate at the north hall at Shouldham to St Edmund's after the death of both of us; and the men are to be free. And I grant to Ely the estate at Wetheringsett, except the land that Æthelric has. He is to hold that freely for his life and his wife's, and after the death of them both, it is to go to the village church and the men are to be free. And I grant the estate at Knapwell to Ely, except the land which Ordheah and the monk Æthelric hold; and the men are to be free. And I grant the estate at Weston to Æthelswith, and after her death to Ely, except the land which Sæwine holds in return for service, which is to go to the village church; and the men are to be free. And I grant half the estate at the middle hall at Shouldham to St Benedict's at Ramsey, and half to St Benedict's at Holme, as it belongs there after the death of both of us; and the men are to be free.

And I grant to my royal lord as heriot two marks of gold and two horses with trappings, and a helmet and a coat of mail and a sword and two shields and two spears. And I desire that the estate at *Bidicheseye* shall be sold, and that two marks of gold shall be taken from that estate for the King's heriot; and Earl Harold [is to receive] half a mark of gold, and Bishop Stigand half a mark of gold, and my partner one mark of gold; and one mark of gold [is to be given] to his child, Thorth's brother, and one mark of gold to Sendi Arfast. And what is left over, the heirs are to distribute it for the sake of his soul in his partner's witness, except that the outermost mill is to go to St Æthelburg's at Barking.

min and Vlfkeles[1] felageschipe stonde to þat forwarde þe wit
speken habben. þat is þat lond at Burg. and Vlfketel hauið leyd
þerwith four marc goldes so wether so leng libbe. buten half
hide at Westle 7 an hide at Dullingham þat ic an Wiking mine
5 knihte. and ic an mine wife Ailgiðe al þe þing þe ic haue on
Norfolke so ic it her hire gaf to mund and to maldage. And þat
lond at Pentelawe 7 at Aesredune[2] buten þat lond at Bromlege
þat schal into þe tunkirke. ouer vnker bother day. and ic an
Agilgið þat lond at Henham buten an half hide þat schal into
10 'þe' kirke. and ic an Alfwi prest and Þurstan mine hirdprest.
and Ordeh mine hirdprest þat he[3] habben þat lond at Kydingtone
after vnker bother day. And ic an Meruyn and his wife and here
bern þat lond at Dunmawe. buten an alf hide þat schal into þe
kirke and an tuft. 7 ic an mine cnihtes þat wude at Aungre buten
15 þat derhage. 7 þat stod þe ic þer habbe. þis is to witnesse innon
Norfolke. Harold erl. and Stigand Bisscop. and Osgote. Clape.
and Godwine. 7 Wlgeat. 7 Eadwine. and Osbern. and Vlf. and
Gouti. And innon Suffolke Lefstan Decan and al se hird on
seynt Eadmundes biri. 7 Eadric and Alfric 7 Vlfketel. and
20 Lemmer. And in Grauntebreggeschire. Leswi abbot 7 al se
hird bynnen Ely. and Aelfwine Abbot 7 al se hird into Rameseye
and Alfwine[4] and Vlfketel Kild. and Osgot Sveyn and Ordger
and oþer Ordger. And innen Essexe. Alfger þe Erles sune. and
Lefkild 7 Osulf File. and Wlwine. and Sendi. and Leuerich
25 discþeng. Se þe þis quide awenden wille. buten ic self it be:✓
god him fordo nu and on domisday. AmeN. þise write sinden
þre. on schal into seynt Eadmunde. And on into Ely. and on
schal ben innon min owen hird. And þat lond at Henham
Þurstan and Agelgið[5]. and Askil vnnen Aegelswide after here
30 aldreday. and after hire day:✓ go þat lond into sce Aetheldrith

---

[1] T. Ulfketeles. [2] T. Æfredune.
[3] T. hi. [4] T. Ælfwine.
[5] T. Ægelgið.

And it is my wish that Ulfketel's and my partnership shall hold good, on the terms to which we have agreed; namely, the estate at Borough [is to go] to whichever of us shall live the longer—except half a hide at Westley and a hide at Dullingham which I grant to my servant Viking—and Ulfketel has laid down on his side four marks.

And I grant to my wife Æthelgyth everything which I have in Norfolk, as I gave it to her before as a marriage payment and in accordance with our contract; and the estate at Pentlow and at Ashdon, except the land at Bromley which is to go to the village church after the death of us both. And I grant to Æthelgyth the estate at Henham, except half a hide which is to go to the church. And I grant to the priest Ælfwig and to my chaplain Thurstan and to my chaplain Ordheah that they shall have the estate at Kedington after our death. And I grant to Merewine and his wife and their children the estate at Dunmow except half a hide which is to go to the church, and a homestead. And to my servants I grant the wood at Ongar, except the deer-enclosure and the stud which I have there.

These are the witnesses in Norfolk: Earl Harold, and Bishop Stigand, and Osgot Clapa, and Godwine and Wulfgeat and Edwin and Osbeorn and Ulf and Gouti; and in Suffolk: Leofstan the dean and all the community of Bury St Edmunds and Eadric and Ælfric and Ulfketel and Leofmær; and in Cambridgeshire: Abbot Leofsige and all the community at Ely, and Abbot Ælfwine and all the community at Ramsey, and Ælfwine and Ulfketel Cild, and Osgot Swegn and Ordgar and the other Ordgar; and in Essex: Ælfgar the Earl's son, and Leofcild and Osulf Fila and Wulfwine and Sendi and Leofric the seneschal.

He who wishes to alter this will, unless it be I myself, may God destroy him now and on the Day of Judgment. Amen.

There are three of these documents: one shall go to St Edmund's, and one to Ely, and one shall be in my own household.

And Thurstan and Æthelgyth and Askil grant to Æthelswith the estate at Henham after their death; and after her death the estate is to go to St Etheldreda's for her own soul and for

for hire owen soule. and for Þurstanes and for Agilwið[1]. 7 for
Lefware and for Askilles boten þo tueye hidan þe Aylmer Parl
haueð. and buten þat on hide þe Wlmare hauede. 7 an girde þe
Lustwine hauede. And ic an Þurgot mine cnihte half hide þe
5 Aelstan on sit at Aungre. 7 Meruin half hide. and þane litle hege
with Meredene. And Sueyn half hide. and þat ouer beth:
ofgon he it on vnker gemede. gif wit aleten willen.

XXXII. THE WILL OF WULFGYTH.

Hyer swuteleð on þesen ywrithe hu Wolgiþ yan hire þing.
efter hire forthsiþe þe hire se almiyti god yuþe on lyue to brukene.
10 þet is þanne herest mine louerde his riyte heriet. and ic yan þet
land at Stistede a godes ywithnesse and mine vrenden into
Xristes cheriche þa muneken to uostre on þan hyrede þet
Elfkitel[2] and Kytel mine bearn bruke þas londes hye dey and
seþþen gange þet land into Xristes cheriche buten ecchere
15 ayentale[3] vor mine saule and vor Elfwines mines louerdes
and for alre mine berne and by hialve þe men vrye efter
here daye ad ic yan into þare cheriche at Stistede to þan þe
ic on lyue yuþe Eldemes land and þertohycken[4] þet þer sy
alles vifty ekeres on wude and on velde efter mine forthsiþe.
20 and ic yan Wulkitele[5] and Kytele mine sunes þet land at
Walsingham[6]. and at Karltune and Herlingham[7]. and ic yan
minen twam doytren. Gode and Bote. Sexlingham[8] and Sumerledetune and into þare cheriche at Sumerledetune sixtene
eker londes and enne eker med. and ic yan Ealgiþe[9] mine
25 doyter þet land at Cheartekere[10] and at Essetesford and þane
wde þe ic leyde þerto. and ic[11] Godwine eorle and Harold erle
Friþetune[12]. and ic yan into Xristes cheriche to Xristes weuede
ane litlene Geldene Rode and ane setrayel. and ic yan seinte

[1] T. Agilgið.
[2] K. Ælfcytel.
[3] K. arentale.
[4] K. Hyekenes.
[5] K. Wolk[ytele].
[6] K. Wælsingaham.
[7] K. Herlingaham.
[8] K. Seaxlingaham.
[9] K. Ælgyðe.
[10] K. Certæcere.
[11] K. supplies gean.
[12] K. Friðtunes.

Thurstan's and for Æthelgyth's, and for Leofwaru's and for Askil's, except the two hides which Æthelmær Parl has, and except the one hide which Wulfmær had, and one yardland which Lustwine had. And I grant to Thurgot my servant a half-hide which Ælfstan occupies at Ongar, and to Merewine a half-hide and the little enclosure near *Meredene*, and to Swegn half a hide; and they may obtain what is left over by agreement with us both, if we are willing to allow them.

XXXII. THE WILL OF WULFGYTH.

Here in this document it is made known how Wulfgyth grants after her death the things which Almighty God has allowed her to enjoy in life.

First to my lord his due heriot. And I grant the estate at Stisted, with the witness of God and my friends, to Christchurch for the sustenance of the monks in the community, on condition that my sons Ælfketel and Ketel may have the use of the estate for their lifetime; and afterwards the estate is to go to Christchurch without controversy, for my soul and for my lord Ælfwine's and for the souls of all my children: and after their lifetime half the men are to be free. And I grant to the church at Stisted, besides what I granted during my life, *Eldemes* land and in addition so much that in all there shall be after my death fifty acres of woodland and of open land.

And I grant to my sons Ulfketel and Ketel the estates at Walsingham and at Carleton and at Harling; and I grant to my two daughters, Gode and Bote, Saxlingham and Somerleyton. And to the church at Somerleyton sixteen acres of land and one acre of meadow. And to my daughter Ealdgyth I grant the estates at Chadacre and at Ashford, and the wood which I attached to the latter. And I grant Fritton to Earl Godwine and Earl Harold.

And I grant to Christ's altar at Christchurch a little gold crucifix, and a seat-cover. And I grant to St Edmund's two ornamented horns. And I grant to St Etheldreda's a woollen gown. And I grant to St Osyth's half a pound of money, and

Eadmunde tueyn yboned hornes. and ic yan Seynte Eþeldrithe
ane wellene kertel. and ic yan seynte Osithe half pund fees and
þe yeue mine barnes. and ic yan seynt Austine an regrayel[1] and
se þe mine quyde beryaui þe ic nu biqueþen habbe a godes
5 ywithnesse beriaued he worþe þises erthliche meryþes and
ashireyi hine se almiyti driyten þe alle sheppe shop[2] and ywroyte
uram alre haleyene ymennesse on domesday. and sy he bytayt
Satane þane deule and alle his awaryede yueren into helle
Grunde and þer aquelmi and[3] godes withsaken bute ysweke and
10 mine irfinume neuer ne aswenche. þisses is to ywithnesse
Eadward king and manie oþre.

XXXIII. THE WILL OF EDWIN.

[O]n min drihtines name Ic Eadwine kithe ihu þat ic an þe
þinge þe me god almithin haue lent on þise liue. þat is þat ic an
þat lond at Eskeresthorp into seint Eadmund buten ten acres ic
15 giue þer into þere kirke. And Lefric habbe þo þre acres þe he
on sit. and ic 'an' þat lond at Lithle Meddeltone[4] into sce
Benedicte 7 ten acres into þe kirke. And ic an þat lond at Beorh
into sce Etheldriðe[5] bi suthen kinges strete buten þat northere
hage at Appelsco. and half þe turfgret ligge into Apetune and
20 þerto weye to rode brod. And ten akres into Beorh kirke be
suthen strete. And ten acres into Apetune kirke bi northen strete.
7 four acres into Huluestone kirke. And four acres into Blitleford[6] kirke. And . x . acres into Sparham kirke. 7 alle mine
men fre eywer. aftir mine tyme. Þis is þat frescet þe Eadwine[7]
25 haueð Crist vnnen and seynte Marie 7 alle Cristes halegen his
sowle to alisidnesse and his sinne tor[8] forgiuenesse. And þis is
þe forward þe Wlfric and Eadwine þa tueye brethere wrouhten
hem bituen. ymbe þa to land at Thorp and at Middeltone þat is
wethe[r][9] here so lenger libbe habbe bothe þe lond. And after
30 here boþere day go þat lond at Middiltone into sce Benedicte for

---

[1] K. sethrægles.
[2] K. gesceafta gesceop.
[3] K. mid.
[4] Addit. MS. Middeltone.
[5] Ibid. Ayldre. K. Æðelðriðe.
[6] Ibid. Blicheleslond.
[7] Ibid. adds þe tueie bretheren wrouthen hem bitwen copying from l. 27.
[8] Sic MS.
[9] K., T. se ðe.

that my children shall give. And I grant to St Augustine's one dorsal.

And he who shall detract from my will which I have now declared in the witness of God, may he be deprived of joy on this earth, and may the Almighty Lord who created and made all creatures exclude him from the fellowship of all saints on the Day of Judgment, and may he be delivered into the abyss of hell to Satan the devil and all his accursed companions and there suffer with God's adversaries, without end, and never trouble my heirs.

Of this King Edward and many others are witnesses.

XXXIII. THE WILL OF EDWIN.

In my Lord's name I, Edwin, make known how I grant the things which God Almighty has lent me in this life. That is, that I grant the estate at Algarsthorpe to St Edmund's except ten acres which I give to the church there. And Leofric is to have the three acres which he occupies. And I grant the estate at Little Melton to St Benedict's, and ten acres to the church. And I grant to St Etheldreda's the estate at Bergh south of King's Street, except the northern enclosure at *Appelsco*. And half the turfpit is to belong to Apton, and a way to it two rods broad. And ten acres south of the street to Bergh church. And ten acres north of the street to Apton church, and four acres to Holverstone church, and four acres to Blyford church and ten acres to Sparham church. And all my men are to be free everywhere after my time. This is the free property which Edwin has granted to Christ and St Mary and all Christ's saints for the redemption of his soul and the forgiveness of his sins.

And this is the agreement which the two brothers, Wulfric and Edwin, made between them about the two estates, Thorpe and Melton: that is, that whichever of them shall live the longer is to have both the estates; and after the death of both of them, the estate at Melton is to go to St Benedict's for the souls of them both: and Ketel is to succeed to the estate at Thorpe after the death of them both on such terms as are set forth there:

here boþere soule. and þat lond at Thorpe:ˊ after here boþere
day:ˊ fange Ketel þerto to swilke forwarde so þer wrouht is.
þat is þat Ketel leste alke iher to pund into seynt Eadmunde
þat is þas londes gouel. 7 for here eyþeres[1] soule ilke day ane
5 messe. and after Keteles day:ˊ go þat lond into seynt Eadmunde
buten alken gentale. and at Metheltone[2] into þere kirke þe
Þurwerd ahte. and þat lond þe Eadwine Ecferþes sune ahte fre
into þe kirke. And of þat lond at Thorp . VIII . acres into
Aescewelle kirke. and of þat lond[3] at Wreningham . VIII . acres
10 into þe elde kirke. and to acres into Fundenhale kirke and to[4]
into Neolondes kirke. þise write sinden þre. on is binnen at sc̄e
Eadmunde. an other at sc̄e Benedicte on Holm. 7 te þridde
haued Eadwine himself.

XXXIV. THE WILL OF KETEL.

Her is on þis write Keteles quide þat is þat ic an Stistede after
15 mine tyme for mine fader soule and for Sefledan into Cristes
kirke. And ic wille þat mine men ben alle fre 7 Mann myne
refe þat he sitte on þe fre lond þat ic him to honde habbe leten:ˊ
his time euer fre. and after his time folege þat lond þen oþere.
And ic an into þere kirke þat lond þat Withrich[5] hauede vnder
20 hande and Lewine and Siric and Goding so so geard goð[6] to
Leueriches hyge. And þat no mam[7] him ne forwerne þan
vtgang. And ic wille þat alle þo men þe ic an fre:ˊ þat he[8]
habben alle þinge þe he vnder hande habben buten þat lond.
And ic an þat lond[9] at Herlinge Stigand Archebisscop mine
25 louerd so it stant buten þo men ben alle fre. and ten acres ic an
into þe kirke. and gif ic ongein ne cume:ˊ þan an ic him to min
heregete an helm and a brenie[10]. and hors. and gereade[11]. and
sverd and spere. and ic wille after þe forwarde þat ic and Eadwine.
and Wlfric after mine time fon to alkere þinge þe min ower is
30 þer on tune buten so mikel so ic an into þe kirke. þat is þat
erninglond[12] þat Alfwold mine man haueð vnder hande. and he

---

[1] Addit. MS. heyres.   [2] Ibid. Middeltone.
[3] at lond written after lond and then deleted.   [4] K., T. omit to.
[5] Addit. MS. Withbrich.   [6] T. Gearagod.   [7] Sic MS. for man.
[8] T. hi.   [9] Addit. MS. omits And ic an þat lond.
[10] Ibid. bronie.   [11] Ibid. goreaude.   [12] Addit. MS. and T. eringlond.

namely, that Ketel is to pay each year to St Edmund's two pounds—that is the rent of the estate—and one mass [shall be said] every day for the souls of both of them. And after Ketel's death, the estate is to go to St Edmund's without controversy; and [that] at Melton to the church which Thurward owned; and the land which Edwin, Ecgferth's son, had, free to the church; and eight acres from the estate at Thorpe, to Ashwell church; and eight acres from the estate at Wreningham to the old church, and two acres to Fundenhall church, and two to Nayland church.

There are three of these documents. One is at St Edmund's: the second at St Benedict's at Holme: the third Edwin himself has.

XXXIV. THE WILL OF KETEL.

Here in this document is Ketel's will: namely, that I grant Stisted to Christchurch after my time, for the sake of my father's soul and for Sæflæd's. And it is my will that all my men shall be free, and that my reeve, Mann, shall occupy the free land which I have given over into his possession, for ever freely during his life, and after his death that estate is to go with the other. And I grant to the church the land which Wihtric had in his possession, and Leofwine and Siric and Goding, to where the fence reaches Leofric's hedge; and [I enjoin] that no one shall refuse him egress. And I desire that all the men to whom I grant freedom shall have all things which are in their possession except the land.

And I grant to Archbishop Stigand, my lord, the estate at Harling just as it stands, except that the men shall all be free, and that I grant ten acres to the church. And if I do not come back again, I grant to him as my heriot a helmet and a coat of mail and a horse with harness and a sword and a spear. And I desire that in accordance with the agreement Edwin and Wulfric shall after my time succeed to everything which is mine everywhere in that village, except so much as I grant to the church; namely, the land let for services which my man Ælfwold holds; and he is to occupy the other during his life-

sitte on þat other his time. And sithen al þat lond þat him to
honde begeð folege mid þe opere into þe kirke. gif Eadwine min
Em wille helden se felageschipe mid me 7 Wlfric min em[1] ymbe
þat lond at Meþeltune gif wit him ouerbiden:ʹ fon we to þat
5 londe at Thorpe into þat forwarde. þat vre boþere time go þat
lond at Metheltone for vre heldren soule. and vre awene soule
into seinte Benedicte at Holm. And þat lond at Thorpe into
seynt Eadmundes biri. And þat is min and mine sustres Boten
'þat' forwarde. gif ic mine day do her his:ʹ þat ic fon to þat lond
10 at Keteringham. and an marc goldes oþer þe wrth. and gif ic
hire ouerbide:ʹ þanne schal ic habben þat lond at Somerledetone.
and þat ilke forwarde Ic and Gode mine suster habbed speken
gif he me ouerbide. gripe he to þat lond at Walsingham. buten
ten acres þo schulen into þere kirke. And gif ic libbe leng þanne
15 hio. þanne schal ic habben þat lond at Prestone. And ic an
Godric mine brother þat lond at Hemfordham[2] so it me on
hande stand. And Kockeshale[3]. And he scal for þat lond at
Strattune[4] gifen Alwy[5] mine cnihte to pund. And Ic and Algif[6]
mine stepdouhter wit habben wrouth þe forwarde ymbe þat
20 lond at Anhus þat so wether vnker so lengere libbe. habbe þat
lond so mikel so wit þer habben. and gif vnc ban fordsith sceot[7]
on Rome weye:ʹ þanne go þat lond for me and for Sefleð[8] and
for Algiue into seint Eadmundes biri. bute þo men ben alle fre.
And ic an Harold erl after mine time þe halue lond at Moran so
25 ful and so forth so ic it richtlike on godes witnesse and mani
manne mid mine wife[9] bigat. and ic it sithen nawer ne forswat
ne forspilde. And ic bidde þe þurh þene drichtin se þe and alle
schefte schop. gif ic ongen ne cume þat þu it nefre ne let welden
mine vnwinan after me þe mid unrichte sitteð þeron. and nittað
30 it me euere to vnþanke. And ic an þe lond at Fretinge after
þat ilke forwarde þat þu þe self and Stigand Archebiscop mine
louerd wrouhten. And ic an Alfric mine prest and mine cuthen þat
lond at Rissewrthe. And gif ani man si so disi þat wille mine
quide bereuen. god him fordo on domesday and alle his halegan.

---

[1] T. *min em Wlfric.*   [2] Addit. MS. *Homfordham.*
[3] Ibid. *Bocchesʹhale.* T. *Keckeshale.*
[4] The MS. has an abbreviation mark standing for *a* and something else.
Addit. MS. *Stantone.*   [5] Ibid. *Aylwy.*   [6] Ibid. *Aylfig.*
[7] Ibid. and T. *sceet.*   [8] Addit. MS. *Selfled.*   [9] Ibid. *wyse.*

time. And afterwards all the land which comes into his possession is to go with the other to the church.

If Edwin my uncle will maintain the partnership with me and my uncle Wulfric with regard to the estate at Melton, if we outlive him we are to succeed to the estate at Thorpe, on condition that after the death of both of us, the estate at Melton shall go to St Benedict's at Holme, for our ancestors' souls and for our own souls: and the estate at Thorpe to Bury St Edmunds.

And this is the agreement between me and my sister Bote: if I end my life before her, that she is to succeed to the estate at Ketteringham and a mark of gold or the equivalent: and if I outlive her, then I shall have the land at Somerleyton. And my sister Gode and I have made a similar agreement: if she survive me, she is to take possession of the estate at Walsingham, except ten acres which are to go to the church: and if I live longer than she, then I shall have the estate at Preston.

And I grant to my brother Godric the estate at Hainford just as it stands in my possession, and Coggeshall. And for the land at Stratton (?) he shall give Ælfwig my servant two pounds. And I and my stepdaughter Ælfgifu have made an agreement about the estate at Onehouse that whichever of us shall live the longer, is to have as much land as the two of us have there. And if death befall us both on the way to Rome, the estate is to go to Bury St Edmunds for me and for Sæflæd and for Ælfgifu, but the men are all to be free.

And I grant to Earl Harold after my time the half estate at *Moran*, as fully and completely as I rightfully acquired it with my wife in the witness of God and many men: and I have since neither lost it by lawsuit (?) nor forfeited it. And I beseech you by the Lord who created you and all creatures, that if I do not come back, you will never let it be possessed after my time by my enemies who wrongfully occupy it and make use of it to my continual injury. And I grant the estate at Frating according to the agreement which you yourself and Archbishop Stigand my lord made. And I grant to Ælfric, my priest and relation, the estate at Rushford. And if anyone be so foolish as to wish to detract from my will, may God and all his saints destroy him on the Day of Judgment.

XXXV. BISHOP ÆTHELMÆR'S BEQUEST TO BURY.

[O]n vre drichtines name ic Ailmer biscop kithe alle manne
ihwat ic habbe vnnen into sc̄e Eadmunde þat is þat lond at
Hindringham. and þat lond at Langham. and þat lond at Hildoluestone 7 þat lond at Suanetone mid[1] alle þe þinge þat ic þerto
5 bigete'n' habbe. and þertoeken half Hundred marc silueres and
ihu so ic Wende mine cuide⸴ ic Wille þat þis stonde euere
vnawent mine soule to lisidnesse. And se þe þise quide wenden
wille⸴ Wende god his ansene him from on domisday.

XXXVI. THE BEQUEST OF THURKIL AND
ÆTHELGYTH TO BURY.

[Þ]urkil and Aþelgit[2] vnnen Wigorham into seynt Eadmunde
10 so ful and so forth so wit it owen. after vnker bother day and
þo men halffre þeowe 7 lisingar[3]. Se þe þis benime. god him
benime heuene riche.

XXXVII. THE WILL OF SIFLÆD.

[H]er sviteleþ ihu Sifled an hire aihte ouer hire day. þat is
erst into seynt Eadmunde Marþingforð for hire leue soule. al
15 buten tuenti acres. and tueye Waine gong wudes. and þere Wude
norþouer. 7 min kirke be fre. And Wlmer prest singe þerat. and
his bearntem so longe. so he þen to þen hode. and fre leswe into
þere kirke. and mine men fre. And be seynt Eadmund mund[4]
þer ouer þene freschot. Se þe þise cuide wille awenden be he
20 amansid from god almichtin 7 from alle hise halegen 7 fram sc̄e
Eadmunde.

---

[1] T. and.
[3] K., T. lisingas.
[2] K., T. Æþelgit.
[4] K. omits mund.

XXXV. BISHOP ÆTHELMÆR'S BEQUEST TO BURY.

In our Lord's name I, Bishop Æthelmær, declare to all men what I have granted to St Edmund's. That is, the estate at Hindringham and the estate at Langham and the estate at Hindolveston and the estate at Swanton, with all the things which I have acquired there, and in addition half a hundred marks of silver.

And however I may change my will, it is my wish that this shall ever remain unchanged for the redemption of my soul. And he who wishes to change this bequest—may God turn his face from him on the Day of Judgment.

XXXVI. THE BEQUEST OF THURKIL AND ÆTHELGYTH TO BURY.

[We] Thurkil and Æthelgyth grant to St Edmund's after the death of both of us Wereham with all the rights with which we possess it, and also the men, [both those who are] half-free and slaves and freedmen.

He who detracts from this, may God deprive him of the kingdom of heaven.

XXXVII. THE WILL OF SIFLÆD.

Here it is made known how Siflæd grants her possessions after her death. First to St Edmund's for her dear soul, Marlingford, all except twenty acres and two wagonloads of wood and the woods over to the north. And my church is to be free and Wulfmær my priest is to sing at it, he and his issue, so long as they are in holy orders. And free meadow to the church. And my men are to be free. And may St Edmund be guardian there over the free property.

He who wishes to alter this will, may he be excommunicated from Almighty God and from all his saints and from St Edmund.

XXXVIII. ANOTHER WILL OF SIFLÆD.

[H]er Switeleþ on þis write ihu Sifled vthe hire aihte þo sche
ouer se ferde. þat is erst into þe tunkirke on Mardingforð
. v . acres 7 ane toft. 7 . ii . acres medwe and to wayne gong to
wude. and ic mine landsethlen here toftes to owen aihte 7 alle
5 mine men fre. And ic an eiþer mine brother ane wayn gong to
wude. And ic an into Northwich to Cristes kirke . iiii . retheren.
and to into sce Marian and on into mine duzme[1]. and ic an into
seynt Eadmunde al þat þere to lafe gesceotte. þat beth on
Mardingforða. hus and hom. 7 wude and feld. 7 on medwe. and
10 on yrue. And gif ic hom cume: þanne wille ic sitten on þat
londe mine day. and after mine day: stonde þat cuide. and wo
so þis awende: god awende his ansene from him on domesday
buten he it here bete.

XXXIX. THE WILL OF ULF AND MADSELIN.

Þis is seo feorewearde þe Vlf 7 Madselin[2] his gebedda worhtan
15 wið[3] 7 wið sce PETER. þa hig to Ierusalem ferdon. þat is þat
land æt Carlatune into Burh. æfter heora dæge heora saule to
alysendnesse. 7 þat land æt Bytham into Sce Guthlace. 7 þat
land æt Sempingaham. into sce Benedicte to Ramesege. 7 þat
land æt Lofintune 7 hæt Heordewican. Ealdrede. ƀ. to fullon
20 ceape. 7 þat land æt Scillintune. 7 æt Houcbig. 7 æt Mortune.
þæron stent þam bisceope eahta marca goldes. 7 gif hig ham
cuman gylde þam. ƀ. his gold. 7 gif heora naðer ne cumð. do
se ƀ for heora saule. swa mycel swa þat land is betere þene þæt
gold sy. 7 gif þam ƀ getid buton eal teala. ga þe aƀƀ Brand to
25 þam ilcan foreweardan. 7 þæt land æt Mannethorp Ic habbe
geunnan þam abbot Brande. 7 þæt land æt Willabyg ic habbe
geunnan Siferðe minen mæge 7 þæt land æt Stoce he[4] hafað
geunnan Lyfgyfan hyre magan. þæt land æt Stroðistune heo

---

[1] Or in. T., K. duzine. [2] K., T. Madselm.
[3] Sic MS. [4] T. heo.

XXXVIII. ANOTHER WILL OF SIFLÆD.

Here in this document it is made known how Siflæd granted her possessions when she went across the sea.

First, to the village church in Marlingford five acres and one homestead and two acres of meadow and two wagonloads of wood; and to my tenants their homesteads as their own possession: and all my men [are to be] free. And I grant to each of my brothers a wagonload of wood. And I grant to Christchurch at Norwich four head of cattle, and two to St Mary's, and one to my.... And I grant to St Edmund's all that may happen to be left of my property, that is house and homestead in Marlingford, with wood and open land, meadow and live stock.

And if I come home, then I wish to occupy that estate for my life; and after my death the will is to take effect. And whosoever alters this, may God turn away his face from him on the Day of Judgment, unless he repent it here.

XXXIX. THE WILL OF ULF AND MADSELIN.

This is the agreement which Ulf and his wife Madselin made with [God] and with St Peter when they went to Jerusalem. That is, the estate at Carlton to Peterborough after their death for the redemption of their souls; and the estate at Bytham to St Guthlac's; and the estate at Sempringham to St Benedict's at Ramsey.

And to Bishop Ealdred the estates at Lavington and Hardwick as a complete purchase, and the estates at Skillington and Hoby and Morton, on which the Bishop has a mortgage of eight marks of gold; and if they return home, the Bishop is to be paid his gold; but if neither of them return, the Bishop is to supply for their souls' sake as much as the land is worth above that gold. And if it should go other than well with the Bishop, the Abbot Brand is to succeed on these same terms.

And I have granted the estate at Manthorpe to the Abbot Brand. And I have granted the estate at Wilby to my kinsman Siferth. And she has granted the estate at Stoke to her kins-

hafað geunnan I[n]gemunde. 7 he hyre¹ þa Westhealle ongean
æt Wintringatune. 7 þ land æt Ofertune syllæ man. 7 do for
heora begra saule. 7 twa land ic habbe geunnen minre modar.
þ is Kitlebig. 7 Cotum. 7 heo hæfð me geunnen Mæssingaham.
5 7 Kytlebi. 7 gif ic ham ne cume. habbe Ingemund þ land æt
Coringatune. 7 þ land æt Cleaxbyg. Ic habbe geunnen Healþene
minan breþer. 7 þ land æt Vrmesbyg Into sce MARIAN stowe.
7 eal þ ic þer ahte. 7 Lindbeor'h'ge habban mine cnihtas gif ic
ham ne cume. 7 þ land æt Lohtune þ heo hafað þ'er'inne². into
10 Þornege.

¹ K., T. supply *an* here.　　　² Sic MS.

woman Leofgifu. And she has granted the estate at Stroxton to Ingemund, and he [has granted] to her in return the west hall at Winterton.

And the estate at Overton is to be sold, and [the money] employed for the souls of both of us. And I have granted two estates to my mother, namely Kettleby and Keelby Cotes, and she has granted to me Messingham and Kettleby. And if I do not come home Ingemund is to have the estate at Kirmington. And I have granted the estate at Claxby to my brother Healden; and the estate at Ormsby and all that I possessed there to St Mary's monastery. And my servants are to have Limber if I do not come home; and the estate at *Lohtun* which she has there [is to go] to Thorney.

NOTES

I.

MS. Cambridge University Library, MS. FF. 2. 33, f. 48. This is the Sacrist's Register of the Abbey of Bury St Edmunds, written about the beginning of the fourteenth century.

EDITIONS. K. 957.
           T. p. 512.
           B. 1008.

DATE. Between 942 and about 951. Theodred bequeathes an estate at Southery, and King Edmund granted this to him in 942 (B. 774). Theodred does not appear as a witness after 951, except in a charter of Edred (B. 910), which is wrongly dated 955. His death must have occurred soon after his last signature, as between the date of this and Bishop Brihthelm's signature in 953 must be placed the episcopate of Wulfstan.

p. 2, l. 1. *þeodred Lundeneware Biscop.* Theodred's signatures occur from 926 to 951. His reference to his see at Hoxne (see p. 102) shows that he was also Bishop of Suffolk. The history of this see is obscure at this date, but we know that later Norfolk and Suffolk formed one diocese under the Bishop of Elmham, and this may have been so already at this time. Theodred is in possession of estates in Norfolk, but does not mention Elmham. His name does not occur in the list of East Anglian bishops in Stubbs (*Registrum Sacrum Anglicanum*, 1897 edition, p. 231), but no name is recorded there between 870, the year of Humbert's death, and 956 when Eadulf's first signature appears. Very little is known about Theodred. W. M. (*G. P.* p. 144) says he was nicknamed 'the Good', and relates a story of his lifelong repentance for having condemned some thieves captured at St Edmund's Abbey by the intervention of the saint himself. The same story is told by Abbo in his *Passio S. Edmundi* (*Memorials of St Edmund's Abbey*, R.S. I, pp. 20 f.). It was by Theodred that King Athelstan sent word to the archbishop that he considered the laws against young thieves too severe (VI Athelstan, 12. 1).

Theodred may be a German name (see Forssner, *Continental-Germanic Personal Names in England*, p. 231). It is noteworthy that two, or perhaps three, of his legatees bear German names (see p. 103).

l. 4. *Eldrene*, or possibly 'parents'. As there is nothing to tell us which the testator meant, I have here, and throughout, translated 'ancestors'.

l. 6. *þat he an.* Changes from the first to the third person, or *vice versa*, are very common in Anglo-Saxon wills.

heregete. The earliest reference to heriot occurs in the will of the Ealdorman Æthelwold (Harmer, xx) between 946 and 955, probably before the end of 947. From this date onwards few wills are without a bequest of this kind. In earlier wills no heriot occurs, but such wills are few in number and in them bequests of chattels of any kind are rare. The written document for the transfer of property was a foreign importation into England and was at first used only for the transfer of land. It is only after the middle of the tenth century that references to other possessions become common in wills. The heriot probably has its origin in the Teutonic custom by which the weapons presented by the lord to his follower reverted to him on the latter's death (see *Beowulf*, ll. 452 f., and cf. Brunner, *Forschungen zur Geschichte des deutschen und französischen Recht*, pp. 22 f., where similar customs among the Lombards and Visigoths are described). By the middle of the tenth century the lord appears to have been expected to respect the will of his follower and prevent its violation in return for this payment of heriot. To obtain this support heriot was paid by ecclesiastics, and sometimes by women. A scale of the amounts due from various ranks of society in payment of heriot is given in II Cnut, 71, but the existence of an earlier standard is implied by Wulfric's phrase *þa wæpna þe þærto gebyriað* (p. 46, l. 8) and the vague instructions in the wills of Bishop Ælfsige and Archbishop Ælfric (p. 16, l. 4; p. 52, l. 23). Cnut does not include ecclesiastics in his list, and possibly it was a voluntary payment from them. Bishop Theodred's heriot is extremely large, more than an earl's, though the horses and weapons are those due from a king's thegn in Cnut's time. A later Bishop of Elmham, the testator of No. xvi, paid only two marks of gold, i.e. rather less than a king's thegn. Bishop Ælfwold of Crediton (see *Crawford Charters*, x) gave as heriot a ship, in addition to the amount due from a king's thegn.

l. 7. *marcas arede goldes*. For O.E. *mancusa reades goldes*. In late copies of O.E. documents the word *mancus* was often replaced by *marc*. The mancus was equivalent to 30 silver pence (see Chadwick, pp. 23 f.), whereas the mark of gold appears to have been equated with 300 West Saxon shillings (see *ibid.* p. 50). 200 marks of gold would therefore be an impossibly high sum for the payment of heriot, fifty times that of an earl as stated by Cnut. The mark was originally a Scandinavian weight, and first occurs in England in Alfred and Guthrum, 2.

l. 10. *Dukeswrthe*. Duxford, Cambridgeshire. D.B. 1, f. 196 a, has *Dochesuuorde*, an estate of 3½ hides held in King Edward's time by Stigand, who had been Bishop of Elmham.

Illyntone. Probably Illington, near Thetford, Norfolk.

l. 11. *Earnningtone*. Arrington, Cambridgeshire.

Eadgiue. Perhaps the queen-mother, the third wife of Edward the Elder. See p. 132.

l. 12. *sče Paules kirke.* The cathedral church of his see of London.

l. 13. *messehaclen*. This occurs as a gloss for *casula* (Wright-Wülker, 327. 22).

l. 16. *Tit* (for *Cic*). Now St Osyth, Essex. It is entered as *Cice* in D.B. II, f. 11 (*V. C. H. of Essex*, I, p. 439), where it is an estate of 7 hides belonging to the Bishop of London.

l. 17. *bedlonde*. This represents O.E. *beodlande*, an estate the income of which was set apart to provide food for the community. (See B.T. *Suppl.*)

ll. 17 f. *þe men þe þer aren fre men alle*. A synod at *Celchyth* in 816 ordained that English men were to be freed on the death of a bishop (see Haddan and Stubbs, *Councils and Ecclesiastical Documents*, III, p. 583). Theodred draws no distinction between slaves enslaved for crime and others, as is done by some testators of the tenth century.

l. 18. *Suthereye*. Southery, Norfolk. Theodred had received land in the island of *Suthereye* from King Edmund in 942 (B. 774).

l. 21. *Tillingham*. Tillingham, Essex. It was still an estate of the canons of St Paul's at the time of the Domesday Survey, and was assessed at just over 20 hides (D.B. II, f. 13: *V.C.H. of Essex*, I, p. 442).

l. 23. *Dunemowe*. Dunmow, Essex.

l. 24. *Mendham*. Mendham, Suffolk.

Osgote. This name is an anglicised form of the O.Icel. *Ásgautr* (see Björkman, p. 14).

ll. 25 f. *buten ic wille...to þere kirke*. This sentence is incomplete and the reading I have supplied may not be the true one. Perhaps we should assume an omission after *minstre* and take the last phrase by itself.

l. 25. *minstre*. In the laws from the second half of the tenth century the term *mynster* is applied to a church, and not confined to a monastic establishment (see II Edgar, 1. 1, 2. 2, 3. 1, V Ethelred, 12. 1, VIII Ethelred, 3, etc., and cf. Liebermann, *Glossar s.v.*; A. J. Robertson, *The Laws of the Kings of England from Edmund to Henry I*, p. 406). The reference in this will is, however, definitely to some sort of religious community, for Theodred speaks of the *hewen* on p. 2, l. 27. As there is no reference elsewhere to a monastery at Mendham, and the will is before the days of the monastic revival, perhaps only a small group of canons is meant. In other wills 'minsters' are mentioned of whose existence we have no evidence elsewhere, e.g. that at Walkhampstead (p. 28, l. 13) and that at Colne, Essex (p. 76, l. 9), which Leofgifu bequeathes to two priests and a deacon some time about 1040. If these were monastic communities, they were apparently of short duration, but it is probable that the word 'minster' is used in the same sense as in the laws.

l. 26. *Scotforð*. Shotford, near Mendham, Suffolk.

l. 27. *Mydicaham*. Mettingham, Suffolk.

l. 28. *þat lond at Silham. 7 at Isestede...* This is an elliptical expression for *þat lond at S. 7 þat lond at I.* I have therefore translated by the plural, 'estates', wherever this construction is used.

Silham. Syleham, Suffolk.

Isestede. This name is preserved in Instead Manor House in Weybread, Suffolk.

Chikeringe. Chickering, near Hoxne, Suffolk.

l. 29. *Aysfeld*. This is more probably Ashfield Green, about 3 miles S.E. of Chickering, than Ashfield near Debenham, some 10 miles to the south.

Wrtinham. I have not been able to identify this place.

þe smale londe. Professor Chadwick has suggested to me the possibility that this means 'strips' of land.

l. 30. *Horham*. Horham, Suffolk.

Elyngtone. Karlström, *Old English Compound Place-Names in -ing*, p. 79, identifies this as Athelington, Suffolk.

l. 31. *Hoxne*. Hoxne, Suffolk. Below, Theodred speaks of his *biscopriche* here, and in Edward the Confessor's time the church of Hoxne was the centre of the diocese of Suffolk (D.B. II, f. 379: *V. C. H. of Suffolk*, I, p. 515). It is clear, therefore, that, although from the middle of the tenth century, at the latest, there was only one bishopric in East Anglia, it had a Suffolk centre at Hoxne as well as a Norfolk centre at Elmham. Just before 1040 a Bishop of Elmham makes bequests to bodies of priests at both places (see p. 72, ll. 20 f.).

sēe Aethelbrichtes kirke. This was dedicated to the East Anglian king whose death at King Offa's hands is mentioned in the Chronicle 792. For later legends see W. M., *G. R.* p. 84, *G. P.* p. 305; *Vita Duorum Offarum*, in Watt's edition of Matthew Paris, Appendix, pp. 23 f.; Matthew Paris, *Chronica Majora*, R.S. I, p. 355; Hardy, *Catalogue*, R.S. I, pp. 494 f.

l. 32. *Luthinglond*. Lothingland, the name of a Suffolk hundred.

p. 4, l. 2. *Osgote mine mey Eadulfes sune*. This is no doubt the Osgot mentioned as the former owner of Pakenham in Edward the Confessor's writ in favour of Bury (K. 851). Later Bury tradition attributed the gift of Pakenham to Osgot Clapa (*Memorials of St Edmund's Abbey*, R.S. I, p. 364), but this is probably a substitution of the name of the more famous man. All the estates left by Theodred to Osgot seem to have come into the possession of Bury by 1066 (see D.B. II, ff. 361 b f.: *V. C. H. of Suffolk*, I, pp. 497 ff.).

l. 3. *Bertune...Rucham...Pakenham*. Great Barton, Rougham and Pakenham, Suffolk.

ll. 4 f. *Newetune...Horninggeshæthe...Ikewrthe...Wepstede*. Nowton near Horningsheath, Horningsheath, Ickworth and Whepstead, Suffolk. These were all held by Bury in 1066 (D.B. II, ff. 356 b f.: *V. C. H. of Suffolk*, I, pp. 492 f.).

l. 5. *sēe Eadmundes kirke*. The Benedictine abbey was not founded until Cnut's reign. Before that time there was a small community of secular canons guarding the relics of St Edmund, which were originally at Hoxne but were transferred to Bury (*Bedericesworth*) some time early in the tenth century.

l. 6. *Waldringfeld*. Waldringfield, Suffolk.

l. 8. *Gypeswich.* Ipswich, Suffolk.
Wrtham. Wortham, Suffolk.
l. 10. *þen Archebiscope.* Oda, Archbishop of Canterbury from 942 to 958.
l. 11. *biscopriche.* The dictionaries do not include episcopal demesne or property among their translations of this word, but it can hardly mean anything else on p. 16, l. 3, and in the present instance if we understand it to mean 'bishopric', 'diocese', it is difficult to know what is meant by *binnen Lundene and buten Lundene.*
ll. 12 f. *at Hoxne at mine biscopriche.* See p. 102.
ll. 14 ff. *7 Ic wille...half for mine soule.* In these clauses Theodred makes arrangements about those estates which he held in virtue of his office. He cannot dispose of the land, but only of the stock which he has added to that already on the estates when he became bishop. It is landed property of this type to which Æthelflæd refers as *bisceophamæ* (see p. 34, l. 27).
l. 21. *Wunemannedune.* Unidentified.
Sceon. Sheen, Surrey.
l. 22. *Fullenham.* Fulham, Middlesex. In D.B. 1, f. 127 b, this is entered as a manor of 40 hides belonging to the Bishop of London, and it is expressly stated that it belongs and belonged to the bishopric.
buten hwe mine manne fre wille. mine manne must represent an O.E. genitive plural. The subject of the clause seems to be the *men* of the principal sentence. *hwe* is apparently for O.E. *hwone.*
l. 23. *Denesige.* Dengie, Essex.
l. 25. *Glastingbiri.* Glastonbury Abbey, Somerset, which had been recently reformed by Dunstan, whom King Edmund made abbot there (Chronicle 943 F and *ibid.* II, p. 144; Fl. Wig. 942).
l. 27. *Gosebricht.* This is not an O.E. name. It represents the German *Gausbert, Gozbert* (see Forssner, *op. cit.* p. 124).
l. 28. *Odgar.* Kemble and Thorpe substitute the more usual name *Ordgar,* but the name *Odgar, Odger* does occur in England and may be either of German or Scandinavian origin (see Forssner, *op. cit.* p. 197).
l. 29. *Gundwine.* This also is a German name (see *ibid.* p. 135).
l. 31. *ic spracacke.* Previous editors have *Spratacke* which they take to be a proper name, assuming the omission of a verb after *ic.* I can find no name resembling this in any Germanic language. I prefer to consider the passage corrupt.

II.

This will should be compared with those of Ælfgar's two daughters (Nos. XIV and XV).

MSS. (*a*) Cambridge University Library, MS. FF. 2. 33, f. 46 (see p. 99).
(*b*) British Museum, Additional MS. 14847 f. 16 b. This MS. is

another fourteenth century Bury cartulary. It is not a copy of (*a*), for in a few instances it has clearly preserved a more original reading. On the whole, however, it is greatly inferior to (*a*), with many omissions, and more misunderstandings of the Old English. The fact that it also has (*a*)'s error of *de brite* for *to brice* shows that both MSS. are from the same source.

The text is from (*a*), but the more important variations in (*b*) are given in the textual notes.

EDITIONS. K. 1222, from (*b*).
T. p. 505, from (*a*).
B. 1012, from (*b*).

DATE. Between 946 and about 951. The Latin rubrics in the cartularies say it is in the time of King Edmund and Bishop Theodred, but this is merely due to the occurrence of these names in the will, where they are mentioned with reference to a past occasion. The phrase 'when I gave to my lord (i.e. the king) the sword which King Edmund gave to me' shows that Edmund was dead before the will was drawn up. Thorpe and Birch date this will 'about 958', probably on account of Ælfgar's signatures in charters (but see following note). Bishop Theodred died soon after 951 and the Ealdorman Eadric does not sign after 949. It seems to me improbable that Ælfgar should have delayed making his will for many years after they informed him of the king's permission.

p. 6, l. 1. *Alfgares*. Ælfgar gives himself no title in his will, but the Chronicle (946 D) calls him ealdorman when referring to the marriage of his daughter Æthelflæd with King Edmund. He first signs *dux* in 945 and continues to do so regularly until 951. After that year the signature *Ælfgar dux* occurs only in two charters of 956 (B. 930, 957), and one of 958 (B. 1027). In the latter it is certainly a mistake for *minister*, referring to the thegn who signs first of the *ministri* in most charters about that time. This thegn is no doubt the king's kinsman who died in Devon in 962 (Chronicle A), and who signs as *regis propinquus* in 958 (B. 1035) and as *consul* in 961 (B. 1074). It is more uncertain whether the two signatures of 956 refer to the testator. Ælfgar appears to have been Ealdorman of Essex, for in his will he is concerned with the eastern counties only, and East Anglia was in the hands of the Ealdorman Æthelstan 'Halfking' throughout this period. We know that later Brihtnoth was Ealdorman of Essex, and as he became an ealdorman in 956 (see p. 106), the occurrence of Ælfgar's name with the title *dux* in 956 may show that Brihtnoth was his immediate successor; but in that case there is difficulty in allotting a sphere of office to an Ealdorman Brihtferth who signs in 955 and 956 (not counting B. 887, which is wrongly dated 950, or B. 1027, a charter of 958 in which Brihtferth *dux* is clearly the man who signs as *minister* both before and after this date). Professor Chadwick (*op. cit.* p. 187) has shown that Brihtferth was probably an ealdorman of one of the eastern provinces, and but for the occurrence of Ælfgar's signature in 956, the most probable explanation would be that he was intermediate between Ælfgar and Brihtnoth in Essex. Unless, however, we regard the title *dux* as applied to Ælfgar in 956 as an error, or, as Chadwick (p. 187) suggests, consider Ælfgar a 'retired earl', we shall have to assume a third province for an ealdorman in the eastern counties about 956.

ll. 1 ff. *þat ic an mine louerd...speren.* This is a smaller heriot than that due from an earl in later days (see II Cnut, 71), even if we include the valuable sword worth altogether 152 mancuses of gold which he had already given to the king (see p. 6, ll. 4 f.).

l. 4. *þeodred bisscop.* The testator of No. 1. See p. 99.

Edric Alderman. He signs as *dux* from 932 till 949. He appears to have been the brother of the Ealdorman Æthelwold whose will is extant (Harmer, xx), and of the Ealdorman Æthelstan of East Anglia.

l. 6. *fetelse*, 'little bag', 'pouch', etc. See B.T.; Grein. B.T. *Suppl.* translates 'belt', but the reasons for this translation are not given.

l. 9. *Athelflede.* The testatrix of No. xiv. See p. 138.

Cokefeld. Cockfield, Suffolk. Cf. p. 36, l. 2; p. 38, l. 30. St Edmund's Abbey held this estate in 1066 (D.B. ii, f. 359: *V. C. H. of Suffolk,* I, p. 495).

Dittone. Fen or Wood Ditton, Cambridgeshire.

l. 10. *Lauenham.* Lavenham, Suffolk.

on þe red. O.E. *on þa* or *þæt gerad.*

l. 12. *aldreday.* In translating this will, I took *aldreday* to represent O.E. *ealdordæg*, 'life-time', but Professor Chadwick has since suggested to me that it is a corruption of O.E. *ealra dæg.* This is more probable, as *ealdordæg* is a purely poetic word. We should, therefore, both here and in l. 24, amend the translation to 'after the death of all of us'.

l. 13. *Beodricheswrthe.* The old name for Bury St Edmunds. See pp. 102, 183.

l. 14. *ouer hire day.* This injunction was not strictly carried out, as Æthelflæd left a life-interest in this estate to her sister and brother-in-law before the estate was to go to a religious community.

l. 19. *Stoke.* Probably Stoke-by-Nayland, Suffolk, near to Polstead and many other of Ælfgar's estates. By the time of D.B. the existence of a religious community there had been forgotten. The manor was held by *Suain* of Essex, and the church there was only in possession of 60 acres (D.B. ii, f. 401: *V. C. H. of Suffolk,* I, p. 538). The estates left by Ælfgar's family to the foundation there were in various hands by 1066. Neither Ælfgar's will nor his daughters' give us any information as to the nature of this religious foundation at Stoke. Ælfflæd recommended it to the protection of the king and the Ealdorman Æthelmær, yet some seventy years later the whole of its large endowment is dispersed among lay-owners.

l. 20. *Babingþirne*. Baythorn, Essex, near Stoke-by-Clare, Suffolk.

l. 21. *min other douhter*. Ælfflæd, wife of the Ealdorman Brihtnoth, and testator of No. xv. See pp. 141 f.

l. 23. *sēe Marie Stowe at Berkynge*. Erkenwald, Bishop of London, founded this nunnery before he became bishop (Bede, *Historia Ecclesiastica*, IV, c. 6–10), but it was probably destroyed by the Danes. Tradition says that it was given by King Edgar to Wulfhild, a nun of Wilton, and restored to its former prosperity (see Capgrave, *Nova Legenda*, *s.v. Wlfhilde*). This authority, however, does not say that it was deserted when Wulfhild received it, and some sort of religious community was no doubt still in existence there, as it is very improbable that this will is as late as Edgar's reign.

l. 24. *Illeye*. Monks Eleigh, Suffolk (cf. p. 38, l. 22). It belonged to Christchurch in 1066 (D.B. II, f. 373: *V. C. H. of Suffolk*, I, p. 509).

l. 25. *Berthnoðe*. Brihtnoth, the hero of the poem on the Battle of Maldon, which describes how he led the local forces against the Viking invaders, and fell in the conflict. This took place in 991 (Chronicle, 991 E, F, 993 A). He is not called ealdorman in Ælfgar's will and does not appear to have reached this dignity until 956, for there is an extant charter of this year (B. 964) granting him an estate at Tadmarton, Oxfordshire, and in it he is called *minister*. But on November 9 of the same year, Edwy granted to him more land at this place, and speaks of him on this occasion as *princeps*, i.e. ealdorman (B. 966). In the later part of his life Brihtnoth was Ealdorman of Essex (see Fl. Wig. 991), and it is possible that he was Ælfgar's successor (see p. 104). *Liber Eliensis*, II, 25, however, shows him holding a shiremoot in Huntingdonshire, and it may be that, as Professor Chadwick (*op. cit.* p. 177) suggests, he held the office of ealdorman there before succeeding to Essex. The *Liber Eliensis* also shows his influence strong in Cambridgeshire, but this may have been on account of extensive estates there. The extant documents in which Brihtnoth appears as the recipient of grants of land do not deal with estates in the eastern counties, but his wife is shown by her will (No. xv) to have possessed lands in Essex, Suffolk and Cambridgeshire, which apparently did not come to her from her own family (see p. 142), and Brihtnoth certainly possessed Rettendon, Essex, at the date of his marriage. It is probable that Brihtnoth was a man of the eastern counties. All the lands we know him to have held elsewhere, Tadmarton (see above), Cookley, Worcestershire (B. 1134), Brayfield, Buckinghamshire (B 1209), Shipford, Oxfordshire (K. 714), and *Micclantun* (*ibid.*), were royal grants. He did not leave any of them to his wife. The history of Tadmarton is curious, for from the very year in which Edwy granted two estates there to Brihtnoth, there is an Abingdon charter (B. 967) stating that Edwy granted to that abbey land at Tadmarton, and this is proved by the boundaries to consist of Brihtnoth's two estates, together with a third which Edwy granted to a *minister* Brihtric, also in 956 (B. 965). If the grant to Abingdon is genuine, we should probably regard it as a confirmation by Edwy of gifts made by Brihtnoth and Brihtric. Brihtnoth is shown by the *Liber Eliensis* and his wife's will to have been a benefactor of Ely also, and a Latin document, according to which he bequeathes Lawling, Eleigh and Hadleigh to Christchurch, is printed by Palgrave (*The Rise and Progress of the English Commonwealth*, 1921 edition, II, p. 314) from the Lambeth MS. 1212. It is dated 991, and, though spurious, may contain information from genuine sources.

l. 28. *Cristes kirke at Caunterbiri.* Canterbury Cathedral.

l. 29. *Colne...Tigan.* Colne and Tey, Essex. There is no means of deciding which places of these names are meant.

p. 8, l. 4. *Piltendone...Mereseye.* Peldon and Mersea, Essex.

l. 5. *lef.* The original may have had *lif*, as on l. 9.

l. 8. *Grenstede.* Greenstead, near Colchester, Essex.

Athelwardes. Perhaps Ælfgar's dead son (cf. p. 6, l. 11).

l. 9. *Wiswiðe.* O.E. *Wigswiðe.* She probably gave her name to the estate first mentioned in Ælfflæd's will (p. 38, l. 16), *Wiswiþetun.* She may have been Ælfgar's wife.

l. 11. *Tidwoldingtone.* D.B. *Tidwoldituna*, an estate of the canons of St Paul's (D.B. II, f. 13 *b*: *V. C. H. of Essex*, I, p. 443). The name is now lost, but the *V. C. H.* identifies the place as Heybridge, near Maldon.

l. 12. *formige*, from the O.E. *feormian*, to provide with a *feorm*, or food-rent.

l. 13. *Paulesbiri.* St Paul's, London.

Totham. Totham, Essex.

l. 15. *wudelond.* This error in the Cambridge MS. is due to the occurrence of *wudelond* in the next sentence.

l. 16. *Aisfeld.* Ashfield, Suffolk.

Eakild. The Additional MS. form (see footnote 15) may represent an O.Icel. *Alfketill*, O.Danish *Alkil* (cf. Björkman, p. 3). *Ayl-* should properly represent O.E. *Æþel-*, but the confusion of the O.E. elements *Ælf-*, *Æþel-* was very great in M.E. The text of this will in the Additional MS. is better than that of most documents contained in that MS., and on the preceding line it has preserved a more original reading. This may be the case here, but if so it is difficult to explain the process of corruption which produced the *Eakild* of the Cambridge MS. I think it more probable that the scribe of the Additional MS. is substituting a name he knows (cf. *Edmund* for the rarer name *Omund* of p. 70, l. 10) and that the document from which both scribes copied had *Ealcild* or *Ealkild*, representing either O.E. *Ealdcild* or *Ealhcild*, with the loss of *d* or *h* between consonants, or more probably, since neither of these combinations occurs elsewhere, an O.E. *Ealhhild*, with loss of initial *h* in the second member of a compound, and the common post-Conquest writing of velar *h* as *c* or *k*. No instance of *Ealh(h)ild* occurs in Searle's *Onomasticon*, but the corresponding name is recorded on the Continent (Forstemann, *Deutsches Namenbuch*, 2nd edition, I, col. 75). The scribe of the Additional MS. could more easily turn *Eal-* into *Ayl-* as the O.E. elements *Eald-, Ealh-, Ælf-, Æþel-* had fallen together at this date (see Zachrisson, *Anglo-Norman Influence on English Place-Names*, p. 109).

l. 17. *Ryssebroc.* Rushbrooke, Suffolk.

l. 18. *Winelme.* This is a masculine name. The *heo* of the next phrase must be a mistake for *he.*

ll. 26 f. *an hide....be hundtuelti acren.* Cf. *Liber Eliensis*, ii, 32: *III hydas de duodecies XX acris* at Horningsea, Cambridgeshire. Evidently some other reckoning of acres to the hide was in use in the east of England in Ælfgar's time, as otherwise he would not have found it necessary to state the number. It is about this time that we begin to find the statement that the hide and the *sulung* are of equal extent, whereas earlier two Mercian or Kentish hides are reckoned to the *sulung* (see p. 130).

l. 26. *Aeulf.* Björkman, p. 36, suggests that this name represents the O.Icel. *Eyiolfr.* In D.B. this name is spelt *Eiulf, Aiolf, Aiulf, Aiulfus.*

III.

ms. British Museum, Harley Charter, viii, 38. This is a single sheet of parchment in a mutilated condition, with several holes, a vertical tear down the middle, and loss of many letters at the edges. Supplied readings are printed between square brackets. The handwriting is considered by the editor of the *British Museum Facsimiles* to be of the eleventh century. The ms. is shown by its frequent insertions and corrections to be a copy, and Keller (*Angelsächsische Paleographie*, in *Palaestra*, xliii, p. 33) says that the scribe is copying an older hand, as certain letters, notably the *y*, are characteristic of documents of the first half of the tenth century. The writing of *st* as *sð, sþ* (see p. 10, l. 9, p. 12, l. 13, p. 14, ll. 9, 15, 18, 21) is also a feature of older West Saxon texts (see Sievers, *Angelsächsische Grammatik*, § 196). On the other hand the fairly frequent writing of *e* for O.E. *ea* (six times in names beginning with *Ead-*, and also in *sem[estran]*, p. 10, l. 30, *bedref*, p. 14, l. 9) show that the diphthong has been monophthongised. Luick considers that this development occurred about the year 1000 (see *Historische Grammatik der englischen Sprache*, § 356). The corrected spelling *re'a'de* on p. 12, l. 12, shows that the *e* spellings are due to the copyist. The document has not been very carefully copied. Some errors have been subsequently rectified, but not all, and one suspects corruption in some words which are inexplicable as they stand, especially the names of the testatrix's slaves.

facsimile. Bond, *Facsimiles of Ancient Charters in the British Museum*, Part iii, No. 38.

editions. K. 1290.
T. p. 533.

date. Perhaps about 950, see following note.

p. 10, l. 1. *Wynflæd*. Kemble, followed by Thorpe and Bond, dates this will 995. This is no doubt due to the identification of Wynflæd with a woman of the same name who was concerned in a legal transaction about 994 (K. 693). To me there seems little evidence for this identification. Wynflæd is not a very uncommon name, and none of the estates concerned in this transaction is mentioned in the will.

In the will, Wynflæd refers to 'the church' (p. 10, l. 2) and the 'refectory' (p. 10, l. 3, p. 12, l. 15) without further distinction, in a way that suggests that she was closely connected with some religious community. In one place she refers to her 'nun's clothing' (p. 14, l. 17). Yet she can hardly have been a cloistered nun, since she is in control of estates and other possessions. Two nunneries are mentioned in the will; the first, Wilton, occurs just after, and is apparently distinct from, the church and refectory which she finds it unnecessary to name. The second nunnery, Shaftesbury, occurs on p. 12, l. 26, and Wynflæd and the community there both have interests in a certain estate. It may well be Shaftesbury with which Wynflæd was connected.

In 942 King Edmund gave two estates to a *religiose sancte conversacionis monialis femine Wenflede* who was probably connected with Shaftesbury, since the grant is preserved in the cartulary of that abbey (B. 775). The estates, Cheselbourne and Winterborne, are in Dorset. It seems to me highly probable that the grantee of this charter is the testatrix of the will. The latter certainly had some connection with a religious community, which would explain the title, and the date would agree well with the palaeographical evidence (see p. 108). The King Edward who had granted the *worþig* to her mother Brihtwyn (see p. 14, ll. 29 f.) would then be identified as Edward the Elder, and Brihtwyn might be the *Beorhtwen*, wife of the brother of Bishop Ælffrith of Sherborne, who was given five hides at Archet in 939 (B. 744).

What Wynflæd's exact relationship was to the nunnery is not clear. Possibly she was a lay-abbess. Little is known about English monastic life at this period, before the reform movement of Edgar's reign. Wynflæd may merely have been a widow who had taken the vow of chastity (see André, *Widows and Vowesses* in *Archaeological Journal*, 1892, pp. 74 f.) and become an associate of the nunnery.

l. 2. *into cyrcan*. Perhaps Shaftesbury. See preceding note.

ofringsceat. Bishop Æthelwold gave *iii offrincsceattas* (for *-sceatas*) to Peterborough (B. 1128), along with altar-cloths, corporals, vestments, etc. No doubt a cloth for use in the Eucharistic service, possibly a chalice-veil, is meant.

l. 4. *saulsceatte*. Wynflæd uses this word generally of any charitable payments for the good of her soul, but often the word is used in a more limited sense, a payment to the religious foundation as a price for burial. This was a church due, not a mere voluntary payment, and was regulated by the laws. These state that it is to be paid 'at the open grave', and to the *mynster* which has the right to it, even if the body is buried elsewhere (I Athelstan, 4, repeated in later codes). Liebermann, *Glossar, s.v. Seelschatz,* quoting Brunner (*Fortleben der Toten,* 9. 12 f.), regards this payment as a survival of the 'dead's portion', a third part of the goods, which was placed in the grave or laid on the pyre. But there is no evidence that in Anglo-Saxon times the *sawolsceatt* was a third of the goods, and it is sometimes paid in land (see e.g. p. 52, ll. 2 f.). The Latin equivalent is *sepultura.* In D.B. we read of powerful churches which had secured the right of *sepultura* over several districts (e.g. D.B. 1, f. 87 *b*: *V. C. H. of Somerset,* 1, p. 443).

godes þeowe. This term included monks and nuns as well as priests (see V Ethelred, 4. 1).

l. 5. *Æþel...þe.* If, with Kemble, we take the first missing letter as *s,* the name is probably Æthelswith, but only one stroke of this letter is visible. The name Æthelfrith is another possibility.

l. 6. *Wiltune.* Wilton Nunnery, Wiltshire. The only information we have concerning the origin of this foundation is the late tradition contained in the fifteenth century *Chronicon Vilodunense* (Cotton Faustina B. III, ed. by R. C. Hoare), where it is stated that the first foundation was due to *Wolstan* (i.e. Weohstan), the Ealdorman of Wiltshire whose death is mentioned in the Chronicle, 800. His foundation was for secular priests, but later King Egbert and his sister turned it into a nunnery. According to the same authority, King Alfred founded a new nunnery there.

Fugele. This name is instanced elsewhere, e.g. as that of a moneyer in the tenth century (see Stenton, *Place-Names in Berkshire,* p. 18, note; Redin, *Studies on Uncompounded Personal Names in Old English,* p. 6).

ll. 7 f. *hyre mentelpreon.* In Wright-Wülker, 152. 37, *fibula* is glossed *preon vel oferfeng vel dalc.* In illuminated MSS. of this period almost every man and woman is depicted wearing a brooch to fasten the mantle or cloak, sometimes at the throat, sometimes on the shoulder. The usual shape is round, but oblong and rectangular brooches also are depicted.

l. 8. *Ebbelesburnan.* Ebbesborne Wake, Wiltshire.

l. 12. *Ceorlatune.* Probably Charlton Horethorne, Dorset.

l. 14. *Mylenburnan.* Probably Milborne Port, Dorset.

l. 15. *Cinnuc...Gyfle.* Chinnock and Yeovil, Somerset.

Eadmære. He is probably Wynflæd's son. On p. 12, l. 11, she speaks of her children, but only one daughter is referred to in the will. On p. 12, l. 28, Wynflæd refers to a son's daughter, Eadgifu. Eadmær is clearly Eadwold's father (see p. 10, ll. 20 f.), and from p. 14, l. 31, we know that Eadwold had a sister. It seems probable therefore that Wynflæd had two children, Æthelflæd and Eadmær, who was the father of Eadgifu and Eadwold. Searle in his *Onomasticon* makes Eadmær Æthelflæd's husband.

l. 16. *C[ol]les[h]ylle*. Coleshill, Berkshire.

Inggeneshamme. Perhaps Inglesham, Wiltshire.

l. 17. *Faccancu[mbe]*. Faccombe, Hampshire.

morgengyfu. The gift made by the husband to his wife on the morning after the marriage. See Young, *Anglo-Saxon Family Law*, in *Essays in Anglo-Saxon Law*, pp. 174 f.; Buckstaff, *Essay on Married Women's Property*, in *Annals of the American Academy of Political and Social Science*, IV, pp. 42 f. A widow retained her *morgengifu* unless she remarried during her first year of widowhood.

ll. 22 f. *he him læte...Ead[b]urggebyrig*. Thorpe assumes an omission after *oþer to*, but this is unnecessary. The *to* completes the sense of *læte*.

l. 23. *Ead[b]urggebyrig*. Adderbury, Oxfordshire.

l. 25. *Waneting*. Wantage, Berkshire.

l. 26. *Scrifenanhamme*. Shrivenham, Berkshire.

l. 27. *Cillariðe*. Childrey, Berkshire.

l. 30. *crencestran*. This is the only occurrence of this word noted in B.T., where it is compared with *cranc-stæf* mentioned in a list of weaving implements.

sem[estra]n. The emendation is Kemble's. The word occurs also on p. 72, l. 9, but there it refers to a male tailor.

p. 12, ll. 1 ff. *freoge man Gerburge 7 Miscin*... These lists of the names of her slaves are peculiar to Wynflæd's will, other wills merely referring to 'all my men' in the manumission clauses. Some of Wynflæd's slaves have very extraordinary names, e.g. *Miscin*, l. 2, *Pifus*, l. 4, *Gurhan*, l. 7. One suspects un-English origin, or corruption by the later scribe.

l. 5. *Sprow*. This name occurs in the *Liber Eliensis*, II, 31.

l. 6. *Gersande*. Forssner (*Continental-Germanic Personal Names in England*, p. 109) considers this a continental name, and compares it with Old German *Gersind(a)*.

Snel. This forms the first element in place-names such as Snelton, Snelsmore (see Stenton, *The Place-Names of Berkshire*, p. 40; Redin, *op. cit.* p. 25).

l. 7. *Bican*. This name occurs also in B. 225, 304. See Redin, *op. cit.* p. 85.

Æffan. Æffa occurs fairly frequently elsewhere. It is probably a short form of the *Ælf-* compounds.

l. 10. *witeþeowman*. In the laws, slavery is the penalty for working on a Sunday (Ine, 3. 2; Edward and Guthrum, 7. 1); for theft under certain conditions (Ine, 7. 1; II Edward, 6; VI Athelstan, 12. 2); for incest (Edward and Guthrum, 4). It is also one of the alternatives for a condemned man who reaches sanctuary (*Be Grithe*, 16). No doubt in many other cases failure to pay a fine or compensation resulted in at least temporary slavery. Ine, 62, deals with the case of a man enslaving himself to a lender who pays the fine for him. When slavery was the penalty for incest, the king owned the man and the bishop the woman. Private owners are in possession of *witeþeowas* already in Ine's time (Ine, 24), and a clause manumitting such slaves is not uncommon in the wills (cf. e.g. p. 16, l. 2, p. 20, l. 8 etc.). It is uncertain whether the private owner held these *witeþeowas* as compensation for theft or other crime committed against him, or as one of the profits resulting from ownership of jurisdiction. Æthelstan Ætheling's phrase *on spræce* perhaps implies the latter (see p. 56, l. 15 and note). The distinction between men enslaved for crime and others is not made in wills after the reign of Ethelred. Wills later than this speak simply of 'men' when they contain manumission clauses. This may, however, be due to the locality of these wills, not the date, as only East Anglian wills are preserved from the later period and the penal slave is not specifically mentioned in East Anglian wills even of an earlier period.

ll. 14 f. *scencingcuppan*. Cf. O.E. *scencan*, 'to give to drink', 'to pour out'. Cups of various shapes and sizes are depicted in illuminated MSS. of the tenth and eleventh centuries, but we do not know how to allot the various names. A 'scencing' cup may have been a specially ornate cup to offer to guests. Cf. Old German *scenche-bechar* glossing *calix* (see B.T. *s.v. scencing-cuppe*).

l. 15. *ieredan*: for O.E. *gieredan*.

l. 21. *gedong*. Apparently a scribal error for O.E. *gedon*.

l. 24. *Hafene*. Avon, Wiltshire.

ll. 24 f. 7 [*h*]*e his fæder syððan*. I do not understand the meaning of this transaction.

ll. 25 ff. *be þan lande æt Cinnuc...7 þa men*. Wynflæd has evidently possessed a life-interest only in this estate.

l. 26. *Sceaftesbyrig*. Shaftesbury, Dorset. See p. 109. This nunnery had been founded by Alfred (see Asser, *Life of King Alfred*, ed. Stevenson, c. 98). Little is known of its history until it became famous as the burial-place of Edward the Martyr (Chronicle, 980 E).

ll. 27 f. *þara gebura þe on þam gafollande sittað*. In Ine's laws the terms *gebur* and *gafolgelda* together appear to cover the whole peasant population. See Attenborough, *The Laws of the Earliest English Kings*, p. 184, and Chadwick, p. 87 note, where it is suggested that the *gebur* was distinguished from the *gafolgelda* because he did not possess land of his own, or at least not so much as a hide. Wynflæd's 'geburs' are evidently not free to choose their own lord, for she disposes of them by will. This means that she transfers to another lord the dues and services which they paid to her. Possibly these were similar to those rendered by the *gebur* in *Rectitudines Singularum Personarum*, 4 f., but the author of this treatise expressly states that customs vary in different parts of the country. In D.B. 1, f. 38, 38 *b*, *buri* are equated with *coliberti*, or freedmen, though *gebur* has not so limited a meaning in Anglo-Saxon times. There are, however, passages in wills which may be taken to show that the freedman, like the *gebur*, can be disposed of by will (see p. 165). We may compare the Treaty of Alfred and Guthrum, 2, where it is stated that the *ceorl ðe on gafollande sit* is to have the same wergild as the Danish freedman.

l. 28. *syna*. Such a form never occurs elsewhere. I take it to be a scribal error, probably due to a repetition of the *y* of the preceding word.

p. 14, l. 2. *Burhwynne Mærtin*. Probably an 'and' has been omitted. Burhwyn is a feminine name.

Hisfig. Kemble emends to *his wif*, but the reading of the MS. is clearly *fig* and it seems unlikely that the scribe should corrupt a word so simple and familiar as *wif*, *g* for *f* being a very unusual error. The name is, however, very extraordinary, and perhaps corrupt.

l. 7. *hyre twilibrocenan cyrtel*. In Sweet's *Oldest English Texts*, 109. 1151, *duplex, biplex* are glossed *tuili*, but the O.E. word does not necessarily mean doubly-woven. B.T. suggests for *brocenan* either 'parti-coloured' (comparing Swedish *brokig*, Danish *broget* or Welsh *brech*, etc.) or 'embroidered'. Another possibility is that the word is a miscopying of O.E. *broccenan*, the writing of a single consonant for a double one, or vice versa, being not infrequent in this document. The word *broccen* occurs in Wright-Wülker, 152. 1, where *melotes vel pera* is glossed *gæten vel broccen rooc*.

l. 9. *ruwan*. This is the only instance of the word as masculine. It evidently refers here to some sort of bed-cover. In Sweet, *op. cit.* 102. 1020, *tapeta* is glossed *ryae*. *Ruwe* is also used as the name of a rough cloak (translating *villosa* in Sweet, *op. cit.* 106. 1080; *lena* in Wright-Wülker, 439. 9. This last word, usually meaning a cloak, is used of a bed-cover in the Rule of St Benedict, c. 55).

l. 11. *gesplottude*. This verb is not recorded as occurring elsewhere. Cf. O.E. *splott*, 'a spot'.

l. 12. *gewiredan*. Cf. O.Icel. *vira-virki*, 'filigree work'. In O.E. poetry the word *wir* is often used in connection with jewelry, no doubt with reference to the filigree work on Teutonic jewelry, examples of which have been preserved. See Baldwin Brown, *Arts and Crafts of our Teutonic Forefathers*, p. 194.

l. 16. *[Æþelf]læde þisse hwitan*. Kemble's emendation is probably correct. It just fits the space in the MS. No doubt the nickname is given to distinguish her from the Æthelflæd, Ealhhelm's daughter, mentioned above. A similar use of the demonstrative in a nickname, *Wulfhun þes blaca*, occurs in B. 591, l. 11, about the beginning of the tenth century, and an *Æþelwold þes greta* is a witness in the *Liber Monasterii de Hyda*, p. 245, to a charter copied from an original of about 990.

cincdaðenan. There is no MS. authority for Kemble's reading, and it is unlikely that the scribe would have mistaken *w* for *d*. The word is evidently an adjective describing *cyrtel*, perhaps the name of a material, possibly a foreign word for a material introduced by trade. The first part looks as if it might be French, but *daðenan* has so far remained a complete mystery. B.T. interprets Kemble's reading as 'purple', literally 'royal woad-coloured', but *cynewædenan* is a long way from what our MS. has.

l. 17. *cuffian*. Like Middle High German *kuffe, kupfe*, it is from the Low Latin *cuphea, cofea*.

hyre nunscrude. See p. 109.

l. 19. *hyru*. This form for O.E. *huru* is no doubt a scribal error due to the occurrence of the word *hyra* just before it.

l. 21. *towmyderce*. 'Box for keeping materials connected with spinning or weaving' is B.T.'s interpretation of this compound, which does not occur elsewhere. Cf. *tow-cræft, tow-tol*, etc.

ll. 29 f. *Eadweard cing*. Probably Edward the Elder. (See p. 109.)

l. 30. *Byrhtwynne*. See p. 109.

IV.

MS. *Liber Monasterii de Hyda*, f. 19. This MS. is in the possession of the Earl of Macclesfield, at Shirburn Castle, Watlington, Oxfordshire. It was compiled in the fourteenth century. Each O.E. document is followed by translations into Latin and fourteenth-century English, which are full of errors and show that the scribe's knowledge of O.E. was very slight.

EDITIONS. Edwards, *Liber Monasterii de Hyda*, R.S. 1866. The will is on pp. 133 f. There is a modern English translation on p. 343.

B. 652: M.E. Version, 653; Latin Version, 654.

Birch, *Liber Vitæ etc. of Hyde Abbey*. Appendix, p. 222.

DATE. 955–958. Ælfsige was Bishop of Winchester from 951 to 958. The Ælfheah who is mentioned in l. 6, became ealdorman in 956 (see p. 121). As he is not given this title in the will it may have been drawn up before 956. It is certainly no earlier than 955, since Ælfsige received *Clere* in that year (B. 905). The rubric in the MS. says it was in the time of King Athelstan, which is clearly impossible.

p. 16, l. 1. *Ælfsiges biscopes*. He is Ælfsige I, who became Bishop of Winchester in 951 and was elected to succeed Oda as Archbishop of Canterbury in 958 (on this date, see Stubbs, *Memorials of St Dunstan*, R.S. pp. xcii f.). He was frozen to death in attempting to cross the Alps to fetch his pallium from Rome (*ibid.* pp. 37, 107, 198). The *Vita S. Oswaldi* (pp. 408 f.) and W.M. (*G.P.*, pp. 25 f.) have a story of an insult committed by him to Archbishop Oda's grave. W.M. (*G.P.* p. 165) says that he bought the archbishopric.

The Chronicle (A) mentions the death of Godwine of Worthy, son of Bishop Ælfsige, in battle against the Danes in Hampshire in 1001. The testator has estates at the Worthys, and is clearly the bishop referred to in this annal. Ælfsige II did not become bishop until 1014. There is no reference in the will to a son, but probably he is the *mægcnafan*, 'young kinsman', of ll. 7, 10, who was to have the reversion of estates at the Worthys and elsewhere. It is conceivable that the Bishop would shrink from directly mentioning a son.

ll. 1 ff. *ic wille...heregeatya*. Note the fluctuation between the first and third person in the opening lines of this will.

l. 2. *ælcne witeþeowne mannan*. See pp. 111 f.

l. 4. *mine heregeatya*. See p. 100.

Tantune. Taunton, Somerset. Edgar in an undated charter (B. 1149) is represented as 'restoring' to Winchester 100 hides at Taunton. Winchester was later in possession of a series of charters relating to this estate which go back to 737 (B. 158), when Æthelheard of Wessex increased an estate at Taunton belonging to Winchester with a gift of other land. The early charters are mainly forgeries, but the cathedral seems to have held land there by Bishop Denewulf's time (B. 611). By 1066 Winchester Cathedral was holding an enormous estate for 100 ploughs at Taunton, assessed at 54 hides 2½ virgates (D.B. 1, f. 87 b: *V. C. H. of Somerset*, 1, p. 442).

l. 5. *Crundelan*. Crondall, Hampshire. Ælfheah gave this estate to the Old Minster in his will (see p. 22, l. 12).

l. 6. *Ælfheage*. The testator of No. IX. See p. 121.

ealden mynstere. The Cathedral Church of Winchester.

l. 7. *mægcnafan*. See p. 114. The M.E. version translates *cosyn mawle*.

Anne. Abbots Ann, Hampshire, which in D.B. is still held by the New Minster (D.B. 1, f. 43: *V. C. H. of Hampshire*, 1, p. 472).

l. 8. *niwan mynstere*. The New Minster, Winchester, which was founded in the reign of Edward the Elder.

ll. 8 f. *æt þan twan Worþigum*. The Worthys are a few miles north of Winchester. Edwards (*op. cit.* p. 343 note) suggests King's Worthy and Martyr Worthy as the two meant here.

l. 11. *Cleran*. Burghclere or Highclere, Hampshire. King Edred granted 10 hides at *Clere* to Ælfsige in 955 (B. 905) with the reservation that the estate was to go to Winchester after four lives. The monks of Winchester held an estate of 10 hides at Clere in King Edward's time (D.B. 1, f. 41), which the *V. C. H. of Hampshire*, 1, p. 465, identifies as Burghclere or Highclere.

l. 12. *Tioceburnan*. Tichborne, Hampshire. See following note.

Wlfrice Cufing. This is evidently the Wulfric who received back Tichborne and other forfeited estates in a charter of 960 (B. 1055). These other estates were Ashbury, Denchworth, Garford, Chieveley, Stanmore, Chaddleworth, Boxford and Benham in Berkshire; Worthing, Stedham, Tillington, Patching, Poyning and Nytimber in Sussex (see Stenton, *Early History of Abingdon*, p. 42). The first five of these estates and Boxford were royal grants to Wulfric, enacted between 940 and 956 (B. 761, 796, 833, 866, 892, 902, 1022). Edwy confirmed the grant of Denchworth in 958 (B. 1034), so that the forfeiture must have occurred after this date. In 947 (B. 823) Wulfric had given an estate at Patching to Christchurch. There is a thegn Wulfric who appears

8-2

as grantee in many other charters of this period and locality (e.g. B. 750, 800, 818, 829, 925), who may be the same man. In 949 (B. 877), King Edred gave him Welford in exchange for land in Cornwall. In 956 Edwy granted Milbrook, Hampshire, to a *princeps* Wulfric (B. 926). There is no charter extant in which Wulfric is granted Benham, but in B. 942, dated 956, 25 hides there are granted by Edwy to his *fideli* Ælfsige. He may be the Bishop, but is more probably the *minister* Ælfsige, who, with his wife Eadgifu, received 33 hides at Ashbury in 953 (B. 899).

l. 13. *Runcwuda.* Ringwood, Hampshire.

l. 15. *Ciltrigtune.* The M.E. version has *Cyltyngtune.* It is possibly Cholderton, Wiltshire, which appears in D.B. as *Celdrintone,* and later as *Childerington* (see Ekblom, *Place-names of Wiltshire s.v. Cholderton*).

Wicham. Perhaps Wickham in Titchfield Hundred, Hampshire.

l. 16. *Lætanlia.* Netley, Hampshire.

V.

MS. British Museum, Additional MS. 15350, f. 61 *b*. This is the *Codex Wintoniensis,* the cartulary of St Swithin's, Winchester, written in the first half of the twelfth century.

EDITIONS. K. 943.
　　　　　T. p. 588.

DATE. There are no means of dating this document unless we can identify the testator with the Ordnoth who witnesses a few charters in the tenth century (see following note).

l. 21. *Ordnoð.* A thegn of this name witnesses two charters in 959 (B. 1046, 1047), and one in 982 (K. 633).

l. 22. *Cendefer.* Candover, Hampshire. According to D.B. the New Minster held an estate of 20 hides there (D.B. 1, f. 42: *V. C. H. of Hampshire,* 1, p. 469).

ealdan cyrican. The Old Minster, i.e. Winchester Cathedral.

p. 18, ll. 3 ff. *þ man unc gefecce....gerysenlic.* The Ealdorman Brihtnoth made a similar arrangement with the monks of Ely, and after his death they fetched his body from the battlefield at Maldon (*Liber Eliensis,* II, 62).

ll. 5 ff. *þis is seo gewitnes....mynstre.* Literally 'This is the witness of God and his community at the Old Minster which Ordnoth wishes to have'.

VI.

MS. *Liber Monasterii de Hyda,* f. 24 (see p. 114).

EDITIONS. Edwards, p. 173, with English translation on p. 351.
B. 989; M.E. version 990; Latin version 991.

DATE. After 957, and probably not much later than 958. See following note.

1. 10. *Æðelgeard.* The preceding charter in the *Liber Mon. de Hyda* (B. 988) is a grant by King Edwy to his faithful *minister Athelgard* of 15 hides at *Stottanwelle* in 957. In 947 he had been granted 10 hides at the neighbouring place, Brightwell, by King Edred (B. 830), and there is another charter extant in which he receives 30 hides there (B. 810). This charter is dated 945, but as the king concerned is Edred, either the date or the king's name is an error. In 948 Edred granted him more land in the same locality, five hides at Mackney and five at *Suttanwlle* (Sotwell) (B. 864). Æthelgeard may also be the grantee in B. 765, 786, 1025, all concerned with estates in Hampshire, the earliest dated 943. In 959 Edwy granted a Hampshire estate to a *princeps* of this name (B. 976). There is no trace of this ealdorman elsewhere, so that perhaps the title is a mistake. The testator may be the *Æþelgeard þréng* whose name occurs in one of the lists of benefactors in the *L.V.H.* (ed. Birch, p. 22). A *minister* of this name signs charters in 934 and 935, and from 942 until 958.

Stottanwelle. The boundaries of this estate are given in Edred's charter (B. 988), and though they cannot now be traced, the occurrence of Mackney and of the Thames in the boundaries makes it probable that Sotwell, Berkshire, is the place meant. The present form, which occurs also in Edred's charter, must be a miscopying. *Suttanwlle* in B. 948 seems to refer to the same place. The D.B. form is *Sotwelle.* An estate of 10 hides belonged to the New Minster in 1066 (D.B. I, f. 59 *b*: *V. C. H. of Berkshire*, I, p. 343).

VII.

MS. Additional MS. 15350, f. 52 *b* (see p. 116). The bequest immediately follows a royal charter of Edred's, granting Rimpton to Brihtric (B. 931).

EDITIONS. K. 628.

       T. p. 518.

       B. 931. He prints the bequest as an addition to Edred's grant.

DATE. Between 964 and 980, while Æthelgar, who is one of the witnesses, was Abbot of the New Minster.

1. 14. *Brichtric Grim.* He is given this second name in the bequest only. The name Grim occurs in place-names in the West of England. See *Place-Name Survey of Worcestershire*, p. 127, where it is suggested that an English name Grim existed beside the Scandinavian name.

Brihtric was perhaps in possession of other estates, as this document may well be a separate bequest like Thurstan's to Christchurch (No. xxx). The name Brihtric is a common one, and more than one *minister* of this name sign charters at this period and later. We cannot therefore identify the testator with thegns of the same name who occur in other charters.

l. 15. *Rimtune*. Rimpton, Somerset. The boundaries of this estate are given in Edred's grant to Brihtric (B. 931). In D.B. the Bishop of Winchester holds five hides there (D.B. 1, f. 87 *b*; *V. C. H. of Somerset*, 1, p. 444).

ll. 16 f. *þa bóc ðe Eadred cyning him gebocode*. That is, Edred's charter, granting Rimpton to Brihtric in 956, which the scribe copied into the cartulary.

ll. 17 f. *to þere ealdan bǽc. þe Æþestan cyning ǽr gebocode*. There is a charter extant (B. 730) in which Athelstan grants an estate at Rimpton to his thegn *Æþǽred* in 938. The boundaries are not identical with those in Edred's grant. They seem to belong to another part of the estate.

l. 20. *gewered*. Vinogradoff (*English Society in the Eleventh Century*, p. 193) translates this 'defended' with reference to taxation. The meaning of the word is, however, shown clearly in a charter of Bishop Denewulf (B. 619) in which he describes an estate as being *nu eall gewæred. and ða hit æst min laford mæ to læt. þa wæs hit ierfælæas*.

l. 22. *Dunstan arcebisceop*. He had become archbishop in 960.

Aþelwold bisceop. St Æthelwold, the leader of the movement for monastic reform. He was Bishop of Winchester from 963 to 984.

l. 23. *Ælfstan bisceop*. This may be the Ælfstan who was Bishop of London from 961 to 995 or 996, or Ælfstan, Bishop of Ramsbury from about 970 to 981.

Æþelgar abbod. He was Abbot of the New Minster, Winchester, from 964 until his consecration to the See of Selsey in 980. In 988 he became Archbishop of Canterbury, but died in the following year.

VIII.

MS. Additional MS. 15350, f. 96 (see p. 116).

EDITIONS. K. 721.

> T. p. 552.

DATE. Between 966 and 975, probably after Edgar's refoundation of Romsey in 967. Newnham and Linslade were obtained by Ælfgifu in 966 (B. 1176, 1189). The will was drawn up in Edgar's lifetime, because the *Liber Eliensis*, II, 47 says he gave to Ely the estate at *Meassewrthe* which *Alfgiva*, when she died, left to him. Kemble's date, 1012, is therefore impossible.

p. 20, l. 1. *Ælfgyfæ*. Kemble calls her Queen Ælfgifu, and Freeman (*Norman Conquest*, 2nd edition, 1, p. 672) suggests that she is the first wife of Ethelred, but the *Liber Eliensis* (loc. cit.) shows that she was dead by 975. There is no evidence for the assumption that she is a queen. It is probably the phrase *for cynescypæ* which gave Kemble this impression, but this refers to the king whom she is addressing (cf. Will of Æthelwold, p. 30, l. 2). Ælfgifu is, however, of royal descent. Edgar refers to her as his kinswoman (B. 1176, 1189). She leaves estates to a certain Æthelweard in the will in a context which implies that he is her brother, and he is very probably the chronicler and future ealdorman (see p. 145), for on p. 20, ll. 32 f., Ælfgifu speaks of her brother's wife Æthelflæd, and we know from a manumission (K. 981) that the wife of the Ealdorman Æthelweard was called Æthelflæd. The chronicler Æthelweard, from his own account (Book IV, cap. 2 of his chronicle), we know to have been the great-great-grandson of King Ethelred I, Alfred's elder brother. We might conjecture that the testatrix was the Ælfgifu whom Archbishop Oda divorced from Edwy because of their kinship (Chronicle, 958 D).

Ælfgifu is in possession of an estate which in 903 belonged to the Ealdorman Æthelfrith (see below) and it may be that she was descended from him, as there is reason to believe that he was of royal descent (see *Crawford Charters*, p. 83, and J. Armitage Robinson, *The Life and Times of St Dunstan*, pp. 45 f., where it is suggested that he was the father of the East Anglian Ealdorman, Æthelstan Half-king).

ll. 5 f. *þæt is æræst...Hrisanbeorgan*. A payment of *sawolsceatt* (see pp. 109 f.).

l. 6. *Hrisanbeorgan*. Princes Risborough, Buckinghamshire. In B. 603, dated 903, an estate of 30 *cassati* here is in the possession of the *dux* Æthelfrith. In 1066 Princes Risborough is still an estate of 30 hides (D.B. 1, f. 143 *b*: *V. C. H. of Buckinghamshire*, 1, p. 232). It was no longer in the possession of the Old Minster.

l. 8. *ælne witæþæownæ mann*. See note on pp. 111 f.

l. 10. *scrín mid hiræ haligdomæ*. The bequest of a shrine occurs also in the will of Æthelmær, p. 24, l. 17. It no doubt refers to a box ornamented with precious metals and gems. In the *L.V.H.* p. 161, reference is made to a 'Greek shrine which the Lady gave', and on p. 162 to a 'shrine which Ælfwold the *ciricweard* made'.

l. 11. *Bleddanhlæwe*. Bledlow, Buckinghamshire.

l. 13. *Hwætædunæ*. Probably Whaddon in Slapton, Buckinghamshire.

Rummæsigæ. The Benedictine Nunnery of Romsey, Hampshire. Edgar re-established this nunnery in 967 (see Fl. Wig.).

l. 14. *Cæstæleshammæ*. This is identified by the *Place-Name Survey of Buckinghamshire* as Chesham.

Abbandunæ. Abingdon, Berkshire. This monastery had been reformed by Abbot Æthelwold, who became Bishop of Winchester in 963. On the previous history of this abbey see Stenton, *The Early History of Abingdon*.

l. 15. *Wicham*. The modern form is Wickham. There are too many places of this name for an identification to be possible.

Baþum. The early history of the abbey of Bath is rather obscure. It was first founded as a nunnery, but by the time of Coenwulf of Wessex it was a house of monks. Probably it was restored or reformed during the revival of Edgar's reign. Edgar was crowned there in 973.

About this time St Ælfheah became a hermit there, and it became famous on his account. See *V. C. H. of Somerset*, II, pp. 69 f.

l. 16. *Weowungum*. Wing, Buckinghamshire. See *Place-Name Survey* of this county.

Hlincgeladæ. Linslade, Buckinghamshire. Edgar granted this estate to Ælfgifu in 966 (B. 1189).

Hæfæresham. Haversham, Buckinghamshire.

l. 17. *Hæðfælda*. Perhaps the Hertfordshire Hatfield.

Mæssanwyrðæ. Masworth, Buckinghamshire. Edgar gave it to Ely after Ælfgifu's death (*Liber Eliensis*, II, 47).

Gyssic. Gussage, Dorset.

l. 19. *sópcuppan*. The word *sop(p)* occurs in O.E. and M.E. with the meaning of a piece of bread soaked in wine or water. It occurs as a gloss for *vipa, offa* and *offulam*. A *sopcuppe* was apparently some special type of drinking-cup in which a *sop* could be made.

ll. 19 f. *syx horsa...spæra*. This reads very like a payment of heriot, but it is not until 1046 that we get the term 'heriot' in a woman's will (see p. 84, l. 10). Cnut's law on heriot (II Cnut, 71) does not mention payment by women. Most women's wills, however, contain a bequest to the king which probably served the same purpose as the heriot (see p. 100).

l. 20. *þam æþelingæ*. Probably Edgar's son, Edward the Martyr.

Niwanhâm. Newnham Murren, Oxfordshire, given to Ælfgifu by Edgar in 966 (B. 1176).

l. 24. *Aþelwoldæ bisceopæ*. Bishop of Winchester, 963 to 984 (see p. 118).

Tæafersceat. I cannot identify this place.

l. 26. *Mundingwillæ*. Mongewell, Oxfordshire.

l. 27. *Beorhþanstædæ*: for *Beorhhamstede*, i.e. Berkhampstead, Hertfordshire.

ll. 27 f. *Ælfwerdæ and Æþelwærdæ and Ælfwaræ*. As the latter is shown by l. 31 below to be Ælfgifu's sister, it is probable that the others are her brothers. In l. 33 Ælfgifu refers to a brother's wife. Two brothers with these names witness a charter of 974 (B. 1301). On *Æþelwærdæ* see p. 119. A *minister* Ælfweard signs frequently from 956.

l. 30. *twa dægfæorman*. A day's *feorm* was a gift of food considered sufficient for the community for one day.

þam twam mynstrum. The Old and New Minsters, Winchester.

ll. 32 f. *Æþælflædæ minæs broþur wifæ*. An Æthelflæd, wife of the Ealdorman Æthelweard, is mentioned in a manumission (K. 981). See p. 119.

l. 33. *bændes*. In Wright-Wülker this word occurs as a gloss for *columbar* (107. 10) and *lunula* (107. 32). *Diadema* is glossed *bend agimmed and gesmiðed* (152. 25). The Latin version of No. xi translates *bend* as *vitta capitis*. In illuminated MSS. of the period, women are sometimes depicted with a yellow head-band over the top of the hood, possibly representing a gold band (e.g. Claudius B. 4, ff. 76, 77 *b*, etc.).

ll. 33 f. *ælchum abbodæ*. Ælfgifu's will was made in the early days of the monastic revival and she is evidently keenly interested in it. On p. 20, l. 24 she leaves a legacy to the leader of the movement, Æthelwold, Bishop of Winchester.

p. 22, ll. 1 f. *þam bisceope and þam abbodæ*, i.e. the Bishop of Winchester and the Abbot of the New Minster, at this date Æthelgar.

IX.

MS. Additional MS. 15350, f. 95 *b* (see p. 116).

EDITIONS. K. 593.

T. p. 526.

B. 1174.

DATE. Between about 968 and 971. Ælfheah refers to two sons of Edgar and Ælfthryth, and the date of their marriage is given in the Chronicle (D), as 965. Fl. Wig, however, places the marriage in 964, and a grant by Edgar to his wife, Ælfthryth, is dated 964 (B. 1143). Fl. Wig. says that Ælfheah's death occurred in 971, but he signs a charter dated 972 (B. 1285). This charter, however, is preserved only in a thirteenth-century Wilton cartulary (Harley MS. 436). Edgar's son, who is mentioned in the will as the elder Ætheling, died in childhood, but as the Chronicles give the year of his death variously as 970, 971 and 972 (see p. 124) we cannot date the will more exactly.

l. 8. *Ælfheah ealdorman*. Ælfheah first signs among the *duces* in 956, and as charters of this year are addressed to him as *minister* he must have been made an ealdorman during the course of the year. One cannot be certain when he first signs as *thegn*, or *minister*, because there are thegns of this name almost continuously from 889. The first signature which can with certainty be assigned to him is in B. 917, a charter of 955, in which he is called Ælfhere's brother, but no doubt his signatures as thegn begin many years earlier. There is another thegn called Ælfheah during the same period, who is perhaps the one who signs *discifer* (B. 941 dated 956) and *cyninges discðegn* (B. 972). The *minister* who signs after 956 is no doubt this other Ælfheah, and not the testator.

Ælfheah was Ealdorman of Hampshire. According to Fl. Wig (971) he died in 971 and was buried at Glastonbury. Edred, Edwy and Edgar all speak of him as their kinsman. Edred granted Compton, Berkshire, to him in 955 (B. 908). In the following year he received *Ellandun* and four hides by the River Nadder from Edwy (B. 948, 1030). In 957 Edwy gave him ten hides at Buckland, Berkshire (B. 1005), and from Edgar, in 962, he received Sunbury (B. 1085), which had been forfeited to the king by Ecgferth (B. 1063), and in 967, 25 hides at Merton and Dulwich (B. 1196). This last estate was given to

Ælfheah's wife, Ælfswith, as well as to him. It is possible that he received a grant of Batcombe from Edmund in 940 (see p. 125). Ælfheah sold Sunbury to Archbishop Dunstan (B. 1063). Some others of his estates are not specifically mentioned in his will, but may be included in the unnamed estates left to his wife.

Ælfheah is shown by his will to have held extremely wide estates. His estate of 120 hides at Worth must have covered many square miles. He also mentions the extent of Sutton and Charlton, and from other sources we know that others of his lands contained as much as twenty or thirty hides (see below).

l. 11. *Ællændune*. Ælfheah had received 30 hides there from Edwy in 956 (B. 948). In D.B. i, f. 65 *b* it occurs as *Elendune*, an estate of 30 hides held by the Bishop of Winchester, but *pro victu monachorum*. The name has now been lost, but from the boundaries given in Edwy's grant, Grundy (*Saxon Land-charters of Wiltshire* in *Archæological Journal*, LXVII, p. 54) identifies the estate as 'lands in the parishes of Wroughton, Lydiard Millicent and probably Lydiard Tregoze', Wiltshire.

Crundelom. Crondall, Hampshire. This estate had been left to Ælfheah by Bishop Ælfsige (see p. 16, l. 5). This is one of the estates entered in D.B. as being for the support of the monks of Winchester. It was then assessed at 50 hides (D.B. i, f. 41: *V. C. H. of Hampshire*, i, p. 465).

l. 12. *Ceorlatunæ*. Charlton near Malmesbury, Wiltshire. Malmesbury Abbey held 20 hides at this place in 1066 (D.B. i, f. 67). Later traditions of the abbey attributed the gift of this estate to King Ethelred of Mercia (B. 59, 59 *a*).

l. 13. *Mealdælmæsbyrig*. W.M. (*G.P.* pp. 251 and 255) says that Malmesbury Abbey was in the hands of secular clergy in the reign of Edwy, and that Archbishop Dunstan restored the monastery in Edgar's time.

Suðtune. Probably one of the Somerset Suttons.

ll. 14 f. *þæra hundtwæntiga hida æt Wyrðæ*. In 1066 the king had an estate at *Ordia* (D.B. i, f. 58: *V. C. H. of Berkshire*, i, p. 334) which the *V. C. H.* identifies as Littleworth, Berkshire. It is assessed at 31 hides. Ælfheah's enormous estate must have included several other villages, which are probably entered separately in D.B.

l. 15. *Coccham*. Cookham, Berkshire. It was a royal manor, assessed at 20 hides, in 1066 (D.B. i, f. 56 *b*: *V. C. H. of Berkshire*, i, p. 327).

þæcham. Thatcham, Berkshire.

l. 16. *Ceolæswyrðæ*. Chelworth, Wiltshire.

Incgenæsham. Possibly Inglesham, Wiltshire. See p. 111. A later Ealdorman of Hampshire, Æthelmær, probably Ælfheah's successor, bequeathes an estate at *Igeneshamme* (see p. 26, l. 5).

Ægelesbyrig. Aylesbury, Buckinghamshire. This and the following estate are entered as royal manors in D.B. i, ff. 143 f. (*V. C. H. of*

Buckinghamshire, 1, pp. 231 ff.). Aylesbury was 16 hides, and Wendover 24.

l. 17. *Wændofron.* Wendover, Buckinghamshire (see preceding note).

ll. 17 ff. *And þreo hund mancusa....scylda.* It is uncertain how much of this huge bequest we should regard as payment of heriot (see p. 100). Ælfheah was the king's kinsman and would no doubt make bequests to him on this account.

l. 19. *handsex.* A short one-edged sword or dagger.

þæræ lecge. B.T. supplies *on* before *þæræ lecge* as some preposition is required by the case. The meaning of *lecg* is very uncertain. Leo, *Angelsächsisches Glossar*, p. 147, l. 13, translates 'gift', Thorpe 'hilt', B. T. 'some part of a weapon, crossbar of the hilt'. But this instance is not, as they thought, the only occurrence of the word. It occurs twice in the *Liber Monasterii de Hyda*, in the will of Æthelwold (cf. p. 30, ll. 8, 13), and none of the above suggestions fit the context there, where it is clear that a *lecg* was an article which could be given by itself. I have guessed 'sheath', for in the present instance it appears to have some connection with a sword. It is strange that, apart from these two Hampshire documents of the second half of the tenth century, the word should have entirely disappeared. Middle Low German has a feminine word *legge* meaning a place where something is kept, e.g. in the combination *linnenlegge.*

l. 21. *Ælfriðæ ðæs cyninges wifæ.* Her name should have been written *Ælfþryðe.* She was Edgar's second wife and mother of Ethelred. Her marriage with Edgar occurred in 964 or 965 (see p. 121). She was the daughter of the Ealdorman Ordgar (Chronicle 965 D) and Fl. Wig. (964) says that she was the widow of Æthelwold, Ealdorman of East Anglia. W.M. (*G.R.* pp. 178 f.) adds a long story according to which Edgar is supposed to have murdered her first husband. Other legends grew up around her. Later chroniclers, led by Osbern (*Memorials of St Dunstan*, R.S. p. 115), make her responsible for the death of her stepson Edward, and the *Liber Eliensis*, II, 56 charges her with the murder, by magic arts, of the Abbot Brihtnoth. Post-Conquest writers believed her foundation of Wherwell to be in expiation for her crimes. None of these stories appear in contemporary writers. She is referred to affectionately in the will of her grandson Æthelstan (p. 62, l. 9). She witnesses charters up to 999, and is appealed to in law-suits (K. 693, 717). She died before the end of 1002, for in this year Ethelred gave lands to Wherwell for her soul (K. 707).

ll. 21 f. *his gefæðeran.* This refers to the relationship between godparents and parents, or between godparents of the same child. It has therefore the same meaning as the original sense of 'gossip', but has no equivalent in modern English.

Scyræburnan. This estate might be Shirburn near Watlington, Oxfordshire, Sherborne near Bourton-on-the-Water, Gloucestershire,

Sherborne in Dorset, Sherborne in Warwickshire or West Sherborne near Basingstoke in Hampshire. Judging by the situation of Ælfheah's other estates, I think either the first or the last suggestion the most probable.

l. 23. *þam yldran æþælingæ*. This is not Edward the Martyr, who was the son of Edgar's first wife, but Edmund, the date of whose death is variously given in the Chronicle, 970 E, 971 A, 972 C.

l. 24. *þam gincgran*. Ethelred, the future king.

l. 25. *Wolcnæsstedæ*. Godstone, Surrey, formerly called Walk-hampstead (see *V. C. H. of Surrey*, II, p. 432, note).

Ælfhære his breðær. This is the Ealdorman of Mercia, the leader of the anti-monastic party. He signs both as *minister* and *dux* in 956, so that he must have become ealdorman in this year. The period of his greatest power was immediately after the death of Edgar, when he led a reaction against the monastic movement. As a result he is given a black character by all the monastic chroniclers. See *Chronicon Abbatiae Eveshamensis*, R.S. pp. 78 f.; Fl. Wig. 975; *Henry of Huntingdon*, R.S. pp. 166 f.; *Vita S. Oswaldi*, pp. 443, 450. He died in 982.

An account of a sale by him of an estate called Kingston is extant (B. 1262), in which it is stated that the estate had been bequeathed to him by his brother Ælfheah. No estate of this name is mentioned in the latter's will, but Stenton (*The Early History of Abingdon*, p. 37), who identifies it with Kingston Bagpuize, suggests that it is included in Faringdon.

ll. 26. *Færndunæ*. Faringdon, Berkshire.

Ealdincburnan. Aldbourne, Wiltshire.

ll. 26 f. *Godwinæ his suna*. He may be the Godwine mentioned in K. 714 as a kinsman of Æthelmær, the son of Æthelweard. Ælfheah speaks of a kinsman Æthelweard in l. 28. Signatures of a thegn called Godwine first appear in 964. The name was not so common at this period as in the next century.

l. 27. *Tudincgatunæ*. Possibly Teddington, Middlesex. See Karl-ström, *Old English Compound Place-Names in -ing*, p. 62.

Wyritunæ. Professor Mawer has suggested to me that this is a mis-reading of *Pyritune*, i.e. Purton, Wiltshire.

l. 28. *Æþelwerdæ his mege*. Perhaps the later ealdorman, the chronicler (see pp. 119, 145). Both he and Ælfheah were kinsmen of King Edgar. The name is, however, a common one.

Wicumun. Wycombe, Buckinghamshire.

l. 29. *Froxafelda*. Froxfield, Hampshire.

ll. 29 f. *Ælfsiþæ minon wifæ*. Nothing is known of her elsewhere, except that she is mentioned in a charter of King Ethelred's, in which he gives to Glastonbury in 987 an estate of forty hides at Kingston which she had bought from King Edgar (K. 659).

l. 30. *it swa gehylt*. There is no antecedent for this *it*. It may refer to her general behaviour (*sic* Thorpe), i.e. 'if she does not marry again'.

p. 24, l. 1. *of þam god geþæncæ*. It is also possible to take *god* as the accusative plural of *gōd*, with the meaning 'good deed', 'benefaction', and to translate the phrase: 'be mindful of benefactions from that (property)'.

l. 2. *Batancumbæ*. Batcombe, Somerset. In a charter of 940 (B. 749) King Edmund left an estate of 20 hides at *Batecombe* to his kinsman and *minister, Elswithe*. But this is a woman's name, and moreover the name of Ælfheah's wife. The most probable explanation is that the estate was given to Ælfheah and Ælfswith jointly and that the copyist omitted Ælfheah's name. Glastonbury Abbey was in possession of an estate of 20 hides at this place in 1066 (D.B. 1, f. 90 b: V. C. H. *of Somerset*, 1, p. 465).

l. 4. *mine broðorn*. I have not succeeded in finding any reference to a brother of Ælfheah except the Ealdorman Ælfhere.

l. 7. *witeþeowne man*. See pp. 111 f.

l. 10. *Aþelwold bisceop*, i.e. of Winchester, 963 to 984. See p. 118.

l. 11. *Æþelwine ealdorman*. This is Æthelwine 'Friend of God', Ealdorman of East Anglia. He was a supporter of monasticism and the chief opponent of Ælfhere's policy after Edgar's death. He signs as ealdorman from 962, and he died in 992 (Chronicle E). As the friend of St Oswold and founder of Ramsey Abbey he figures prominently in the *Vita S. Oswaldi* (especially pp. 428 f., 445, 467 f., 474 f.) and in the *Historia Ramesiensis*. See also *Liber Eliensis*, II *passim*.

Ælfwinæ. Perhaps the sister's son mentioned above.

ll. 11 f. *Æscwig abbod*. A grant was made by Edgar to an Abbot Æscwig of Bath in 970 (B. 1257). He is probably the abbot of this name who signs regularly from 963 to 975, and in an undated charter of the reign of Edward the Martyr (K. 1277). He certainly ceased to be Abbot of Bath some time before 984, as his successor, Abbot Ælfheah, became Bishop of Winchester in that year. It is possible that Æscwig became Bishop of Dorchester, as a bishop of this name signs from 979 to 1002, not counting B. 1296, in which an Æscwig appears as bishop in the reign of Edgar. In this document Æthelgar, Bishop of Selsey from 980, is also called bishop. The document is preserved only in the *Textus Roffensis* and Æscwig's name as well as Æthelgar's may be a later insertion.

X.

MS. *Liber Monasterii de Hyda*, f. 35 b (see p. 114).

EDITIONS. Edwards, p. 254, modern English translation, p. 363.

DATE. Between 971 and 982 or 983. See following note.

l. 13. *Æðelmær ealdorman*. There were two ealdormen of this name. The earlier was Ealdorman of Hampshire (Fl. Wig. 982) and according to the Chronicle C. and Fl. Wig. died in 982, and was buried at the

New Minster, Winchester (Fl. Wig.). The second was Ealdorman of the Western Provinces and died some time about 1017 (see pp. 144 f.). It is the earlier ealdorman who is the testator of this will. On p. 24, ll. 15 f. he leaves instructions that he is to be buried at the New Minster. In the *L.V.H.* (ed. Birch, pp. 21, 54), an Ealdorman Æthelmær occurs twice among the benefactors. He signs as *dux* from 977. Ælfheah, who was Ealdorman of Hampshire, died in 971, and Æthelmær may have been his immediate successor. It seems probable that 983, and not 982, is the correct date of his death, since a charter of Ethelred's of this date grants an estate of 10 hides at *Clife* to a *dux* Æthelmær (K. 638). K. 636 is a charter exactly identical with this one, except that the grantee is a *minister* Æthelwine. In K. 692 (a charter of 995) an Æthelwine, son of the Ealdorman Æthelmær, is mentioned, so that it is probable that the grantee of *Clife* is Æthelmær's son, and that he obtained a new charter after his father's death. The will seems to have been drawn up before Æthelmær received *Clife*, which is not included among the bequests to his sons.

l. 14. *his cwyde wæs.* In my translation I have assumed the omission of an interrogative pronoun before this phrase.

l. 16. *into Niwan Mynstre, þære ic me restan wille.* We know from Fl. Wig. 982 that this wish was fulfilled.

l. 17. *min scrin.* See p. 119.

l. 20. *Cyrthugtune.* The place meant here may be Chirton, Wiltshire, which occurs in the fourteenth century as *Chirughton* (see Ekblom, *Place-Names of Wiltshire, s.v. Chirton*).

l. 21. *Aþelwoldes bysceopes.* Bishop of Winchester, 963 to 984.

l. 22. *Tudanwyrðe.* Perhaps Tidworth, on the border of Hampshire and Wiltshire.

l. 24. *into Ealdan Mynstre into sēe Trinitate.* In early charters the most usual dedication of Winchester Cathedral is to St Peter and St Paul, sometimes to St Peter alone. There are, however, some documents in which the Holy Trinity is named as well as these saints in the dedication (B. 398, 625, 627, 628, 690, 831), while in B. 705, dated 934, and K. 626, dated 980, the Holy Trinity alone is mentioned. The New Minster was dedicated to the Holy Trinity, St Mary and St Peter, and is often referred to as 'the Holy Trinity'.

l. 26. *Nunnena Mynstra.* The Nunnery of St Mary, Winchester.

mæssepreosta gylde. This was perhaps an association in Winchester similar to that which had its centre at York and of which the statutes are preserved in the first half of the code called *Norðhymbra Preosta Lagu*. Liebermann (III, p. 220) considers that only chapters 1 to 45 are the priests' laws proper. The code shows the priests bound together into an association for mutual protection. Any priest who commits an offence is to pay compensation to his *geferan* as well as to the bishop, and for certain offences the priest forfeits the 'friendship' of the association. For the breach of certain rules it is stated that a deacon pays half the sum due from a priest in compensation. Such an association is possibly referred to in the laws (VIII Ethelred, 27 = I Cnut, 5, 3) where it is stated that a priest who is a false witness or accessory to a theft is to forfeit *ægðer ge geferscipes ge freondscipes* and every dignity.

l. 27. *diacona gylde.* In York the deacons seem to have been included in the same gild as the priests (see preceding note).

Cristes cyricun. Canterbury Cathedral.

l. 28. *sce Agustyne.* The monastery founded by Augustine at Canterbury was originally dedicated to St Peter and St Paul, but was later more often referred to by the name of its founder.

l. 29. *Hrofeceastere.* Rochester.

l. 32. *Cracgelade.* Cricklade, Wiltshire. By the time of D.B. the church at this place was in the possession of Westminster Abbey (D.B. 1, f. 67).

l. 33. *Burnan.* As the Cottesmore mentioned below in the will is apparently Cottesmore in Rutland, it is possible that *Burnan* is Bourne in Lincolnshire, about ten miles from Cottesmore.

hiredcnihtum. The precise meaning of the term *cniht* at this date is uncertain. It is sometimes used in the sense 'boy', 'young man', but in the wills, where it is always used with a possessive, it clearly refers to some sort of servant or follower. Wulfwaru, on p. 64, ll. 19 ff., speaks of her four 'knights' and all her *hiredwifmannum.* On the other hand, Bishop Ælfwold of Crediton (*Crawford Charters*, x) makes a distinction between his *hiredcnihtas* and his *hiredmen*, and a charter of Edmund Ironside (K. 1302) is witnessed by his *discþegn*, two of his 'knights' and all the other *hiredmen.* It seems to me probable, therefore, that the term *cniht* was applied only to the higher officials of the household. Æthelstan the Ætheling once refers to a certain man as his *cniht*, once as his *discþegn* (see p. 170) and the latter official was a sort of seneschal. The *cniht* was admitted to the Cambridge thegns' gild (see T. pp. 610 f.), but not to full membership, and his lord was responsible for his good behaviour. A distinction between the *cniht* and the gildsman is drawn also in the statutes of the Exeter gild (T. p. 613). Thurstan's *cniht*, Viking, to whom in 1044 he left one hide of land, is entered among the 'socmen' of D.B. (see p. 194).

p. 26, l. 1. *cynehlaforde.* The M.E. scribe translates this word *cosyn*, no doubt connecting it with O.E. *cynn*, 'kin'.

to heregeatuwum. See p. 100. Æthelmær gives the exact number of horses and weapons stated in II Cnut 71 as due from an earl, but his money payment is a hundred mancuses in excess of the amount stated in this law.

l. 2. *beagus.* The M.E. version translates this *baggys!*

l. 5. *minan yldran suna.* Perhaps Æthelwine (see p. 126).

Igeneshamme. Possibly Inglesham, Wiltshire. See p. 122. Professor Mawer has also suggested that Eynsham, Oxfordshire, may be meant.

l. 6. *Cottesmore.* Cottesmore, Rutland, is a long way from Æthelmær's other estates, but no other place of this name is known.

l. 8. *ðæs ðe ic gean.* As it is possible to read sense retaining this phrase as it stands, I have done so in the translation, but *gean* may be a scribal error due to the occurrence of the word just before. The original perhaps had *læfe*, in which case we may translate the sentence: 'And finally, I grant to my wife all that I leave, whether estates or goods, according to the terms, etc.'

l. 9. *þam forewordun.* Perhaps a marriage agreement of the kind referred to in the code called *Be Wifmannes Beweddunge.* See pp. 135 f.

XI.

MS. (*a*) *Textus Roffensis,* f. 144. The will is contained in the cartulary which forms the second portion of this codex, and is immediately followed by a Latin translation. The handwriting is twelfth-century.

(*b*) British Museum, Stowe MS. 831, a late paper copy of (*a*). The text is from (*a*).

EDITIONS. Hickes, *Dissertatio Epistolaris,* p. 51, in *Thesaurus,* I. Hearne, *Textus Roffensis,* pp. 110 f. K. 492, Latin version 1242. T. p. 500, Latin version, p. 503. B. 1132, Latin version 1133.

DATE. Between 973 and 987. The later limit is certain because Rochester was then in possession of Bromley, an estate which was to go to them after the death of the Brihtwaru mentioned in the will. On the earlier date, which depends on the evidence of the Rochester document B. 1296, see the following note.

l. 11. *Byrhtrices.* He is evidently the kinsman of Brihtwaru concerned in the litigation about Snodland, Bromley and Fawkham, which is described in B. 1296 (from the *Textus Roffensis*). Brihtwaru had another kinsman called Brihtric (cf. l. 16), but as the testator mentions these three estates, there can be no doubt that it is he who figures in the litigation about them.

The account of this litigation given in B. 1296 from the Rochester point of view, is as follows: the title-deeds of Snodland had been given to Rochester Cathedral by Æscwyn, but were stolen by the priests and secretly sold to her son Ælfric. When the bishop discovered the loss, he demanded the deeds from Ælfric, but at that point the latter died. The bishop then took legal action against his widow, Brihtwaru, and a meeting in London, over which King Edgar presided, gave a decision in his favour, awarding him the title-deeds of Snodland and compensation for theft, and declaring the widow's estates, Bromley and Fawkham, forfeit to the king. The document does not give the grounds for this sentence. Probably it was held that Ælfric had wittingly received stolen goods, or instigated the theft. The record goes on to describe how the bishop, at Brihtwaru's entreaty, bought back Bromley and Fawkham, allowing her a usufruct, but retaining

the title-deeds. After the death of Edgar, however, Brihtwaru's kinsman Brihtric compelled her to attempt to recover these title-deeds
(the Rochester scribe calls this robbery), and when the suit was brought
up before the ealdorman and the people of Kent, the bishop was forced
to give them up. The Rochester scribe represents this as an entirely
illegal proceeding, but he is a biassed authority. Possibly Brihtwaru
and Brihtric succeeded in performing an oath that Ælfric was ignorant
of the theft.

Brihtric's will gives not the merest hint that there has been litigation
over these estates, although it is later than Ælfric's death and therefore
than the beginning of the conflict. From it we learn that the reversion
of all three estates had been granted to Rochester by Ælfric's father,
Ælfhere. Ælfric's purchase of the deeds of Snodland was, therefore,
perhaps an attempt to violate this bequest. When Edgar declared the
other two estates forfeit, the Cathedral would lose its right of reversion,
which was no doubt the reason why the bishop was ready to buy back
the estates. Considering the friendly tone of the will as regards
Rochester, it seems to me that it could have been drawn up only at
two points in the conflict; either just after the bishop had bought
back the two estates and allowed Brihtwaru the use of them, or after
the events related in the Rochester record, in which case we should
perhaps assume that a friendly settlement had finally been arrived at.
The bishop's purchase of Bromley appears from an extant charter
(B. 1295) to have taken place in 973, as the list of witnesses belongs to
this year, though the charter is dated 955. The record of the suit also
gives a list of witnesses of the purchase of the estates, but the witnesses
belong to the year 975, except that Bishop Æthelgar's name must be
a later insertion, as he was not bishop until 980.

The main difficulty, however, in reconciling the evidence of the
Rochester document with that of the will, is to account for Brihtric's
naming of the estates in question in his will. They had belonged to
Brihtwaru's husband's family, and she was left a life-interest in them.
It is difficult to see what right Brihtric had over them, but possibly
he had obtained some share in them as a price for his assistance in
the suit, or he may have managed the estates as Brihtwaru's *mund*
and taken this opportunity of restating the arrangements made concerning the succession to these estates.

l. 12. *Meapaham.* Meopham, Kent.

on heora maga gewitnæsse. Wills only occasionally mention the
names of the witnesses. It is probable that they were generally drawn
up at some big assembly. When only a few witnesses are present,
as in this instance, the will was perhaps drawn up during illness.

l. 13. *Wulfstan Ucca.* He occurs as Wulfstan *Uccea* in B. 1131,
a document relating an exchange between him and Bishop Æthelwold
of Winchester. Æthelwold gave Washington, Sussex, in exchange for
Yaxley (afterwards given to Thorney) and Ailsworth, Huntingdonshire (afterwards given to Peterborough). The latter estate had been

forfeited by a widow and her son on the charge of attempting to encompass the death of Wulfstan's father, Ælfsige, by witchcraft. This forfeiture apparently occurred in 948, as Ælfsige had received Ailsworth from Edred in that year (B. 871). He may be the Ælfsige who received Haddon, Huntingdonshire, in 951 (B. 893) and Kettering in 956 (B. 943), and possibly identical with a thegn called Ælfsige Hunlafing, who was given five hides at Alwalton, Huntingdonshire, in 955 (B. 909). Wulfstan himself may be King Edwy's grantee in B. 1003, dated 957, where a thegn Wulfstan receives nine hides at Conington, Huntingdonshire.

Sired Ælfredes suna. Perhaps the Sired Siweard's brother, who witnessed K. 929, 847, somewhere about the end of the century. A 'Sired the old' witnesses a marriage agreement in Cnut's reign (K. 732), and an Ælfgar, Sired's son, is a surety in the same document. These are all Kentish charters.

ll. 15 f. *Byrhtwara Ælfrices laf.* See pp. 128 f.

l. 16. *Bryhtric hyræ mæg.* See p. 128.

Ælfstan bisceop. Probably Ælfstan, Bishop of Rochester. There was, however, a Bishop Ælfstan of London from 961 to 995 or 996. The date of the accession of Ælfstan of Rochester is uncertain. He signs from 964, and his predecessor's last signature occurs in 946. Ælfstan was succeeded by Godwine in 995. He was, therefore, the bishop who carried on the suit about the Bromley and Fawkham charters (see above).

ll. 17 ff. *ænne beah.....headorhundas.* This is a large heriot. The number of horses and swords is that of a king's thegn's heriot in Cnut's time (see II Cnut, 71, 1), but the whole payment is probably considerably in excess of this. For the inclusion of hawks and hounds we may compare the passage in D.B. 1, f. 56 *b*, which states that the Berkshire thegns paid to the king as 'relief' all their hawks and hounds if he wished to have them.

l. 19. *gefetelsode.* The Latin version mistranslates *optime adornatos.*

l. 22. *scē Andreæ.* Rochester Cathedral, which was dedicated to St Andrew.

l. 23. *sulung.* Land in Kent is usually reckoned in *sulungs* instead of hides. A charter of Coenwulf of Mercia of 812 equates the *sulung* with 2 hides (see Vinogradoff in *E.H.R.* xix, pp. 282 f.), but in a charter of King Edmund (B. 780), the phrase *VI mansas quod Cantigene dicunt VI sulunga* occurs. Similar expressions are to be found in B. 791, 869 and 1295, belonging to the reigns of Edmund, Edred and Edgar respectively. Some time before the middle of the tenth century the small hide of half a *sulung* had been superseded by one which was identical with the *sulung.* See also p. 108.

Denetune. Denton near Gravesend, Kent, D.B. *Danitone.* Rochester had two *solins* there (D.B. 1, f. 5 *b*).

l. 24. *Langanfelda.* Longfield, N.W. of Meopham, Kent. It occurs as an estate of one *solin* belonging to Rochester in D.B. 1, f. 5 *b*.

l. 26. *bænd*. The Latin version has *vittam capitis*. See p. 120.

l. 27. *twegra daga feorme*. See p. 120.

Hæslholte. This cannot now be identified.

Woðringaberan. Wateringbury, Kent.

l. 28. *Bærlingan*. Birling, Kent.

Hærigeardeshamme. Harrietsham, Kent.

p. 28, l. 1. *ðam biscope*. The Archbishop of Canterbury is meant.

l. 3. *Meapaham*. Christchurch had here an estate for 30 ploughs, assessed at 10 *solins*, in 1066 (D.B. 1, f. 4 *b*).

sc̄e Augustine. St Augustine's Abbey, Canterbury.

l. 5. *Dæræntan*. Darenth, Kent.

l. 7. *7 he selle x hund pænega*. The Latin version inserts *omni anno*. It is possible that the Anglo-Saxon version has omitted an *ælce geare*. In the time of Edward the Confessor, Birling, an estate of 6 *solins*, had a value of £12 (D.B. 1, f. 7 *b*).

l. 8. *innon þ gecynde*. This is one of the limitations in the alienation of land referred to in the laws (Alfred, 41). Land so bequeathed could not be alienated except with the consent of the kindred, in the presence of king and bishop.

ll. 10 f. *inland....utland*. The *inland* was the portion of the estate retained by the lord and worked for his use, the *utland* that leased out to tenants.

l. 11. *Wolcnesstede*. This is now Godstone, Surrey (see p. 124).

l. 12. *ân handsecs on ðrim pundan*. The Latin version omits this.

l. 13. *Strættune*. Stratton in Godstone, Surrey.

þæm mynstre. See p. 101.

l. 14. *Fealcnaham*. Fawkham, Kent.

Ælfric. See pp. 128 f. He was the son of Ælfhere and Æscwyn. Hickes (*op. cit.* p. 56) assumes that this Ælfhere is the ealdorman of that name, as he had a son Ælfric, who was banished in 985. This identification is impossible as the Ælfric mentioned in this will was dead before 975 (B. 1296).

l. 15. *Bromleah*. Bromley, near Chiselhurst, Kent. In 987 Rochester Cathedral was despoiled of this estate by King Ethelred, who gave it to Æthelsige (K. 657). Ethelred restored it in 998 (K. 700) and Rochester held it as an estate of 6 *solins*, but with land for 13 ploughs, in 1066 (D.B. 1, f. 5 *b*).

l. 17. *Snodingcland*. Snodland, Kent. In Bishop Godwine's time, soon after 995, Rochester Cathedral had another lawsuit about this estate (K. 929), with a certain Leofwine, Ælfheah's son, who was in possession of the estate while the Cathedral had the title-deed. The suit ended in a compromise by which the Cathedral secured the reversion. Rochester holds an estate of 6 *solins* in D.B. 1, f. 5 *b*.

ll. 18 f. *Ælfere...Ælfrices fæder*. See above. In the Latin version he is wrongly called Ælfric's son.

l. 19. *7 he seoððan*. The date of this confirmation by Ælfric of his father's bequest is earlier than the death of Archbishop Oda. The

Chronicle F places this in 961, but 958 is probably the true date (see p. 114).

Eadgife ðære hlæfdian. She was the third wife of Edward the Elder and mother of Edmund and Edred. She was the daughter of the Kentish Ealdorman Sigelm, and held lands in Kent (see Harmer, XXIII and notes). King Edred leaves her all his 'booklands' in Sussex, Surrey and Kent, as well as some other estates (*ibid.* XXI). She was despoiled of her estates in Edwy's reign, but recovered them in Edgar's. It is improbable, therefore, that Ælfric's confirmation took place in Edwy's reign, when she was in disfavour.

l. 20. *Odan arcebisceopes.* He became Archbishop of Canterbury in 942. On the date of his death, see p. 114. An account of him is given in the *Vita S. Oswaldi,* pp. 401–411, 419, and his life was written by Eadmer (Hardy, *Catalogue,* I, 566–568).

ll. 20 f. *Ælfeges Ælfstanes suna 7 Ælfrices his broðor.* These brothers are concerned in the document relating to Rochester Cathedral's estate at Wouldham (B. 1097). Ælfheah inherited his father's estates and, after the death of his brother Ælfric and the latter's son Eadric, he let Archbishop Dunstan draw up his will, in which he left Wouldham and other estates to Rochester. Eadric's widow and her second husband attempted to violate this will, but the suit was brought up before a shiremoot and decision given in favour of Rochester, some time during the archepiscopate of Dunstan.

l. 21. *Fecham.* Fetcham, Surrey.

l. 22. *Hó.* Hoo, on the north bank of the estuary of the Medway. *Crogdæne.* Croydon, Surrey.

l. 25. *Tydiceseg.* Titsey, Surrey.

l. 26. *7 II spuran on III pundan.* This is omitted in the Latin version.

XII.

MS. *Liber Monasterii de Hyda,* f. 33 *b.* See p. 114.

EDITIONS. Edwards, p. 236, with a modern English translation on p. 357.

DATE. Not before 987, as Ethelred granted Manningford to Æthelwold in this year (see preceding charter in the *Liber Mon. de Hyda*). Apart from this we have no means of dating the will.

p. 30, l. 1. *Apelwoldis.* The rubric calls him *viri Dei,* possibly confusing him with the Bishop, St Æthelwold.

l. 2. *for his cynescipe.* Cf. p. 20, l. 2.

l. 6. *sawelsceatte.* See pp. 109 f.

ll. 6 f. *his gebroþrun into Abbandune.* Æthelwold may have been admitted to confraternity with the monks of this abbey. Cf. Harmer, p. 72.

l. 7. *heregeattewan.* See p. 100. The uncertainty as to the meaning of *lecg* prevents us from estimating the value of this heriot. In the number of horses and weapons it is nearest to the heriot of the highest king's thegn in the Danelaw as stated in II Cnut, 71, 4. See p. 147.

l. 8. *lecga*. See p. 123.

l. 10. *Maningforda*. Manningford Abbots, Wiltshire. Ethelred had granted Æthelwold ten hides there, and these were held by the New Minster in 1066 (D.B. 1, f. 67).

l. 13. *Uptune*. Possibly Upton Scudamore, Wiltshire.

XIII.

MS. British Museum, Stowe Charter 36. This is the top portion of a 'cyrograph' (see p. 151), written about the end of the tenth century. Its endorsement, *Westmonasteriensi—Brikandon*, shows it to have belonged to Westminster Abbey. Thorpe has also a reference to Harley 311, f. 316, but this MS. does not contain so many folios, and no version of Ælfhelm's will is contained in it. It is a paper MS. containing copies of documents relating to Ramsey Abbey, among which is that by which Ælfhelm and Æffe gave Hatley and Potton to the abbey (B. 1062, *Historia Ramesiensis*, R.S. chapter XXX) and perhaps Thorpe's reference is due to confusion with this. I cannot find a second version of the will, and Thorpe appears to have taken his text from Kemble, who quotes the Stowe MS. as his only authority. Madox, who in his *Formulare Anglicanum*, p. ii footnote, has a reference to this will, knew of the Stowe MS. only.

FACSIMILE. *Ordnance Survey Facsimiles*, Part III, No. 37.

EDITIONS. Lye, *Dictionarium Saxonico et Gothico Latinum*, II, Appendix II, 1.
K. 967.
T. p. 596.
B. 1306.

DATE. After 975, and certainly before 1016. The will is later than the foundation of Ramsey Abbey, and the Ramsey historian gives the date of the dedication as 974. Ælfhelm speaks of his services to the father of the reigning king and probably, therefore, drew up his will in the reign of Edward the Martyr or Ethelred. He witnesses a charter of 989, and if he had served King Edmund he would have been an old man by this date. He is mentioned in the *Liber Eliensis* in connection with events of Edgar's reign. A *minister* Ælfhelm appears fairly frequently in lists of witnesses up to 974, and between 982 and 990, but this may be the Ælfhelm who signs as ealdorman from about 990, and was killed in 1006. After 990 the name Ælfhelm occurs only twice among the *ministri* in Ethelred's reign, in 1007 and 1008, but we have no means of deciding whether this is the testator.

l. 16. *Ælfhelm*. In B. 1305 Edgar refers to him as his faithful *minister* and grants him an estate at Wratting. The *Liber Eliensis*, II, 73, records Ælfhelm's gift of land at this place to the abbey, calling him *miles divitiis abundans*, but does not identify him with the Ælfhelm *Polga* who is spoken of elsewhere in the *Liber Eliensis*. The spurious Westminster charter (B. 1050), however, referring to Ælfhelm's gift of Brickendon, calls him *Polga*, and this is not a statement likely to have been invented by a forger. The Ælfhelm *Polga* of the *Liber Eliensis* (II, 10, 11, 29) acts as witness in the counties in which the estates of this will are situated. He had a brother who was also called Ælfhelm (*ibid.* II, 10). This naming of brothers by the same name may be due to Scandinavian influence; it is not infrequently met with in Icelandic Sagas. The Ælfhelm mentioned on p. 32, l. 21 is probably the testator's brother. Two Ælfhelms, one called *Polga*, witness a document in the *Liber Monasterii de Hyda* (p. 245) which can be dated 989 by its list of witnesses.

There is also an extant document in which Ælfhelm grants a hide of land at Potton to his goldsmith (K. 1352), and among the witnesses, besides the grantor, occur another Ælfhelm, 'the young', and his sons Æthelric and Ælfwold. No doubt these are the people who occur in this will (see below), probably the brother and nephews of the testator. Other witnesses are Wulfmær, the bishop's brother, Ælmær *Cild*, and Godric, the son of Leofric of *Holewelle*. These also may be legatees in the will.

Ælfhelm occurs also in the *Historia Ramesiensis*. In chapter xxx he and his wife *Affa* are said to have given Hatley and Potton to Ramsey Abbey, yet in his will Ælfhelm bequeathes land at these places to two brothers, Ælfstan and Ælfmær, with no mention of a reversion to Ramsey. In chapter xxix an abstract is given of the will of a certain Æthelstan, Mann's son, and according to this, Æthelstan left two hides at Hatley to his sister and the rest to *Lefsius*. The latter is called Ælfhelm's relation in chapter xxx, and is no doubt the Leofsige of Ælfhelm's will: Æthelstan, Mann's son, left Potton to his brother's son after the death of Ælfhelm's wife Æffa. The history of these estates is therefore very confused. It may be that the name Æthelstan is an error for Ælfstan, one of the legatees who are to receive these estates according to the present will, and that he drew up his will after Ælfhelm's death. Æthelstan, the son of Mann, is, however, also mentioned in the *Liber Eliensis*, II, 13, 33, so that it is not only the Ramsey scribe who gives the name in this form. In any case the grant to Ramsey Abbey remains unexplained, unless it concerns different estates at these places. Ramsey was not holding land at either place in 1066, according to D.B.

l. 17. *for gode 7 for wurulde*. Literally 'for the sake of God and the world'.

ll. 17 ff. *ærest his hlaforde....ungerædode*. This is almost the heriot of the king's thegn who is nearest to him (see II Cnut, 71, 1). He pays double the money payment, but no helmets or coats of mail.

l. 20. *Wrættincge*. Wratting, Cambridgeshire. Ælfhelm had received 2½ hides (3 according to the boundaries) from Edgar in 975

(B. 1305), but he must have held more land there than this or he would have expressed his bequest to Ely differently. This bequest is mentioned in the *Liber Eliensis*, II, 73, and the exception of the 2 hides is accurately noted. Ely may have possessed one copy of the will. In D.B. I, f. 190 *b*, Ely is in possession of 4½ hides at Wratting.

l. 21. *sēe Æþeldryðe*. The original foundress of Ely. (See Bede, *Historia Ecclesiastica*, IV, 19.)

l. 22. *Brycandune*. Brickendon, Hertfordshire. In the spurious Westminster charter B. 1050, Ælfhelm *Polga* is mentioned as the donor of 5 hides at Brickendon.

ll. 22 f. *sēe Petre to Westmenstre*. The legends of the founding of Westminster are collected in J. Armitage Robinson's introduction to Flete's *History of Westminster Abbey*. Tradition ascribes its refoundation to Dunstan (Flete, chapter XVI). It had certainly been refounded by 998, when bequests were made to it by a certain Leofwine (*Crawford Charters*, IX).

ll. 23 f. *þ man mæste minum wiue...þider hire leouest sy*. I owe to Professor Chadwick the suggestion that *þider* refers to a religious foundation. This word would hardly have been used to express 'in whatever place'.

l. 25. *Hwipstede*. Whepstead, Suffolk.

l. 26. *Wealtune*. Perhaps Walton near Felixstow, Suffolk.

p. 32, l. 1. *morgengyue*. See p. 111.

Beadewan 7 Burgestede. Baddow and Burstead, Essex.

Strætford. Probably Stratford St Mary, Suffolk.

l. 2. *Heanhealan*. Skeat (*Place-Names of Cambridgeshire*, 1911 edition, p. 43) identifies this as Enhale, an old parish now absorbed into West Wickham. It occurs in the boundaries of the grant of Wratting (B. 1306), where it is shown to be near Balsham.

ll. 2 f. *þa wyt ærest togædere comon*. Besides the *morgengifu*, it appears that Ælfhelm had made another gift to his wife. This no doubt corresponds with the gift which, according to the code *Be Wifmannes Beweddung*, 3, the bridegroom was to pay in order to obtain the bride's consent. In this code, however, no *morgengifu* is mentioned. It appears to have been replaced by an agreement concerning succession in the event of the wife outliving her husband. There is an extant marriage agreement which corresponds closely with Ælfhelm's will as regards this question. It is an eleventh-century Kentish document (K. 732), and it first states what the bridegroom gave to the bride 'in order that she might accept his suit', and then names two estates with stock, which were probably the *morgengifu*, and finally mentions an arrangement by which the survivor shall succeed to the stock on all their lands. If we assume that Ælfhelm's wife's right of succession to half the stock on their lands, mentioned on ll. 27 f., was by virtue of an agreement made at the time of her marriage, the parallel between the will and the Kentish contract is very close. It seems as if a *morgengifu* could exist by the side of an agreement concerning succession, and its omission from the *Be Wifmannes Beweddung* is perhaps only accidental. On the other hand Thurstan in his will of 1044 or 1045 (p. 82, l. 6) states what he gave to his wife ' as bride-payment and by agreement' and does not mention *morgengifu*, though this does not prove that he had not given one. As is pointed out below (see p. 195) he uses a Scandinavian legal phrase, and the introduction of the agreement concerning succession may be due to Scandinavian influence. Agreements between husband and wife, which may have been marriage contracts, are mentioned in the wills of the Ealdorman Æthelmær (p. 26, ll. 7 ff.) and Thurketel of Palgrave (p. 68, l. 8).

l. 3. *Wilburgeham.* Wilbraham, Cambridgeshire.

Hrægenan. Rayne, Essex.

l. 4. *Carletunes.* Carlton, Cambridgeshire, about 2 miles N.E. of Wratting.

l. 5. *heauodbotles.* This passage shows clearly that *heafodbotl* denotes not only the house but also the land attached to it.

Gyrstlingaþorpe. Gestingthorpe, Essex.

.l 6. *Godrice.* Probably Ælfhelm's son-in-law, and perhaps the son of Leofric of *Holewelle* who witnessed K. 1352 (see p. 134).

l. 7. *7 be felda.* Not 'field' in the modern sense but land not included in the arable, woodland, or meadow.

l. 9. *Cunningtune.* Conington, Cambridgeshire.

l. 10. *Æþelrice 7 Alfwolde.* See p. 134.

l. 11. *minum cnihte.* See p. 127.

l. 12. *Ælfmære 7 his breðer Ælfstane.* Ælfmær may be the *Ælmær Cild* who witnesses K. 1352. On p. 134 I have suggested that Ælfstan is the same person as the Æthelstan, son of Mann, who bequeathed Hatley and Potton.

l. 13. *æt Hættanlea 7 æt Pottune.* Cockayne Hatley, and Potton, Bedfordshire. See p. 134.

l. 14. *Leofsige.* See p. 134.

l. 15. *Lytlanbyrig.* Littlebury, near Saffron Walden, Essex.

l. 16. *þan ealdormen.* Probably Æthelwine of East Anglia.

l. 17. *Stoctune.* Possibly Stockton near Bungay, Norfolk. This is rather a long way from Ælfhelm's other estates, but I cannot find a place of this name nearer at hand.

l. 19. *minum þrym broþron.* One we know to have been called Ælfhelm, who had sons called Ælfwold and Æthelric (see p. 134).

Trostingtune. Troston, Suffolk.

l. 21. *Ælfhelme.* See p. 134.

Icelingtune. Ickleton, Cambridgeshire.

l. 22. *Mawyrþe.* The MS. is corrupt at this point. There may have been a letter before the *m*. The place cannot be identified.

Wulfmære. Perhaps the Bishop's brother who witnesses K. 1352 (see p. 134).

Byornham. Probably Barnham, Suffolk. (For the spelling *yo*, cf. *Byorcing* in the will of Æthelflæd, p. 34, l. 24.)

l. 23. *minre scæðe.* O.Icel. *skeið*, 'a ship of the largest kind', 'a long-ship' (see Fritzner, *Ordbok, s.v. skeið*). The word is feminine in Ice-landic, but this will contains the only recorded instance of the feminine in O.E. In the will of Bishop Ælfwold of Crediton (*Crawford Charters*, x), the bishop grants to the king *ænne scegð lxiiii ǽre.* This shows that the Chronicle 1008 F. is right in speaking of *scegþ* as *unam magnam nauem.* Yet *scapha, vel trieris* is glossed *litel scip, uel sceigð* in Wright-Wülker, 165. 40. Evidently it was the shape, not the size, which was the distinguishing feature of the *scegþ.*

Ælfhelm's bequest is probably for the purpose of lessening the burden of a ship-tax. We may compare the Chronicle 1008 E (cf. also *ibid.* II, p. 185) where it is stated that the king ordered the building of ships 'over all England', *þ is þonne [of] þrym hund hidum. 7 of x. hidon ænne scegð, 7 of viii hidum helm 7 byrnan.* It is possible that Ælfhelm's will is later than this annal, but it is not necessary to assume this, as the bequest by Archbishop Ælfric in 1003 or 1004 of ships to two counties, one of them an inland one, shows that some sort of ship-tax was known before the date of this notice in the Chronicle, which perhaps marks an increase in the amount (see p. 163).

Hramesege. This monastery was founded by Bishop Oswold of Worcester and Ealdorman Æthelwine of East Anglia, and dedicated to St Benedict. See *Vita S. Oswaldi*, pp. 429 f.; *Historia Ramesiensis*, chapter XVIII f. The latter authority gives 974 as the date of its dedica-tion, but says it was begun in 968.

ll. 25 f. *minan geferan...þe me mid ridað.* These may have been fellow-members of some association like the London gild whose statutes are given in VI Athelstan. One of its chief functions was the riding after stolen cattle. In Athelstan's second code the term *geferan* is applied to the men who were jointly responsible for carrying out the sentence of forfeiture on a man in their district (cf. e.g. 20, 2, *gif hwa þonne nylle ridan mid his geferan*).

l. 28. *swa hio to forgyuen wæs.* No compound verb *toforgifan* is recorded, and I therefore take *to* to be adverbial. The construction is, however, unusual, and I suspect that something has been omitted. The phrase may refer to a marriage agreement (see p. 135).

p. 34, l. 2. *on mode 7 on mægene.* An alliterative phrase which can-not be literally translated. Alliterative expressions containing these words continue down into M.E. (see N.E.D. *s.v. mood*).

XIV.

With this will, cf. Nos. II, xv.

MSS. (*a*) British Museum, Harley Charter 43, C. 4, a sheet of parchment containing this will and No. xv. The handwriting is of the early eleventh century. The endorsement, *Ceorleswoðe 7 Cokefeld*, shows that it was a Bury charter, since these two estates are left to Bury.

(*b*) Cambridge University Library, MS. FF. 2. 33, f. 46 *b* (see p. 99). Probably the original of this fourteenth-century version was the Harley charter, since the boundaries in the later version cease just where the Harley charter becomes illegible. This version of the will has therefore no independent value.

The text is from (*a*).

FACSIMILE of (*a*). Bond, *Facsimiles of Ancient Charters in the British Museum*, Part III, No. 35.

EDITIONS. Wotton, *Short View of Hickes' Thesaurus*, 2nd edition,
      1737, pp. 95 f., from (*a*).
      K. 685, from (*a*).
      T. p. 519, from (*a*).
      E. p. 364, from (*a*).
      B. 1288, from (*a*), 1354, from (*b*).
      Sweet, *A Second Anglo-Saxon Reader*, p. 209, from (*a*).

DATE. Between 962 and 991, probably after 975. The will is certainly no earlier than 962, the year in which Edgar granted to Æthelflæd the estate at Chelsworth (B. 1082). It is earlier than Brihtnoth's death in 991. Probably Edgar was dead when the will was made, since Æthelflæd gives Damarham to Glastonbury for his soul as well as for Edmund's.

l. 13. *Æþelflæde*. She was the daughter of the Ealdorman Ælfgar (see No. 11) and second wife of King Edmund, who could not have married her more than two years before his death in 946, as his first wife died in 944 (Ethelwerd, Bk IV, c. 6). The Chronicle, 946 D, speaks of her as *Æþelflæd at Domerhame*. There is an undated charter of Edmund (B. 817) in which he grants her this estate.

Her will is mentioned in the *Liber Eliensis*, II, 64, and here she is called the wife of the Ealdorman Æthelstan. If the Ely scribe is not making a wrong identification here, this ealdorman must have been her second husband. Two ealdormen of this name sign in the first part of the tenth century, one being Æthelstan 'Half king' of East Anglia, whose signatures first appear in 923. Both sign together from 940 till 956, then one only signs until 974, and it is no doubt the East Anglian ealdorman who ceases to sign in 956. It is more probable that Æthelflæd's husband was the second Æthelstan, whose sphere of office is unknown. Æthelstan 'Half king's' wife was called Ælfwen (*Historia Ramesiensis*, c. 111), and if he had married Æthelflæd as his second wife it is probable that this would have been mentioned in the *Historia Ramesiensis*, which gives us much information concerning his family. The *Liber Eliensis* knows nothing of Æthelflæd's marriage with Edmund, but this must have been of short duration. The same authority states that she outlived her husband and remained a widow until her death.

Æthelflæd makes no reference to her husband Æthelstan in her will. She does not leave a bequest for his soul and one cannot be certain whether she is holding estates left by him. She leaves an estate at Ham to Christchurch, and in 958 King Edgar granted *Hamme* to Æthelstan, his *comes* (B. 1037); but these estates need not be identical, for Ham is a common name. Æthelflæd's estate is more probably that given by an *Agylflaeda*, with the consent of her lord, Edmund, to Christchurch (B. 698). This charter, it is true, bears the date 933 or 934, but it is preserved in the late cartulary, Lambeth 1212, and the date may be an error for 944. It is at least a coincidence that we should find the names of Æthelflæd and her husband connected with a grant to Christchurch of an estate of the same name as one that Æthelflæd actually bequeathed there.

Of the other estates of Æthelflæd's mentioned in her will many were bequeathed to her by her father, and others we know from Ælfflæd's will to have been granted by other ancestors. Damerham and Chelsworth were royal gifts to her. There remain seven estates in the eastern counties, and Lambourn, Cholsey and Reading, which might have come into Æthelflæd's possession from her second husband. Lambourn, however, had been a royal estate (see Harmer, p. 18, l. 9) and the estates in the east lay closely intermixed with those which came to her from her family.

l. 14. *Lamburnan.* Lambourn, Berkshire. In 1066 it was a royal estate of 20 hides (D.B. 1, f. 57 b: *V. C. H. of Berkshire*, 1, p. 331).

Ceolsige. Cholsey, Berkshire. This is entered in D.B. as a royal estate of ' 23 hides assessed at 22 ' (D.B. 1, f. 56 b: *V. C. H. of Berkshire*, 1, p. 328).

Readingan. Reading, Berkshire. This also is a royal estate in D.B., assessed at 43 hides (D.B. 1, f. 58: *V. C. H. of Berkshire*, 1, p. 334).

ll. 15 f. *7 feower beagas...7 IIII hors.* This serves the same purpose as the heriot (see p. 100).

l. 15. *pellas.* O.E. *pæll* is derived from Latin *pallium* and is used in the sense 'mantle', 'cloak', but with special reference to the costly garments worn by the wealthy. It is also used of valuable material and coverings. See examples in B.T. *s.v. pæll.*

l. 16. *bleda.* Some sort of vessel to carry liquids, generally wine. Cf. Cockayne, *Leechdoms*, R.S. 11, 118. 24, etc. It is used as a gloss for *fiola, fiala* in Wright-Wülker, 122. 38, 282. 8, 405. 27, and for *patera*, 329. 21.

l. 19. *Domarhame.* Damerham, Wiltshire. The estate was given to her, with reversion to Glastonbury, by her husband King Edmund, and his donation charter is extant (B. 817).

ll. 19 f. *into Glestingabyrig for Ædmundes cinges sawle.* King Edmund was buried at Glastonbury (W.M. *G.R.* p. 160; Fl. Wig. 946), which had lately been restored by Dunstan (see Chronicle, 11, p. 144).

l. 20. *7 for Æadgares cinges.* Edgar also was buried at Glastonbury (Chronicle, 1016 D, E). This reference to him in connection with a bequest to Glastonbury, and nowhere else in the will, makes it probable that the will is later than his death.

l. 21. *Hamme*. There are too many places called *Ham* for us to identify this estate. It might be the Essex, Kentish, or Surrey Ham.

l. 23. *Wudaham*. One of the Essex Woodhams.

Bæorhtnoðe æaldormen. See p. 106.

mire swustær. Ælfflæd, whose will is No. xv.

l. 24. *sca Marian cyrcan æt Byorcingan*. Barking Abbey. See p. 106.

l. 25. *Hedham*. Hadham, Hertfordshire. Æthelflæd had also given an estate at this place to Ely (*Liber Eliensis*, ii, 64). In 1066 the Bishop of London had 7½ hides at this place (D.B. i, f. 133 b: *V. C. H. of Hertfordshire*, i, p. 305) and the Abbot of Ely 4 hides (D.B. i, f. 135: *V. C. H. of Hertfordshire*, i, p. 312).

l. 27. *to bisceophamæ*, i.e. the property set apart for the use of the bishop. See p. 103.

Dictunæ. Fen or Wood Ditton, Cambridgeshire. Cf. p. 6, ll. 9, 15 and p. 40, l. 9.

p. 36, l. 1. *scæ Æþælðryð*. See p. 135.

hire geswustran. See pp. 143 f.

l. 2. *Cohhanfeldæa*. Cockfield, Suffolk, the *Cokefeld* of Ælfgar's will, p. 6, ll. 9, 13, where it was left to Æthelflæd with reversion to Bury on her death, but she grants it to Bury only after the death of her sister and her brother-in-law.

Cæorlesweorþe. Chelsworth, Suffolk. This estate had been given to Æthelflæd by King Edgar in 962 (B. 1082). Bury was in possession in 1066 (D.B. ii, f. 368 b: *V. C. H. of Suffolk*, i, p. 505).

l. 4. *scæ Eadmundes stowe to Bydericeswyrðe*. See p. 102.

l. 5. *Fingringahó*. Fingringhoe, Essex.

·l. 6. *scæ Pætres cyrcan æt Myresigæ*. West Mersea church is now dedicated to St Peter and St Paul. Its tower is said to be late Anglo-Saxon (see Baldwin Brown, *The Arts in Early England*, ii, p. 340).

l. 7. *Polstede*. Polstead, Suffolk. The boundaries of this estate are given on p. 40, ll. 27 ff.

l. 8. *Stocy*. Stoke-by-Nayland, Suffolk. See p. 105. The form with y does not occur in No. xv. It is very curious. Can it be a dialectal survival of a locative? Forms in -*i*, -*y*, occur in the first part of the Rushworth MS., a text of about the same period as the original of this will. See Sievers, *Angelsächsische Grammatik*, § 237, note 2.

l. 9. *Hwifersce*: a scribal error for *Hwifermersce*, now Withermarsh, about a mile east of Polstead.

l. 10. *Strætforda*. Stratford St Mary, Suffolk.

l. 12. *Lauanham*. Lavenham, Suffolk.

l. 13. *Byligesdynæ*. Professor Mawer identifies this as Balsdon Hall, one mile S.W. of Lavenham. The boundaries which are given on p. 40, ll. 21 ff., do not support Skeat's identification of this estate with Bildeston (*Place-Names of Suffolk*, p. 94).

l. 15. *æt Peltandune 7 et Myresige 7 æt Grenstede*. Peldon, Mersea and Greenstead, Essex.

l. 17. *Ylmesæton*. Elmsett, Suffolk.

l. 19. *þorpæ*. Perhaps Thorpe Morieux, Suffolk. This is the nearest Thorpe to Hadleigh, and is close to Cockfield, Lavenham and other estates of Æthelflæd's.

Hedlæge. Hadleigh, Suffolk, not far north of the Polstead estate. The Domesday entry (D.B. 1, f. 372 *b* : *V. C. H. of Suffolk*, 1, p. 509) says that it had a church with one carucate of free land, which is perhaps the hide at Thorpe granted by Æthelflæd.

l. 21. *Wicforda*. Wickford, Essex.

Sibrihte minum mægæ. Possibly he is the Sibriht whose brother Ætheric fought at Maldon (*Battle of Maldon*, ll. 280 ff.).

l. 22. *minum geræfan*. The reeve was an official who looked after the management of the estate. His duties are set out in the document *Gerefa* (Liebermann, 1, pp. 453 ff.).

IIII hida. There is uncertainty about this number. Kemble read it IIII, but there is a faint line joining the first two strokes and Bond and Birch read UII. The scribe of the Cambridge MS. read the number as IIII. In either case, it is an unusually large grant to a reeve.

l. 24. *minum cnihtæ*. See p. 127.

l. 25. *Dunninclande*. Donyland, Essex.

l. 30. *Wæaldingafælda*. Waldingfield, Suffolk.

Crawa mira magan. Æthelflæd leaves this gift to Crawe without any reservation, and yet Ælfflæd is able to dispose of the estate after Crawe's day according to her sister's agreement (see p. 40, ll. 3 ff.). There must, therefore, have been some separate arrangements about this estate which are left unmentioned in the will.

XV.

With this will cf. Nos. 11, xiv.

MS. AND FACSIMILE. See pp. 137 f.

EDITIONS. Wotton, *op. cit.* pp. 103 f., from (*a*).
    K. 685, from (*a*).
    T. p. 522, from (*a*).
    E. p. 366, from (*a*).
    B. 1289, from (*a*).
    Sweet, *A Second Anglo-Saxon Reader*, p. 210, from (*a*).

DATE. 1002, or a year or two earlier. The Ealdorman Æthelmær mentioned in the will is never given this title before 996, and then probably erroneously. I consider it improbable that he was ealdorman before 998. His first certain signature is 1002 (see pp. 144 f.). The queen-mother Ælfthryth, a legatee of the will, died before the end of 1002 (see p. 123).

p. 38, l. 1. *Ælfflæd*. She was Ælfgar's younger daughter and wife of the Ealdorman Brihtnoth. She is mentioned as a benefactress in the *Liber Eliensis*, 11, 63. The same authority, 11, 88, says that Brihtnoth had a daughter, Leofflæd, and gives a Latin version of her will, in which she leaves estates to three daughters. If she had been Ælfflæd's daughter, many estates left by Ælfflæd to religious communities should by the terms of Ælfgar's will have reverted to her (see, e.g. p. 6, ll. 20 ff.). She is not even mentioned in Ælfflæd's will. It is, of course, possible that she was dead by this date, but if so it is curious that Ælfflæd makes no bequests to any of Leofflæd's children. It seems most probable that Leofflæd was Ælfflæd's step-daughter only. On the descendants of this Leofflæd see pp. 189 f.

Ælfflæd at the date of this will was in possession of numerous estates left to her by her father and her sister. Most of these she was to have for her lifetime only. Besides these she had some estates obtained from her ancestors which are not mentioned in the wills of her father and sister. Another estate, Rettendon, was her *morgengifu* from Brihtnoth, and she had eleven estates of which we do not know the origin. They all lie in the eastern counties, mainly Essex, and probably she inherited them from her husband. Seven of them she leaves to the king.

ll. 2 ff. *Ærest þ ic an minum hlaforde....* A similar bequest to her sister's on p. 34, ll. 13 ff. See p. 139.

l. 4. *Douorcortæ.* Dovercourt, near Harwich, Essex.

Fulanpettæ. This place is entered in D.B. II, f. 77 *b* as *Fulepet.* *V. C. H. of Essex,* I, p. 396, identifies it as Beaumont, a few miles from Dovercourt.

Ælesforda. D.B. II, f. 11 *b, Elesforda. V. C. H. of Essex,* I, p. 440, identifies it as Alresford.

Stanwægun. Stanway, Essex.

l. 5. *Byrætune.* Perhaps the unidentified Domesday manor of *Bertuna* in Barstable Hundred (D. B. II, f. 94: *V. C. H. of Essex,* I, p. 558).

Læxadyne. Lexden, Essex.

Ylmesætun. Elmsett, Suffolk. This is the only estate of the eight left to the king which we know to have come to Ælfflæd by inheritance from her kindred. See p. 36, l. 17.

Bucyshealæ. Buxhall, Suffolk.

l. 7. *leof*: a title of address. See Harmer, p. 117.

l. 9. *Stocæ.* See p. 105.

l. 10. *sæadon.* This probably represents the O.E. *sealdon,* the 'l' having been omitted by a copyist's error.

ll. 10 f. *a to freogon godæs rihte.* For the order of the words in this phrase, cf. Wülfing, *Syntax Alfreds des Grossen,* I, p. 50: e.g. *mid ryhtum Godes dome; mistlica Godes gesceafta.*

ll. 13 f. *þonæ wuda æt Hæþfælda þæ min swystar gæuþæ.* There is no mention of this wood in Æthelflæd's will; she must therefore have granted it to Stoke on a separate occasion. The place is perhaps Hatfield Peverel, Essex, or Hatfield, Hertfordshire.

ll. 14 ff. *þa land....7 ofær minne.* In this list of estates are some which should have gone to Stoke immediately on Æthelflæd's death.

l. 16. *Stredfordæ*. Probably Stratford St Mary, Suffolk. Cf. p. 36, ll. 10 f.

Fresantun. Freston, Suffolk. This estate has not occurred in Ælfgar's will or Æthelflæd's.

Wiswyþetun. Wiston, or Wissington, Suffolk. This estate is first mentioned in this will. See p. 107.

l. 17. *Lauanhamæ.* Lavenham, Suffolk.

Byliesdyne. Balsdon Hall, Suffolk. See p. 140.

Polstyde. Polstead, Suffolk.

Wifærmyrsc. Withermarsh, Suffolk.

Boundaries of these three estates are appended to the will.

ll. 17 f. *Grænstydæ 7 Peltandune 7 Myræsegæ.* Greenstead, Peldon and Mersea, Essex. See p. 8, ll. 4 f.

ll. 18 f. *þ wudæland æt Totham...into Myresiæ.* See p. 8, ll. 13 ff.

l. 19. *Colne 7 Tigan.* Colne and Tey, Essex. See p. 6, l. 29.

l. 22. *Illanlege.* Monks Eleigh, Suffolk.

l. 23. *Hedham.* See p. 34, l. 25 and note.

biscophame. See pp. 103, 140.

l. 24. *Tidwoldingtune.* Ælfgar had left this estate to a certain Ælfwold (p. 8, ll. 11 f.) on condition of paying a rent to St Paul's. In a St Paul's charter of doubtful authenticity (B. 737), the gift of this estate is attributed to King Athelstan. No doubt by the date of the fabrication of this charter the true origin of the Cathedral's possession of this estate had been forgotten.

l. 25. *Beorcingan.* Barking Abbey. See p. 106.

Babbingþyrnan. Baythorn, Essex. Ælfgar had left it to Æthelflæd, with reversion to Ælfflæd (see p. 6, ll. 19 f.), but it is not mentioned in Æthelflæd's will.

l. 26. *Ælfþræðe minæs hlauordæs medder.* This refers, not to Brihtnoth's mother, but to the king's mother, Ælfthryth (see p. 123). The form of the name here is due to the fact that the scribe's dialect clearly had *e* for O.E. *y* (cf. e.g. *brece*, p. 38, ll. 22, 24, 25, 31, *gefelste*, p. 40, l. 20), and that he regarded *e* and *æ* as equivalent symbols.

l. 27. *Wuduhamæs.* Woodham, Essex.

l. 30. *Cæorlesweorþæ 7 Cochanfelde.* Chelsworth and Cockfield, Suffolk.

l. 32. *Hnyddinge.* Nedging, near Bildeston, Suffolk.

Crawan. See p. 36, l. 30.

p. 40, l. 2. *Fingringaho.* Fingringhoe, Essex.

l. 3. *Wealdingafelda.* Waldingfield, Suffolk.

l. 4. *into Suðbyrig to scæ Gregoriæ.* Sudbury, Suffolk, had a 'church of St Gregory with 50 acres of free land' at the time of Domesday (D.B. II, f. 286 *b*: *V. C. H. of Suffolk*, I, p. 426). The Essex thegn Æthelric also makes a bequest to this church. (See p. 42, l. 20.)

l. 5. *scæ Æþældryþe.* See p. 135.

l. 6. *sce Wihtburhe.* She was a younger sister of St Etheldreda, and founded a monastery at Dereham (see *Liber Eliensis*, I, 2; Capgrave,

Nova Legenda s.v. *Withburga*). Her body was translated to Ely in Edgar's reign (*Liber Eliensis*, II, 53).

scæ Sexburhe. St Etheldreda's sister, and successor as abbess of Ely (Bede, *Historia Ecclesiastica*, III, 8, IV, 19; Capgrave, *Nova Legenda* s.v. *Sexburga*).

sce Æormenhilde. She was Sexburg's daughter, and wife of Wulfhere of Mercia. She succeeded her mother as abbess of *Minster*, then of Ely.

ll. 6 f. *þer mines hlafordes lichoma rest*. *Liber Eliensis*, II, 62, after a legendary account of the Battle of Maldon, states that the monks fetched Brihtnoth's body from the battlefield and buried it at Ely, in accordance with a promise given to him in return for nine estates, thirty mancuses of gold and other presents.

l. 7. *þara þreo landa*. The *Liber Eliensis*, II, 63 relates that *Ælfleda Domina*, the wife of the *dux* Brihtnoth, gave to them *Ratendune*, *Saham* and *Dittune*, after her husband's death. In the preceding chapter it says that *Rettendun* and *Sægham* were given by Brihtnoth to Ely in return for hospitality shown to him on his way to Maldon. Probably Brihtnoth and Ælfflæd had granted the reversion of these estates to Ely.

l. 8. *Rettendune*. Rettendon, Essex.

morgangyfu. See p. 111. The *Liber Eliensis*, *loc. cit.*, says that *Ratendune* was *de dote sua*. In post-conquest Latin texts the O.E. *morgengifu* is translated by *dos*, because there was nothing corresponding to the Anglo-Saxon gift after the Conquest. The *morgengifu*, however, was a gift by the husband to the bride, and the true *dos* was a gift by the bride's guardian.

l. 9. *Sægham*. Soham, Cambridgeshire.

Dictune. Fen or Wood Ditton, Cambridgeshire.

ll. 10 f. *þaræ anre hide æt Cæafle þe min swystar begeat*. Cheveley, Cambridgeshire. Æthelflæd does not mention it in her will. The *Liber Eliensis*, *loc. cit.*, says that *Ælfleda* gave one hide at *Chefle*.

l. 11. *þes bæahges gemacan*. The ring given as *sawolsceat* to Ely must be the 'torque' of gold mentioned in the *Liber Eliensis*, *loc. cit.*, as given by *Ælfleda* after her husband's death. According to the same authority, she also gave a curtain showing the deeds of her husband, apparently a tapestry of the Bayeux type.

ll. 11 f. *minum hlaforde to sawlescæatte*. Not '*as soulscot to my lord*' (Thorpe). (For *sawlescæatte*, see pp. 109 f.)

l. 12. *Æðelm[æ]re æaldorman*. He is to be distinguished from the Ealdorman of Hampshire, the testator of No. x, who died in 982 or 983 (see p. 125). The ealdorman in this will is the one mentioned in the Chronicle, 1013 D, E, when he, with the western thegns, submitted to Swegn at Bath. He appears, therefore, to have been Ealdorman of the Western Provinces. His first signature as *dux* occurs in K. 1291, dated 996, but is probably a scribal error. In this charter all the signatures after the bishops have the title *dux*, including Wulfgeat who certainly was never an ealdorman. Æthelmær's next signature with the title *dux* is in 1002 (K. 1296). His predecessor was Æthelweard, Ealdorman of the Western Provinces. He signs until 998, but he is still alive in the episcopate of Bishop Burhwold (K. 981, and cf. p. 119). The date of this bishop's accession is uncertain, but his predecessor's last signature is in 1002. Unless Æthelmær became ealdorman during Æthelweard's lifetime, 1002 must be the date of his accession. If so, the present will can be dated 1002, since the queen-mother, Ælfthryth, was dead before the end of that year (see p. 123). In any case it is improbable that Æthelmær became ealdorman before 998, when Æthelweard was taking part in the affairs of the kingdom. Æthelmær was probably succeeded by the Ealdorman Æthelweard who was exiled in 1020 (Chronicle, C, D, E), and who appears to have been Æthelmær's son-in-law (*Crawford Charters*, p. 79).

The editors of the *Crawford Charters* (pp. 87 f.) hesitate to identify Æthelmær the Ealdorman with the Æthelmær who was the son of his predecessor Æthelweard. They prefer to identify Æthelmær, Æthelweard's son, with the other Æthelmær mentioned in Ælfflæd's will (l. 17 below), assuming him to be Brihtnoth's kinsman, though the *hlafordes mæge* on which this assumption is based is supplied by the transcription in the *British Museum Facsimiles* to fill an illegible space in the MS. It seems to me more probable that the Ealdorman Æthelmær was the son of Æthelweard. It was an ordinary thing for the office of ealdorman to descend from father to son in the tenth century (cf. the retention of East Anglia by the family of Æthelstan). The fact that Æthelmær the Ealdorman had a son called Æthelweard (Chronicle, 1017 D, E) is in favour of this identification.

Æthelmær, son of Æthelweard, is a prominent figure at this period. He founded the monasteries of Cerne and Eynsham (K. 656, 714) and was a patron of Ælfric the Homilist (see the latter's Preface to his *Lives of Saints*).

l. 13. *Lellinge*. Lawling, Essex; D.B. *Lellinge*. It is a coincidence that Æthelmær, the son of Æthelweard, should have been in possession of an estate called Little Compton in *Lellincge* some time before 1005 (K. 714). This cannot be the place in Essex, because no instance of the name 'Compton' has been recorded in that county.

l. 17. *Lissingtune*. Liston, Essex.

Eðelmere mines... The final letters of the last missing word may be -*ge*. The first missing word was evidently illegible when the Bury scribe copied the document. More than one thegn of this name sign charters at this period. One signs as 'my lord's *discthegn*' in 1006 (K. 715). See also note to l. 12 above.

l. 21. *þa landmearca*. Ælfflæd's will is the only extant Anglo-Saxon will to which boundaries are attached. They are added in a different hand from the rest of the document, but one that is contemporary, or nearly so. Boundaries of three estates only are given, all of them estates left to Stoke. The original from which our manuscript was copied may have been intended for the use of Stoke, or the other estates of the will may have had their boundaries defined on other title deeds.

A large proportion of royal charters have attached to them a description of the boundaries, usually in English. A record of an appeal made to the boundaries of the original charters during a law-suit is contained in B. 574 (Harmer, xiv).

þa landmearca to Byligesdyne. These cannot now be traced, as some of the places mentioned cannot be identified.

l. 22. *Humelcyrre....Heregeresheafode.* These cannot be identified.

l. 25. *Acantune.* Acton, near Lavenham, Suffolk.

l. 26. *Rigendune.* This name has survived in Roydon Drift, just east of Long Melford.

ll. 27 f. *þa landgemæra to Hwifermirsce 7 to Polestede.* Enough of these boundaries can be traced to show that the estate consisted of the corner of land bounded by the Brett on the east and the Stour on the south, stretching as far west as Nurstead and north to some place between Kersey and Shelley.

l. 28. *Loppandune.* This cannot now be identified.

Scelfleage. Shelley.

l. 29. *Mercyl.* Probably the *Mearcella* which occurs in the boundaries of Æthelflæd's estate at Chelsworth (see p. 140). It seems therefore to be an old name for the River Brett.

Sture. The River Stour.

l. 31. *Amalburnan.* Probably the River Box.

ll. 31 f. *Norðfelda...Bindhæcce...Tudanhæcce.* I have not been able to find these places.

p. 42, l. 1. *Giddingforda.* Dr O. K. Schram has identified this as Giffords Hall, one mile south-west of Shelley, Suffolk.

Hnutstede. Nurstead.

l. 2. *Hwitincghó...Wudemannestune.* These cannot be identified.

l. 3. *Cæresige.* Kersey.

l. 4. *Hædleage.* Hadleigh.

Hligham. Layham.

XVI (1).

MSS. (*a*) Christchurch MSS.; The Red Book of Canterbury, No. 20, a contemporary parchment. It is quoted by Thorpe as *Chart. Antiq. Cantuar.* B. i.

(*b*) Cambridge University Library, MS. FF. 2. 33, f. 50. See p. 99. The text is taken from (*a*).

FACSIMILE. (*a*) *Ordnance Survey Facsimiles*, I, No. 16.

EDITIONS. K. 699, from (*a*).
T. p. 516, from (*a*) and (*b*).
E. p. 215, from (*a*).

DATE. The MS. is endorsed with the date 997, in a late hand, but this is clearly wrong. Bishop Ælfstan, who is mentioned in the will, last signs in 995 and his successor signs in 996. From the confirmation charter it is clear that a bequest of Bocking to Christchurch, if not this particular will, had been made before Archbishop Sigeric's death in 995. In a late Canterbury list of benefactors, attributed by Dugdale to Gervase of Canterbury, reference is made to Æthelric's will under the year 1006, which is impossible. (See Dugdale, 1, p. 97.)

997 may be correct for the date of Ethelred's confirmation charter, which must be between 995, when Ælfric became Archbishop of Canterbury and Godwine became Bishop of Rochester, and 999, when Abbot Lyfing became Bishop of Wells.

l. 6. *Æþeric*. It would be interesting if we could identify him with the Ætheric, Sibriht's brother, who fought at Maldon (*Battle of Maldon*, ll. 280 f.). His estates lie close to Maldon. The name is, however, a common one.

ll. 7 ff. *þ is ærest...francan.* Except for an additional 10 mancuses in the money payment, Æthelric's heriot is identical with that demanded by Cnut from the highest king's thegn in the Danelaw (II Cnut, 71, 4), although Æthelric is an Essex thegn. The king's thegn outside the Danelaw should, according to this law, pay twice the number of horses and weapons. Æthelwold's heriot (see p. 133), as far as we can judge, approximates to that of a Danelaw thegn, and in the time of Edward the Confessor the thegns of Berkshire paid only two horses, their weapons and their hawks and hounds (D.B. 1, f. 56 *b*). It would seem that there was more than one standard of payment for the king's thegn outside the Danelaw, and that Cnut's law states only the highest.

l. 9. *targan*. Probably a small round shield. It is equated with *parma*, *pelta* (Napier, *O.E. Glosses*, 726, 2958). Cf. O.Icel. *targa*, a round shield.

francan. From the *Battle of Maldon*, ll. 77, 140 f., it is clear that this was a throwing spear.

l. 11. *Boccinge*. Bocking, Essex. This was afterwards held by Christchurch (D.B. 11, f. 8; *V. C. H. of Essex*, 1, p. 436).

ll. 13 f. *buton anre hide...þeowaþ.* This is probably a payment of *sawolsceatt*. See pp. 109 f.

l. 14. *Rægene*. Rayne, Essex.

be westan. The reading of the Cambridge MS., which adds *strete*, may be by analogy with the phrase *be eastan stræte* on l. 18, but it is possible that the Canterbury charter is guilty of an omission, in which case the road meant is no doubt the Roman road which passes through Chelmsford, Little Waltham and Bocking. The 'Stane Street' which passes through Rayne itself runs almost due east and west.

l. 15. *þam bisceope*: i.e. of London.

l. 17. *mid healfum punde 7 mid anre garan*. O.E. *gara*, 'a triangular piece of land', etc., is always masculine, and does not give a very satisfactory sense here. A feminine word *gare* is not recorded. B.T. *Suppl.* suggests 'javelin', but this as a yearly rent does not seem very probable.

T. suggests reading *mid acre garen*, which he considers to be the reading of the Cambridge MS., but this has *are*, not *acre*, and therefore represents the reading of the Canterbury MS.

l. 18. *stræte*. Perhaps the Roman road from London through Chelmsford to Colchester. Copford is just S.E. of this road.

ll. 18 f. *Ælfstane bisceope*. Bishop of London from 961 to 995 or 996.

l. 19. *Coppanforde*. Copford, Essex. The Bishop of London had an estate of 1½ hides there in 1066 (D.B. II, f. 10 *b*: *V. C. H. of Essex*, I, p. 439).

þæs heges. An enclosure for hunting purposes. Cf. p. 84, l. 5 and *derhage*, p. 82, l. 15.

Glæsne. Professor Mawer identifies this as Glazenwood in Bradwell by Coggeshall, Essex.

l. 20. *Norðho*. This cannot be identified.

Suþbyrig. Sudbury, Suffolk. See p. 143.

XVI (2).

MS. Christchurch MSS.: The Red Book of Canterbury, No. 18. It is a contemporary parchment, with halves of the word *cyrograph* at the top and bottom, thus supporting the statement on p. 46, ll. 2 ff. that there were three copies, one at Christchurch.

FACSIMILE. *Ordnance Survey Facsimiles*, I, No. 17.

EDITIONS. K. 704.
T. p. 539.
E. pp. 216 f.
Essays in Anglo-Saxon Law, Appendix, No. 26.

DATE. See note on the date of Æthelric's will, p. 147.

p. 44, ll. 2 f. *hit wæs manegon earon ær Æðeric forðferde*. The accusation must at the latest have been made in 995, the year of Sigeric's death. The first invasion of Swegn in the Chronicle is in 994, E, F. In his note on this annal (II, p. 177), Plummer suggests that an earlier unrecorded invasion must be meant here, since he thinks that insufficient time elapses between the accusation and this confirmation of the will to be called 'many years'. But this document may well be four years later than the accusation, perhaps five, which is a long time for a man to live secure under suspicion of a capital crime.

l. 4. *on þam unræde*. The meanings given by the dictionaries for *unræd*, 'ill-advised course', 'folly', 'bad counsel', etc., are hardly adequate in this instance. In Icelandic the word *úráð* has a stronger meaning. It is sometimes applied to a plan of treacherous murder (e.g. in the Prose Edda, *Skáldskaparmál*, c. 39, where Regin and Fafnir's plan to murder their father for his gold is called an *óráð*). Scandinavian usage has evidently influenced the English word. In an eleventh-century agreement (K. 745) the phrase occurs, *gif hi mid ænegan unræde wið hine ðas forwyrd to-brecen*, in which *unræde* undoubtedly means 'false dealing', and I have no doubt that the idea of treachery is contained in the word as applied to Æthelric's conduct.

Swegen. The King of Denmark, Cnut's father, who was accepted as king by the English in 1014 and died in the same year. See Chronicle, 994 to 1014.

l. 5. *ða he ærest þyder mid flotan com.* According to the Chronicle this was in 994 (see p. 148). The same authority states that the fleet consisted of 94 ships.

l. 6. *Sigerice arcebisceope.* He had been Abbot of St Augustine's (see Thorne, *De rebus gestis Abbatum S. Augustini*, in Twysden's *Decem Scriptores*, col. 1780) and Bishop of Ramsbury. He became Archbishop of Canterbury in 990 (Chronicle C). He is accused of being the first to advise payment of Danegeld (*ibid.* 991 E, F).

l. 7. *Boccinge.* See p. 42, l. 11.

l. 9. *ungeladod ge ungebétt*: i.e. he had neither cleared himself, by oath or ordeal, nor payed compensation. In II Cnut, 64, however, treason is called a *botleas* crime, i.e. one which cannot be atoned for with money. To clear himself from a charge of treason Æthelric would have had to produce an oath of the value of the king's wergeld, or go to the three-fold ordeal (V Ethelred, 30).

hergeatu. See p. 100. A widow was bound to pay the heriot within a year of her husband's death (II Cnut, 73. 4).

l. 10. *Cócham.* Cookham, Berkshire.

widan. This may refer to a particularly large gathering of the *witan*, to deal with the urgent question of defence against the Danes, possibly to the meeting in 999 which according to the Chronicle E organised offensive operations against the enemy on land and sea.

l. 12. *Leofsige ealdorman.* Ealdorman of Essex (K. 698), perhaps in succession to Brihtnoth. In 1002 he killed the king's high-reeve, Æfic, and was banished. He witnesses charters from 994 to 1001, not including the spurious charter K. 715, which is dated 1006.

l. 13. *Ælfric arcebisceop.* The testator of No. XVIII.

l. 14. *Æðelmær.* He may be the same Æthelmær as the one in Ælfflæd's will whom she asks to be her protector (see p. 40, l. 17). Both documents are concerned with Essex and belong to the same period.

l. 15. *morgengyfe.* See p. 111.

In the list of benefactors to Christchurch in Dugdale, 1, p. 96, *Ethelric* and *Leofwina* are said to have given Bocking and Mersea to Christchurch. As Mersea is not mentioned in the will, it may be Leofwyn's *morgengifu*. The estate in question is the two hides at Mersea entered with Bocking in D.B. 11, f. 8, and later known as Bocking Hall.

l. 22. *costes.* Scandinavian *kostr*.

ll. 22 f. *þeos swutelung...gewriten.* Judging from the tone of the document, it would seem to have been written by a Christchurch scribe.

l. 25. *Ælfheh ð on Wintaceastre.* He became Bishop of Winchester in 984, and succeeded Ælfric as Archbishop in 1006. He was killed by the Danes in 1012 and was regarded as a martyr. See Chronicle, 1012; W.M. *G.P.* pp. 33, 164, 169 f. His life by Osbern is contained in *Anglia Sacra,* II, pp. 122 ff.

ll. 25 f. *Wulfsige ð on Dorsæton.* He was Bishop from 992 to 1001. On *Dorsæton* refers to the see of Sherborne, which was established in 705 as the bishopric of Western Wessex. Edward the Elder created the bishoprics of Ramsbury, Wells and Crediton, for Wiltshire, Somerset and Devon, so that the diocese of Sherborne was limited to Dorset.

l. 26. *Godwine ð on Hrofeceastre.* There may have been two successive bishops of this name. Signatures occur from 995 to 1045.

l. 27. *Leofwine ealdorman.* According to K. 698, a document of 997, he was the Ealdorman of the Hwicce. He was the father of Leofric, Earl of Mercia. (See Freeman, *Norman Conquest,* I, pp. 717 f.) He signs until 1024.

Ælfsige abð. Perhaps of Peterborough. Ælfsige was abbot there for 50 years, dying in 1041. There is also an Abbot of Ely of this name who was abbot from 981 to 1019.

Wulfgar abð. He was Abbot of Abingdon from 989 or 990, till 1016. He signs from 993 to 1015.

l. 28. *Byrhtelm abð.* This may be the Byrhtelm who occurs third in W.M.'s list of six abbots of Malmesbury between 980 and 1016 (*G.P.* p. 411). An Abbot Byrhtelm of Exeter signs a doubtful charter of 993 (K. 684).

Lyfincg abð. Lyfing, whose other name was Ælfstan (Chronicle, 1019 D) or Æthelstan (Fl. Wig. 1005), was Abbot of Chertsey before he became Bishop of Wells in 999. He was Archbishop of Canterbury from 1013 to 1020.

Alfwold abð. An abbot of this name signs in 958, 963, and from 980 to 1002, but his abbey cannot be identified.

Æðelmær. See note to l. 14 above.

l. 29. *Ordulf.* He may be the founder of Tavistock (Chronicle, 997 C, D, E), who was the son of the Ealdorman Ordgar and brother of Edgar's wife Ælfthryth. He signs from 980 to 1006.

Wulfget. A thegn of King Ethelred called Wulfgeat was deprived of his possessions in 1006 (see p. 164).

Fræna. Björkman, p. 43, derives this name from a Scandinavian *Fræni, Fráni,* which is not extant. A Fræna is mentioned in the Chronicle, 993, as leading the flight from the Danes.

Wulfric Wulfrune sunu. K. 692, a grant to this man, proves that he was the wealthy North-West Midland thegn, the testator of No. XVII. See p. 152.

p. 46, l. 1 f. *Westsexan...Englon.* This fourfold division is recognised in Cnut's law on heriot (see II Cnut, 71).

ll. 2 ff. *þissa gewrita....wíduwe.* This is the first occurrence in the wills of a clause which is common in the eleventh century. It refers to a practice of writing two or more versions of a document on the same parchment, divided from one another by some word in large capitals, usually *cyrograph*. The parchment is then divided by cutting through the capital letters so that half are left on each portion, and thus by fitting them together one can prove two documents to be from the same parchment. Bresslau (*Handbuch der Urkundenlehre für Deutschland und Italien*, I, pp. 502 f.) considers that this device originated in England, and mentions a charter of 855 as the earliest example of a parchment cut in this way that he is able to discover. A description of the process is contained in the *Liber Eliensis*, II, 11, in connection with the will of a certain Siferth, who lived in the reign of Edgar. Copies of a document were generally given to the parties concerned in the transaction, but sometimes one was entrusted to a disinterested monastery (see K. 738, 745, 773, 1347).

l. 3. *æt þæs cinges haligdome*. This is the earliest reference to the keeping of documents with the king's relics. Larson (*The King's Household in England before the Norman Conquest*, p. 132) gives no reference before the reign of Cnut. The phrase *mid þise kinges halidome* occurs in the Will of Leofgifu (see p. 78, l. 9) and equivalent phrases in K. 956, 1327. The expression *in thesaurum regis* in the *Liber Eliensis*, II, 88, is no doubt a translation of this phrase.

XVII.

MSS. (*a*) A large parchment in the possession of the Marquis of Anglesey. The upper portion is occupied by King Ethelred's charter to Burton Abbey (K. 710), and the will is on the lower half. W. H. Stevenson considered this MS. to be a copy made about 1100.

(*b*) The Burton Abbey Register, also in the possession of the Marquis of Anglesey.

The text is from the facsimile of (*a*). The gaps in the MS. are filled in with the help of Thorpe's version from (*b*).

FACSIMILE of (*a*) in *Ordnance Survey Facsimiles*, Part III, last plate.

EDITIONS. Dugdale, III, p. 37, from (*b*), with a Latin translation.
K. 1298, from (*b*).
T. p. 543, from (*b*).
E. pp. 218 f., from (*b*).
Bridgman, *Wulfric Spot's Will*, in *Historical Collections for Staffordshire* (William Salt Archaeological Society), 1916, pp. 1 ff., from (*a*), with an English translation.

Modern English versions only are contained in:
John Nichols, *History of Leicestershire*, 1811, vol. IV, Part II, p. 426.
Stevenson and Duignan, *Anglo-Saxon Charters relating to Shropshire* in *Shropshire Archaeological Society Transactions*, 4th series, I, p. 14.

DATE. Between 1002 and 1004. John of Brompton (Twysden, *Decem Scriptores*, col. 885) gives 1002 as the date of the foundation of Burton, Matthew Paris (*Chronica Majora*, R.S., 1, p. 480) 1003, the Burton Annals (*Annales Monastici*, R.S. 1, p. 183) 1004. The charter by which the abbey received official recognition from Ethelred is dated 1004. The abbey was already in existence before Wulfric drew up his will (cf. p. 46, ll. 14 f.). His wife, who is not mentioned in the will and was presumably dead, was buried there (see following note). Wulfric does not witness charters after 1002, and as Ethelred's charter to Burton repeats the list of lands left to that abbey by Wulfric, the will must have been drawn up before 1004.

l. 5. *Wulfric*. The question of his identity is dealt with by Stevenson, *Shropshire Archaeological Society Transactions*, 4th series, 1, pp. 20 f.; Freeman, *Norman Conquest*, 1, note 00; Bridgman, *op. cit.*; *Dictionary of National Biography*.

Wulfric is nicknamed *Spot(t)* in the *Chronicon Abbatum* (Dugdale, III, p. 47), in the Burton Annals (*Annales Monastici*, R.S. 1, p. 183) and in the *Historia de Abingdon* (R.S. 1, p. 411). He is called Wulfrun's son in K. 692, a charter of 995 in which Dumbleton is granted to him (see p. 153), and a *Wulfric, Wulfrune sunu*, witnesses No. XVI (2), about 997. He must have been an old man by the time of his will if the Wulfric who receives Austrey from King Edred in B. 1021 is the same person, and as he bequeathes this estate in his will the identification is probable. It is true that in this charter the name of the king does not agree with the date, but the list of witnesses shows it to be no later than 956. There are also two charters in the Wynne Collection (see *2nd Report of the Historical MSS. Commission*) in which Wulfric receives estates. They are both dated 993, and the estates concerned are *Bedintun* and Bromley, which are disposed of by Wulfric in his will. It is uncertain when Wulfric's signatures begin to appear in charters, as the name is common and occurs on charters throughout the century. Often two men of this name sign. From 988, however, only one Wulfric witnesses charters, and he is no doubt the testator. His signatures cease in 1002.

Wulfric's mother was probably the Wulfrun who was taken prisoner by the Danes in 943 at Tamworth (Chronicle D). Wulfric himself held land at Tamworth and was interested in the religious community there. This Wulfrun may at the end of her life have endowed the church of canons at Wolverhampton, for this place received in 994 a number of estates from a certain Wulfrun (see Duignan, *The Charter of Wulfrun to Wolverhampton*) and it is in the part of the country in which Wulfric held so much land. Fl. Wig. 1035 speaks of a Wulfrun who was the wife of Ælfhelm, the Ealdorman of Northumbria, and the mother of Ælfgifu of Northampton, but there are strong reasons for believing the Ealdorman Ælfhelm to be Wulfric's brother (see below), and so it is probable that Fl. Wig. has confused Ælfgifu's mother with her grandmother. In any case, it can hardly be Ælfgifu's mother who endowed Wolverhampton, for the charter mentions an only daughter, *Elfthryth*, who was dead in 994.

Wulfric's wife was called *Elswitha*, according to the *Chronicon Abbatum*, which records her burial at Burton. The Ælfhelm, Wulfric's brother, who is mentioned in the will in connection with Wulfheah and Ufegeat, is very probably the Ealdorman of Northumbria who witnesses charters from 990 to 1005 and who was murdered in 1006 (Chronicle E). The same authority says that Wulfheah and Ufegeat were blinded and Fl. Wig. gives the additional information that they were Ælfhelm's sons. Ælfhelm's daughter, Ælfgifu, was the mother of Harold Harefoot. Bridgman (*op. cit.*) thinks that the Morcar mentioned in the will was related to Wulfric by marriage, but it is also possible that he was his sister's son.

Neither in the will nor in charters is there any sign that Wulfric held an official position, and only late authorities, such as the *Chronicon Abbatum*, give him the titles *consul* and *comes*. The same chronicle says that he was mortally wounded in a battle near Ipswich in 1010, and died on the 10th of November, and was buried in the monastery, his brother the *dux Alwinus* and the *comes* Morcar being present. There are, however, difficulties in accepting this information (see Stevenson, *loc. cit.*); his estate at Rolleston was in the king's possession in 1008, apparently through the forfeiture of Ælfhelm's lands after his murder. Bridgman (*op. cit.*) thinks that the document with which we are dealing is not really a will, but was meant to have immediate effect. It is, however, couched in the terms usual for a will, but not for a grant meant to take effect during the grantor's lifetime. It is more probable that, as Stevenson suggests, the date 1010 is an addition by a scribe who saw from the Chronicle that a Wulfric was killed in this year. This Wulfric is called Leofwine's son. The identification of the *dux Alwinus* presents another difficulty. If the name represents Ælfwine or Æthelwine, the title is probably an error, as there is no evidence of an ealdorman of either of these names at this period. It may, however, be a mistake for Ælfhelm, and if so, Wulfric must have died before or during 1006. The *comes* Morcar is the legatee of the will, no doubt called *comes* by confusion with the later earl, Edwin's brother.

hleofan. A slip of the pen due to the following word. By this time *hl* was pronounced *l*. Cf. *to hlafe* in the Will of Wulfgeat, p. 56, l. 6.

ll. 6 ff. *twa hund mancessa goldes…þærto gebyriað.* This is the money payment of an earl as heriot, but the number of horses is that of an English king's thegn only. The weapons belonging to it would, in Cnut's time at least, be two swords and four spears and shields and a helmet and coat of mail (II Cnut, 71. 1).

l. 12. *Ælfrice arcebis[ceope].* See his will, No. XVIII, and notes, pp. 160 ff.

l. 13. *Dumeltan.* Dumbleton, Gloucestershire. Wulfric obtained 2½ hides there in 995 by exchange with a certain Hawase who had received it from King Ethelred after its forfeiture by a thief called Æthelsige (K. 692). In 1002 King Ethelred granted 24 hides at the same place to Archbishop Ælfric (K. 1295), and it is probably to this estate that Wulfric refers as 'the other'. The Archbishop left the whole to Abingdon (see p. 52, ll. 7 f.), and on this account Wulfric's will is mentioned in the *Historia de Abingdon* (*loc. cit.*).

ll. 14 f. *þære stowe þe ic geworht hæbbe*: i.e. Burton-on-Trent (see below).

l. 15. *Ælfhelme*. This is probably the brother referred to on p. 50, l. 12. The kinsman of the same name on p. 48, l. 13, is no doubt a different person. It is probable that this brother is to be identified with the Ealdorman of Northumbria (see p. 153).

Wulfage. See p. 153.

l. 16. *betwux Ribbel 7 Mærse*. This is the name given to South Lancashire in D.B., where it is surveyed immediately after Cheshire. It had been held by Roger of Poitou, but before that had belonged to the king. It is probable that King Ethelred took possession of the estates of Ælfhelm and his sons in 1006.

[*Wir*]*halum*. Wirral, the promontory between the estuaries of the Dee and the Mersey.

l. 17. *dælan*. This verb seems to be used here in the sense of 'share the profits'.

l. 18. *sceadd*. Shad, a kind of herring.

l. 20. *Rólfestun*. Rolleston, Staffordshire. According to the Burton Annals (*Annales Monastici*, I, p. 184) it was in the king's possession in 1008, as in this year the Abbey of Burton obtained it from him in exchange for two estates, *Ælfredington* and *Ealdesworth*, given to them by Wulfric (see p. 48, l. 33, p. 50, l. 1). The Annals add that the Count *de Ferrariis* held it, and in D.B. I, f. 248 b it is entered among his estates, but he is said to have succeeded Morcar. The abbey had apparently alienated the estate between 1008 and 1066.

Héorlfestun. Harlaston, near Elford, Staffordshire.

l. 21. *Beorelfestune...Mærchamtune*. Barlaston and Marchington, Staffordshire.

l. 22. *Cunugesburh*. Conisbrough, Yorkshire.

l. 25. *Alewaldestune*. Either Alvaston or Elvaston, Derbyshire.

Ufegeate. See p. 153.

Norðtune. This might be Norton in Hales, or Norton Bridge near Eccleshall, Staffordshire, or Norton Cuckney, Nottinghamshire.

l. 27. *Elleforda*. Elford, near Tamworth, Staffordshire.

l. 28. *Acclea*. Duignan (*Notes on Staffordshire Place-Names*, p. 109), suggests Oakley, a farm near Elford.

l. 30. *to forwyrcenne*. This may mean merely 'to injure', but I consider the expression equivalent to one in K. 1327, where a life-interest in a Christchurch estate is granted with the proviso that the holder may *ne forspecan ne forspillan ut of ðam halgan mynstre*, i.e. neither lose it by a law-suit nor forfeit it.

p. 48, l. 1. *þa hwile þe heo hit geearnigean cann.* Perhaps we should translate 'as long as she is capable of holding it'. Wulfric's references to this daughter are rather mysterious. He appears to think it probable that she will forfeit her estates.

l. 4. *Tamwurþin.* Tamworth, Staffordshire. Wulfric may have inherited it from his mother. See p. 152.

hire. The sense is clearest if we take this as the optative present of *hiran*, 'to belong'. This verb is elsewhere spelt with an *e* in this document, but in this instance the copyist might be influenced by the occurrence of *hire* in the same sentence.

l. 6. *cnihte.* See p. 127.

Baltryðeleage. Balterley, Staffordshire.

l. 7. *Morcare.* No doubt the thegn of the Seven Boroughs who was killed along with his brother Siferth in 1015 (see Chronicle, Fl. Wig.). Fl. Wig. calls them sons of Earngrim. Morcar receives more estates than any other legatee, except the Abbey of Burton. Wulfric also leaves an estate to his wife and one to his daughter, Wulfric's goddaughter, with some article of jewelry which had been her grandmother's. Wulfric's possession of this suggests some relationship between them, as Bridgman (*op. cit.*) points out. Morcar's signatures occur in 1001, 1004, 1005, 1012 and 1013. Three charters of Ethelred's, granting estates to him, are preserved in the Wynne MS. 150. In 1009, he received six estates, in 1011 one, and another in 1012. Morcar's fall from favour cannot have been connected with that of Ælfhelm, Wulfheah and Ufegeat, when he receives so many estates after 1006. He may have had something to do with the submission of the people of the Five Boroughs to Swegn in 1013 (Chronicle). The thirteenth-century French life of St Edmund (*Memorials of St Edmund's Abbey,* II, p. 246) may be preserving a genuine tradition when it states that Swegn came to England on the invitation of Ælfhelm and Morcar.

After Morcar's death his estates and his brother's were seized by Edmund Ironside. By 1066 seven of those left to Morcar by Wulfric, and the one estate left to his daughter, together with estates he had received from Ethelred, were held by a certain Leofnoth, who was succeeded by Ralf, the son of Hubert (D.B. I, f. 277: *V. C. H. of Derbyshire,* I, pp. 348 f.).

l. 8. *Waleshô.* This cannot be identified with certainty, but it may, as Bridgman suggests, be Wales, Yorkshire, some 2 miles from Beighton, which Wulfric left to the same legatee.

Þeogendeþorpe. Unidentified.

Hwitewylle. Whitwell, Derbyshire.

l. 9. *Clune...Barleburh...Ducemannestune.* Clowne, Barlborough and Duckmanton, Derbyshire.

l. 10. *Moresburh..Eccingtune..Bectune.* Mosbrough, Eckington, Beighton, Derbyshire.

Doneceastre. Doncaster, Yorkshire.

l. 11. *Morlingtun.* Unidentified.

Aldulfestreo. Austrey, Warwickshire. Perhaps the estate held in
D.B. by Henry de Ferrieres is the one meant here (D.B. 1, f. 242:
V. C. H. of Warwickshire, 1, p. 327). Henry had succeeded to other
estates which had been Wulfric's (see below).

l. 13. *Ælfhelme minan mæge*. Probably a different person from the
Ælfhelm mentioned above. His estate at Palterton passed into the
possession of Leofnoth, the predecessor of Ralf, the son of Hubert,
who succeeded to many of Morcar's estates. See p. 155.

Paltertune. Palterton, Derbyshire.

l. 14. *Scegð*. This is one of the forms in which the O.Icel. *skeið* was
transcribed in O.E. (see p. 137). I have not found any occurrence of
this word as a personal name elsewhere.

Wibbe[to]fte. Wibtoft, Warwickshire.

l. 15. *Twongan*. Tong, Shropshire, or Tonge, Leicestershire.

l. 17. *þa land þe ic geann into Byrtune*. The *Historia de Abingdon*
(*loc. cit.*) values the estates given by Wulfric to Burton Abbey at £700.
The abbey was in possession only of a portion of these estates in 1066,
according to D.B. Even when we assume that several small estates
are included in the Domesday entries of larger ones, there remain
several lands in alien hands. Morley, Breadsall, Burton Hastings and
perhaps Harbury had been held by Siward, the predecessor of Henry
de Ferrieres, Ogston, Morton and Pilsley by *Suain cilt*. Various
holders held other estates left to Burton.

l. 18. *Stræt[tu]n*. Stretton, near Rolleston, Staffordshire, about 2
miles north of Burton-on-Trent. The abbey was in possession at the
time of the Domesday Survey (D.B. 1, f. 247 *b*).

Bromleage. Abbots Bromley, Staffordshire, held by Burton Abbey
in D.B. 1, f. 247 *b*. Wulfric had received this and the following estate
from Ethelred in 993 (see p. 152).

Bedintun. This is entered as an estate of Burton Abbey in D.B. 1,
f. 247 *b*. The name has since disappeared. Duignan identifies it with
Pillaton, near Penkridge, Staffordshire (see *Notes on Staffordshire Place-
Names*, p. 119).

l. 19. *Gageleage*. Gailey, near Penkridge, Staffordshire. It is not
mentioned separately in D.B. as an estate of Burton, but probably
was included in some other estate.

Witestan. Whiston, near Penkridge, Staffordshire. It is held by
Burton in D.B. 1, f. 247 *b*.

Langanford. Probably Longford, near Newport, Shropshire, which
is some 7 miles from Stirchley.

Styrcleage. Stirchley, near Shifnal, Shropshire.

ll. 19 f. *Niwantun æt þære wi[c]*. No Newton is entered in the
Domesday Survey of the Burton possessions. Probably the place
meant here is Newton in Cheshire, by Middlewich, one of the salt-
towns which are described in D.B. 1, f. 268. The term applied to them
is *wich* (cf. Will of Wulfgeat, p. 56, l. 8).

l. 20 *Wædedun*. Unidentified.

ll. 20 f. *oðer Niwantune.* Probably Newton Solney, Derbyshire, which adjoins Winshill.

l. 21. *Wineshylle.* Winshill, near Burton-on-Trent, Staffordshire, but surveyed under Derbyshire in D.B. i, f. 273 (*V. C. H. of Derbyshire*, i, p. 335.) It had been held by Burton.

Suttun. Sutton-on-the-Hill, Derbyshire. One carucate at Sutton was held by Burton (D.B. i, f. 273: *V. C. H. of Derbyshire*, i, p. 334).

Ticenheale. Ticknall, Derbyshire. Burton Abbey held it in 1066 (D.B. i, f. 273: *V. C. H. of Derbyshire*, i, p. 335).

l. 22. *Scen[ct]une.* Bridgman suggests Shankton or Shangton, Leicestershire. There is no trace in D.B. of its having belonged to Burton.

Wicgestane. Little Wigston, Leicestershire. Burton had lost it by 1066.

Halen. There is no evidence that an estate of this name belonged to Burton Abbey. West or Kirk Hallam, Derbyshire, and Sheriff Hales, Staffordshire, are possibilities, but the mention of Romsley and Shipley immediately afterwards makes it probable that Halesowen, Worcestershire, is the place meant.

Hremesleage. Probably Romsley, near Bridgenorth, Shropshire.

l. 23. *Sciplea.* Shipley, 6 miles N.E. of Bridgenorth.

Suðtune. Probably this is Sutton Maddock, Shropshire, as this is not many miles from Shipley.

Actune. Perhaps Acton Round, west of Bridgenorth. There is no record of Burton's having held land at any of these last four places.

ll. 23 f. *tw[egra] manna dæg.* This is an unusual condition for land left to a religious foundation. It perhaps refers to the lives of two tenant-holders.

ll. 24 f. *Deorlafestun...Rudegeard...Cotewaltune.* Darlaston, Rudyard and Cotwalton near Stone, Staffordshire. Only the first is entered among the Burton estates in D.B. i, f. 247 *b*, but the others are probably included in it. They are not near to Darlaston, Rudyard being the whole length of the county distant. Only about 2 miles from Cotwalton there is a place called Darlaston Hall, perhaps owing its name to this connection between Cotwalton and Darlaston.

l. 26. *Lege...Ácofre.* Leigh, near Uttoxeter and Okeover, Staffordshire. They are entered as estates of Burton Abbey in D.B. i, f. 247 *b*.

l. 27. *Hílum. ⁊ Celfdun. ⁊ Cætesþyrne.* Ilam, Caldon and Castern, near Okeover. Probably these three estates are included in Okeover in the Domesday Survey of the Burton estates.

þ heregeatland. This may mean that Wulfric had the right to receive the heriot of the tenants on this land. D.B. shows that the ownership of rights over heriot could be complicated. The heriot of 70 socmen at Stamford always remained with the king, although they were free to choose their lord (D.B. i, f. 336 *b*), whereas at Thetford there were burgesses whose customs, except heriot, remained with the king, whatever lord they sought (D.B. ii, f. 119). In Well Wapentake,

Lincolnshire, the heriot of the thegns was divided between the earl and the Abbey of Stow (D.B. I, f. 376). In view of these passages it seems probable that this estate at Sutton belonged to men who were obliged to pay heriot to Wulfric. It is, however, possible that it is land which Wulfric has received in payment of heriot.

l. 28. *Suðtune*. Wulfric had estates at two Suttons. Probably it is Sutton-on-the-Hill (see note to l. 21) that is meant here, as Wulfric deals immediately afterwards with Derbyshire estates.

Morlege. 7 *Bregdeshale.* 7 *Mort[u]n.* Morley, Breadsall, and Morton, Derbyshire. The first two were held by Siward, the predecessor of Henry de Ferrieres, the last by *Suain cilt*, in 1066 (D.B. I, ff. 275 *b*, 276 *b*: *V. C. H. of Derbyshire*, I, pp. 343, 347).

l. 29. *socna*. By this Wulfric means that he bequeathes the profits resulting from the exercise of jurisdiction (see Liebermann, *Glossar*; Maitland, *Domesday Book and Beyond*, pp. 80 f.; Adams, *The Anglo-Saxon Courts of Law* in *Essays in Anglo-Saxon Law*, pp. 40 f. The latter contends that a grant of *socn* does not imply a private court of justice). Professor Stenton (*Types of Manorial Structure in the Northern Dane-law*, pp. 21 f.) suggests that this passage in Wulfric's will may show the existence at the beginning of the eleventh century of the arrange-ment so common at the time of Domesday in this part of England, by which a manor had attached to it 'sokeland', i.e. land from which the lord received the profits of jurisdiction, although he did not own the soil. He also points out (*ibid*. pp. 79 f.) that the word *soc* was apparently used as early as the middle of the tenth century, in this part of the country, as it occurs in charters from different sources.

Pilleslege. 7 *Oggodestun.* Pilsley, and Ogston, Derbyshire. In 1066 these estates belonged to *Suain cilt* (D.B. I, f. 276 *b*: *V. C. H. of Derby-shire*, I, p. 347). The *soc* belonged to Wingfield.

l. 30. *Wynnef[eld]*. Wingfield, Derbyshire. This estate did not belong to Burton in 1066.

Snodeswic. This appears in D.B. I, f. 276 (*V. C. H. of Derbyshire*, I, p. 346) as *Esnotrewic*. The name is now lost. It appears to refer to some place near South Normanton and Glapwell. Kemble suggested Pinxton.

Taðawyllan. Tathwell, Lincolnshire. This is a long way from Wulfric's other estates, but no other place of this name is known.

l. 31. *Æppebbyg.* Appleby, now in Leicestershire, but surveyed in the Derbyshire portion of Domesday (D.B. I, f. 273: *V. C. H. of Derbyshire*, I, p. 334). Burton held 5 hides there, and had given one to the Countess Gode.

l. 32. *Westune.* 7 *Burhtun.* These are common names, but their occurrence in connection with Sharnford and Wigston makes it possible to identify them with Weston in Arden and Burton Hastings, Warwickshire. These are also close to Wulfric's estate, Wibtoft. Burton Hastings was later held by Siward, Henry de Ferrieres' predecessor (D.B. II, f. 242: *V. C. H. of Warwickshire*, I, p. 327).

Scearnforda. Sharnford, Leicestershire. There is no mention of this hide among the Burton lands in D.B.

l. 33. *Hereburgebyrig.* Harbury, Warwickshire. D.B. does not enter it among the Burton estates. It is held by various owners. Perhaps the estate held in 1066 by Siward Barn, the predecessor of Henry de Ferrieres, is the one left by Wulfric (see D.B. 1, f. 242: *V. C. H. of Warwickshire*, 1, p. 327).

Ealdeswy[rðe]. Either Awsworth, Nottinghamshire, or Aldsworth, Gloucestershire. This was one of the estates exchanged by Burton with the king for Rolleston, in 1008 (see p. 154).

p. 50, l. 1. *Ælfredingtune.* Alvington, Gloucestershire (D.B. *Alvredintune*), or Alfreton, Derbyshire. See p. 154.

Eccleshale. There is nothing to show whether Exhall, Warwickshire (D.B. *Ecleshelle*), Eccleshall, Staffordshire, or Ecclesall near Sheffield, Yorkshire, is meant here. The abbey had apparently no land at any of these places by 1066.

Waddune. Perhaps Whaddon, Gloucestershire.

l. 2. *Sceon.* Sheen, Staffordshire. It is king's land by the time of D.B. (D.B. 1, f. 246 *b*).

þam hirede in Tom[wy]rðin. No religious community at Tamworth is entered in D.B., but this borough is only incidentally mentioned in D.B. and is not fully surveyed.

l. 3. *Langandune.* Probably Longdon, N.W. of Lichfield, Staffordshire.

l. 5. *se bisceop.* Either Ælfheah, Bishop of Lichfield, or his successor Godwine. Ælfheah's last signature is in 1002, Godwine's first in 1004.

l. 6. *Bubandune.* Bupton, Derbyshire, near Longford. In D.B. 1, f. 273 (*V. C. H. of Derbyshire*, 1, p. 334) it is in the possession of the Bishop of Chester, to which place the see of Lichfield had been moved.

l. 11. *7 to wurðmynta minan hlafor[de].* The Burton Register has *for* after *wurðmynta*, so that the passage would read 'for the praise and honour of God, on behalf of my lord'.

l. 12. *Ælfhelm min broðor.* See p. 153.

l. 16. *Strættune.* Probably Stretton in North Wingfield parish, Derbyshire, which was held in 1066 by Leofnoth, who succeeded to many of Morcar's estates also. See p. 155.

ðo[ne] búle. The final *e* is probably a scribal error. The existence of a strong form *bul* is shown by the gloss *bulas* for *murenulas* in the *Rituale Ecclesiæ Dunelmensis* (Surtees Society, x, p. 4, l. 3). Wright-Wülker, 360. 25, has a weak noun *bula* which is equated with the Latin *bulla* (cf. also *bulum* 359. 40), which may be weak or strong. This Latin word had a variety of meanings, 'boss', 'stud' or anything rounded. It was also applied to an amulet worn at the neck. As the *murenula* also was a neck ornament, it is possible that it is some sort of pendant that is meant here.

ll. 25 ff. *Endorsement*. This is the endorsement of the whole document and concerns the first portion, King Ethelred's charter, rather than Wulfric's will.

l. 27. *geédstaðelode*. The use of a word meaning reestablish here is no doubt due to the tradition that an earlier religious house was founded in Burton-on-Trent by St Modwenna, to whom Wulfric's foundation was dedicated. The history of this saint is very confused. She appears to have founded a nunnery at Burton in the late sixth or seventh century. Her life was written by monks of Burton-on-Trent in the eleventh and twelfth centuries (see Hardy, *Catalogue*, I, pp. 94–100). See also *Dictionary of Christian Biography*, *s.v. Modwenna*.

l. 28. *mid munecon gesette*. The first monks and their abbot, Wulfgeat, were brought from Winchester (see Dugdale, III, p. 47, from the *Chronicon Abbatum* of Burton Abbey).

XVIII.

MS. British Museum, Cotton Claudius B. VI, f. 103, a thirteenth-century Abingdon cartulary. It is immediately followed by a Latin version, which is also given in another Abingdon cartulary, Cotton Claudius C. IX, f. 125 *b*.

EDITIONS. Hickes, *Dissertatio Epistolaris*, p. 62.
Dugdale, I, pp. 517 ff.
K. 716.
T. p. 549 f., Latin version, p. 551.
Historia Monasterii de Abingdon, R.S. ed. Stevenson, I, p. 416.

There is a modern English translation of the will in Hook's *Lives of the Archbishops*, I, p. 452.

DATE. 1003 or 1004. Wulfstan II became Archbishop of York in 1003, and the last signature of Wulfstan, Bishop of London, occurs in the same year. His successor signs in 1004. Archbishop Ælfric's will, therefore, must have been drawn up between 1003 and 1004. His death is entered in the Chronicle, 1005 A, 1006 E.

p. 52, l. 1. *Alfric arcebisceop*. Ælfric first became a monk at Abingdon (*Historia Monasterii de Abingdon*, I, p. 415). W.M. says he was abbot there (*G.P.* p. 32), but there is no mention of this in the Abingdon History. He was afterwards Abbot of St Albans. Our evidence for this does not rest alone on the confused account in the *Gesta Abbatum* of this monastery, for we are told in Eadmer's *Life of St Oswald* (see Raine, *Historians of the Church of York*, R.S. II, p. 22) that Oswold appointed him Abbot of St Albans. In the *Gesta Abbatum Monasterii S. Albani*, R.S. I, pp. 31 ff., Ælfric is represented as the eleventh abbot, but many features of the account given there are impossible and he has probably been confused with a later abbot, perhaps one of the same name. It is stated that he was the younger brother of

Leofric, the tenth abbot, and the son of a *Comes Cantiae*; that he succeeded Leofric as abbot when the latter became Archbishop of Canterbury, though at first he had refused the see in favour of Ælfric; that the latter's abbacy continued into the reign of Edward the Confessor. There is no doubt that the position of the two abbots has been interchanged. Ælfric preceded Leofric, who probably became abbot in 990 when Ælfric was made Bishop of Ramsbury. Leofric was never archbishop (MS. Nero D. I. of these *Gesta* corrects the statement of the other MS. on this point). The majority of the stories related of Ælfric probably belong to Leofric's abbacy or even later, but I see no reason for doubting the statement that Ælfric and Leofric were brothers.

Ælfric became Bishop of Ramsbury in 990. Plummer considers that the Bishop Ælfstan mentioned in the Chronicle, 992 E, as a leader of the fleet, is a mistake for Ælfric, but there was a Bishop Ælfstan of London at this date. Ælfric succeeded Sigeric in the see of Canterbury in 995 and went to Rome for the *pallium* two years later. The Chronicle (995 F) has an account of how he replaced the canons of Christchurch by monks, though this has already been attributed to Sigeric. MS. F is a late authority, and W.M. (*G.P.* p. 32) disbelieves the story. No doubt Ælfric favoured the party of the monastic revival, for he had been trained at Abingdon, one of the earliest reformed monasteries. His death is entered in the Chronicle, 1005 A, 1006 E. In the will, he leaves bequests to all the religious foundations with which he has been connected.

He used to be identified with Ælfric the Homilist. For reasons against this, see Dietrich, *Abt Ælfric*, in Niedner's *Zeitschrift für historische Theologie*, 1855, summarised by Wülker, in *Grundriss zur Geschichte der angelsächsischen Litteratur*, pp. 453 f.

l. 2. *saulsceate*. See pp. 109 f.

l. 3. *Wyllan*. D.B. I, f. 5, *Welle*, probably Westwell, Kent, which was held by Christchurch as an estate of 7 *solins*.

Burnan. Probably Bishopsbourne, Kent.

Risenbeorgas. Monks Risborough, Buckinghamshire. This had been in the possession of Christchurch until Archbishop Sigeric gave it to Æscwig, Bishop of Dorset, in return for money with which to bribe the Danes to spare Christchurch (K. 689). Æscwig later returned the the estate to Archbishop Ælfric and Christchurch (K. 690). This estate, therefore, was not the Archbishop's private property. It is entered in D.B. I, f. 143 b, as an estate of 30 hides held by the Archbishop.

ll. 3 ff. *he becwað his laford...beornena*. This is not a payment of heriot, as the Archbishop leaves instructions about this later in the will (see l. 23 below).

l. 4. *his beste scip....* In the Chronicle, 992 E, we find two bishops as leaders of the fleet, and Plummer believes one of these to be Ælfric himself (but see above). Bishop Ælfwold of Crediton also leaves a ship in his will (*Crawford Charters*, x) and so does the Cambridgeshire thegn, Ælfhelm of Wratting (see p. 137). Later in the will the Archbishop leaves a ship to Kent and one to Wiltshire.

ll. 5 ff. 7 *he wilnode...Eadulfingtune.* K. 672, a St Albans charter starred by Kemble and bearing an impossible date, states that Ethelred gave 55 hides at *Eadulfingtun* and 6 at Flamstead and St Albans to the abbey in return for £200 with which to bribe the Danes, and that St Albans afterwards gave back *Eadulfingtun*, retaining only the 6 hides at the other places. The *Gesta Abbatum S. Albani*, I, p. 33, merely mentions that the abbey received Oxhey and *Eadulfingtun* as a pledge for 1000 marks. The charter attributes the transaction to Leofric, the *Gesta* to Ælfric, but as we have seen above this authority constantly confuses the two abbots. It seems to me that the charter preserves a genuine tradition, though the reason for the surrender of *Eadulfingtun* has been forgotten. This can be supplied from Ælfric's will; it was in order to obtain the royal confirmation of the abbey's possession of Kingsbury. This estate, according to the *Gesta*, I, p. 32, had been bought from the king by Ælfric. Liebermann (*Glossar, s.v. folcland*) assumes that the reason that the royal consent is necessary is that the estate is *folcland*. Other explanations are, however, possible, e.g. the estate may have been transferred by a charter reserving a right of reversion to the king.

l. 6. *sce Albane.* The chronicles of this abbey are very unreliable for the early period and the early history of the abbey is obscure. It no doubt underwent the same period of decline that affected other monasteries in the ninth and early tenth centuries. It was one of three places offered by Edgar to Oswold for him to make into a monastery of the revived type. He did not accept it then, but later appointed Ælfric, the testator of this will, as abbot (see Eadmer, *loc. cit.*).

Cyngesbyrig. Kingsbury, Middlesex. St Albans was not holding this in Edward the Confessor's reign, for it is entered as an estate of Westminster Abbey in D.B. I, f. 128 *b*.

l. 7. *Eadulfingtune.* Unidentified.
Dumeltun. Dumbleton, Gloucestershire. See p. 153.

l. 8. *Abbandune.* Abingdon, Berkshire. Ælfric had become a monk at this abbey (see p. 160).

l. 10. *filgan hi þam lafordscype....* They are not to be given or sold away from the estate.

l. 11. *Wealingaforda.* Wallingford, Berkshire.

l. 12. *Ceolesige.* The Abbey of Cholsey, Berkshire, was a foundation of Ethelred's, according to tradition in expiation of the murder of his brother Edward. It was perhaps destroyed by the Danes in 1006. (See John of Wallingford, in Gale, *Scriptores xv*, I, p. 546; Roger of Hoveden, R.S. 1006.)

l. 13. *Tiwan.* Not Tewin, Herts. (*sic* Hook, Thorpe), but Tew, Oxfordshire. An estate of 16 hides at *Tewam* was held by Odo of Bayeux in 1086 (D.B. I, f. 155 *b*), and in the *Gesta Abbatum S. Albani*, I, p. 53, we are told that *Tiwa,* which had belonged to the abbey in King Edward's time, was afterwards held by Odo of Bayeux.

l. 17. v *pundun*: of silver is understood.

l. 18. *Osanig.* Osney, Oxfordshire.

l. 23. *hergeatwæn.* See p. 100. It is nowhere stated what an archbishop was expected to pay as heriot.

l. 24. *anes scipes.* This bequest is no doubt to assist these counties in the payment of a ship-tax (see p. 137).

Wiltunescire. Ælfric had been bishop of this county.

l. 26. *Uulfstan bisceop.* He was Bishop of London from 996 to 1003 or 1004.

Leofric abbud. Abbot of St Albans, and Ælfric's brother. See pp. 160 f. The *Gesta Abbatum S. Albani,* 1, pp. 28 f. speaks well of him, but blames him for giving the treasures of the monastery to the poor, and for admitting none but men of noble birth to the monastery.

l. 27. *Fittingtune.* Fiddington, near Tewkesbury, Gloucestershire.

Niwantune. Newton near Tewkesbury, Gloucestershire, about one mile from Fiddington.

l. 29. *à on his cyn.* Here we have an instance of what Alfred refers to in his law (Alfred, 41), i.e. a clause by a transmittor of an estate preventing its free alienation (cf. p. 131).

Uulfstane ærcebiscope. This is Wulfstan II, Archbishop from 1003 to 1023. He is usually identified with the writer of the homilies. (See Napier, *Über die Werke des altenglischen Erzbischofs Wulfstan,* pp. 4 f.) He was a benefactor, and perhaps a monk, of Ely, where he was buried. (*Liber Eliensis,* 11, 87.)

p. 54, l. 1. *Alfheage biscope.* This is the Bishop of Winchester who succeeded Ælfric as Archbishop of Canterbury and was killed by the Danes in 1012. See p. 150.

ll. 2 f. *And he forgeaf...foresceat.* Probably these debts were incurred during the Danish raids, in order to bribe the invaders.

ll. 4 f. *ælene witefæstne man...forgylt wære.* See pp. 111 f. In a synodal decree of 816 (see p. 101), it is stated that at the death of a bishop, besides gifts to the poor for his soul, every English man is to be freed, *qui in diebus suis sit servitute subvictus.*

XIX.

MS. British Museum, Harley Charter 83 A. 2, a single sheet of vellum, the bottom portion of a cyrograph, written in a hand of about the early eleventh century. It originally belonged to Worcester Cathedral.

FACSIMILE. Bond, *Facsimiles of Ancient Charters in the British Museum,* Part IV, No. 42.

EDITIONS. B. 1317.

Modern English translations only are given in:

Cockayne, *Shrine*, p. 159.

Duignan, *The Will of Wulfgate, of Donnington*, in *Shropshire Archaeological Society Transactions*, 2nd series, III, p. 36.

Duignan and Stevenson, *Anglo-Saxon Charters relating to Shropshire*, *ibid.*, 4th series, I, pp. 10 f.

Bridgman, *Staffordshire Pre-Conquest Charters*, in *Historical Collections for Staffordshire* (William Salt Archaeological Society), 1916, pp. 119 f.

DATE. The will is undated, and none of the persons in it can be identified with certainty. The *Heantun* of the will is probably Wolverhampton, where a religious house received large gifts from Wulfrun, if it was not actually founded, in 994 (see below). We cannot, however, be certain that there was no religious establishment there before this date, to which a bequest might be made. The date 1006 usually given to this will rests on the assumption that the testator is Ethelred's thegn whose estates were forfeited in this year (see following note).

l. 7. *Wulfgates*. There was a king's thegn of this name whose estates were forfeited in 1006 (Chronicle, C, D, E) and who is called Leofeca's son by Fl. Wig. (1006). Two extant charters refer to this forfeiture. In one, K. 1305, dated 1008, Ethelred grants to Abingdon an estate at Moredon near Swindon, Wiltshire, which had been held by his reeve Ælfgar. The latter's widow, Ælfgifu, had married Wulfgeat, and the document states that all their estates were forfeited on account of their crimes. The second charter (K. 1310) belongs to 1015 and is a grant to Bishop Brihtwold of Ramsbury of land at Chilton, Berkshire, forfeited by Wulfgeat because of his being leagued with enemies of the king. The testator of the present will has no estates in these localities, and, as Wulfgeat is by no means an uncommon name, I consider that the identification of the testator with this thegn of King Ethelred rests on a very slender foundation. There is, however, one small piece of evidence that might be held to support the identification, namely that we know that King Ethelred held land at Tardebigge, for Heming's cartulary (ed. Hearne, p. 276) says that a dean *Ægelsius* of Worcester purchased it from Ethelred; but in D.B. Tardebigge is assessed at 9 hides, and according to the will Wulfgeat had only 3 hides there. It need not, therefore, be Wulfgeat's land which was in Ethelred's possession.

There are also a few references to a Wulfgeat who lived in the same part of England as the testator. Wulfrun (see p. 152) bequeathed 10 hides to Wolverhampton for the soul of her kinsman Wulfgeat, on account of his offences, mentioning him along with her dead daughter in a way that implies that he was dead by the date of the charter, 994 (see Duignan, *The Charter of Wulfrun to Wolverhampton*). Among the estates she grants to Wolverhampton is *Earnleie* (Upper Arley, Worcestershire), and therefore it is probable that her kinsman is the Wulf-geat to whom King Edgar granted an estate at *Ernlege* along with Duddeston, Warwickshire, in 963 (B. 1100). The name Wulfgeat occurs among the *ministri* in lists of witnesses from 965 to 974 and again from 986 to 1005. The latter group undoubtedly belongs to the thegn who suffered forfeiture in 1006. I think it probable that the earlier signatures are those of a different person, the grantee of Edgar in 963 and kinsman of Wulfrun. Of the two men I think this earlier Wulfgeat is more probably the testator, who, we may notice, made a bequest to *Heantun*, probably Wolverhampton, but I do not consider that the evidence is sufficient to justify either identification. We should have to assume that the testator, if identical with Edgar's grantee, disposed of Duddeston and Arley separately, or drew up his will before he received them, as neither estate is mentioned in the will.

Dunnintune. Donington near Albrighton, Shropshire, to judge by its being mentioned along with Kilsall.

l. 8. *sawelscættas*. See pp. 109 f. The will does not state to what church this payment is to be made. Presumably Wulfgeat intends it to be paid to the church at Donington, his principal estate.

Tærdebicgan. Tardebigge, Worcestershire. Heming (*loc. cit.*) relates that Ethelred sold this with other estates to Worcester, but that *Ævic* the *vicecomes* of Staffordshire usurped them. It was held by King Edward in 1066 (D.B. 1, f. 172 *b*: *V. C. H. of Worcester*, 1, p. 287), and was assessed at 9 hides.

l. 9. VI 7 *twentig freotmonna for his sawle*. It seems to me possible to take this phrase either as a manumission clause, or as a grant of rights over certain freedmen to the legatee who is to receive Tarde-bigge. In Kent in early times the lord had the right to his freedman's inheritance, *wergeld* and *mund* (Wihtred, 8). Whether this held good in Wessex in the tenth century is uncertain, but Wulfgeat may be bequeathing some similar rights. In an eleventh-century East Anglian will (No. xxxvi), freedmen (*lisingar*) are bequeathed along with an estate. On the other hand I think it most natural to interpret the phrase relating to freedmen in the Will of Wulfwaru (p. 64, ll. 23 f.) as a manumission clause.

l. 10. *Wigeracæstre.* Worcester Cathedral.

an bryþen. B.T. *Suppl.* gives this example under *byrþen*, a 'load'. *Byrþen* is, however, elsewhere always feminine and I follow the earlier B.T. and Sweet (*A Student's Anglo-Saxon Dictionary*) in taking *bryþen* here to mean a 'brewing'. The word occurs in the poem on St Guthlac, l. 953, and though Grein enters it in his *Sprachschatz* as feminine, his only reference tells us nothing about the gender.

l. 11. *Cylleshale.* Kilsall, near Donington, Shropshire.

sce Æþelbrihte. Hereford Cathedral was dedicated to the East Anglian saint, King Ethelbert, who was supposed to have been buried there. See p. 102.

l. 12. *sce Guðlace.* A church of secular canons at Hereford, dedicated to the East Anglian saint, Guthlac, the patron saint of the abbey of Crowland.

Leomynstre. Leominster, Herefordshire. There was a nunnery here in Edward the Confessor's reign (Fl. Wig. 1048), which was suppressed before the date of the Domesday Survey. Symeon of Durham (*Historia Regum*, 1057) and Roger of Hoveden (R.S. 1057) include it among the religious foundations of Earl Leofric of Mercia, but this is hardly sufficient evidence to justify the assumption that there was no religious foundation already. There is evidence of a monastery in early days, traditionally ascribed to an under-king of Mercia, Merwald (Capgrave, *Nova Legenda, s.v. Milburga*), and we are ignorant of the fate of this. In any case, Wulfgeat's bequest may have been to a church there, not necessarily to a religious community.

l. 13. *Bromgearde.* Bromyard, Herefordshire.

Cliftune. Clifton-on-Teme, Worcestershire.

l. 14. *Heantune.* Duignan's suggestion, Wolverhampton, is very probable.

Pencric. Penkridge, Staffordshire. This is held by the clerks of Wolverhampton in D.B. 1, f. 247 b.

l. 15. *Tweongan.* Tong, Shropshire.

ll. 19 f. II *hors* 7 II *sweord...coltan.* This heriot is probably a little smaller than that described in II Cnut, 71. 1, as due from a king's thegn. The latter was to give four horses, not two, and 50 mancuses of gold where Wulfgeat gives ten mares and ten colts. According to the *Geræcdnes betweox Dunsætan* 7, a mare was worth 20 (Mercian) shillings, i.e. 2⅔ mancuses. The *wilde weorf* which is valued in the same passage at 12 (Mercian) shillings is probably an unbroken colt (see Liebermann, III, p. 219). Ten mares with ten colts would according to this document be worth almost 43 mancuses. The *Geræcdnes* is undated, but probably belongs to the tenth century.

l. 22. *Eowniglade.* Evenlode, Worcestershire.

Hrodene. Roden, Shropshire.

l. 24. *nehste.* Birch has *ne liste* but in the MS. the horizontal stroke of the *h* can be seen, though faintly.

l. 25. *þornbyrig.* Thornbury, north of Bromyard, Herefordshire.

p. 56, l. 1. *Ingewyrðe.* Ingardine or Ingwardine, Shropshire.

l. 3. *on wedd gesealdon.* This is evidently an agreement of the type frequently met with in eleventh-century wills (cf. pp. 194, 203), by which two persons agree that whichever of them outlives the other is to have a certain portion of the deceased's property. It is a feature common to all these agreements that the testator does not give instructions for the disposal of the property which may come to him in this way.

l. 4. *Wrotteslea.* Wrottesley, Staffordshire.

l. 6. *hlafe.* For O.E. *lafe*, showing that the distinction between *hl* and *l* had been lost.

l. 7. *minre dohtran.* The noun is plural but the pronoun is singular.

In the next line *mine*, as dative singular, and *ealle mine freondum* in l. 9, as dative plural, are also departures from the O.E. inflectional system.

ll. 7 f. *þeo wellinc æt þære wic.* In the Domesday account of Donington five salt-pits in *Wich* are entered as belonging to it (D.B. i, f. 253 b: *V. C. H. of Shropshire*, i, p. 317). The *wich* meant is probably Droitwich, Worcestershire. The salt-towns of Cheshire also are called *wich* in D.B. (cf. also p. 48, l. 20).

l. 8. *Æþelsige. leof.* On the use of *leof* as a method of address see Harmer, p. 117.

XX.

MSS. (*a*) British Museum, Stowe Charter, 37. This is a single sheet of vellum, in an early eleventh-century hand. It has the upper halves of the letters CYROGRAPHUM at the bottom, showing that at least one other contemporary copy existed. See pp. 150 f.

(*b*) Christchurch, Canterbury, MS. AA. H. 68. A single sheet of vellum in a handwriting approximately contemporary with that of (*a*). It is endorsed in a late hand with the date 1015.

(*c*), (*d*) Additional MS. 15350, ff. 43 b, 50. On this MS. see p. 116. The will of Æthelstan has been copied into this cartulary twice. Version (*c*) is very incorrect, with several inversions and repetitions. Version (*d*) is copied, either from the Stowe Charter itself, or from an almost identical version. Except that the language has been to a certain extent modernised, it keeps very close to the original.

The text is taken from (*a*).

FACSIMILES. (*a*) *Ordnance Survey Facsimiles*, III, No. 38.
     (*b*) *Ibid.* I, No. 18.

EDITIONS. Somner, *A Treatise of Gavelkind*, pp. 198 f.
   Lye, *Dictionarium Saxonico et Gothico Latinum*, II, Appendix, II, 5, from (*a*), with a Latin translation.
   K. 722, from Lye and (*d*).
   T. p. 557, mainly from (*d*).
   E. pp. 224 f., from (*b*).

DATE. The date of the endorsement to the Canterbury MS., 1015, though in a late hand, is apparently correct. Bishop Ælfsige of Winchester was consecrated in 1014, which is therefore the earliest possible date for this will, and if my identification of Morcar and Siferth with the thegns of the Seven Boroughs is correct, the will cannot have been drawn up later than 1015 (see p. 155). Signatures of the Ætheling Æthelstan do not occur after 1013, with the exception of one in the doubtful Evesham charter, K. 723, which is dated 1016.

l. 10. *Æþestan æþeling.* He was the son of King Ethelred by his first wife, whom Fl. Wig. (ed. Thorpe, I, p. 275) calls Ælfgifu, daughter of the Ealdorman *Æthelberht.* An ealdorman of this name witnesses a doubtful charter of 981 (K. 629), but is otherwise unknown. Ailred of Rievaulx (Twysden, *Decem Scriptores*, col. 362, 372) says she was a daughter of the *comes* Thored. W.M. (*G.R.* p. 213) does not know her name. Fl. Wig. (*loc. cit.*) makes Æthelstan appear as the second son, but his information with regard to Ethelred's family is very incomplete. In charters Æthelstan signs first of the king's sons, as if he were the eldest. His name first occurs among the witnesses in three doubtful charters (K. 643, 672, 684) dated 984, 990, 993. As his father could not have been born before 966 these dates are impossible. From 997 to 1013 his name occurs frequently among the witnesses to charters. After that date it occurs only in the doubtful charter K. 723, which is dated 1016. In 1014 four of Ethelred's sons witness K. 1309, but not Æthelstan, and again in 1015 his name does not appear when his brothers Edmund and Edward witness K. 1310. No doubt he was ill or dead by this time. There is, however, a story in the contemporary continental chronicler Thietmar, VII, c. 28, in which he is mentioned as being alive after his father's death, but this story is so confused—for example Archbishop Ælfheah is confounded with Dunstan—that it can hardly be trusted in this instance. Æthelstan may have been confused with his brother Eadwig, whom we know to have survived his father.

It seems probable that illness was the cause of the drawing up of the will. Æthelstan cannot have been more than thirty years of age. Yet none of his bequests, even those to his father, contain the clause 'if he live longer than I'. Three of Ethelred's six sons by his first wife appear to have been dead by this date. At least they are not mentioned in Æthelstan's will, and their names do not appear in later charters.

l. 13. *þe ic hit æt geearnode.* As often in O.E., *hit* has no definite antecedent. Here it can only refer to the phrase *mine dre 7 mine æhta.*

l. 14. *witefæstne mann.* An alternative expression for *witeþeow.* See pp. 111 f.

ll. 14 f. *þe ic on spræce ahte.* Perhaps as profits resulting from a right of private jurisdiction (see note on *witeþeowman,* p. 111), but it may mean no more than that he obtained these men through their failure to pay compensation due to him after he had won a suit against them.

l. 15. *ic geann in mid me.* This is in payment of *sawolsceatt.* See pp. 109 f.

ll. 15 f. *þær ic me reste. Criste 7 sče Petre.* The Old Minster, Winchester, is meant. On its dedication see p. 126. It was in possession of Adderbury in 1044 (K. 768).

l. 16. *Eadburgebyrig.* Adderbury, Oxfordshire. 14½ hides there were held by the Bishop of Winchester in 1066 as belonging to his church (D.B. I, f. 155).

l. 17. *mid twam hund mancosan goldes be gewihte.* The 'mancus' was the regular term for expressing weight in gold. It was originally about 70 grains. (See Chadwick, pp. 11, 47 f.)

l. 18. 7 *þ land æt Mereldfan*.... The punctuation of the MS. leaves it doubtful whether this should be taken with the preceding or following sentence, that is, whether it forms part of the *sawolsceatt* or not. *Mereldfan*. Marlow, Buckinghamshire.

l. 20. *Mórdune*. Morden, Cambridgeshire. In D.B. 1, f. 190, it is entered as an estate of 8 hides which 'belonged and belongs' to St Peter of Winchester (the Old Minster).

l. 27. *for hyre are*. Thorpe translates 'for her honour'. O.E. *ár* also has the meanings 'property', estates', 'income'.

p. 58, l. 1. *Ælfsige bisceope*. This is Ælfsige II, Bishop of Winchester from 1014 to 1033.

l. 2. XII *pund be getale*. 240 pence were counted to the pound.

l. 3. *Holungaburnan*. Hollingbourne, Kent. This bequest is mentioned in a list of benefactors to Christchurch (Dugdale, 1, p. 97), but wrongly dated 980. In D.B. 1, f. 4 *b*, an estate of 6 *solins*, but with land for 24 ploughs, is held by the monks of the Archbishop of Canterbury.

l. 4. *þære anre sulunge*. See p. 130.

Siferðe. Considering the smallness of the grant and the locality I should be inclined to doubt whether he is the same as the Siferth on p. 60, l. 11, who is probably the thegn of the Seven Boroughs (see p. 155).

l. 5. *Garwaldintune*. Karlström, *Old English Compound Place-Names in -ing*, p. 59, identifies this as Garrington in Littlebourne, Kent.

l. 6. *Hryðerafelda*. Rotherfield. Perhaps the Oxfordshire place of this name, near Henley-on-Thames. There is also a Rotherfield in Sussex. The Nunnery of Winchester did not possess an estate of this name at the time of D.B.

nunnan mynstre. The Abbey of St Mary, Winchester.

ll. 7 f. *niwan mynstre*. The New Minister, Winchester, afterwards Hyde Abbey. See p. 155. In the *L.V.H.* (ed. Birch, p. 14) *Æþelstan filius Æþelredi regis* occurs as one of the benefactors for whose soul the monks are to pray, along with Eadmund, Ecgbyrht, Eadred, Eadwig and Eadgar, evidently his brothers, though Birch identifies them otherwise.

l. 8. *hwer*. This seems to have been some sort of cauldron or cooking vessel. In Wright-Wülker, 123. 39, *lebes* is glossed *hwer uel cytel* and among the glosses edited by Bouterwek in Haupt's *Zeitschrift für deutsches Altertum*, IX, on p. 503, l. 34, *hweres vel cyteles* is equated with *sartaginis*.

ll. 8 f. *on þære halgan þrymnesse naman*. The original dedication of the New Minster. Edward's first charter (B. 596) is dedicated to the Holy Trinity, his second (B. 602) to St Mary and St Peter in addition. In D.B. the minster is referred to as St Peter.

l. 10. *Sceaftenesbyrig*. Shaftesbury Abbey was originally dedicated to the Blessed Virgin, but was later more often known as St Edward's. In D.B. it appears with either dedication. I have not found any other reference to the holy cross there. Possibly Shaftesbury received a portion of the wood of the true cross sent to Alfred (Asser, chapter 71), or it may have possessed a famous crucifix like the Holy Cross of Waltham.

sēe Eadwearde. Edward the Martyr, Ethelred's half-brother, who was murdered in 978 or 979 (see Chronicle, and Plummer's note, II, p. 166). The *Vita S. Oswaldi* (p. 449) says his murder was by a party wishing to put Ethelred on the throne. Later authorities make Ælfthryth, Ethelred's mother, the instigator of the crime (see p. 123). Edward was first buried at Wareham (Chronicle, 979 E), but the Ealdor-man Ælfhere transferred the body to Shaftesbury (*ibid.* 980 E). Miracles were performed at his tomb (*Vita S. Oswaldi*, pp. 451 f.). In Ethelred's fifth code (c. 16) his festival is appointed for March 18th.

l. 11. *Eadmunde minon breðer*. Edmund Ironside, who succeeded Ethelred as king. His wars with Cnut, the division of the kingdom, and his death in 1016 are told in the Chronicle and later historians. Later chroniclers, e.g. Henry of Huntingdon (p. 185) and W.M. (*G.R.* p. 217), declare him to have been murdered, but there is no hint of this in the Chronicle or Fl. Wig.

l. 13. *Cealhtune*. Chalton, Hampshire.

Ælmære minon cnihte. The name Ælmær occurs four times in this will, but I am inclined to think that three, if not all, of the references refer to the same person. Here, eight hides of the estate at Chalton, which is bequeathed to the king, have been given to Æthelstan's *cniht* Ælfmær. On p. 60, ll. 9 f. Æthelstan states that he gives to his seneschal Ælfmær eight hides at Catherington. As Catherington is only about two miles from Chalton and would be included in a large grant of land round Chalton, it seems to me highly probable that we have here two references to the same gift, and that Ælfmær, the *cniht*, is Ælfmær the seneschal. He may be the Ælmær on p. 58, l. 30, who receives Hambledon, probably the Hampshire Hambledon which is less than five miles west of Chalton. We have no evidence to help us to decide whether the Ælmær, Ælfric's son, of p. 62, l. 2, is the same man or not.

l. 14. *Norðtune*. There are too many Nortons for this estate to be definitely identified. Chipping Norton, Oxfordshire, is a possibility.

l. 15. *Mollintune*. Mollington, Oxfordshire.

Ulfcytel. This is perhaps the Ulfcytel of East Anglia who fought against the Danes in 1004, and again in 1010 (Chronicle), and fell at *Assandun* in 1016. He appears also in Scandinavian authorities for this period, the *Knytlinga Saga*, the *Saga of St Olaf*, and the *Jóms-vikinga Saga*. In the latter he is said to have married Ethelred's daughter.

l. 16. *Morkære*. This is an uncommon name at this period, and I have little doubt that here it refers to the *Morcær* whose murder is related in the Chronicle 1015 (see p. 155). The Siferth to whom a bequest is made in this will, on p. 60, ll. 11 ff., I take to be Morcar's brother who was murdered with him. W.M. (*G.R.* p. 213) lays the blame of the murder on Ethelred, so that it is of interest to find them on friendly terms with his son in this will. After their murder Edmund Ironside married Siferth's widow against his father's will, and took possession of the estates of both brothers (Chronicle, 1015 E). He made a bequest to the New Minster for Siferth's soul (K. 726).

Þurbrand. O.Icel. *Þorbrandr.* In this period the only person of this name of whom we have any record is the slayer of Earl Uhtred in 1016 (Symeon of Durham, R.S. 1, pp. 216 f.), but there is no reason to identify him with the legatee of this will.

l. 17. *Leofwine.* The name is too common for identification. He may be the ealdorman of this name.

l. 18. *Þæs swurdes þe Offa cyng ahte.* Offa reigned from 757 to 796, so that the sword had been handed down for over two hundred years.

l. 19. *pyttedan.* This does not occur elsewhere. B.T. connects it with *pytt*, 'pit', 'hollow'. It perhaps refers to some stamped pattern (cf. pictures of swords of the Viking period in Du Chaillu, *The Viking Age*, II, pp. 65–72).

anes brandes. The dictionaries recognise *brand* as a poetical word for sword, but it is clear from this passage that there is some distinction in meaning. What this is I have been unable to discover. Possibly *brand* refers to the blade alone.

l. 21. *Pedcesdele.* This cannot be identified with certainty. Professor Mawer suggests that it is the valley of the Peak, Derbyshire. This district, which was royal demesne in 1066, is described by Professor Stenton in his *Types of Manorial Structure in the Northern Danelaw*, pp. 72 f.

l. 22. *ane dægfeorme.* See p. 120.

l. 23. *Sce Æþeldryðe mæssedæg.* June 23rd.

l. 28. *Eadwige minon breðer.* He survived his father and brothers. He was banished by Cnut in 1017, and murdered in the same year (Chronicle, C; Fl. Wig.).

l. 29. *Ælfsige bisceope.* See p. 169.

l. 31. *Hamelandene.* Probably Hambledon in Hampshire, near Chalton (see p. 170). There are also Hambledons in Buckinghamshire and Surrey.

p. 60, ll. 2 f. *Godwine Wulfnoðes suna.* This may be the great Earl Godwine, as all authorities agree in calling him Wulfnoth's son (see Freeman, *Norman Conquest*, I, p. 705), but Godwine is a very common name at this period. Freeman discusses the identity of this Wulfnoth. As he points out, if he is the outlaw, Wulfnoth *Cild*, the South Saxon (Chronicle, 1009 E), it is easy to see why his son should not be in possession of his father's land.

l. 3. *Cumtune.* It is impossible to state with any certainty which of the numerous Comptons is meant here. If Wulfnoth, who apparently forfeited this estate, is Wulfnoth *Cild*, probably one of the Sussex Comptons is meant (see Freeman, *op. cit., loc. cit.*).

l. 5. *Westune*. Weston is too common a name for identification.

l. 7. *Heorulfestune*. Perhaps Harleston in Suffolk. There are also places of this name in Norfolk, Devonshire and Staffordshire.

l. 8. *þæs malswurdes*. Cf. O.Icel. *málasax*, *málaspjót*, and see Fritzner, *s.v. mál*. 15. This word was used of the patterns of inlay of precious metals on weapons.

Æthelstan leaves this sword to his chaplain, though a priest was technically not allowed to wear weapons (*Canons of Ælfric*, 30, in Thorpe's *Ancient Laws and Institutes of England*).

Wiðer. A *Wiðer* witnesses a charter (K. 714), dated 1005. The name represents the O.Icel. *Víðarr*.

l. 9. *Ælmære minon discþene*. See p. 170.

discþene. This official appears to have been a seneschal in royal households. The Latin equivalent is *discifer*. He is mentioned in King Edred's will, where he is a higher official than the stewards (see Harmer, pp. 121 f.). From signatures we know the *discthegn* to have been a *minister* or king's thegn. The office is first mentioned in Athelstan's reign and the latest occurrence of *discthegn* is as the title of a witness to the Will of Thurstan in 1044 (see p. 82, l. 25).

l. 10. *Cateringatune*. Catherington, Hampshire. See p. 170.

ll. 10 f. *þæs sceardan swurdes*. B.T. translates *sceard* 'notched', 'hacked', 'having gaps or rifts'. If this refers to the blade of the sword, Æthelstan is perhaps bequeathing the weapon for the sake of precious metals on the hilt. Possibly, however, the adjective describes some kind of ornamentation.

l. 11. *mines targan*. See p. 147.

Siferðe. See pp. 155, 169. Signatures of Siferth occur in 1005, 1012, 1013.

l. 12. *Hocganclife*. Hockliffe, Bedfordshire.

mines bohscyldes. *boh* is the form in the two early MSS. The Winchester Codex has *boc*, which Thorpe translates as 'beechen'. But the Winchester scribe ordinarily has *c* for O.E. guttural *h*. I suggest tentatively 'curved', 'arched', as *boh-* could well have been written for *bog-* at this date, but I am by no means clear what was the distinguishing feature of this shield, for, judging by the pictures in illuminated MSS. of the period, notably Claudius B 4 and Harley 603, the normal shield of this date is round and convex, usually with a pointed boss. The earlier Anglo-Saxon shield, that of the heathen period, was flat, but this is never delineated in eleventh-century MSS. Lye translates *humerale scutum*, apparently meaning a shield slung over the shoulder, the ordinary Anglo-Saxon shield being grasped by the hand. I have found no pictures of such a shield, except that in the Bayeux tapestry it is shown that the long kite-shaped shield could be carried in this way; but the introduction of this into England is generally taken to date from the middle of the century, and in any case one would expect a more descriptive term for this very distinctive shield.

l. 13. *Æþelwerde Stameran*. Æthelweard is a particularly common name at this time. A son of the Ealdorman Æthelwine bore it, and also a son of the Ealdorman Æthelmær. There was also an Ealdorman Æthelweard who was banished in 1020. The name does not occur with this nickname elsewhere. The nickname *Stamera* occurs in a manumission (E. pp. 261 f.).

l. 14. *Tywingan.* Tewin, Hertfordshire. D.B. *Tewinge.*

l. 15. *Cwattes.* I can offer no explanation of this curious nickname.

l. 16. *Leommære æt Biggrafan. Biggrafan* is Bygrave, Hertfordshire. In B. 1297 (Edgar's foundation charter to Thorney), we are told that Leofwine, son of Athulf, sold 6 hides at Bygrave to Thorney Abbey. He may have been father to Leofmær, since the custom of giving the son one element of his father's name was often followed. In 1066 Bygrave was still held by a man called Leofmær (*Lemar*), under Stigand. (D.B. 1, f. 135: *V. C. H. of Hertfordshire*, 1, p. 311.)

l. 17. *Godwine Dreflan.* The name is too common for identification. It does not occur with this nickname elsewhere.

Lutegaresheale. This may be either Ludgershall, Wiltshire, Ludgershall, Buckinghamshire, Ludgarshall, Gloucestershire, or Lurgashall, Sussex. The latter place is about 15 miles from Æthelstan's estate of Chalton, Hampshire.

ll. 18 f. *þæs swurdes þe seo hand is on gemearcod.* I take this to refer to the symbol which appears frequently on the coins of the period, especially on Ethelred's coinage, namely an open hand representing the hand from heaven (see Keary, *Catalogue of Anglo-Saxon Coins in the British Museum*, vol. 1, pl. XXVIII, vol. 11, pls. VIII, XVI, and pp. 192, 203 f.).

l. 22. *Colungahrycge.* Unidentified.

ll. 22 f. *gehealde mon...Ælfric.* For this construction of *gehealdan* with the accusative, in the sense of 'satisfy', 'pay', see *Crawford Charters*, p. 23, l. 21, and p. 131, and also B.T. *Suppl. s.v. gehealdan*, XI.

l. 23. *Bertune.* The name Barton is too common to be identified.

l. 27. *middessumeres mæssedæge.* June 24th, the Nativity of John the Baptist.

l. 28. *þ wæs þ...worde.* Literally 'namely, that he (i.e. Ælfgar) informed me...'. The sequence of ideas is a little confused in the original. My translation is not literal, but does, I think, express what Æthelstan means.

p. 62, l. 2. *Byrhtmær abb.* Abbot of the New Minster, Winchester, from 1008 to 1021.

l. 3. *ealle þa witan...rædan.* The Ealdorman Alfred addresses his will to the witan as well as to the king (Harmer, x), and King Alfred brought his father's will before the witan in a case of dispute (Harmer, XI). Usually, however, there is no reference to the witan, and it is hardly likely that the wills of lesser people were read there.

ll. 5 f. *Swa mines fæder leaf. On minon Cwyde stænt.* The Christchurch MS. has a variant reading, which I translate 'in accordance with my father's permission and the terms of my will'.

l. 9. *Ælfþryðe*. See p. 123.

l. 10. *þe me to þyson godan gefylstan*. As the endings -*en*, -*on*, -*an*, are not kept apart at this date it is possible to take *gefylstan* as a preterite plural and to translate the phrase: 'who have helped me to [obtain] these possessions'.

XXI.

MS. Corpus Christi College, Cambridge, MS. CI, f. 88. This is a twelfth-century Bath Cartulary and has been edited by W. Hunt (see following note).

EDITIONS. Hickes, *Dissertatio Epistolaris*, p. 54.
K. 694.
T. p. 528.
W. Hunt, *Two Chartularies of the Priory of St Peter at Bath*, p. 32.

DATE. Between 984 and 1016.

The will was drawn up in the reign of Ethelred, and after Ælfhere became Abbot of Bath.

l. 13. *Wulfwaru*. I have not been able to identify her or her children with people who appear elsewhere.

l. 19. *blede*. See p. 139.

l. 21. *hricghrægles*. Cf. p. 86, l. 3. The word also occurs in the will of Bishop Ælfwold of Crediton (see *Crawford Charters*, x, l. 22, and note, p. 131).

l. 22. *wahryfte*. Perhaps for the walls of the bed-chamber.

hoppscytan. B.T. *Suppl.* gives an instance from Ælfric's *Homilies* (ed. Assman, IX, 307) in which *hopscytan* translates the *conopeum* of the Vulgate in the story of Judith.

l. 23. *Ælfere abbode*. Abbot Ælfere of Bath witnesses a charter of 993 (K. 684) and another of 997 (K. 698). Probably he is the Ælfhere who signs as abbot twice in 985 (K. 1283, 648) and also in 990 (K. 673) and 1007 (K. 1304). He may be the abbot of this name who brought the King's *insegel* to a shiremoot between 990 and 992 (K. 693). He was perhaps successor to Ælfheah who became Bishop of Winchester in 984. The Abbot Ælfhere who signs in 1019 (K. 730) and in 1031 (K. 744) may be a different person.

l. 24. *Ferscesforda*. Freshford, Somerset.

l. 26. *Clatfordtune*. Claverton, 2 miles S.E. of Bath.

l. 27. *Cumtune*. There are several Comptons in Somerset. This may be Compton Dando, about 7 miles from Winford, or Compton Martin near Butcombe.

l. 28. *Budancumbe*. Butcombe, Somerset.

p. 64, l. 1. *heafodbotl*. See p. 136.

l. 4. *Leage*. W. Hunt (*op. cit.* p. 79) suggests Leigh-on-Mendip, Somerset.

l. 5. *Healhtune.* Holton near Blackford, Somerset. See *ibid.*, *loc. cit.*

l. 6. *Hocgestune.* Unidentified.

l. 9. *Wunfrod.* Winford, Somerset.

l. 10. *anes bendes.* See p. 120.

l. 11. *twegea preonas.* See p. 110.

l. 17. *anes heallreafes.* Probably an alternative term for the *heall-wahriftes* of the preceding line.

l. 18. *burreafes.* A tapestry for a 'bower', i.e. one of the smaller chambers than the hall, used as bedrooms or women's quarters, etc.

l. 19. *cnihtum.* See p. 127.

ll. 23 f. *þ hi fi[n]don....westan.* The original probably had a horizontal stroke over the *i* to represent the *n*. Thorpe reads *fedon* and translates 'feed', but it is unusual to find *i* as an error for *e* and *fedon* does not give a probable sense. For *findan* in the sense 'provide', see examples in B.T. *Suppl.* The phrase perhaps means 'manumit twenty slaves'.

freotmanna. See p. 165.

l. 25. *ane feorme.* See p. 120.

XXII.

MS. K. and T. quote as their authority *Reg. B. pen. Dec. et Cap. St Paul*, f. 20 *b*, but I cannot find this MS. at St Paul's. Birch, who prints from K. two charters out of this register (B. 735, 736), was also unable to find the MS.

My text is taken from K.

EDITIONS. K. 972.

T. p. 542.

DATE. Probably between 1004 and 1014. The document has an impossible list of witnesses, but it is drawn up with the permission of King Ethelred, and if we ignore all the more famous personages in the list, such as a later scribe might insert, the date appears to be about the first decade of the eleventh century. The names of many witnesses do not agree with this date. The Ealdorman Ælfhere died in 983, Æthelnoth became Archbishop of Canterbury in 1020 and the Ealdormen Brihtnoth and Eadric did not hold office together. Yet there is nothing in the phrasing of the bequest to suggest that it is spurious, and we know of no motive for its forgery, as there is no trace that either Laver or Cockhampstead were ever owned or claimed by St Paul's. I suggest that the list of witnesses in the original had been damaged and that the gap was filled in by a later copyist.

A Latin document which purports to be a confirmation by Ethelred of this bequest is contained in the St Paul's MS., W.D. 4 (*Liber L*), f. 10. It is K. 1300. This has variations from the bequest in the list of witnesses. The abbots *Wigard* and *Ælsi* are omitted, and so is Ufegeat, and three names, *Hargodus presbyter, Ælfricus diaconus, Wuluricus presbyter*, are added.

p. 66, l. 1. *Ægelfled*. Thorpe calls her queen, and says she was the first wife of King Ethelred, giving as his authority Lappenberg (*History of England under the Anglo-Saxon Kings*, II, p. 163), but Freeman (*Norman Conquest*, Note SS) points out that Lappenberg had misunderstood the Scholiast on Adam of Bremen. Fl. Wig. gives Ælfgifu as the name of Ethelred's first wife (see p. 167).

The testatrix is probably not the Æthelflæd of No. XIV, since neither the latter nor her sister mentions Laver or Cockhampstead. She may be the Æthelflæd, sister of Leofsige, Ealdorman of Essex, whose estates were forfeited for aiding her brother after his banishment in 1002 (K. 719). This would explain why St Paul's apparently did not obtain possession of the estates granted to them.

l. 3. *Lagefare*. Laver, Essex. D.B. *Laghefara*.

l. 4. *Cochamstede*. Cockhampstead, Hertfordshire.

l. 8. *Ægelnoð arcebiscop*. He held the see of Canterbury from 1020 to 1038.

l. 9. *Wulfstan arcebiscop*. Archbishop of York, 1003 to 1023.

Ælfun biscop on Lundene: i.e. from 1004 to 1014.

l. 10. *Ælfric abbot*. This may be the homilist, but several monasteries, including Malmesbury, Abingdon, Evesham and St Albans, had abbots called Ælfric at some time during the period covered by this list of witnesses.

Wigard abbot. This abbot also appears in K. 715, a Christchurch charter of doubtful authenticity. It is dated 1006. Even if spurious, it proves that he was not an invention of the St Paul's scribe.

ll. 10 f. *Ælsi abbot on Cowwaforde*. No religious foundation called *Cowwaforde* is otherwise known, and as Peterborough, Ely and the New Minster, had abbots called Ælfsige at this period, we cannot assign other signatures to this witness.

l. 11. *Ælfere ealdorman*. See p. 124. He died in 983.

Briðnoð ealdorman. See p. 106.

l. 12. *Eadric ealdorman*. Eadric Streona, Ealdorman of Mercia from 1007 to 1017 (see Chronicle, E).

Ælfsige cynges þegn. Ælfsige is too common a name in the tenth and eleventh centuries for this witness to be identified.

l. 13. *Ufegeat scireman*. I have found no reference to him elsewhere. The name is a rare one. The only other instances in Searle's *Onomasticon* refer to the son of the Ealdorman Ælfhelm (see p. 153).

scireman is equivalent to *scirgerefa*, 'sheriff'. See p. 191.

Frena. No doubt the *Fræna* who witnesses No. XVI (2). See p. 150.

XXIII.

MS. (a) The Red Book of Thorney. This cartulary was in the possession of the Earl of Westmorland in 1879. It has unfortunately been inaccessible to me. I have therefore been obliged to print from

(b) British Museum, Additional MS. 5937, f. 133 b (quoted by

K., T. as f. 180 b). This MS. is a paper book containing extracts from (a), made in the reign of Elizabeth or James I by Strangeman and St George.

EDITIONS. *Collectanea Topographica*, IV, p. 58, from (b), with an English translation which is also printed in Warner's *History of Thorney Abbey*, p. 51.

K. 1329, from *Collectanea Topographica*.

T. p. 555, from (b).

DATE. The will is addressed to Cnut, who reigned from 1017 to 1035, but it is evident from the language that it is preserved only in a late and corrupt form. It is not without suspicious features, and therefore the inaccessibility of the cartulary version is particularly to be regretted. The use of the first person plural is unparalleled, and so is the name Mantat, though possibly this is to be explained as a corruption of a foreign name. The use of the title *ancer* in connection with Thorney at this late date looks like a piece of exaggerated antiquarianism. One of the estates named in the will was in the possession of Thorney Abbey at the time of D.B. and according to the Red Book (see below) the abbey considered that the other had been wrongfully taken from them. Yet if we assume that the abbey forged a title-deed to strengthen their claim, it is difficult to see why they did not merely fabricate a royal grant on the pattern of others in their possession. There must have been at least a tradition that these estates were given by Cnut to a hermit, and that the latter left them to the abbey in return for right of burial there. There is nothing improbable in the transaction, and it is possible that we ought to regard the will as the result of the tampering of later copyists with a genuine original. The writ form in which it is couched also occurs in a copy of a will of about 1040 (see following note).

l. 16. *Mantat ancer...greteð Cnut cing.* Only one other will (No. XXIX) begins in this way. It is due to the influence of a form of charter which became common in the eleventh century, and is generally known as a 'writ'. It approaches an epistolary form, beginning with a greeting and generally ending with a valediction. Both this will and No. XXIX show the influence of the writ in their endings also (cf. p. 66, ll. 27 ff., with p. 78, l. 8).

Mantat. This can hardly be an O.E. name, unless it is hopelessly corrupt. The first element occurs in Continental German names , e.g. *Mangod* (cf. Forssner, *Continental-Germanic Personal Names in Old English*, p. 186), and -*tat* may perhaps represent the German -*taita* (see Förstemann, *Deutsches Namenbuch*, I, col. 1387).

Emma hlæfdie. Ælfgifu Emma, the widow of Ethelred. She married Cnut in 1017 (Chronicle, D, E).

l. 20. *Twiwell.* Twywell, Northamptonshire. Thorney Abbey held this estate in 1066 (D.B. I, f. 222 b: *V. C. H. of Northamptonshire*, I, p. 319).

þornige. Thorney Abbey, Cambridgeshire, was originally founded as a community of anchorites and was a subordinate house to Peterborough (Dugdale, II, p. 571, from Harley 5071). It was restored by Bishop Æthelwold in Edgar's reign (Hugo Candidus in Sparke, *Historiae Anglicanae Scriptores Varii*, p. 27).

Cunintun. Conington, Huntingdonshire. Thorney Abbey let this estate to *Turchil* of Harmworth at a rent, but when his estates were forfeited to the Crown, it was granted to Earl Waltheof. The monks explained that it was not Turchil's property and it was arranged that Waltheof should keep it on the same terms as Turchil had it. After his death, the Countess Judith held the estate and paid no rent. After her death it was lost to the abbey. (See Warner, *op. cit.* pp. 58 f., from the Red Book of Thorney.)

In D.B. this estate is held by the Countess Judith. It is stated that *Turchillus* had held 9 hides, of which 6 belonged to Thorney, and that he paid a *caritas* to the abbey. The Hundred did not know how much he paid (D.B. I, f. 206 b: *V. C. H. of Huntingdonshire*, I, p. 351).

l. 21. *prestes 7 diaknes.* This must have replaced a dative plural.

earnodon. The only meanings recognised by the dictionaries for O.E. *(ge)earnian* are 'deserve', 'earn', 'acquire', 'gain by labour', 'win' and the like. My own opinion is that the word when used in connection with land sometimes refers to sub-tenure, and means 'to hold land under some-one else', possibly only when services were rendered in return for the land. This meaning would fit the context here, but as it is doubtful I have translated with the established meaning. In B. 1097 where we read that a certain Ælfheah, who has succeeded to his father's estates, 'denied his brother Ælfric estates and possessions unless he "earned" anything from him', it seems to me that the sense might be 'to hold under his brother', rather than 'deserve' or 'acquire'. The document goes on to say that Ælfheah allowed Ælfric certain estates for his lifetime. I take it that the land which *Sewine* had *to earninge* (p. 80, l. 17) was land for which he rendered services rather than land given to him as a reward, and that the same meaning is contained in the *erninglond* of p. 88, l. 31. There seems to me no authority for rendering this last word, with B.T., 'land earned or made freehold', '*bocland*'. The only other occurrence I know of is in K. 679, where Bishop Eadulf gave a *curtam* in Worcester, which had reverted to the Cathedral, as *earnignclande* to whoever he chose. This can be variously interpreted, but it does not seem to me necessary to assume that he alienated it permanently from the Cathedral by giving up the title-deeds. If *earningland* is the same as land held *to earninge*, it is certainly not *bocland*, for Thurstan could not have bequeathed the *bocland* of *Sewine*.

XXIV.

MSS. (a) Cambridge University Library, MS. FF. 2. 33, f. 48 b.
  (b) Additional MS. 14847, f. 18 b.
On these MSS. see pp. 103 f. The text is from (a).

EDITIONS. K. 959, from (a).
  T. p. 579, from (a).
  B. 1020, from (b).

DATE. Before 1038, if, as seems probable, Thurketel's wife *Lefwen* to whom he bequeathes Roydon is the Leofwyn who sold an estate at that place to Bishop Ælfric, the testator of No. XXVI (see p. 184).

p. 68, l. 1. *þurketel.* There is no reason to identify him with any of the other Thurketels who make grants to Bury. Thurketel is a common name in East Anglia at this period.

l. 2. *Palegraue.* Palgrave, Suffolk. According to B. 1084, St Edmund's had received 4 *cassati* from a certain Wulfstan in 962. As the abbey was holding only 4 carucates in 1066 (D.B. II, f. 361 : *V.C.H. of Suffolk*, I, p. 497), the estate granted by Thurketel may have been alienated from St Edmund's.

Witingham. Whittingham near Fressingfield, Suffolk.

l. 4. *toft.* This refers to the dwelling and the yards, outbuildings, etc. round it.

his metecu 7 his metecorn. Cf. *Rectitudines Singularum Personarum*, 8, where the amount of food due to a servant (*esne*) is stated as *xii pund godes cornes 7 ii scipæteras 7 i god metecu.*

Reydone. Roydon, near Diss, Norfolk, which is only about 2 miles from Palgrave, is clearly the place meant here. Below Thurketel leaves land at this place to his wife, who probably sold it to Bishop Ælfric (see p. 72, l. 17 f.). Roydon is only some 2 miles from the Bishop's estate of Fersfield.

l. 5. *forlong.* The acre strips of the arable fields were arranged in parallel groups, the number of strips to a group varying with the lie of the land. These groups were called furlongs, one of their dimensions being the length of a furrow. See Seebohm, *The English Village Community*, 4th edition, p. 4, and Maitland, *Domesday Book and Beyond*, p. 380.

Scortland. Perhaps this is a field-name.

l. 6. *Lefwen min wif.* See note on the date.

l. 7. *Simplingham.* Shimpling, Norfolk, is more probable than the Suffolk Shimpling, as the former is only about 4 miles from Palgrave, and all Thurketel's estates lie near the Norfolk and Suffolk boundary, near Diss and Eye.

þat ic mid hire nam. This sounds like a reference to dowry brought by the wife. This is foreign to Anglo-Saxon marriage customs and may be due to Scandinavian influence, for dowry (O.Icel. *heimanfylgia*) regularly occurred in a Scandinavian marriage.

l. 8. *þat forwarde*. This may have been a marriage agreement. See pp. 135 f.

l. 9. *Wingefeld*. Wingfield, Suffolk.

l. 13. *Osebern*. This represents O.Icel. *Ásbiorn*.

l. 14. *Thrandestone*. Thrandeston, near Palgrave, Suffolk.

ll. 17 f. *er daye ⁊ after daye*. This expression also occurs in K. 898, where a bishop buys land *to geofene ⁊ to syllanne ær dæge ⁊ æfter dæge*. An almost identical phrase is found in K. 789, where land is bought *to gyfanne ⁊ to syllanne on dæge ⁊ æfter dæge*. It is clear from the context that the phrases are identical in meaning, i.e. that the land can be alienated both during the lifetime of the purchaser and afterwards.

ll. 20 f. *þise write..himself*. See pp. 150 f.

XXV.

MSS. (*a*) Cambridge University Library, MS. FF. 2. 33, f. 45. See p. 99.

(*b*) Additional MS. 14847, f. 15. See pp. 103 f.

The text is taken from (*a*).

EDITIONS. K. 960, from (*a*).

T. p. 578, from (*a*).

B. 1017, from (*b*).

DATE. First half of the eleventh century (see following note). Probably later than Cnut's foundations of Holme and Bury, i.e. than 1020.

p. 70, l. 1. *Thurketel*. There would be no means of dating this will if it were not for the accidental circumstance that Hermann in his *Miracles of St Edmund* (Liebermann, *Ungedruckte anglo-normannische Geschichtsquellen*, p. 234) refers to a certain *Thurcytel*, the father of *Aelfwen* who was a recluse at St Benedict's at Holme. This is clearly the same man, and the identification is made more certain by Hermann's connecting him with the district called *Flec*, that is Flegg in Norfolk. The testator of this will bequeathes estates in East Flegg Hundred. Hermann relates that Thurketel collected a tax for Swegn just about the time of the latter's death, but when he heard of his death he paid back the money. This was in 1014. We do not know how long after this the will was made. The story was told to Hermann by Thurketel's daughter, Ælfwyn, herself.

Thurketel is given the cognomen *Heyng* in the Latin rubric. This is the O.Icel. *Hæing*, 'salmon'.

l. 2. *Castre*. Caister, in East Flegg Hundred, Norfolk. The Abbey of St Benedict at Holme held one carucate there in 1066 (D.B. II, f. 221: *V. C. H. of Norfolk*, II, p. 144).

Thorpe. There is now no Thorpe in the neighbourhood of Thurketel's other estates. Bury owned two estates of this name in Norfolk in 1066, Thorpe Abbots (D.B. II, f. 210 b) and Morningthorpe (*ibid.* f. 212).

ll. 4 f. *sēe Benedicte...to Holm.* An abbey of Benedictine monks was founded near the R. Bure at a place then called *Holm*, just west of Thurne, by Cnut, probably about 1019. It was from here that the prior Ufi was sent with twelve monks to form the nucleus of Bury in 1020. There was an earlier foundation, traditionally assigned to 800, which was destroyed by the Danes, and refounded in the next century. See *Chronica Johannis de Oxenedes*, R.S. p. 19.)

l. 5. *mine wyues del.* Possibly there had been an agreement before their marriage stating what proportion of her husband's goods the wife was to have on his death. See pp.135 f. In Scandinavian law this under ordinary circumstances was one-third of the goods and purchased land.

l. 6. *heregete.* See p. 100.

l. 7. *Alfwen.* See p. 180.

Ormisby. Ormesby, East Flegg Hundred, Norfolk. In D.B. it is stated to have been held by *Guert* under St Benet of Holme (D.B. II, f. 115 b: *V. C. H. of Norfolk*, II, p. 45).

l. 11. *Scrouteby.* Scratby, near Ormesby.

mine nefe kild Swegner sunen 7 Alemundes. It is necessary to take *nefe* as a genitive plural to make sense of this phrase. The present form, for O.E. *nefena*, may be due to Scandinavian influence. The *r* in *Swegner* is a scribal error. Elsewhere this scribe confuses O.E. *s* and *r* (see p. 187). The variant reading of the Additional MS. is no doubt due in the first place to a misreading of *un* of *sunen* as *im*. *Alemundes* is O.E. (Anglian) *Alhmund*, with *e* in error for *c*.

l. 13. *ihernen.* Elsewhere in this MS., *ih* represents O.E. *h* (cf. *ihu*, l. 1 above) or O.E. *g* (cf. *ihere*, p. 8, l. 12, for O.E. *geare*). It is possible therefore that this word represents O. West Saxon *giernan*, 'desire', 'ask for', but I do not consider that this gives a very plausible sense. In my translation I have taken the word to represent O.E. *(ge)earnian.* The Addit. MS. *heruen* may be merely a miscopying, with the common error of *u* for *n*. If not, it must represent the O. West Saxon *ierf(i)an*, 'inherit', but this again gives an unsatisfactory meaning in this context.

ll. 15 f. *þise write...seluen.* See pp. 131 f. *and* for *an*, or vice versa, is a common error of this MS.

XXVI.

MSS. (*a*) British Museum, Cotton Augustus, II, 85, a single parchment in an eleventh-century hand.

(*b*) Cambridge University Library, MS. FF. 2. 33, f. 48. See p. 99.

(*c*) Additional MS. 14847, f. 18. See pp. 103 f.

The text is from (*a*), which has clearly been in the possession of Bury, for the cartulary versions are copied from it (see note to p. 72, l. 9), and it has a marginal note against the part dealing with bequests to Bury, drawing attention to the bequest further on in the will of a mill to the Abbey (see p. 72, footnote 2, and cf. l. 18). It has some insertions and corrections above the line, and it looks to me like a copy. I also hesitate to believe that as early as 1040 a bishop's will would be written in such ungrammatical O.E., when such good O.E. as that of No. xxx could be written in 1044. There the O.E. inflectional system is preserved, whereas here, to name only a few divergences, *mine cnihtas* (p. 72, l. 7) represents a dative plural, *minas lafordas* (p. 70, l. 21) a genitive singular, *a* is written as the ending of the optative singular several times, *e* for the ending of the genitive plural in *punde* (p. 72, l. 2). It seems to me probable that the will is a Bury copy of a somewhat later date. A date of some twenty or thirty years later is not excluded by the paleographical evidence, though the handwriting could be contemporary.

FACSIMILE of (*a*) in Bond, *Facsimiles of Ancient Charters in the British Museum*, IV, No. 21.

EDITIONS. K. 759, from (*a*).
T. 567, from (*a*).
Sweet, *A Second Anglo-Saxon Reader*, p. 213, from (*a*).

DATE. During the reign of Harold Harefoot, 1035 or 1037 (see note to p. 70, ll. 19 f.) to 1040.

p. 70, l. 17. *Ælfric ð.* According to the Chronicle C, D, E, an Ælfric, Bishop of East Anglia, died about Christmas, 1038, and W.M. (*G.P.* p. 150) says that he was succeeded by another Ælfric. Fl. Wig. (1038, 1047) says, however, that Grimketel became Bishop of East Anglia in 1038, and this is supported by two writs of Edward the Confessor in favour of Bury (K. 832, 1342), which are addressed to him. One of these, at least, is spurious, being addressed also to Earl Ælfgar, who did not become earl until nine years after Stigand's accession to the see of Elmham, but Grimketel's name would not have been used had he never been Bishop of Elmham. As Stigand succeeded to the see in 1043, and there is a writ of Edward the Confessor addressed to a Bishop Ælfric (K. 868), Grimketel could not have held the see long. It seems most probable that he relinquished it when he became Bishop of Selsey in 1039. It is therefore just possible that the testator is the second Ælfric, though the earlier one is more probable. The date of the first Ælfric's accession is uncertain. It was not before 1022, as his predecessor Ælfwine occurs as a witness in that year.

ll. 19 f. *Haralde cyncge.* Harold Harefoot, said to be the son of Cnut and Ælfgifu of Northampton, though this was disputed already in his own day (see Chronicle, 1035, C, D). He ruled England from 1035, but Plummer (Chronicle, II, p. 209) thinks that he was not crowned king till 1037. In this year he drove out Ælfgifu Emma, the mother of his younger brother and rival, from England. He died in 1040. (See *Encomium Emmae*, Liber III; Chronicle, 1035 to 1040; Fl. Wig. 1035.)

l. 20. *Wilrincgawerþa.* Worlingworth, Suffolk. Bury held 6 carucates there in 1066 (D.B. II, f. 368: *V. C. H. of Suffolk*, I, p. 504).

l. 23. *Hunstanestune*. Hunstanton, Norfolk.

Holme. Holme-next-the-sea, near Hunstanton, Norfolk.

p. 72, l. 1 *on Byrig*. The old name for Bury St Edmunds, *Bederices-wyrth*, was being supplanted in the eleventh century by *Sancte Eadmundes burh*. I think the present will is the earliest example of *byrig* used alone to refer to this foundation. The old name is used in Æthelric's will about 995, and in Ælfflæd's about the same period. I know no later instance of its use except in the doubtful charter of Cnut (K. 735). In eleventh-century wills the name 'St Edmund's Bury' occurs frequently, and though these wills are not in their original form, I think it unlikely that the scribe has substituted the more familiar name when he did not do so in his copies of tenth-century documents.

l. 2. *Ticeswelle...Doccyncge*. Tichwell and Docking, Norfolk.

l. 3. *Leofstane dæcane*. No doubt he is the same person as the dean of Bury who witnessed Thurstan's will in 1043 or 1044 (see p. 82, l. 18). A 'dean' was originally set over every ten monks.

Grimastune. Grimston, Norfolk.

ll. 4 f. *ic gean...*II *marc gol*. See p. 100. Two marks are equal to 100 mancuses.

l. 5. *mire hlefdigen*. It would seem from this that Harold Harefoot had a wife, though there is no reference to her elsewhere. The bishop would hardly make a bequest to the reigning king's greatest enemy, Cnut's widow, Ælfgifu Emma.

l. 6. *fatfylre*. Literally 'cup-filler'. In the Anglo-Saxon version of Gregory's *Dialogues* (Grein, *Bibliothek der angelsächsischen Prosa*, v), p. 186, l. 19, *fætfylleres* translates *fusoris*. The usual English word for cup-bearer or butler was *byrele*, cf. *þæs bisceopes byrele*, *ibid.* p. 186, ll. 21 f.

l. 7. *stiwardas*. This official is also mentioned in the will of Leofgifu (p. 76, ll. 14, 16, 17) and in that of King Edred (Harmer, xxi), where he is clearly a lesser official than a *discþegn*. The latter official, however, is apparently confined to royal households, and the steward in private households may have been a seneschal, like the *discþegn*. *Stigweard* is once equated with *discifer* (Wright-Wülker, 223. 7), once with *economus* (*ibid.* 129. 13).

l. 9. *sæmestre*. See p. 111. The other MSS. have not noticed that *se* has been erased.

l. 10. *Walsingaham*. One of the Norfolk Walsinghams.

l. 12. *Fersafeld*. Fersfield, Norfolk.

ll. 12 f. *iungere Brun*. *iungere* could represent either the comparative of the adjective *geong*, or the noun, O.E. *gingra*, *geongra*. In either case we should have expected a definite article and a weak ending, but this will is very ungrammatical throughout. The O.E. noun *gingra* had various meanings, e.g. 'disciple', 'pupil', 'vassal', 'inferior' (see B.T. *Suppl.*), but in the laws it refers to a subordinate official, and is translated *Beamte* by Liebermann. An ealdorman's *gingre* is mentioned in Alfred, 38, 2, and in the eleventh-century document *Judex*, 8

(Liebermann, *op. cit.* 1, p. 475), the word is used to refer to the ealdorman's officials, where it is considered by Liebermann to be equivalent
to the *gerefan* of *ibid.* 13; and in *ibid.* 10, it refers to officials under
the *gerefan*. There was a Brun who was reeve of Ipswich in Edward
the Confessor's time, but as he was alive in 1086, nearly fifty years
after the date of this will, his identity with the legatee here is doubtful.
He was holding 17 acres in Baylham, and had held 60 in Stonham
(D.B. 11, f. 337 *b*: *V. C. H. of Suffolk*, 1, p. 475).

l. 15. *Eggemera.* Egmere, Norfolk. In 1066, 3 carucates were held
by Bishop *Ailmar* of Elmham (D.B. 11, f. 192 *b*: *V. C. H. of Norfolk*,
11, p. 115). It appears to have been an episcopal estate.

Uui is the O.W.N. *Ûfi.* The first abbot of Bury bore this name.
He had been prior of St Benedict's of Holme, but as he became abbot
of Bury in 1020 he cannot be the person meant here.

prouast. The provost (O.E. *præfost*) was the monastic officer second
under the abbot, later called the prior. See *Rule of St Benedict* in
Grein, *Bibliothek der angelsächsischen Prosa*, 11, pp. 124 f.

l. 16. *Gæssǽte.* Guist, Norfolk. It was one of the estates belonging
to the bishopric of East Anglia in Domesday Book (D.B. 11, f. 193:
V. C. H. of Norfolk, 11, 115).

l. 17. *Rygedune.* Roydon, near Diss, Norfolk.

l. 18. *Leofwenne.* It seems probable that this former owner of
Roydon is the *Lefwen*, wife of Thurketel, who was left an estate at
Roydon by her husband in his will. See p. 179.

l. 19. *Mulantune.* This may be either the Suffolk or the Norfolk
Moulton, more probably the former, as Bishop Ælfric's successor is
entered in D.B. as having held land there (D.B. 11, f. 372 *b*: *V. C. H.
of Suffolk*, 1, p. 509).

l. 20. *þurlac.* An Anglicised form of the O.Icel. *þorleikr.*

Ælmham. Elmham, Norfolk, the Norfolk seat of the bishopric.
Though there was only one bishop for East Anglia, Suffolk still had
a separate episcopal centre at Hoxne. See p. 102.

l. 21. *Hoxne.* Hoxne, Suffolk.

an þusend werð fen. Presumably a thousand pence is meant.

l. 22. *into Holme.* The abbey of St Benedict at Holme.

l. 23. *Norðwic.* In D.B. 11, f. 116 *b* (*V. C. H. of Norfolk*, 11, p. 46),
the Abbot of Bury is said to have half the church of St Laurence and
one house in Norwich. A late list of benefactors of the abbey (see
Dugdale, 111, p. 140) says that Bishop Ælfric gave a *mansio* 'where
now the Church of St Laurence is'.

hit. This may refer, not to the *hage*, but loosely to all his property.

ll. 24 f. *þan hage into scē Petre binnon Lunden.* I take the *binnon
Lunden* with *hage*, parallel with *þon hage binnon Norðwic* just mentioned.
St Peter's might then be Westminster Abbey. If, however, we are
meant to understand that the church also was in London, I suggest
St Peter's in Cornhill, but the early history of London churches is
very obscure.

XXVII.

MSS. Cambridge University Library, MS. FF. 2. 33, f. 50. See p. 99. The Additional MS. 14847, f. 19 *b*, gives a short Latin summary of the bequest to Bury, followed by the O.E. anathema.

EDITIONS. K. 979.
T. p. 556.

DATE. Between 1022 and 1043. The will was made during the episcopate of an Ælfric. There were two Bishops of Elmham of this name. See p. 182.

p. 74, l. 1. *Wlsi*. Nothing is known of him apart from this will.

l. 2. *Wiken*. This might represent Wyken near Ixworth, Suffolk, Ash Wicken or Wick in Garboldisham, Norfolk. There is no evidence that the Abbey of Bury held any of these places.

l. 3. *Alfric Biscop*. See note on the date.

ane girde. A quarter of a hide. See Maitland, *Domesday Book and Beyond*, pp. 384 f.

l. 4. *Wlwine*. The feminine name, Wulfwyn, is evidently intended.

ll. 6 f. *II hors...spere*. This heriot does not tally with any of those stated in II Cnut, 71. It seems nearest to the 'middle' thegn, but the gold-inlaid spear is an unknown quantity.

l. 7. *goldwreken*. The past participle of the O.E. verb *wrecan* 'drive', 'press', is not instanced elsewhere with this meaning, but the corresponding O.Icel. *rekinn* is frequently used in this sense. See Fritzner, *s.vv. reka*, 5, and *gullrekinn*.

l. 8. *marc*. See p. 100.

ann ore wichte. 8 ores were reckoned to the mark.

l. 11. *sadelgarun*. Literally 'saddle-trappings', from O.E. *gearwe* 'dress', 'equipment'.

XXVIII.

MS. Cambridge University Library, MS. FF. 2. 33, f. 45. See p. 99.

EDITIONS. K. 970.
T. p. 566.

DATE. Probably 1042 or 1043. The will was drawn up in the episcopate of a Bishop Ælfric, apparently one of the two Bishops of Elmham of that name (see p. 182). It cannot therefore be later than 1043, when Stigand became bishop. A Latin entry in a Bury St Edmunds Register (Cambridge University Library, MS. MM. 4. 19, f. 167) says that Ælfric's bequest of Loddon, etc., was in the time of King Edward. If this is trustworthy the will can be dated 1042 or 1043. There is an extant writ of Edward the Confessor, confirming the bequests to Bury (K. 882), which cannot be earlier than 1051, since it is addressed to Earl Ælfgar and Bishop Æthelmær.

l. 14. *Alfric.* His nickname *Modercope, -coppe,* occurs in the Latin rubric and in the MS. MM 4. 19 (*loc. cit.*) and in two writs of Edward the Confessor concerning him. One (see preceding note) is a confirmation of his gifts to St Edmund's, the other (K. 877) gives him permission to 'bow' (i.e. commend himself) to the abbots of Bury and Ely. It would appear from this that Ælfric was originally a king's man and in the position of those men of whom D.B. states that they could not 'go where they would' without permission.

l. 15. *Lodne.* Loddon, Norfolk. 3 carucates and 10 acres were in St Edmund's possession in 1066 (D.B. II, f. 211 *b*: *V. C. H. of Norfolk*, II, p. 133).

l. 16. *so ful* 7 *so forth.* Literally 'as fully and to the same extent'. From Edward's confirmation writ we know that Ælfric held Loddon with *sac* and *socn.*

l. 17. *Birthe.* Probably Bergh Apton, Norfolk.
seynt Apeldrithe. The Abbey of Ely.

l. 19. *Berton.* Barton Turf, Norfolk. St Benet's held ½ carucate there in 1066 (D.B. II, f. 219: *V. C. H. of Norfolk*, II, p. 143).

l. 21. *þurwineholm...Fuglholm.* These places cannot be identified.

l. 23. *heregete.* See p. 100. A mark of gold was worth 50 mancuses (see *ibid.*). Ælfric therefore does not pay as much as a king's thegn, who, according to II Cnut, 71, should pay horses and weapons as well as 50 mancuses, but he pays three times as much as the lesser thegn.

l. 24. *Alfric biscop.* See p. 182.

l. 26. *Tofi Prude.* He married Gytha, the daughter of Osgot Clapa (see p. 196) in 1042. According to the *De Inventione S. Crucis... Waltham* (ed. Stubbs) he was the founder of the first church of Waltham. The holy cross had been found on his estate at Montacute, Somerset, in the reign of Cnut. The same authority relates that Tofi's son *Adelstanus* lost Waltham, which was afterwards given by King Edward to Harold. *Adelstanus* it states to have been the father of Esgar Staller, but if so Tofi must have been an old man at the time of his marriage with Gytha. The *De Inventione* calls Tofi 'staller', and says that he was *regiis implicitus negotiis*, and this is borne out by K. 755, where he came to a shiremoot in Herefordshire, on the king's errand. The information that he was the first man in the kingdom after the king we may put down to the chronicler's desire to honour the founders of his house.

þrunni. Perhaps the stroke over the *i* is misplaced and we should read *þrimm,* which would represent O.Icel. *þrymr.*

XXIX.

MSS. (a) Cambridge University Library, MS. FF. 2. 33, f. 45. See p. 99.

(b) Additional MS. 14847, f. 15. See pp. 103 f.

The text is taken from (a).

EDITIONS. K. 931, from (a).

T. p. 569, from (a).

DATE. During the episcopate of Ælfweard of London, i.e. 1035 to 1044.

p. 76, l. 1. [L]*eofgiue gret hyre leuedi*. This is the manner of beginning characteristic of the writ. The valediction, *God þe healde*, at the end of this will is also due to the influence of the writ-form. See p. 177. I have not been able to find any reference to Leofgifu elsewhere.

l. 3. *þer ic self resten wille*. This is a payment of *sawolsceatt* (see pp. 109 f.).

l. 4. *Hintlesham*. Hintlesham, Suffolk.

l. 5. *Gristlyngthorp*. Gestingthorpe, Essex. Neither this nor the preceding estate was held by Bury in 1066.

l. 6. *ilc þridde aker*. Cf. *Liber Eliensis*, II, 36, *omnem octavam acram in Brandune*, and also K. 674, where Bishop Oswold of Worcester makes an arrangement with two brothers by which the elder is to have three acres, the younger one acre, out of every four leased to them. This is a reference to the acre-strips of an open-field system of agriculture, but the reference in Leofgifu's will is not so clear, as it is apparently woodland which is concerned. Perhaps the passage refers to a cultivated clearing in the wood.

l. 7. *Ailri*. The *r* is a misreading of an original *s*. In Anglo-Saxon writing *s* was often very similar to the *r* of this MS. The name probably represents O.E. *Æþelsige*.

l. 9. *þat minstre at Colne*. There is no evidence elsewhere for the existence of a monastery at any of the Colnes. It is therefore probable that *minster* here merely means church (see p. 101). D.B. shows many churches in private ownership and regarded as a source of income, so there is nothing strange in Leofgifu's bequeathing it in her will. Even monasteries could be granted as private property (see instances in Liebermann, *Glossar*, *s.v. Kirchenherr*). Wulfric, in his will (p. 50, l. 14), thought it necessary expressly to state that the *mund* of his foundation of Burton are not to treat the monastery as their own property.

l. 11. *loh*. Apparently some office in the above mentioned 'minster'.

ll. 11 f. *And be se mund…opere*. An alternative translation would be 'and may that minster be entitled to the same protection as all others'.

l. 12. *to marc goldes*: i.e. 100 mancuses. Perhaps we should regard this as a payment of heriot (see p. 100).

ll. 12 f. *for min eruenumen to 7 gealaeste þat gold.* This is clearly corrupt. Thorpe's reading, *fon* for *for*, is perhaps the original reading (cf. the same error on p. 24, l. 4). It is not unusual in this MS. to have *min* for O.E. *mine* or the verb in the singular instead of the plural.

l. 14. *Belhcham.* One of the Essex Belchamps. As none of these estates were held by a woman in King Edward's time, according to D.B., we have no means of deciding which of them is meant here.

l. 15. *Alfward bisscop.* Bishop of London, 1035 to 1044.

Benetleye. Bentley, Essex.

l. 17. *Berric.* This may represent O.E. *Beornric.*

l. 18. *Borham.* Boreham, Essex.

l. 19. *Alfric mine mey Withgares sone.* He was an important land-owner in the eastern counties, especially Suffolk, and the founder of a house of secular canons at Clare. He and his son Wihtgar are entered in D.B. as pre-Conquest holders of wide estates, but Bramford is not included among them. Wihtgar, Ælfric's son, had, however, a church in Ipswich to which were attached 100 acres and 5 villeins, and these were claimed by the sheriff as belonging to the royal manor of Bram-ford (D.B. II, f. 393: *V. C. H. of Suffolk,* I, p. 530). Ælfric also occurs in K. 874, 883, 905 and in *Historia Ramesiensis,* cap. CXIV, where he disputes a will made by his kinsman Æthelwine the Black in favour of Ramsey Abbey.

Bromforde. Bramford, Suffolk.

l. 20. *Stigand.* No doubt the Stigand who became Bishop of Elmham in 1043.

Willauesham. Willesham, Suffolk.

l. 21. *Stonham.* We have no means of deciding whether Stonham Aspall, Earl Stonham, or Little Stonham, Suffolk, is meant here. Among the numerous pre-Conquest land-owners at Stonham in D.B. is one called *Aluric,* who may be Leofgifu's legatee, as the Additional MS. calls him *Alfric,* not *Ailric,* and the confusion of the two names is very common. This Domesday landowner was a freeman of Eadric of Laxfield and held 90 acres as a manor (D.B. II, f. 438: *V. C. H. of Suffolk,* I, p. 572). There was also an *Ailmar* with 3 acres (D.B. II, f. 305: *V. C. H. of Suffolk,* I, p. 445) and he may be the *Aylmer* of the will (see l. 24).

Waldingfeld. Waldingfield, Suffolk.

Lithtletic. I cannot identify this name, which appears to be corrupt. The Addit. MS. form *Licheletic,* may be better, *t, c* and *e* being frequently confused. It seems to me possible that the extraordinary ending *-tic* may be an error for *-cic* and the place represent one of the manors at St Osyth, the old name of which was Chich (see p. 101). The Cambridge MS. form looks as if it might be a corrupt form meaning 'little Chich' (cf. *Lithle Meddeltone,* p. 86, l. 16), but the reading of the Addit. MS. is against this.

l. 22. *Hagele.* Haughley, Suffolk.

l. 23. *aðum.* Either brother-in-law or son-in-law.

Werle. Probably one of the Essex Warleys.

l. 24. *Aylmer.* See note to l. 21 above.

l. 25. *to reflande.* Possibly land that had been let to him while he was reeve in return for his services (see Vinogradoff, *English Society in the Eleventh Century*, p. 372; on p. 225 of his *Growth of the Manor* he gives a different interpretation).

p. 78, ll. 1 ff. *And Ailric min hirdprest....heren willen.* The chaplain was not likely to have been counted among her 'knights', and the passage is probably corrupt. The plural form may be a mistake, or perhaps we should insert an 'and' between *Alric* and *mine chihtes.* On *cniht*, see p. 127.

l. 2. *Lalleford.* Lawford, Essex. D.B. *Laleforda.*

l. 3. *Forendale.* Neither this nor the Additional MS. variant *Frendenhale* can be identified.

l. 8. *God þe healde.* See p. 177.

ll. 8 ff. *Nu....seluen.* See pp. 150 f.

l. 9. *mid þise kinges halidome.* Literally 'with the king's relics' See p. 151.

XXX.

MSS. (a) A parchment contained in the Red Book of Canterbury, Christchurch, Canterbury.

(b) British Museum, Cotton Augustus, II, 34.

Both MSS. are in contemporary writing. Both have the top halves of the letters of the word 'cyrograph' in the bottom margin. The Christchurch MSS. contains a fuller account of the transaction, while the Cotton MS. has two witnesses who are missing in the other MS., namely, Ælfric, Archbishop of York from 1023 to 1051, and Ælfgar, son of Earl Leofric, but the name of this witness is a later insertion. The text is taken from (a).

FACSIMILES. (a) *Ordnance Survey Facsimiles of Anglo-Saxon MSS.*, Part I, No. 25.

(b) Bond, *Facsimiles of Ancient Charters in the British Museum*, Part IV, No. 33.

EDITIONS. Madox, *Formulare Anglicanum*, p. 238, from (b).

K. 788, from (b).

T. p. 577, from (b).

Sweet, *Anglo-Saxon Reader*, 8th edition, p. 59, from (b).

DATE. The will is undated, but a date of 1042 or 1043 is required by the list of witnesses; that is, after Edward became king in 1042 and before Stigand was made bishop in 1043.

l. 11. *þurstan.* In his will he is called Wine's son, and on p. 84, l. 4, a certain Lustwine is mentioned. This is an uncommon name, and when in *Liber Eliensis*, II, 89, we find that a Lustwine was in possession of many estates held by Thurstan in the will, we can hardly doubt that Thurstan inherited from him. Thurstan's estates of Knapwell,

Borough Green, Weston, Kedington, Pentlow, Wimbish and Ashdon
were all held at one time by Lustwine. In the *Liber Eliensis* (*loc. cit.*)
we are told that Lustwine was the husband of Leofwaru, the daughter
of Leofflæd and granddaughter of the Ealdorman Brihtnoth, and
in the preceding chapter the will of Leofflæd is quoted in which she
leaves an estate at Wetheringsett to Leofwaru. The latter also is
mentioned in Thurstan's will (p. 80, l. 4) and he is in possession of the
estate at Wetheringsett. There can be no doubt that Thurstan had
inherited from Lustwine and his wife Leofwaru. It is probable that
he was their son, since Wine may well be a shortened from of Lustwine.
There is, however, one difficulty about the descent of these estates.
According to the *Liber Eliensis*, they were all left by Lustwine to Ely,
and no mention is made of any violent seizure of them. Thurstan may
have bought them back from the abbey. He leaves some of them to
Ely, but not all.

In a list of benefactors to Bury, Cambridge University Library MS.,
MM. 4. 19, Thurstan is called *vir strennuus Heing Thurstan*. If this
is not a mistake for thegn, it must represent the Scandinavian nickname *hæing* (see p. 180). Thurstan is the anglicised form of O.Icel.
Þorsteinn, and Scandinavian influence is seen in the will. It is interesting that this influence is so marked in the will of a man who appears
to be of English descent. A Thurstan who may be the testator witnesses
a charter of 1022 (K. 734) and one of 1024 (K. 741).

l. 12. *Wimbisc*. According to D.B., Wimbish, Essex, was in the
possession of Thurstan's wife, Æthelgyth, in 1066. Christchurch
never obtained it, as it passed to her Norman successor (D.B. II,
f. 69 b: *V. C. H. of Essex*, I, p. 523).

Leofware. See above.

l. 13. *Æþelgyðe*. Thurstan's wife (see p. 82, l. 5). She appears in
D.B. as 'a certain freewoman, *Ailid*', who held in King Edward's
reign the estates left to her in Thurstan's will, and also Dunmow and
Ongar which he bequeathed to other legatees, Shimpling in Suffolk,
and many estates in Norfolk. She was succeeded by Ralf Bainard
in many of her estates, including those mentioned in the will, except
Ongar. An *Ailid* also held some lands in Norfolk which went to
Reynold, the son of Ivo, and as these lie intermixed with those held by
Æthelgyth, she is probably the same woman. On p. 205, it is suggested
that Reynold's predecessor is the Æthelgyth who along with Thurkil
granted Wereham to St Edmunds (cf. No. XXXVI). If so, she may
have married Thurkil after Thurstan's death, but we need not assume
that, as co-grantors of an estate, Thurkil and Æthelgyth were necessarily
husband and wife.

l. 16 f. *be getale*. See p. 169.

l. 18. *Ælfgifu seo hlæfdige*. The queen-mother, wife of Cnut.
Edward despoiled her of her estates in 1043. She died in 1052.

Eadsige arceb. He became Archbishop of Canterbury in 1038
(Chronicle, E, F). He had been one of Cnut's chaplains (*ibid*. F and

cf. K. 745, 1327) and two Kentish writs of Cnut's are addressed to him as bishop only. Stubbs (*Registrum Sacrum Anglicanum*, p. 35) suggests that he was Bishop of St Martin's. In 1044 he resigned his duties because of ill-health (Chronicle, C), but resumed them in 1048 (*ibid.*). He died in 1050 (*ibid.* A, C).

l. 19. *Godwine eorl.* This is the great Earl of Wessex, who first signs *dux* in 1018. He died in 1052.

Leofric eorl. He witnesses charters as *eorl, dux* from 1023. His earldom was Mercia, which he held until his death in 1058.

Ælfwærd b on Lundene. He was bishop from 1035 to 1044. He occurs as a legatee in the Will of Leofgifu, p. 76, l. 15.

l. 20. *Ælfwine b on Winceastre.* He succeeded to the bishopric in 1032 and died in 1047. Later legends depict him as the lover of the Queen Ælfgifu Emma (see *Anglia Sacra*, I, pp. 233 ff.).

Stigand þ. He is called Cnut's priest in the Chronicle (1020 F) when the church at Ashingdon was committed to him. He became Bishop of Elmham in 1043, but was deposed in the same year and reinstated in 1044 (see Chronicle, *sub anno* and also II, p. 223). From 1047 he also held the bishopric of Winchester. When he became Archbishop of Canterbury in 1052 he relinquished Elmham, but not Winchester. His appointment was not looked on with favour by the Pope, and he did not receive his pallium till 1058. William deposed him in 1070.

Eadwold þ. He witnesses K. 745, 746, 751 (dated 1033) and 767 (dated 1043).

ll. 20 f. *Leofcild scirgerefa.* He is shown to have been Sheriff of Essex by two writs of Edward the Confessor (K. 869, 870) addressed to Bishop Ælfweard and the thegns of Essex as well as to him. The earliest occurrences of the title *scirgerefa* are from the reign of Cnut, but it is probable that this official is sometimes meant when the simple word *gerefa* is used, e.g. in Athelstan's sixth code where the *gerefa* is spoken of in connection with the *scir.* An official called the *sciresman* is shown presiding over a shiremoot not later than 1005 (K. 929) and already in Dunstan's time there is a reference to a *scirigmann* apparently holding a shiremoot (B. 1097). In Cnut's time *scirman* and *scirgerefa* were equivalent terms (cf. K. 731 with K. 732). The origin of the office and the nature of the sheriff's duties are discussed by W. A. Morris in *E.H.R.* XXXI, pp. 20 ff., where it is shown that he was partly the deputy of the earl or ealdorman, partly the representative of the royal power, with judicial, fiscal and police functions, and that the office probably arose in the early tenth century. See also Liebermann, *Glossar, s.v. sheriff*; Chadwick, pp. 229 ff.

l. 21. *Osulf Fila.* He also witnesses Thurstan's will, among the Essex thegns. The *Place-Name Survey of Buckinghamshire*, p. 207, suggests that a personal name *Fila* is contained in Fillington.

Ufic. This is an uncommon name, but does occur elsewhere. There was a cleric of this name in Worcester in Bishop Oswold's time (B. 1139,

1232). See Redin, *Studies on Uncompounded Personal Names in Old English*, p. 152.

Ælfwine Wulfredes sunu. He also witnessed K. 978 and K. 962, both concerned with the eastern counties.

l. 22. *Ælfric Wihtgares sunu*. See p. 188.

ll. 23 f. 7 *na stinge...χp̄es circean*. Royal writs of this period often include a phrase restricting authority on the estate to the grantee. The phrase here probably implies that Thurstan had the *socn* on this estate.

l. 25. *yrfan*. This is the only recorded example of this verb, which apparently means 'to inherit'.

ll. 25 ff. *þissera gewritu...sylfan*. See pp. 150 f.

XXXI.

MSS. (*a*) Cambridge University Library, MS. FF. 2. 33, f. 49. See p. 99.

(*b*) Additional MS. 14847, f. 19. See pp. 103 f. Only a fragment of the will is contained here, down to 'Ely' on p. 80, l. 12, followed by the anathema on p. 82, ll. 25, 26.

The text is from (*a*). (*b*) has variants in spelling but no important differences.

EDITION. T. p. 571, from (*a*).

DATE. The will cannot be later than 1045 because in this year Abbot Leofsige of Ely died. The earliest possible date is 1043, when Stigand became Bishop of Elmham and Ælfwine became Abbot of Ramsey. If Leofstan, Dean of Bury, is the Leofstan who became Abbot there in 1044, the will cannot be later than that date, but we know it to be later than Thurstan's bequest of Wimbish because Stigand is now a bishop.

p. 80, ll. 3 ff. *þat lond at Wimbisc...into seynt Augustine*. This is an abstract of the separate bequest. Like the Cotton MS. of the latter, it makes no mention of the pound to be paid yearly or the alternative of paying 2 hides instead of £12.

l. 4. *Lefwares*. She is also mentioned on p. 84, l. 2. See p. 190.

Egelsithes. A comparison with Thurstan's bequest shows that this represents O.E. *Æþelgyth*, which also appears in this will as *Ailgiðe*, p. 82, l. 5, *Agelgið*, p. 82, l. 29, *Agilwið*, p. 84, l. 1. The scribe has been confused by the occurrence of the name *Æþelswith* in the will, e.g. p. 80, l. 16.

l. 7. *Herlawe*. Harlow, Essex. St Edmund's held this later as a manor and as 1½ hides (D.B. II, f. 19 *b*: *V. C. H. of Essex*, I, p. 451).

l. 8. *Gildenebrigge*. Professor Mawer tells me that this is Ealing Bridge in Harlow.

l. 9. *hóó*. See *Introduction to the Place-Name Survey*, II, *s.v.*

l. 10. *Sculham at þe Northhalle*. Below on l. 19, *lond at þe Middelhalle* is mentioned. In D.B. Æthelgyth was in possession of two estates at Shouldham, Norfolk, both of 2 carucates. The first is not definitely called a manor, but it is entered separately from the other, with a separate valuation. The second is called 'the other Shouldham', and is called a manor. See D.B. II, f. 250: *V. C. H. of Norfolk*, II, p. 174. As one would expect from the nomenclature 'Middle hall', there was a third estate at Shouldham (D.B. II, f. 155: *V. C. H. of Norfolk*, II, p. 231), which no doubt would be known as the land at the south hall. This third estate is also called a manor in D.B. and was held by *Turchill*, possibly the testator of No. XXXVI (see p. 205).

l. 12. *Wetheringsete*. Wetheringsett, Suffolk. This estate was left by Leofflæd to Leofwaru, who left it to Ely (see p. 190). Thurstan may have had a life-interest in it which the Ely scribe does not mention. In 1066 Ely held 4 carucates there (D.B. II, f. 384 *b*: *V. C. H. of Suffolk*, I, p. 521).

l. 14. *Cnapwelle*. Knapwell, Cambridgeshire, was one of the estates left by Lustwine to Ely (see p. 189). Ramsey Abbey, not Ely, held it in 1066 (D.B. I, f. 192 *b*).

l. 16. *Westone*. Probably near Pentlow, Essex. It was another of the estates left by Lustwine to Ely (see p. 190).

Agilswiðe. She also occurs on p. 82, l. 29. Leofwaru's sister was called *Æthelswith* (*Liber Eliensis*, II, 88), but the name is common.

l. 17. *to earninge*. See p. 178. Thorpe takes this as a place-name.

l. 22. *Hergete*. As far as the number of horses and weapons is concerned, Thurstan pays a heriot equivalent to that allotted in II Cnut, 71. 4 to the highest king's thegn among the Danes. The sum of money is twice that demanded by Cnut and the whole payment must therefore have amounted to that of the highest king's thegn elsewhere (see p. 153).

sadelfate. Thorpe translates 'saddle-vessels' and suggests in a note 'bottles hung from the saddle-bow'. From other information concerning the constitution of the heriot, however, it is clear that it is harness that Thurstan means. The O.E. *fæt* always means vessel of some kind, but Thurstan has no doubt been influenced by the Scandinavian usage in which *fat* can also mean baggage, or clothing.

l. 24. *Bidicheseye*. I have been unable to identify this name.

ll. 25 f. *þe erl Harold*. Harold was Earl of East Anglia until he succeeded his father in Wessex in 1052. I know of no occurrence of his name with the title 'earl' before the date of this will.

l. 26. *Stigand bisscop*. See p. 191.

l. 27. *felage*. The O.Icel. *félagi*, meaning a person who has goods in common with another. It also occurs in a more general sense of 'comrade', but here probably has its original sense. It probably refers to the Ulfketel who had a *felageschipe* with Thurstan (see p. 82, l. 1).

his berne. I see no reason to take this as a personal name as Thorpe does. No such name occurs elsewhere. The omission of the name is unusual, but may be a copyist's error.

þorþes. This is the O.Icel. *þorþr*. A *þorð, þurcylles nefa*, witnesses

K. 745. The name occurs frequently in lists of signatures from about 1023 to 1035. Two sign in 1023 and 1024 (K. 739 and 741). A *Thored steallere* occurs in K. 1327.

l. 28. *Sendi*. This name also occurs in the list of witnesses, p. 82, l. 24. Björkman (*Zur englische Namenkunde*, p. 73) suggests O.Icel. *Siaundi*, or O.Icel., O. Swedish *Siunde*, as the origin of this name. Double names are not unknown at this period: an Osgot Sveyn occurs on p. 82, l. 22. It is however possible that 'and' has been omitted after Sendi.

Arfast. The scribe first wrote *bisscop* after this name, and then deleted it. Arfast, or Herfast, was the name of a Bishop of Elmham from 1070 to 1084, and as he occurs frequently in the Bury cartulary, the scribe first wrote the usual title after the name. Björkman (*Zur englische Namenkunde*, p. 46) compares this name with the O. Swedish *Hærfast*.

ll. 28 f. *delen le eruene men*. This is a corruption representing O.E. *dælen þa ierfenuman*. Over the top of *eruene* is written *pouere* by someone who found the passage incomprehensible as it stood. He probably connected it with O.E. *earm*.

l. 30. *sče Aethelburg at Berkynge*. Æthelburg was sister to the Bishop Erkenwald of London who founded the abbeys of Barking and Chertsey. She was the first abbess of Barking. See p. 106.

p. 82, l. 1. *Vlfkeles*. This is a Scandinavian name common in this period. Two Ulfketels witness Thurstan's will, one in Suffolk and the other, Ulfketel *Kild*, in Cambridgeshire. Either of these may be the *Ulfkel* mentioned here. The estates concerned in the agreement are in Cambridgeshire, but close to the Suffolk border.

felageschipe. This word corresponds to the O.Icel. *felagskapr*, which means any kind of partnership. D.B. is full of examples of estates held jointly by several owners.

to þat forwarde. The terms Thurstan and his partner have made are similar to arrangements made in Wulfgeat's will (see p. 166), and in Ketel's (see p. 203), namely that the one who lives the longest is to have a certain portion of the other's property.

l. 2. *Burg*. Borough Green, Cambridgeshire, which is very near to the Dullingham and Westley mentioned in this agreement.

l. 3. *þerwith*: literally, 'in return'.

l. 4. *Westle*. Westley Waterless, Cambridgeshire, about 2 miles from Dullingham.

Dullingham. Dullingham, Cambridgeshire.

Wiking. This represents the O.Icel. *Vikingr*. He is no doubt the *Wichinz* who is entered in the *Inquisitio Comitatus Cantabrigiensis*, f. 90 *b* (ed. Hamilton, p. 18), as the holder in 1066 of one hide at Dullingham. He was at that date a 'man' of Earl Harold, and could not alienate his land. Probably he had commended himself to Harold's protection after Thurstan's death. In the corresponding entry in D.B. 1, f. 195 *b*, this man and two others are entered as 3 *sochemanni, non potuerunt recedere.* Though it is interesting to find that an Anglo-Saxon *cniht* is a 'socman' twenty years later, one cannot argue from an isolated instance.

l. 5. *knihte.* See preceding note and also p. 127.

ll. 5 f. *al þe þing þe ic haue on Norfolke.* In 1066 Æthelgyth was certainly holding in Norfolk Fincham, Barton, Boughton, Bradenham, Merton and Wilby (D.B. II, ff. 250 *b* f.: *V. C. H. of Norfolk*, II, pp. 173 f.), in all of which she was succeeded by Ralf Bainard. Ely was laying claim to Fincham and the Hundred supported their claim. Æthelgyth may be identical with a woman of this name holding estates in the same part of Norfolk which went to another Norman successor (see p. 190).

l. 6. *to mund and to maldage.* This is a Scandinavian expression. Cf. the older *Gulaþingslögr*, 25: *varr skal hverr eina kono eiga, þa er hann hever mundi keypt ok maldaga...* and also *ibid.* 27. A corresponding phrase, *mæþ mund ok mæþ mæli*, is used in the older *Vestgötalag*, *Arfþær Bolkær*, 7, 8. The *mundr* was the price to be paid before the marriage, originally to the bride's guardian. The O.E. *mund* does not occur with this meaning. *Máldaga* refers to the agreement concerning succession to property (see pp. 135 f.).

l. 7. *Pentelawe.* Pentlow, Essex. The freewoman who held 4 hides, 3 virgates in King Edward's time and was succeeded by Ralf Bainard was probably Æthelgyth (D.B. II, f. 69 *b*: *V. C. H. of Essex*, I, p. 523).

Aesredune. Ashdon, Essex, at which place Æthelgyth afterwards held 2 hides (D.B. II, f. 71: *V. C. H. of Essex*, I, p. 525). It was one of the estates Lustwine had held (see p. 190).

Bromlege. From the context, one would expect this Bromley to be near to Ashdon. The places in Essex which still bear this name, Great Bromley and Little Bromley, are near Colchester, at the other end of the county.

l. 9. *Henham.* Henham, Essex. Æthelgyth's estate here was one of 13½ hides less 10 acres (D.B. II, f. 71: *V. C. H. of Essex*, I, p. 525).

l. 11. *Kydingtone.* Kedington, Suffolk, one of the estates given by Lustwine to Ely. Æthelgyth held 5 carucates with *sac* and *soc*, 'except the six forfeitures of St Edmund' (D.B. II, f. 413 *b*: *V. C. H. of Suffolk*, I, p. 550).

l. 12. *Meruyn.* This may be O.E. *Mær-* or *Merewine* or the Welsh name *Merfyn*. A *Meruin* held 12 acres in Swavesey, Cambridgeshire, in 1066 (D.B. I, f. 194 *b*), but the name does not occur in connection with the estates of the will.

l. 13. *Dunmawe.* (Little) Dunmow, Essex. It was held by Æthelgyth in 1066 as 4½ hides (D.B. II, f. 69: *V. C. H. of Essex*, I, p. 522).

l. 14. *þat wude at Aungre.* In D.B., Ongar, Essex, is entered as having woodland for 1000 swine. It is the only one of the estates bequeathed to Æthelgyth in which she is not succeeded by Ralf Bainard (D.B. II, f. 30 *b*: *V. C. H. of Essex*, I, p. 467). Thurstan only disposes of the wood and half a hide there, so possibly the main estate belonged to Æthelgyth in her own right. This was assessed at only one hide, though it had 5 ploughs.

l. 15. *derhage*. An enclosure for hunting purposes.

l. 16. *Stigand Bisscop*. See p. 191.

Osgote. Clape. In the Chronicle he is called *Stallere* or marshall. He was outlawed in 1046 (Chronicle, C) and in 1049 he attempted to return with a fleet (*ibid*. C). His death is entered in the Chronicle, 1054, C, D. He is connected with the eastern counties in a story of Hermann's (*Memorials of St Edmund's Abbey*, I, pp. 54 f.), where he is called *majordomus*. He had a house at Lambeth in which Hardacnut died at the marriage feast of Osgot's daughter and Tofig the Proud (Fl. Wig. 1042). See also Freeman, *Norman Conquest*, II, pp. 63, 89 f.

Osgot is the O.Icel. *Ásgautr*, and *Clapa* may be Scandinavian also. See Björkman, pp. 14, 81.

l. 17. *Eadwine*. Perhaps the testator of No. XXXIII, who held many estates in Norfolk.

Osbern. This is an anglicised form of O.Icel. *Ásbiorn*. See Björkman, p. 10.

l. 18. *Gouti*. O.Icel. *Gauti*, O. Danish, Gøti. There was a landowner of this name in Nettlestead in King Edward's time (D.B. II, f. 294 b: *V. C. H. of Suffolk*, I, p. 435).

Lefstan Decan. It is probable that he is the future abbot of Bury, who succeeded Ufi in 1044. The Abbot Leofstan had been a monk in the abbey since its foundation. As no abbot signs for Bury, the will was perhaps drawn up during the abbot's illness or during an interregnum.

l. 19. *Eadric*. Perhaps Eadric of Laxfield, who figures prominently in the Domesday Survey of Suffolk (see especially D.B. II, f. 304 b to f. 330).

Alfric. Probably Ælfric, Wihtgar's son, who witnesses Thurstan's bequest to Christchurch. See p. 188.

Vlfketel. See p. 194.

l. 20. *Lemmer*. A man of this name witnesses K. 978.

Leswi abbot. This is a mistake for *Lefsi*, O.E. *Leofsige*. See *Liber Eliensis*, II, 84 to 94. He was succeeded by Wulfric in 1045 (*ibid*. II, 94).

l. 21. *Aelfwine Abbot*. He was abbot from 1043 to 1049. He was one of the English churchmen at the Council of Reims. (See Chronicle, 1046 E; *Historia Ramesiensis*, chapters LXXXII, CIII to CXIX.)

l. 22. *Alfwine*. Perhaps Ælfwine, Wulfred's son, who witnessed the bequest to Christchurch. See p. 192.

Vlfketel Kild. See p. 194.

Osgot Sveyn. The name of this Cambridgeshire thegn is also preserved in the *Historia Ramesiensis*, chapter XC. He held an estate of Ramsey Abbey.

ll. 22 f. *Ordger and oþer Ordger*. One of these may be the witness of K. 978. The sheriff of Cambridgeshire in King Edward's day bore this name (D.B. I, f. 199).

l. 23. *Alfger þe Erles sune*. The son of Earl Leofric of Mercia.

l. 24. *Lefkild*. Probably the sheriff who witnessed the bequest to Christchurch. See p. 191.

Osulf File. See p. 191.

Sendi. See p. 194.

ll. 24 f. *Leuerich discþeng*. He does not occur elsewhere. For *discþeng*, see p. 172.

ll. 26 ff. *þise write...hird*. See pp. 150 f.

ll. 28 ff. *And þat lond*.... From here to the end is perhaps a later addition.

l. 28. *Henham*. See p. 195.

l. 30. *aldreday*. See p. 105. The translation should be amended to 'after the death of all of them'.

sĉe Aetheldrith. See p. 135.

p. 84, l. 2. *Aylmer Parl*. I cannot explain this nickname.

l. 3. *girde*: i.e. a quarter of a hide.

l. 4. *Lustwine*. See pp. 189 f.

Þurgot mine cnihte. His name represents O.Icel. *Þorgautr*. He is perhaps the freeman who was in possession of half a hide at Ongar in 1066 (D.B. II, f. 30 b: *V. C. H. of Essex*, I, p. 467).

l. 5. *Aungre*. See p. 195.

l. 6. *Meredene*. I have not identified this.

l. 7. *on vnker gemede. gif wit aleten willen*. This change to the dual number is very curious. Since these arrangements are apparently not meant to take effect until after Thurstan's death, it seems most probable that *wit* refers to the two surviving owners, Æthelgyth and Askil.

XXXII.

This will should be compared with those of her son Ketel (No. xxxiv) and his uncle Edwin (No. xxxiii).

MS. Christchurch, Canterbury, Register C, v, f. 11. This is a twelfth-century version.

EDITIONS. Somner, *A Treatise of Gavelkind*, p. 211.

        K. 782. He quotes as his only authority the above MS., but he has normalised the text, sometimes obscuring the meaning (see notes to p. 84, ll. 15, 18).

        T. p. 563, from K.

DATE. 1046, if the Latin heading in the register can be relied on. It fits well with the internal evidence, as the will was made in Edward's reign and before the death of Godwine in 1053.

l. 8. *Wolgiþ*. She was sister of the Edwin who appears in D.B. as a king's thegn (see p. 199). Her husband's name was Ælfwine (see

l. 15 below). She is referred to as Ælfwine's widow in Thorne's *De rebus gestis Abbatum S. Augustini* (Twysden, *Decem Scriptores*, col. 2224), where it is stated that Stisted and Coggeshall were given by her and *Godwinus* to Christchurch. In the will she mentions three daughters and three sons, one of them the testator of No. xxxiv, Ketel. He refers to a brother Godric in his will, who does not occur in Wulfgyth's will, and who may therefore have been Ketel's half-brother only.

l. 10. *his riyte heriet*. See p. 100. This is the only occurrence of the term heriot in a woman's will.

l. 11. *Stistede*. Stisted, Essex. In D.B. this estate is entered as a manor of the Holy Trinity (i.e. Christchurch) at Canterbury. It was assessed at only half a hide, though there were in all 9 plough-teams there in King Edward's time (see D.B. ii, f. 8: *V. C. H. of Essex*, i, p. 437). Wulfgyth's estate was probably only a portion of the land afterwards held there by Christchurch, as the latter had been given some land at this place by a certain Godwine (see above).

l. 12. *on þan hyrede*. O.E. *on þam gerade*.

l. 13. *Elfkitel*. He does not occur again either here or in Ketel's will. His name is an anglicised form of a Scandinavian *Alfketill* (see Björkman, pp. 3 f.).

Kytel. The testator of No. xxxiv. See p. 201.

l. 15. *ayentale*. O.E. *(on)geantalu*. Kemble has *arentale*, which is meaningless.

l. 18. *Eldemes*. This looks like a corruption of O.E. *Ealdhelmes*.

and þertohycken. This represents O.E. *and þærtoeacan*. *h* is redundant as in *herest* (l. 10 above), and as the Kentish dialect had *e* for O.E. *y*, the latter is here written for M.E. *e* from O.E. *ea*. Kemble has emended here, taking *hycken* as a proper name.

l. 20. *Wulkitele*. O.Icel. *Ulfketill*, but it is possible that the name is an error and that the Elfkitel of l. 13 is meant.

l. 21. *Walsingham*. Ketel mentions this estate in his will (p. 90, l. 13). In D.B. there were two Norfolk Walsinghams, both held by landowners called Ketel, but only the Walsingham in East Carleton, Humbleyard Hundred (D.B. ii, f. 254: *V. C. H. of Norfolk*, ii, p. 177) is held by the Norman landowner who succeeds Ketel in other estates, Ranulf Peverel. Ketel is a common name in the Norfolk Domesday Survey, and the man with two estates in Walsingham in Greenhoe Hundred (D.B. ii, f. 233: *V. C. H. of Norfolk*, ii, p. 157) does not appear to be identical with Wulfgyth's son.

Karltune. East Carleton, in Humbleyard Hundred, Norfolk. Ketel does not mention it in his will, but in D.B. ii, f. 254 (*V. C. H. of Norfolk*, ii, p. 177) we are told that it was held in King Edward's time by Godric, a freeman of *Kitel*.

Herlingham. East Harling, Norfolk. Cf. p. 88, l. 24.

l. 22. *Gode and Bote*. These also occur in Ketel's will. See p. 90, ll. 8, 12.

Sexlingham. Saxlingham, Norfolk.

Sumerledetune. Either Somerleyton, near Lowestoft, or Somerton, Suffolk (D.B. *Sumerledetuna*), which is near Chadacre, another estate of Wulfgyth's.

l. 24. *Ealgiþe*. O.E. *Ealdgyþ*. She does not occur in Ketel's will, and is not mentioned in D.B. as owner of Chadacre in 1066 (D.B. II, f. 430 *b*: *V. C. H. of Suffolk*, I, p. 565).

l. 25. *Cheartekere*. Chadacre, Suffolk.

Essetesford. Ashford, Kent, appears in D.B. I, f. 13, in exactly this form. Wulfgyth possessed no other estates in Kent, but I can find no trace of the name elsewhere.

l. 26. *Godwine eorle*. The great earl of Wessex. The bequests to him and his son are no doubt to secure their support in the carrying out of the will.

Harold erle. See p. 193.

l. 27. *Friþetune*. Either Fritton, north-west of Lowestoft, Suffolk, or Fritton near Long Stratton, Norfolk. D.B. preserves no memory of either place having been in the possession of Godwine's family.

p. 86, l. 1. *yboned*. Cf. O.E. *bon*, 'an ornament'.

Seynte Eþeldrithe. See p. 135.

l. 2. *seynte Osithe*. The patron saint of the church of *Chich*, Essex, now St Osyth. Her life is contained in Capgrave's *Nova Legenda*, where she is said to have been the daughter of Frithwald of Surrey and Wilburg, a daughter of Penda. She was buried at St Osyth.

l. 3. *seynt Austine*. St Augustine's Monastery at Canterbury.

regrayel. Kemble has *sethrægles*, but the original probably had *hrycghrægl*. Cf. p. 62, l. 21.

XXXIII.

With this will cf. Nos. XXXII, XXXIV.

MSS. (*a*) Cambridge University Library, MS. FF. 2. 33, f. 45. See p. 99.

(*b*) Additional MS. 14847, f. 15 *b*. See pp. 103 f.

The text is from (*a*).

EDITIONS. K. 921, from (*a*).
          T. p. 589, from (*a*).

DATE. The will cannot be dated from internal evidence. Edwin was alive in 1066 (see below). His sister, Wulfgyth, made a will about 1046, and his nephew, Ketel, made his before 1066.

l. 12. *Eadwine*. He appears in Domesday Book as a demesne thegn (*teinus dominicus*) of King Edward (D.B. II, f. 203: *V. C. H. of Norfolk*, II, p. 125). Elsewhere in D.B. he is called thegn, and freeman. He is succeeded by Godric the Dapifer. With the exception of Blyford, his estates are in Norfolk, and besides those bequeathed in the will, he possessed in 1066 45 acres in Wramplingham, 2 carucates in Alpington,

2 in Sparham and 2 in Blyford. He mentions these last two places in his will, but only to make small bequests to the churches there. He may have acquired these estates after the drawing up of this document, or, what seems to be more probable, we ought to regard the document not as a complete will, but as a list of bequests to religious foundations for the good of his soul. It is unusual for a will to have no mention of the heriot at this date.

The will never took effect, as Edwin lost all his possessions at the Norman Conquest.

l. 14. *Eskeresthorp*. Algarsthorp, in Melton, Norfolk. I am indebted to Dr O. K. Schram for the identification of this name and of *Apetune* in l. 19 below.

l. 16. *Lithle Meddeltone*. Little Melton, Norfolk. D.B. states that Edwin held this estate as 2 carucates under the abbey of Holme 'on such terms that he had granted it to the abbot after his death'. The abbot had not succeeded in obtaining possession, as it is held by Godric the Dapifer (D.B. II, f. 204 *b*: *V. C. H. of Norfolk*, II, p. 126). Later, however, Godric granted it to the abbey (Dugdale, III, p. 87).

l. 17. *Beorh*. Bergh Apton, Norfolk. D.B. does not mention Edwin's possession of this estate, but the *Inquisitio Eliensis*, f. 54 (ed. Hamilton, p. 136) states that Godric the Dapifer holds it under the abbey of Ely as his 'antecessor' (i.e. Edwin) held it. From Edwin's will alone we should not know that he had not an independent tenure of this estate.

l. 19. *Appelsco*. This name has now disappeared.

turfgret. This is probably a corruption of the O.Icel. *torfgröf*.

Apetune. (Bergh) Apton, Norfolk. The parishes of Bergh and Apton were at one time separate. Godric the Dapifer, Edwin's successor, is entered on f. 213 of the *Inquisitio Eliensis* (ed. Hamilton, p. 195) as the holder of Bergh and Apton.

l. 22. *Huluestone*. Holverstone, Norfolk. Edwin had freemen at this place commended to him (D.B. II, f. 203: *V. C. H. of Norfolk*, II, p. 125).

Blitleford. *tl* is written in error for *th*, and the place meant is Blyford, Suffolk, where Edwin held 2 carucates (D.B. II, f. 355 *b*: *V. C. H. of Suffolk*, I, p. 491). His successor is in possession of the *soc* there. D.B. also mentions a church with 12 acres.

l. 23. *Sparham*. Sparham, Norfolk. At this place also Edwin had 2 carucates (D.B. II, f. 204: *V. C. H. of Norfolk*, II, p. 126). There was a church with 40 acres there.

l. 24. *frescet*, 'free property', B.T. 'property at one's own disposal'. Perhaps the distinction here is between the foregoing estates and those which Edwin could dispose of only in accordance with the agreement made with his brother and nephew. It is possible, however, that the term is applied to estates held in such a way that the holder could, to use the D.B. phraseology, 'go where he would with his land'; but we may note here that, according to the *Inquisitio Eliensis*, Edwin held one of the estates he calls *frescet* under the abbey of Ely (see note to *Beorh*, p. 200).

l. 27. *þe forward.* This agreement is stated also on p. 90, ll. 2 ff.

Wlfric. Cf. Will of Ketel, p. 90, l. 3. He may be the unnamed freeman, 'who was also a thegn', mentioned in D.B. as holding a carucate as a manor in the two Meltons in the time of Edward the Confessor (D.B. II, f. 204 b: *V. C. H. of Norfolk*, II, p. 126).

l. 28. *Thorp.* Probably Thorpe near Fundenhall, which was afterwards joined to Ashwell as Ashwell Thorpe. This was held in King Edward's time by a thegn of Stigand, who may have been Ketel Alder (D.B. II, f. 151 b: *V. C. H. of Norfolk*, II, p. 77).

Middeltone. Great Melton, Norfolk. Edwin held 2 carucates there (D.B. II, f. 204: *V. C. H. of Norfolk*, II, p. 126) and another 2 carucates were held by Ketel (D.B. II, f. 254 b: *V. C. H. of Norfolk*, II, p. 177).

p. 88, l. 2. *Ketel.* The testator of No. XXXIV.

ll. 6 f. *at Metheltone...þe þurwerd ahte.* Something may have been omitted before *at Metheltone*, such as an expression defining the size of the grant.

l. 9. *Aescewelle.* Ashwell Thorpe, Norfolk.

Wreningham. Wreningham, Norfolk.

l. 10. *Fundenhale.* Fundenhall, Norfolk.

l. 11. *Neolondes.* Nayland in Wreningham, now lost.

ll. 11 ff. *þise write...himself.* See pp. 150 f.

XXXIV.

With this will cf. Nos. XXXII, XXXIII.

MSS. (a) Cambridge University Library, MS. FF. 2. 33, f. 45 b. See p. 99.

(b) Additional MS. 14847, f. 20. See pp. 103 f.

The text is taken from (a).

EDITIONS. K. 1339, from (b). Kemble gives a translation of this will in *Norfolk Archaeology*, III, p. 253.

T. p. 581, from (a).

DATE. The will was made after Stigand had become Archbishop in 1052, and before the accession of Harold in 1066.

l. 14. *Keteles.* He is given the nickname *Alder* in the Latin headings in the cartularies, and in the list of benefactors to Bury in the Cambridge MS. MM. IV. 19, f. 167. This may represent O.E. *ealdor*, but more probably at this date (fourteenth century) means 'the elder'. He is the son of Wulfgyth, the testatrix of No. XXXII. In D.B. he is entered as a holder of estates in King Edward's time, and in one entry, referring to his estate at Walsingham, he is called a thegn of Stigand's. This information is borne out by his will, where he speaks of Stigand as his lord and leaves his heriot to him. Yet in the Suffolk portion of

D.B., where he is in possession of Onehouse, he is called King Edward's thegn. On this estate, and this only, he is mentioned as possessing the *soc*.

There are several Ketels in the Norfolk portion of D.B., but it is certainly Ketel Alder who is succeeded by Ranulf Peverel in Great Melton, Ketteringham and Walsingham in East Carleton, all of which estates he mentions in his will (see below). Outside Norfolk he was succeeded by Ranulf Peverel in Frating, Essex, and Onehouse, Suffolk. Hainford and Harling, Norfolk, and Rushford, Suffolk, went to other Norman holders. It may be the same Ketel who held a few acres in Stoke Holy Cross under Stigand (D.B. II, f. 264 *b*: *V. C. H. of Norfolk*, II, p. 187), but the landowner with extensive estates who was succeeded by Reynold, son of Ivo (D.B. II, ff. 230 *b* f.: *V. C. H. of Norfolk*, II, pp. 154 ff.), is no doubt a different person.

Stistede. Stisted, Essex. Ketel had only been left a life-interest in this estate by Wulfgyth (see p. 84, ll. 10 ff.), and that is probably the reason why Christchurch succeeded in retaining possession after the Conquest and is entered as pre-Conquest holder in D.B. (see p. 198).

l. 15. *Sefledan*. Perhaps she was Ketel's wife. She does not occur in Wulfgyth's will or Edwin's. On p. 90, l. 22, the name occurs in a strong form, as is usual. The present form is probably due to Latinisation, as the element *-flæd* is generally written *-fleda* in mediæval Latin documents.

l. 20. *so so geard goð*. I take the second *so* to be an error for *se*, *e* and *o* being frequently confused by this scribe.

l. 21. *hyge*. O.E. *hege*. The inverted spelling of *y* for *e*, due to the dialectal development of O.E. *y* to *e*, occurs also in the Bury document containing Nos. XIV, XV (e.g. *Ylig*, p. 36, l. 1; *Ylmesætun*, p. 38, l. 2).

l. 24. *Herlinge*. East Harling, Norfolk, the *Herlingham* of p. 84, l. 21. Ketel held 2 carucates there in 1066 (D.B. II, f. 223: *V. C. H. of Norfolk*, II, p. 146).

Stigand Archebisscop. See p. 191.

ll. 26 f. *min heregete*. See p. 100. Ketel pays the heriot of the *medeme* thegn of II Cnut, 71. 2, for which may be substituted £2 in East Anglia and Mercia, and he pays it, not to the king, but to an intermediate lord. A sum of £2 is also the heriot of the man of smaller means (*se ðe læsse maga sy*) in the Danelaw (II Cnut, 71. 5), and this clearly corresponds with the 3 marks of silver paid as 'relief' in Edward the Confessor's time in Derbyshire, Nottinghamshire and Yorkshire, by the thegns with six manors or less (D.B. I, ff. 280 *b*, 298 *b*), as 3 silver marks, allowing 20 pence to the ore, amount to £2 precisely. There is also a class in the land between the Ribble and Mersey which pays 40 shillings (D.B. I, f. 269 *b*). This lower thegn in the three counties mentioned above, paid not directly to the king, but to the sheriff. We do not know how old this arrangement was, but as in Cnut's law the higher thegn is distinguished by his closer relation to the king, it seems probable that already at this date the men from whom the lower heriot is due were in general under the sheriff or some intermediate lord. Also, we have no means of knowing whether the six manor distinction was a recent one, and whether it was confined to the three counties about which we have information. Ketel appears to have been holding nine manors in D.B.

ll. 28 ff. *þat ic and Eadwine...kirke.* This passage cannot be right as it stands. The reference to himself is out of place in an arrangement concerning succession to his property. Perhaps there has been an omission. The original may have had *þe ic and Eadwine and Wulfric wrohton þæt Eadwine and Wulfric...fon,* etc. The scribe might easily have made the error of following on after the second *Wulfric* instead of the first. Otherwise we must take *ic and* as an insertion.

l. 28. *Eadwine.* See p. 199.

l. 29. *Wlfric.* See p. 201.

l. 31. *erninglond.* See p. 178.

p. 90, l. 3. *felageschipe.* See p. 194. According to D.B., Ketel, Edwin, and a thegn who may have been Wulfric, all held lands in Great Melton (see p. 201). The partnership may have been an arrangement to hold these estates in common.

l. 4. *Meþeltune.* Great Melton, Norfolk.

l. 7. *Thorpe.* See p. 201.

l. 8. *Boten.* Cf. p. 84, l. 22.

l. 9. *forwarde.* Ketel has made several agreements of this type. The same practice is shown in other wills (see p. 166).

gif ic mine day do her his: þat ic fon... This passage is clearly corrupt. I suggest that *his* is a miscopying of *hio,* but it is difficult to explain how the scribe came to write *ic fon* instead of the *hio fo* that the original must have had.

l. 10. *Keteringham.* Keteringham, Norfolk. Ranulf Peverel succeeded Ketel to 1½ carucates there (D.B. II, f. 254 b: *V. C. H. of Norfolk,* II, p. 177).

oþer. A scribal error, either for *oþþe* or for *ofer.* If the latter, we must translate 'a mark of gold above the value'.

l. 11. *Somerledetone.* Somerleyton, near Lowestoft, or Somerton, Suffolk. It was one of the estates bequeathed by Wulfgyth to her daughter. See p. 84, l. 22.

l. 12. *Gode.* See the Will of Wulfgyth, p. 84, l. 22.

l. 13. *Walsingham.* Walsingham in East Carleton, Norfolk. See p. 198.

l. 15. *Prestone.* Probably Preston, near Lavenham, Suffolk.

l. 16. *Hemfordham.* In D.B. II, f. 243 b, Ketel is holding an estate, *Hamforda,* as one carucate under Stigand. The *V. C. H. of Norfolk,* II, p. 167 identifies this as Hainford. I think there can be no doubt that this is Ketel's estate of *Hemfordham. e* for *o* is a common error in this MS.

l. 17. *Kockeshale.* Coggeshall, Essex. Wulfgyth, Ketel's mother, had possessed land in this place (see p. 198). The Additional MS. form might be Buxhall, but is, I think, merely due to a misreading.

l. 18. *Strattune*. Probably Stratton Strawless, near Hainford. 30˙ acres there, held before the Conquest by five men, are entered in D.B. along with Ketel's estate at *Hamforda* (D.B. II, f. 243 *b*: *V. C. H. of Norfolk*, II, p. 167).

cnihte. See p. 127.

l. 20. *Anhus*. Onehouse, Suffolk. Ranulf Peverel succeeded Ketel, King Edward's thegn, to an estate of 1½ carucates and 20 acres there (D.B. II, f. 416 *b*: *V. C. H. of Suffolk*, I, p. 553). This is the only one of Ketel's estates over which he is stated to have had the *soc*.

l. 24. *Harold erl*. See p. 193.

Moran. I cannot identify this with certainty, but it is probably the D.B. *Mora* in the Hundred of Blofield, Norfolk. This is not held by Ketel, but from the will it appears that Ketel was not in possession, but claimed it. In the time of King Edward it was held as 2 carucates by Siric, a freeman (D.B. II, f. 269 *b*: *V. C. H. of Norfolk*, II, p. 191). The *V. C. H.* (*loc. cit.*, footnote) identifies it with Mousehold Heath.

l. 26. *mid mine wife begat*. This phrase is ambiguous. It may merely refer to a transaction carried out by Ketel and his wife acting together, but it could also mean that he received the estate as part of his wife's portion when he married her. We may compare p. 68, l. 7, where Thurketel mentions land *þat ic mid hire* (i.e. *his wife*) *nam* (see p. 179).

ll. 26 f. *ne forswat ne forspilde*. *forswat* does not occur elsewhere. B.T. *Suppl.* suggests *forspæc* on the analogy of K. 1327, *He hit ne mæg naðer gifan ne syllan, ne forspecan ne forspillan*. The emendation is a very simple one, as *w* was liable to be confused with *p*, and *c* with *t*.

l. 30. *Fretinge*. Frating, Essex. Ketel held it as a manor and 2 hides, and was succeeded by Ranulf Peverel (D.B. II, f. 75 *b*: *V. C. H. of Essex*, I, p. 532).

l. 33. *Rissewrthe*. Rushford, on the border between Norfolk and Suffolk. 2 carucates there were held by *Alti* and Ketel in 1066, as two manors. They are described as freemen and thegns (see D.B. II, f. 421: *V. C. H. of Suffolk*, I, p. 557). The soke of the whole hundred belonged to St Edmund's Abbey.

XXXV.

This document reads more like a record of a grant which has already taken effect than a bequest, except for the last phrase, which calls it a *quide*. Domesday Book, however, also shows that the gift was not intended to take effect until after the Bishop's death, for he was still in possession of three of the four estates at the time of his deposition. In l. 6 he implies that he has made, or intends to make, a will. This document is merely a pious bequest of a portion of his property, similar to Thurstan's bequest to Christchurch.

MS. Cambridge University Library, MS. FF. 2. 33, f. 49. See p. 99.
EDITION. T. p. 599.
DATE. Between 1047 and 1070.

p. 92, l. 1. *Ailmer biscop*. Æthelmær succeeded Stigand, his brother, as Bishop of Elmham when the latter became Bishop of Winchester in 1047. He retained the see until 1070, when William deposed him. He received two of the estates mentioned in the bequest, Swanton and Hindolveston, from Bury before he became bishop. A copy of the agreement on this occasion is preserved in MS. FF. 2. 33, f. 49, and can be assigned to 1043 or 1044 by the list of witnesses. The lands were to return to the abbey on Æthelmær's death, but his successor, Bishop William, succeeded in retaining them (see D.B. II, ff. 192 f.: *V. C. H. of Norfolk*, II, pp. 115 f.).

ll. 3 f. *Hindringham ... Langham ... Hildoluestone ... Suanetone*. Hindringham, Langham, Hindolveston and Swanton Novers, Norfolk.

XXXVI.

MS. Cambridge University Library, MS. FF. 2. 33, f. 50. See p. 99.
EDITIONS. K. 980. MS. wrongly quoted as FF. 3. 33.
        T. p. 591.
DATE. Uncertain. See following note.

l. 9. *þurkil and Apelgit*. Thurkil does not appear as owner of Wereham in D.B., nor is it hinted there that St Edmund's had ever held land in this place. Wereham was held in 1066 by a 'freeman', *Toli*, and he was succeeded by Reynold, son of Ivo (D.B. II, f. 230 *b*: *V. C. H. of Norfolk*, II, p. 155). The same Reynold succeeded a certain *Turchill* in Boughton, Shouldham, Crimplesham and Barton in the same hundred as Wereham, that is, Clackclose Hundred, and a woman, *Ailid, Alid* (i.e. Æthelgyth) in Crimplesham and in Yaxham in Midford Hundred. This may be coincidence, but it may be that this *Turchill* and this *Ailid* are the testators of this document, which would then belong to the period just before the Conquest. In any case, the document is probably a bequest of a portion of their possessions only, like Thurstan's bequest to Christchurch.

It seems probable that this *Ailid* is the woman of the same name who was Ralf Bainard's predecessor in Boughton, Shouldham, Barton, Fincham and Wiggenhall in Clackclose Hundred and in other estates elsewhere (D.B. II, ff. 250 *b* f.: *V. C. H. of Norfolk*, II, pp. 173 f.). In the first three of these places, as we have seen, *Turchill* held land also. But Ralf Bainard's predecessor we have elsewhere identified with Æthelgyth, the wife of the Thurstan who made his will in 1043 or 1044 (see p. 190).

The objection to this identification of Thurkil and Æthelgyth with the landowners mentioned in D.B. is that Wereham was in the possession of neither in 1066, nor is it held by their legatee. The *Toli* who held it also had 6 carucates at Barton Bendish, where *Turchill* had 3 and *Ailid* 2 (D.B. II, ff. 230, 250 b: *V. C. H. of Norfolk*, II, pp. 154, 174). It is possible that the estate at Wereham had been divided among the three of them in a similar way, and that the account in D.B., whether through the forgetfulness of the jurors, or through omission by the compiler, does not give all the details of the ownership of this estate. Or secondly, Thurkil and Æthelgyth may have inherited the estate from Toli either just before or just after 1066.

Wigorham. Wereham, Norfolk. I am indebted to Dr O. K. Schram for this identification.

l. 11. *þo men halffre.* Thorpe takes this phrase as equivalent to *half þe men fre*, 'and half the men are to be freed'. Liebermann (*Glossar, s.v. Halbfreie*) compares one of Wulfstan's homilies (ed. Napier, p. 171, note) in which a distinction is drawn between *freotmen* and *healffreon.* Toli's estate at Wereham (see p. 205) had on it 15 villeins, 8 bordars and 6 slaves in 1066. The slaves correspond to the *þeowe* of the bequest. *halffre* probably refers to men who were obliged to render service to the lord of the manor and who were unable to leave their lord. Such, no doubt, were the villeins and bordars in the Domesday account of the estate, and Thurkil and Æthelgyth's freedmen were probably included among the bordars.

lisingar. O.Icel. *leysingi*, or *leysingr*, 'a freedman'. Apparently our text retains the O.Icel. plural in *-ar*, but there are instances in this MS. of *r* written in mistake for *s* (cf. p. 76, l. 7).

XXXVII AND XXXVIII.

There is nothing to show which of these two wills is the earlier. It may be that the one made before her journey is an enlarged and amended version of the other.

MSS. Cambridge University Library, MS. FF. 2. 33, f. 49 b; see p. 99. The longer will follows immediately after the shorter.

EDITIONS. K. 946, 947.
T. p. 592.
B. 1015, 1014.

DATE. There are no means of dating these wills. From the wording they appear to be late tenth or eleventh century. St Edmund's Abbey was in possession of Marlingford by 1066.

l. 13. *Sifled.* She cannot be identified with anyone else of this name.
l. 14. *Marþingforð.* Marlingford, Norfolk. St Edmund's Abbey held this estate in the Confessor's time (D.B. II, f. 209 b: *V. C. H. of Norfolk*, II, p. 131).

There is no mention whatever of the church. It is perhaps included in the remark, 'others hold land there', which closes the description of the estate, as the only holder in Marlingford, apart from the Abbey, is Count Alan with two sokemen holding 16 acres (D.B. II, f. 145 b: V. C. H. of Norfolk, II, p. 71).

ll. 14 f. *al buten tuenti acres.* She does not make it clear for whom she reserves these acres.

l. 15. *tueye Waine gong.* This represents an O.E. *twegra wægna gang,* 'a going of two waggons', but the genitive afterwards in place of the preposition *to* shows that the original meaning was lost. Cf. B. 496, dated 858, II *wena gang mid cyninges wenum to blean ðem wiada;* B. 539 (A.D. 875) *an cinges bocholte fif wena gang fram lacum oð sumermessan;* B. 1071, dated 961, *twega wæna gang on clætinc to wuduredenne.* The O.E. construction is retained on p. 94, ll. 3, 5.

þere Wude. This must represent an O.E. genitive plural. I am uncertain whether, like *wudes* on the same line, it should be taken with *wainegong,* or whether it is a remnant of the genitive construction after *unnan.*

l. 17. *þen to þen hode.* O.E. *(ge)þeon to þæm hade,* literally, 'thrive as far as that order'.

l. 19. *freschot.* See p. 200.

p. 94, ll. 4 f. *alle mine men fre.* The one serf in the Domesday account of this estate must have been added by the Abbey.

l. 6. *into Northwich to Cristes kirke.* Neither Christchurch nor St Mary's at Norwich are mentioned by name in the Domesday description of the town (D.B. II, f. 116 b: V. C. H. of Norfolk, II, p. 46), but they may be included in the fifteen churches held by the burgesses.

l. 7. *sce Marian.* See preceding note.

duzme or *duzine.* This word must be a corruption. It cannot be interpreted whichever way one reads the MS.

XXXIX.

MS. The Society of Antiquaries of London, MS. LX. f. 50 b. This MS. is a twelfth-century cartulary of the Abbey of Peterborough.

EDITIONS. K. 953.

T. p. 594.

DATE. Between November, 1066, and about 1068. Brand did not become abbot until the November of 1066, and both he and Archbishop Ealdred died in 1069. The latter before his death had been in possession of Lavington and Skillington, which are mentioned in the will; had been disseised, and had obtained the king's writ and been reseised of the estates (D.B. I, f. 376 b: F. and L. p. 227). All this must have taken some time, so that the will must have been drawn up at least several months before the Archbishop's death.

l. 14. *Vlf.* He occurs fairly frequently in the Lincolnshire portion of D.B. On f. 376 b, where his transaction with Archbishop Ealdred concerning Lavington, Hardwick, and Skillington is recorded, he is called *Tope sune*. Tope occurs once as a landowner in Lincolnshire in King Edward's time. He had held an estate at Kirmington which passed into the possession of Hugh the son of Baldric (D.B. i, p. 356: F. and L. p. 116). Ulf himself also held land at this place (see p. 211). In the will Ulf speaks of two estates, Messingham and Kettleby, as belonging to his mother, and probably therefore the *Eddiva* (O.E. Eadgifu) who held these estates in 1066 (D.B. i, f. 362: F. and L. pp. 150 f.) was Ulf's mother. The same *Eddiva* held Melton Ross, Brocklesby and Grayingham, and was succeeded in all these estates by Erneis de Burun. Ulf speaks also of a brother *Healþene*, clearly the Halden, son of Tope, mentioned in a twelfth-century list of benefactors to Peterborough (Hugo Candidus, ed. Sparke, p. 43). He is there called a kinsman of Abbot Brand.

It is clear from D.B. that Ulf's will never took effect. Most of his lands are in the hands of Norman lords, and the predecessors of these are not Ulf's legatees. There is an apparent exception with regard to the estates which Bishop Ealdred was to have; he succeeded in obtaining possession of them, but this was because Ulf sold them to the Bishop and the reference to them in the will is merely a record of the sale.

Ulf himself is entered as the pre-Norman holder of many of the estates mentioned in the will; in Kettleby, Kirmington, Claxby, Ormsby and Limber, and also in Hoby, Leicestershire, he was succeeded by Drew de Beuere. Besides the estates of which he disposes in his will, he also held Witham-on-the-Hill (but possibly this estate is included in the Manthorpe bequeathed in the will). Drew succeeded an Ulf who may be the testator in many estates in Holderness, Yorkshire (D.B. i, p. 324: *V. C. H. of Yorkshire*, ii, pp. 266 f.), but Ulf is a common name in this part of England in D.B.; two men of this name had held Drew's estate of Burton, Holderness. In Chadstone, Northamptonshire (D.B. i, f. 228: *V. C. H. of Northamptonshire*, i, p. 349), Drew's predecessor was Ulf, a man of Earl Waltheof's. The Countess Judith, Waltheof's wife, was laying claim to this estate. It is possible that Ulf had held this estate under the Earl, which would explain its omission from the will if this Ulf is identical with the testator. Two estates in the will, *Heordewican* and *Willabyg*, if the identification of them with Hardwick and Wilby, Northamptonshire, is correct, were held by the Countess Judith at the time of the Domesday Survey. Why they are in her possession must remain a mystery; one might guess that they were given by Ulf to Waltheof as a price for his protection, if both the evidence of the will and D.B. (see p. 209) did not agree that Ulf had sold Hardwick to Archbishop Ealdred.

Many estates belonging to Ulf and his wife at the time when the will was made are entered in D.B. as the property of Morcar in King Edward's time. Drew de Beuere had succeeded him in Carlton-le-Moorland, Bytham, Stoke and Stroxton (D.B. i, f. 360: F. and L. pp. 141 f.). In Sempringham, however, he was succeeded by Alfred of Lincoln (D.B. 1, f. 358 *b*: F. and L. p. 130). The jurors state that they leave to the King's decision the claims of Drew upon Morcar's land. Whether Ulf had acquired these estates only a short time before he made his will, or whether he held them under Morcar, it is impossible to ascertain.

An *Vlf filius Tope* witnesses a charter of William I late in 1066 (Dugdale, 1, p. 383), after which he does not appear again. Probably his lands were seized at the same time as those of his brother Halden (see p. 211). We do not know if he ever carried out his project of going to Jerusalem.

Madselin. The only suggestion I can offer for this very curious name is that it is a corrupt spelling of the German name which is variously spelt *Mazelin, Macelin, Matzilin* (see Förstemann, *Deutsches Namenbuch*, 1900 edition, col. 1120). This, however, was a man's name.

l. 16. *Carlatune.* Probably Carlton-le-Moorland, Lincolnshire. 12 carucates there were held by Ulf's successor in D.B., but Morcar is entered as the pre-Conquest holder, not Ulf. See p. 208.

Burh. The Abbey of St Peter at *Burg*, afterwards called Peterborough.

l. 17. *Bytham.* Probably Castle Bytham, D.B. *Westbitham*, which had been held by Morcar. See p. 208.

Sēe Guthlace. Crowland Abbey, Lincolnshire, of which St Guthlac was the patron saint.

l. 18. *Sempingaham.* Sempringham, Lincolnshire. F. and L. p. 130 understand the *Stepingeham* of D.B. 1, f. 358 *b*, to be a mistake for this name. It had been held by Morcar. See p. 208.

ll. 18 f. *þat land æt Lofintune 7 hæt Heordewican.* Lavington, Lincolnshire, and perhaps Hardwick near Wellingborough, Northamptonshire. In D.B. it is stated that Archbishop Ealdred bought Lavington, with the berewick of Hardwick and also Skillington, from Ulf, Tope's son, in the presence of the wapentake (D.B. 1, f. 376 *b*: F. and L. p. 227). Lavington and Skillington are both entered among the lands of the Archbishop of York (D.B. 1, f. 340: F. and L. pp. 29 f.). The former is definitely stated to have belonged to Ulf, but it is Morcar and not Ulf who is said to have owned the estate at Skillington. The Archbishop is not entered in possession of an estate at Hardwick. F. and L. suggest the Northamptonshire place because an Ulf held one hide there which the Countess Judith had in 1086, and there is another estate there which might be the berewick in question (D.B. 1, f. 229: *V. C. H. of Northamptonshire*, 1, p. 354). This is also of one hide, and in the possession of the Countess, but the name of the pre-Conquest holder is not given.

The Archbishop was afterwards disseised of these estates by Hilbold, but the wapentake declared that it had seen the king's seal by which the Archbishop was reseised.

l. 19. *Ealdrede b.* He had become Archbishop in 1061 though he is only referred to as bishop in this will. The Archbishop of York is called bishop in other documents, e.g. the *Norðhymbra Preosta Lagu* (Lieber-mann, I, p. 380). Ealdred had previously held the see of Worcester from 1044 until 1062 when it was given to Wulfstan.

l. 20. *Scillintune.* Skillington, Lincolnshire. See p. 209. D.B. im-plies that Ealdred bought this estate outright. The will leaves it ambiguous whether this was the case or whether he receives it in pledge for money lent.

Houcbig. Hoby, Leicestershire. In 1066 Ulf held this estate and was afterwards succeeded by Drew (D.B. I, f. 236: *V.C.H. of Leicester-shire*, I, p. 332).

Mortune. I cannot identify this Morton. The only place of this name which D.B. notes as having belonged to Archbishop Ealdred is an estate of 2½ carucates at Murton in Sutton-on-the-Forest, in the North Riding of Yorkshire. This is stated to have been held by Ulf, but this Ulf is clearly the same as the man who preceded the Archbishop in many estates in this locality (D.B. I, f. 303: *V. C. H. of Yorkshire*, II, p. 212) and he is no doubt the Ulf, son of Thorald, who gave many estates in the North and East Ridings, together with a horn, to York Minster (see *V. C. H. of Yorkshire*, II, p. 151).

l. 21. *þæron stent....goldes.* It is not clear to me whether this mortgage is on the estate of Morton alone, or on Skillington and Hoby as well.

l. 24. *þe abb Brand.* He was a kinsman of Ulf (see p. 208). He be-came Abbot of Peterborough after the death of Leofric on November 1st, 1066, having before been monk and provost there. The Chronicle relates that the monks sent to Edgar Ætheling to have the election confirmed, and that because of this it required the intervention of 'good men' and a substantial gift to persuade William the Conqueror to confirm Brand's election. He obtained a charter from William (see Dugdale, I, p. 383) confirming to the abbey lands which had been held by his brothers and kinsmen. This charter was witnessed by Ulf, Tope's son, among others. In a list of benefactors in Hugo Candidus, p. 44, the estates given by Brand and his brothers, Askil, Siric and Siworth, are enumerated. They are of wide extent and mainly in North Lincolnshire. Professor Stenton in his introduction to F. and L., p. xl, compares this passage with the Domesday evidence, which partly confirms it. Brand had a fourth brother, Godric, a later Abbot of Peterborough.

l. 25. *Mannethorp.* Manthorpe, Lincolnshire. Perhaps the berewick in Witham, Manthorpe and Toft with Lound, held by Peterborough in 1086 (D.B. I, f. 345 b: F. and L. p. 55), is the estate granted by Ulf, but if so the abbot was more fortunate than Ulf's other legatees. It is, however, possible that the estate of Ulf's entered in D.B. as Witham is the one called Manthorpe in the will. The two places are less than a mile apart. Drew held Witham in 1086 (D.B. I, f. 360 b: F. and L. p. 142).

l. 26. *Willabyg.* Perhaps Wilby, Northamptonshire. This estate was held by the Countess Judith in 1086 (D.B. 1, f. 228: *V. C. H. of Northamptonshire*, I, p. 351).

l. 27. *Stoce.* Stoke Rochford, Lincolnshire. According to D.B. Drew succeeded Morcar in this estate. See p. 208.

l. 28. *Stroðistune.* Stroxton, Lincolnshire. This estate also was first held by Morcar and then by Drew. See p. 208.

p. 96, l. 1. *I[n]gemunde.* A man of this name is entered in D.B. as preceding Count Alan in Beesby, Lincolnshire, and as holding land under the Count after the Conquest (D.B. 1, f. 347 *b*: F. and L. p. 94); but as the name does not occur in connection with Winterton, the estate mentioned in the will, I hesitate to identify this landowner with the legatee here.

l. 1 f. *þa Westhealle ongean æt Wintringatune.* According to Domesday evidence, Winterton consisted, in addition to berewicks and sokelands attached to other manors, of an estate of 12 bovates held before the Conquest by a certain Fulcheric (D.B. 1, f. 361 *b*: F. and L. p. 147) and an estate of 11 bovates held by Grimbold and Fulcheric (D.B. 1, f. 371 *b*: F. and L. p. 203). There is no mention of an Ingemund as the pre-Conquest holder. Both these entries have a marginal note stating them to be 'two manors', but there is no indication as to which of them included the 'west hall'.

l. 2. *Ofertune.* Probably Cold Overton, Leicestershire. Drew held this in 1086, but the name of his predecessor is not given (D.B. 1, f. 236: *V. C. H. of Leicestershire*, I, p. 332).

l. 3. *minre modar.* See p. 208.

l. 4. *Kitlebig.* Kettleby, near Wrawby, Lincolnshire. Ulf had one carucate here (D.B. 1, f. 360: F. and L. p. 139) and *Eddiva*, probably Ulf's mother, had another.

Cotum. Keelby Cotes, or Nun Coton. It was held by Drew in 1086, but his predecessor is not called Ulf but Rolf (D.B. 1, f. 360: F. and L. p. 140).

Mæssingaham. Messingham, Lincolnshire, which was held by *Eddiva* in 1066.

l. 6. *Coringatune.* I consider that Professor Stenton's identification of this with Kirmington, Lincolnshire, D.B. *Chernitone*, where Ulf had 4 bovates (D.B. 1, f. 360: F. and L. p. 139), is very probable (see Introduction to F. and L. p. xlii). The present form must be corrupt, with omission of the nasal, which may have been represented only by a stroke over the *r*, and probably with *o* for *e*, a common error.

Cleaxbyg. Claxby by Normanby, Lincolnshire, where Drew succeeded Ulf to 6 bovates (D.B. 1, f. 360 *b*: F. and L. p. 143).

Healþene. See p. 208. Hugo Candidus, p. 43, states that Halden's kinsman Brand let the Peterborough estate of Dunsby to him because King William had given all his estates to the Bishop of Lincoln. He is therefore identical with the *Aldene* who preceded the Bishop in many estates (D.B. 1, f. 344: F. and L. pp. 49 f.), including Grayingham, where *Eddiva*, probably his mother (see p. 208), also held land, and

Dunsby, which the Abbey of Peterborough said the Bishop had usurped. The wapentake, however, said that the abbey did not hold Dunsby in King Edward's time (D.B. 1, f. 377: F. and L. p. 231). *Healþene* is for *Healdene* representing the O.Icel. *Halfdan*, O. Danish *Haldan*.

l. 7. *Vrmesbyg.* North Ormsby, Lincolnshire. D.B. 1, f. 376 (F. and L. p. 219) says that Ulf of Ormsby sold 4½ carucates to St Mary of Stow and that that foundation was holding it when King Edward died. If it is this estate to which Ulf refers in his will, he is there confirming a transaction of some previous date, but D.B. records that Drew de Beuere is in possession of 4 carucates and 7 bovates which had belonged to Ulf and *Scemund* (D.B. 1, f. 360 *b*: F. and L. p. 141).

sēe MARIAN stowe. This was a foundation for secular priests established by Eadnoth, Bishop of Dorchester from 1034 to 1050 (Roger of Hoveden, R.S. 1057). It was endowed by Leofric Earl of Mercia and his wife Godgifu in 1052 or 1053, and the charter they made to this place is extant (Dugdale, III, p. 13). In the time of Bishop Remigius monks were established there and later they were removed to Eynsham.

l. 8. *Lindbeorhge.* Limber, Yarborough Wapentake, Lincolnshire. Ulf held one carucate there and was succeeded by Drew (D.B. 1, f. 360: F. and L. p. 139).

l. 9. *Lohtune.* There is now no place of this name near Limber. Laughton near Folkingham, which appears in D.B. as *Loctun*, is at the other end of the county. If this is the place meant here, *þerinne* must imply that it was an outlying estate attached to Limber.

INDEX NOMINUM

Clarendon figures refer to pages, plain figures to lines of text

INDEX LOCORUM

INDEX RERUM

Accusation. *See* Onspæc, Spæc

Acquirement of property '*begietan*', '*(ge)earnian*', **2**, 2 ff.; **18**, 16; **30**, 3 f.; **42**, 12; **48**, 7; **70**, 18; **74**, 17 f.; **76**, 6. *See also* Purchased land

Advocacy, advocate '*forespræc*', '*foresp(r)eca*', **26**, 21; **40**, 15 f.; **44**, 6, 14; **50**, 13

Æhta. *See* Goods, Livestock, Possessions, Property

Ælmesse 'alms', 'charity', 'charitable bequests', **2**, 5; **54**, 18; **58**, 25 f.; **62**, 14; **66**, 18

Agreements. *See* Contract, Marriage agreements

Aldreday, **6**, 12 ff.; **82**, 30; **105**, **197**

Alienation, **8**, 27; **10**, 9; **70**, 5 f.; *see also* Frescet: of an estate from a religious foundation forbidden, **18**, 13: other restrictions on, *see* Kindred, Men

Anathema, xi n. 2, xvi; **4**, 32 f.; **8**, 22 ff.; **16**, 18 ff.; **28**, 28 ff.; **34**, 4 ff.; **50**, 19 ff.; **54**, 5 f.; **62**, 10 ff.; **64**, 27 ff.; **66**, 13 ff.; **68**, 18 f.; **70**, 13 ff.; **74**, 11 ff., 27 f.; **78**, 6 ff.; **82**, 25 f.; **86**, 4 ff.; **90**, 33 f.; **92**, 7 f., 11 f., 19 ff.; **94**, 11 ff.

Andluman 'utensils', **14**, 28

Ar 'estate', **56**, 11; **60**, 29: 'income', **54**, 17; **56**, 27; **169**: 'property', *see* Property

Archives. *See* Documents

Association. *See* Gild

Aðum, **76**, 23; **188**

Attestation. *See* Witness

Bænd 'headband', **20**, 33; **26**, 26; **28**, 4; **64**, 10, 20; **120**, **131**

Bayeux tapestry, **144**, **172**

Beag 'armlet', **6**, 2; **12**, 19; **20**, 18 ff.; **127**, **144**: agrafenan beah, **10**, 7

Bedreaf 'bedclothing', **12**, 22; **14**, 9; **62**, 22; **74**, 25

Bedwahrift 'bed-curtain', **14**, 9

Beodreaf 'table-cover', **64**, 18

Binde 'headband', **14**, 16 f.

Biscopham. *See* Episcopal property

Biscoprice. *See* Episcopal demesne

Bishop, for archbishop, **28**, 1; **94**, 19; **131**, **209** f.: Englishmen to be freed at the death of, **101**, **163**: to own the woman enslaved as a punishment for incest, **111** f.: son of, **114** f.: to be witness when restriction limiting bookland to kindred is broken, **131**

Blædhorn, seolforhammenne 'silver-coated trumpet', **58**, 20

Bledu 'bowl', **34**, 16; **62**, 19; **139**

Boc. *See* Books, Title-deed

Bohscyld, **60**, 12 f.; **172**

Bookland '*bocland*', xix, xx, xxix, xxxii and n. 4, xxxiii, xxxv n. 1, xxxvi, **132**, **178**

Books, bequest of, **14**, 23; **52**, 20: mass books, **2**, 14; **4**, 27. *See also* Psalter, Title-deed

Borg. *See* Debts

Boundaries '*landgemæra*', '*-mearca*', **40**, 21 ff.; **145** f.

Brand, **58**, 19; **171**

Broccen 'of badger skin', **113**

Brooch '*(mentel)preon*', **10**, 8; **14**, 12; **64**, 11; **110**. *See also* Bul

Bryce 'use', 'usufruct', **6**, 29; **8**, 9; **18**, 19; **38**, 22 ff.; **48**, 1; **50**, 4. *See* Usufruct

Bryþen 'brewing', **54**, 10; **165**

Bul, **50**, 16; **159**

Bullocks '*hryðra*', bequest of, **54**, 13 ff.; **94**, 6

Burgesses, heriot of, **157**

Burial fee. *See* Sawolsceatt

Burreaf 'tapestry for a chamber', **64**, 18; **175**

Byrne. *See* Coat of mail

Calves, bequest of, **12**, 31

Carta, xxiv, xxxii and n. 4: carta primitiva, xxxii n. 4, xxxv n. 1: cartae excisae, xxiv n. 2. *See also* Levatio cartae, Traditio cartae. Cf. Notitia

Castenere 'chest', **64**, 22

CAMBRIDGE: PRINTED BY W. LEWIS, M.A., AT THE UNIVERSITY PRESS

CAMBRIDGE: PRINTED BY W. LEWIS, M.A., AT THE UNIVERSITY PRESS